Core Java
Career Essentials

Focusing on

Java platform, language, classes, objects, OO concepts & principles, data structures, algorithms, and pattern matching essentials

By

Arulkumaran Kumaraswamipillai
Sivayini Arulkumaran

Core Java Career Essentials

Focusing on platform, language, classes, objects, collections, and logic essentials

Please e-mail feedback & corrections (technical, grammatical and/or spelling) to
java-interview@hotmail.com.

More Java/JEE career resources are availabale at
http://www.lulu.com/java-success

First Edition : April 2011

Thanks to the reviewers: Ankit Garg, Devaka Cooray, Roberto Perillo, Rod Good, and Sean Clynes.

Table of Contents

Section-1:

Getting Started …...

- How can this book help you?
- Why is this a PERFECT companion?
- What are the technical key areas?

So you have a java interview coming up in a few days or you want to impress your peers and superiors with your technical strengths during code review sessions, team meetings, and stand-ups, and concerned about how to make a good impression? you don't need to worry if you are familiar with the fundamentals. Most Java interviews and technical challenges you face at work are structured around the fundamentals and how well you communicate those fundamentals. So regularly brushing up on these fundamentals really pays off.

Your analytical, problem solving, and coding skills will also be under scrutiny along with your ability to get the job done with the right tools. If your fundamentals are clear and know what tools to use, you can tackle any questions, and find solutions to any problems and challenges you face. Even if you don't have the exact answer for a problem, you will know how to go about solving them with a little research if you have a solid grounding in the fundamentals covered in this book.

A little preparation can make a huge difference to your career success. Preparation can help you communicate your thoughts more clearly with examples and illustrations. Preparation can make a good and lasting impression on those who talk with you during your interviews and team meetings. This impression will be partly influenced by how prepared you are and how knowledgeable you are about your industry and the challenges it faces. It will also be influenced by your appearance, attitude, enthusiasm, and confidence. Good preparation breeds confidence and it shows in the interviews and team meetings. So prepare well in advance if you just begun to see yourself in your dream company or would like to go places in your chosen field.

How can this book help you?

This unique "questions and answers approach" with tagged technical key areas, diagrams, code snippets, and examples can help you excel in your chosen Java based profession. This is more than just an interview preparation guide. Let's look at ways in which we believe this book can benefit a reader.

- Helps you brush up or be aware of the basics in software development that you must know. <u>Preparing for the most common interview questions</u> will increase your chances. If you fail to answer these basic questions, your chances of succeeding in interviews will be very slim. In fact, 40% - 60% of the professionals irrespective of their level of experience fail to make an impression in one or more of the following most common areas.

    - ◆ **Coding**: You may have to write some simple code, with correct syntax and logic in Java. You might be asked to explain and critique on snippets of code. You might be asked to demonstrate both recursive and iterative approaches to a given problem. You will be assessed on your ability to think about the exceptional cases, exit conditions, and algorithms.

    - ◆ **OO design**: You will be asked to define basic OO concepts and principles, and come up with the classes and interfaces to model a simple problem. A good weeder question would be to judge your ability to decide when to use attributes, inheritance, and composition. You might be asked to critique a system or platform you had worked on. A good OO design question can also test your coding skills and domain knowledge.

    - ◆ **Language fundamentals and best practices**: You must have a solid grasp of the language fundamentals. You might be asked what parts of Java you don't like and why? You must know about the common pitfalls, anti-patterns, and how to avoid them. You must know the differences between abstract classes and interfaces, how the garbage collection works?, etc and relevant best practices.

    - ◆ **Data structures**: You must demonstrate basic knowledge of the most common data structures. Most candidates know about arrays, sets, lists, and maps but fail to mention trees and graphs. You will be quizzed on real life examples of where to use a particular data structure and big-O performance (e.g. linear, logarithmic, exponential, etc) of various operations like find, insert, and delete. It is also worth knowing the basic sorting and searching algorithms.

- ◆ **Bits, bytes, and data types:** You must demonstrate how good you are technically. You must know the logical operations like AND, OR, NOT, and XOR and where to use them in real life examples for things like setting or testing for a specific bit. Using the wrong data types in your program can bring the whole application down. You must also know the difference between signed and unsigned data types and narrowing versus widening conversions.

- ◆ **Right tools to use**: Knowing the right tools will make you more productive without having to reinvent the wheel, and get the job done more effectively and on time. These tools can vary from harnessing the power of Unix scripts with regular expressions or embedded groovy scripts to tools like Wireshark to sniff the packets.

The prospective employers generally determine if you "know it", "knowledgeable enough to learn it on the job" or "have no clue at all". You surely don't want to be in the category of "have no clue at all".

- • Helps you refresh your memory or learn answers to the technical questions that are frequently asked in interviews. This can build up your confidence and it really shows in interviews. Software development field is very vast and competitive, and it pays to jog your memory even if you are an experienced professional.

- • All the other applicants may have much the same degrees, certifications, skills, and experience. But those who are in the know how can make it all come alive and seem real by selling their practical and technical competencies with illustrations, examples, and enthusiasm. If you don't relate your qualifications, skills, experience, and abilities to demonstrated results, most employers will tend to think that you have a great deal of raw potential – but limited immediate usefulness.

- • Helps you think aloud for some of the more difficult to tackle scenario based and open-ended questions where the interviewers will be more interested in evaluating your thought process and approach than expecting a detailed solution or answer.

- Helps you progress in your career a lot quicker by enabling you to pro-actively learn and apply the core technical key areas that will otherwise take years to fully understand if you rely on your experience alone. Some mistakes are too expensive to learn on the job.

This book complements our previously published book in 2005, entitled "Java/J2EE Job Interview Companion", which was well received, and the purpose of this book is to keep up with the recent developments, cover more on coding, open-ended, and scenario based interview Q&A, and to incorporate some of the constructive criticisms from the readers and reviewers. The "Java/J2EE Job Interview Companion" gives an overview of many topics from Java to J2EE, XML to UML, and frameworks to emerging technologies. The "Core Java Career Essentials" as the name implies, focuses solely on the essentials in more depth. The ensuing career essentials series will cover the topics not covered here.

> "Knowledge is knowing what to do, skill is knowing how to do,
> virtue is getting it done. " – Norman Vincent Peale

Why is this a PERFECT companion?

The primary objective is to make your learning or brushing up a PERFECT experience, which stands for **P**ractical, **E**njoyable, **R**ewarding, **F**ocused, **E**xamples driven, **C**oncise, and **T**hought-provoking.

- **Practical**: What is the point in learning bitwise operators without knowing where to apply and when to use them? This book is full of practical examples, workable code, best practices, and potential pitfalls.

- **Enjoyable**: Nothing is more enjoyable as a developer than cutting quality and workable code. That is why there are 100+ executable code samples as opposed to just code snippets. Feel free to experiment with the code samples.

- **Rewarding**: The basics described here with examples and sample code can bring success in job interviews, technical tests, code reviews, and performance appraisals by learning to sell yourself more effectively.

- **Focused**: Our last book entitled "Java/J2EE Job Interview Companion" was providing a bird's eye view of a vast range of technologies and frameworks. While this approach was well received and provided a road map for job interviews, it lacked some level of details. This book is focused on more details to extend its usefulness beyond just interviews by covering a limited number of topics in more depth.

- **Examples driven**: Prospective employers are not just looking for professionals with just academic qualifications. They are looking for professionals with experience. You cannot drive a car with just theoretical knowledge. Software development is no different. So use these examples to code, code, and more code.

- **Concise**: Who wants to read pages after pages about a single topic. There is always Google to perform additional research on a as needed basis.

- **Thought-provoking**: The questions and answers approach gives a different perspective to learning and brushing up. It will get you thinking and asking the right questions when you are working on a project. Asking the right questions and spotting the potential pitfalls can present you in a better light for potential promotions and pay rises.

What are the technical key areas?

Writing a quality software is a very complex process. It must not only meet all the functional requirements to satisfy the business needs, but also should be robust, maintainable, testable, and flexible enough to adapt to growing and changing business needs. It must also address non-functional aspects like,

- Adequate logging, auditing, and alarms to provide better problem diagnostics and customer support.
- Security, data integrity, data retention, fail over and disaster recovery strategies.
- Being up 24x7, performance metrics, and adherence to SLAs (Service Level Agreements) like response times, timeouts, etc. Service assurance can help improve customer trust and experience in the system.

If you just take technical design alone, there are many pros and cons for each approach along with likely trade-offs to be made in your design decisions. Understanding the key areas will help you not only write quality software, but also excel in your chosen career. How do you excel in your career by understanding the key areas you may ask?

Firstly, in your regular job,

- You can earn the appreciation of your superiors and peers by pro-actively and retro-actively solving everyday problems by understanding the key areas. For example, you can resolve problems relating to performance, memory, concurrency, language fundamentals, etc. Some of the subtle issues can be hard to understand, reproduce and solve without the adequate technical skills, and it really pays to have the experience and good understanding of the basics in these key areas.

- Understanding some of the nuances and best practices can help you write less error-prone and more robust code. Writing maintainable, supportable, readable, and testable code will not go unnoticed in code reviews and can also earn you the much needed recognition. You can also come up with intelligent questions or suggestions in team/stand-up meetings and group discussions. You can pro-actively identify potential issues not only in your own code or design, but also in others' code and design to become a great contributor.

- You can build up a reputation as a "go to person" by complementing your technical skills in these key areas with soft-skills and personal attributes to mentor others and get things done.

Secondly, in your job interviews,

- You can impress your interviewers by highlighting your past achievements in these key areas. For example, you can make use of open-ended questions like "Tell me about your self?" or "Why do you like software development?" to highlight your strengths and accomplishments.

- Many software projects face performance bottlenecks, design inefficiencies, concurrency issues, inadequate software development processes, etc. Hence the prospective employers will make sure that they hire the right candidate by asking questions relating to these key areas. Even if they don't cover any particular key area you are good at like performance tuning or concurrency management, you can bring it up yourself by asking intelligent questions like "What are the challenges faced by your current software? and do you face any performance issues or customer complaints that are hard to reproduce? ".

• Better candidates will control the interview in a nicer way as they understand it is a two way process. They will quickly understand what the prospective interviewer is looking for and reflect back on their past experience to relate how they went about resolving problems and adding value.

Let's look at the key areas relating to software development. Please be aware that not all key areas are covered in this book.

1. Language Fundamentals `LF`
2. Specification Fundamentals `SF`
3. Design Concepts `DC`
4. Design Patterns `DP`
5. Performance Considerations `PC`
6. Memory Considerations `MC`
7. Transaction Management `TM`
8. Concurrency Considerations `CC`
9. SCalability `SC`
10. Exception Handling `EH`
11. Best Practices `BP`
12. Software Development Processes `SP`
13. SEcurity `SE`
14. COding for readability, maintainability, supportability, extendability, and testability `CO`
15. Quality of Service `QS`
16. Platform Fundamentals `PF`

Most of the questions are tagged with relevant technical key area(s) shown above. Some questions are also tagged with question type and/or its popularity as shown below:

• Open-Ended Question `OEQ`
• Scenario Based Question `SBQ`
• COding Question `COQ`
• IMpossible Question `IMQ`
• Frequently Asked Question `FAQ`

Getting Started ......

Speaking the same language as your prospective employers from both technical and business perspective will help you establish a level of comfort with them. Discuss things in simple terms so that anyone can understand. It is okay if you struggle a little and then figure it out with minor hints or prompting from the interviewers. It is natural to be a bit rusty as the technologies are pretty vast these days. But it is not a good sign to be completely clueless or badly confused, especially with the core fundamentals. These career companions and career essentials will boost your knowledge and confidence to succeed in your career.

Take the initiative to grasp a potential employer's problems, challenges, and requirements to marry them with your past experience and accomplishments. This is more important than just having the necessary experience or understanding in the technical key areas. The ensuing sections will elaborate on this.

Important:

- Sample code in this book is making use of static methods and other approaches in many places for illustration purpose and to keep things simple. This should not be construed as a best practice.

- A commercial standard code will make use of unit tests using either *JUnit* or TestNG instead of public static main(String[ ] args) methods for testing and most of the methods except a fewer utility methods will be non-static. You will hardly see main methods required except for initial bootstrapping of applications that are run stand-alone. It will also be making use of Object Oriented principles, Dependency Injection, Law of Demeter principle, Don't Repeat Yourself (DRY) principle, etc to make the code more reusable, testable, maintainable and readable.

- The *System.out.println(....)* statements should be replaced with a logging framework like log4j. For example,

```
private static final Log logger =  LogFactory.getLog(MyClass.class);

logger.info("logging text goes here .................. ");
```

- Comments are over used to explain concepts, and real code should not be cluttered with comments. The classes, methods, and variables should have meaningful names and the code should be self-explanatory.

Getting Started …...

Section-2:

Platform Essentials

- Why use Java?
- Java platform basics – JDK, JRE, JVM, etc.
- Setting up and running Java
- How are your classes loaded?
- Compile-time vs runtime

This section is mainly for a beginner level, but I am very surprised to see even some intermediate to senior level developers lack good understanding of these platform essentials. This section is a must read for a beginner level. The intermediate and senior level candidates are highly recommended to brush up on the following frequently asked questions,

Q1, Q2, Q3, Q7, Q8, Q9, Q10, Q17, Q18, Q19, Q20, Q21, Q22, Q24 and Q25.

Even if you have limited experience, it is better to have an idea as to how to go about getting it done than to have no idea at all. This will differentiate yourself from others who have similar experience as you. Good Java interview questions are designed in a way to analyze if you are capable of applying the basics of a programming language.

Why use Java?

Q1   Give a few reasons for using Java? `LF PF FAQ OEQ`

A1   One needs to use the best tool for the job, whether that tool is Java or not. When choosing a technology to solve your business problems, you need to consider many factors like development cost, infrastructure cost, ongoing support cost, robustness, flexibility, security, performance, etc.

Java provides client technologies, server technologies, and integration technologies to solve small scale to very large scale business problems.

- If you want to target multiple platforms, Java is the best solution. Although the notion of "Write Once Run Anywhere (WORA)" does not always hold true, but it is true that the majority of the code you write in Java will run almost anywhere.

- The emergence of open-source technologies has truly made Java a powerful competitor in the server and integration technology space. You can always find a proven framework that best solves your business problems. For example,

  http://java-source.net/, http://projects.apache.org/indexes/category.html http://www.springsource.org/

- The Java platform has been around for a while and has been tested and deployed in many industries. It is mature both in terms of implementation as well as APIs. There's less risk that there's some bug in the platform that poses security risks, or has some intrinsic flaw in its architecture.

- The Java platform is standardized and the specifications are publicly available from various sources. There are many books, on-line resources, tutorials, and training courses on how to develop on it. Hence, it'll be easier to find developers who can be productive sooner.

- There are plethora of design, development, and deployment tools both open-source and commercial to choose from.

- The platform also comes with a rich set of APIs. This means developers spend less time writing support libraries, and more time developing content for their applications.

- Finally, the usual benefits of the Java platform and its APIs

    - Built-in support for multi-threading, socket communication, and automatic memory management (i.e. automatic garbage collection).

    - Object Oriented (OO).

    - Supports Web based applications (Servlet, JSP, etc), distributed applications (sockets, RMI, EJB, etc), and network protocols (HTTP, JRMP, etc) with the help of extensive standardized APIs (Application Programming Interfaces).

    - Security checking is built into the libraries and virtual machine.

    - Supports Unicode for ease of internationalization (i18n - where 18 stands for the number of letters between the first i and last n in internationalization).

    - Similar to C++ and C#, so it is familiar to commercial programmers. It does not include the dangerous parts of C++. So it is safer and simpler.

Q2 What is the difference between C++ and Java? `LF FAQ`

A2 Both C++ and Java use similar syntax and are object oriented, but that is where the similarity ends:

- Java does not support pointers. Pointers are inherently tricky to use and troublesome.

- Java does not support multiple inheritances because it causes more problems than it solves. Java supports multiple **interface** inheritance, which allows an object to inherit many method signatures from different interfaces with the condition that the inheriting object must implement those inherited methods. The multiple interface inheritance also allows an object to behave polymorphically on those methods.

17

- Java does not support destructors, but adds a finalize( ) method. Finalize methods are invoked by the garbage collector prior to reclaiming the memory occupied by the object, which has the finalize( ) method. This means, you do not know when the objects are going to be finalized. Avoid using finalize( ) method to release non-memory resources like file handles, sockets, database connections, etc because the platform has only a finite number of these resources, and **you do not know when the garbage collection is going to kick in to release these resources** through the finalize( ) method.

- Java does not include structures or unions because the traditional data structures are implemented as an object oriented Java Collections framework.

- All the code in Java program is encapsulated within classes therefore Java does not have global variables or functions.

- C++ requires explicit memory management while Java includes automatic garbage collection.

- Generics in Java provides a simple compile-time type safety check whereas in C++ whenever a template class is instantiated with a new class, the entire code for that class is reproduced and recompiled for the new class.

Q3 Is Java 100% object oriented? If yes, why? And if not, why not? `LF FAQ OEQ`

A3 I would say Java is not 100% object oriented, but it embodies practical OO concepts. There are 6 qualities to make a programming language to be pure object oriented. They are:

1. Encapsulation – data hiding and modularity.
2. Inheritance. – you define new classes and behavior based on existing classes to obtain code reuse.
3. Polymorphism – the same message sent to different objects results in behavior that's dependent on the nature of the object receiving the message.
4. All predefined types are objects.
5. All operations are performed by sending messages to objects.
6. All user defined types are objects.

The main reason why Java cannot be considered 100% OO is due to its **existence of 8**

primitive variables (i.e. violates point number 4) like int, long, char, float, etc. These data types have been excused from being objects for simplicity and to improve performance. Since primitive data types are not objects, they don't have any qualities such as inheritance or polymorphism. Even though Java provides immutable wrapper classes like Integer, Long, Character, etc representing corresponding primitive data as objects, the fact that it allowed non object oriented primitive variables to exist, makes it not fully OO.

Another reason why Java is considered not full OO is due to its **existence of static methods and variables** (i.e. violates point number 5). Since static methods can be invoked without instantiating an object, we could say that it breaks the rules of encapsulation.

Java does not support multiple class inheritance because different classes may have different variables with same name that may be contradicted and can cause confusions and result in errors. We could also argue that Java is not 100% OO according to this point of view. But Java realizes some of the key benefits of multiple inheritance through its support for multiple interface inheritance. The multiple interface inheritance gives simplicity by avoiding ambiguity, complexity, misuse, and potential increased memory usage that is present in multiple class inheritance.

Operator overloading is not possible in Java except for string concatenation and addition operations. String concatenation and addition example,

```
System.out.println(1 + 2 + "3");          //outputs 33
System.out.println("1" + 2 + 3);          //outputs 123
```

Since this is a kind of polymorphism for other operators like * (multiplication), / (division), or - (subtraction), and Java does not support this, hence one could debate that Java is not 100% OO. Working with a primitive in Java is more elegant than working with an object like *BigDecimal*. For example,

```
int a,b, c;
//without operator overloading
a = b – c * d
```

What happens in Java when you have to deal with large decimal numbers that must be accurate and of unlimited size and precision? You must use a *BigDecimal*. *BigDecimal* looks verbose for larger calculations without the operator overloading as shown below:

```
BigDecimal b = new BigDecimal("25.24");
BigDecimal c = new BigDecimal("3.99");
BigDecimal d = new BigDecimal("2.78");
BigDecimal a = b.subtract(c.multiply(d));          //verbose
```

Java 7 may have operator overloading for *BigDecimal*, and it would make your code more readable as shown below.

```
BigDecimal a = b − (c * d);                         //much better
```

Q4   What does Java comprise of? `BP PF LF`

A4   Java comprises three components:

- **Java language** comprising the syntax and semantics for programming has 3 editions – Java SE (Standard Edition), Java ME (Micro Edition), and Java EE (Enterprise Edition).

- **Java API** (Application Programming Interface) is nothing but a set of classes and interfaces that come with the JDK. All these classes are written using the Java language and contains a library of methods for common programming tasks like manipulating strings and data structures, networking, file transfer, etc. The source *.java files are in the src.zip archive and the executable *.class files are in the rt.jar archive. There are 3 types of APIs available in Java technology.

  Firstly, the official **Java core API** (i.e. src.zip and rt.jar) that is part of the JDK download. Secondly the **optional Java APIs** that can be downloaded separately. The specifications of the API is defined according to the Java Specification Request (**JSR**). For example, JSR 270 is the Java SE 6, JSR 168 is the portlet specification and so on. Finally, the **third party libraries**, which are unofficial APIs that are developed by third parties and and can be downloaded from the owner website. For example, http://www.apache.org/ where a number of handy APIs like Apache Commons, Apache Logging, and many more can be downloaded. Spring Framework, Hibernate, Struts, etc to name a few more.

  `BP`   It is a best practice to reuse proven and well tested APIs from Java

Core, Java Optional, and third party APIs from Apache, Spring foundation, etc. It is also highly recommended to have these API documentation handy while coding to reuse appropriate well tested methods where possible without having to write your own.

- **Java Virtual Machine** (JVM) is where all the classes written using the Java language and the API run on. The Java classes and API are platform independent but the JVM is not platform independent. You will find different downloads of the JVM for each Operating System (OS).

Java platform basics – JDK, JRE, JVM, etc.

Q5 What is the main difference between the Java platform and the other software platforms? `PF`

A5 The Java platform is a software only platform, which runs on top of other hardware based platforms like Unix, Windows, etc.

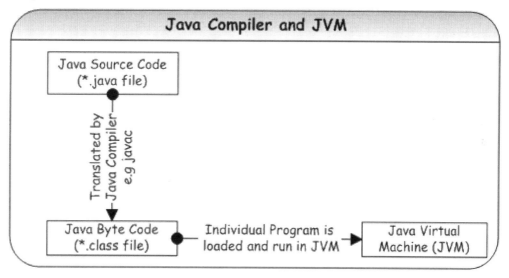

- Java source code is compiled into byte code that is understood by the JVM. Byte codes are the machine language of the JVM. The source code is easy for humans to understand. This enables a programmer to write programs. The byte code is very difficult for humans to understand. The first four bytes of every Java class (i.e the byte code) file are specified to be 0xCAFEBABE, a magic number that can help tools quickly differentiate likely class files from

21

non class files.

- Java Virtual Machine (JVM) – is a software that can be ported onto various hardware platforms. JVM interprets Java programs that have been compiled into byte code and usually stored in a "*.class" file. Byte code can be run on any computer that has Java interpreter (i.e the JVM). The JVM converts the byte code into platform (i.e. OS) specific executable machine language – a language understood by computers (i.e. binary 0s and 1s). The machine language is almost impossible for humans to understand. Every OS has its own machine language.

Q6 How would you differentiate JDK, JRE, JVM, and JIT? **PF**

A6

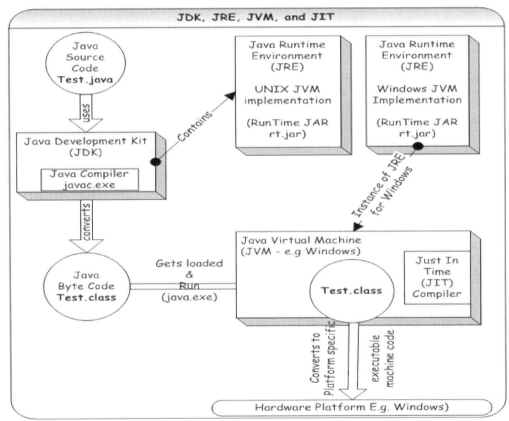

JDK: You can download a copy of the Java Development Kit (JDK). Be sure to download a copy that is appropriate for your operating system and processor. The JDK contains the compiler (i.e. javac) and other programs and libraries (i.e. jar files)

useful for Java development.

JRE: Java Runtime Environment is an implementation of the JVM. The JDK typically includes the Java Runtime Environment (JRE) which contains the virtual machine and other dependencies to run Java applications. The JRE is also available as a separate download if you have no interest in development and just want to be able to run Java applications. Remember to download a copy that is appropriate for your operating system and processor.

JIT: A JIT is a code generator that converts Java byte code into native machine code. Java programs invoked with a JIT generally run much faster than when the byte code is executed by the interpreter. The JIT compiler is a standard tool that is part of the JVM and invoked whenever you use the Java interpreter command. You can disable the JIT compiler using the -Djava.compiler=NONE option to the Java VM. You might want to disable the JIT compiler if you are running the Java VM in remote debug mode, or if you want to see source line numbers instead of the label (Compiled Code) in your Java stack traces.

Q7   Is it possible to convert byte code into source code? `PF FAQ`
A7   Yes. A Java **decompiler** is a computer program capable of reversing the work done by a compiler. In essence, it can convert back the byte code (i.e. the .class file) into the source code (i.e the .java file).

There are many decompilers that exist today, but the most widely used JD - Java Decompiler (http://java.decompiler.free.fr/) is available both as stand-alone GUI program and as an eclipse plug-in.

`SE` If you want to protect your Java class files from being decompiled, you can take a look at a Java **obfuscator tool** like yGuard or ProGuard, otherwise you will have to kiss your intellectual property good bye.

Q. When would you use a decompiler?
A.

- When you have *.class files and you do not have access to the source code (*.java files). For example, some vendors do not ship the source code for java class files or you accidentally lost (e.g deleted) your source code, in which case you can use the Java decompiler to reconstruct the source file. Another scenario is that if you generated your .class files from another language like a groovy script, using the groovyc command, you may want to use a Java decompiler to inspect the Java source code for the groovy generated class files to debug or get a better understanding of groovy integration with Java.

- To ensure that your code is adequately obfuscated before releasing it into the public domain.

- Fixing and debugging .class files when developers are slow to respond to questions that need immediate answers.

- To learn both Java and how the Java VM works.

Q8   What are the two flavors of JVM? `PF  PC  MC`

A8

- **Client** mode is suited for short lived programs like stand-alone GUI applications and applets. Specially tuned to reduce application start-up time and memory footprint, making it well suited for client applications. For example:

```
c:\> java -client MyProgram
```

- **Server** mode is suited for long running server applications, which can be active for weeks or months at a time. Specially tuned to maximize peak operating speed. The fastest possible operating speed is more important than fast start-up time or smaller runtime memory footprint.

```
c:\> java -server MyProgram
```

Q. How do you know in which mode your JVM is running?

```
c:\> java -version
```

```
java version "1.6.0_07"
Java(TM) SE Runtime Environment (build 1.6.0_07-b06)
Java HotSpot(TM) Client VM (build 10.0-b23, mixed mode, sharing)
```

Note: -client or -server must be the first argument or option of the JVM.

Q9   What are the two different bits of JVM? What is the major limitation of 32 bit JVM?

A9 JVMs are available in 32 bits (-d32 JVM argument) and 64 bits (-d64 JVM argument). 64-bit JVMs are typically only available from JDK 5.0 onwards. It is recommended that the 32-bit be used as the default JVM and 64-bit used if more memory is needed than what can be allocated to a 32-bit JVM. The Sun Java VM cannot grow beyond ~2GB on a 32bit server machine even if you install more than 2GB of RAM into your server. It is recommended that a 64bit OS with larger memory hardware is used when larger heap sizes are required. For example, >4GB is assigned to the JVM and used for deployments of >250 concurrent or >2500 casual users.

Q10 How do you monitor the JVMs?

A10 Since Java SE 5.0, the JRE provides a mean to manage and monitor the Java Virtual Machine. It comes in two flavors:

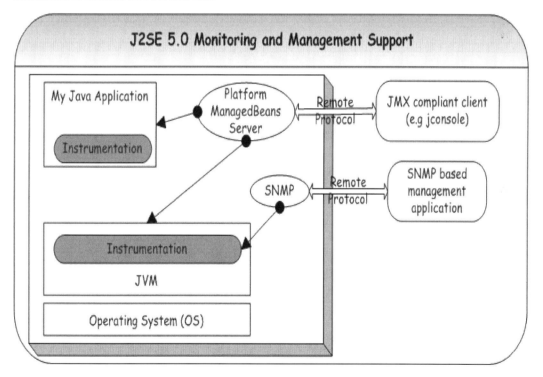

- The JVM has built-in instrumentation that enables you to monitor and manage it using Java Management eXtension (**JMX**). You can also monitor instrumented applications with JMX. To start a Java application with the management agent for local monitoring, set the following JVM argument when

25

you run your application.

$JAVA_HOME/bin/java **-Dcom.sun.management.jmxremote** MyApp

To start the JConsole:

$JAVA_HOME/bin/jconsole

- The other is a Simple Network Management Protocol (**SNMP**) agent that builds upon the management and monitoring API of the Java SE platform, and exposes the same information through SNMP.

Proactive application monitoring is vital to detect and respond to problems - before an end user is even aware that a problem exists, especially for revenue-generating production environments. it's also important to be able to gather metrics about performance and resource consumption, especially for long-running applications like websites. While you can get some information from the operating system (such as CPU and memory usage), you will often need much more detailed information.

Problem	Symptom	Tool
Insufficient memory	*Java.lang.OutOfMemoryError* indicating out of heap space, perm gen space or native swap memory space.	jhat
Memory leaks	Frequent garbage collection and growing use of memory indicated by saw tooth shaped graph. This can cause the application to slow down.	jconsole, jstat, jmap, JAMon, VisualVM, and commercial tools such as Wily's Introscope or YourKit Java Profiler.
Deadlocked threads waiting for each other, endlessly looping threads, and racing threads ending up waiting for other long running	Threads blocked on object monitors or *java.util.concurrent* locks. Deadlocked threads can cause a part or the whole application to become unresponsive. Looping threads can cause the application to hang.	jconsole, jstack, and jmap, VisualVM, and commercial tools such as Wily's Introscope or YourKit Java Profiler.

thread to release the monitor (known as thread contention).	Thread contention issues can adversely affect performance and scalability.	
JVM abruptly going down and other network fault monitoring.	Causing an application or service to be down.	tools such as Wily's *Introscope*, capable of monitoring the JVM environment and emitting SNMP traps to an IBM's *Tivoli* console to raise alarms. network switches and routers, with built-in SNMP capabilities to send traps when network faults occur.

QS Many organizations use commercial tools like Wily's Introscope, Tivoli Monitoring, etc and SNMP trap handling tools like Nagios to provide quality of service (QoS) on their mission critical applications.

Q11 What are some of the JVM arguments you have used in your projects? **PF**

A11
- To set a system property that can be retrieved using System.getPropety("name");

  ```
  -Dname=value
  ```

- To set the JVM mode:

  ```
  -client or -server
  ```

- To set the classpath:

  ```
  -cp or -classpath
  ```

- To set minimum and maximum heap sizes:

  ```
  -Xms1024 -Xmx1024
  ```

- To set garbage collection options:

  -Xincgc

- To enable assertion:

  -ea

Note: A collection of JVM arguments or options can be found at
http://blogs.sun.com/watt/resource/jvm-options-list.html

Q12 Can you briefly describe the JDK and JRE file structures? PF
A12

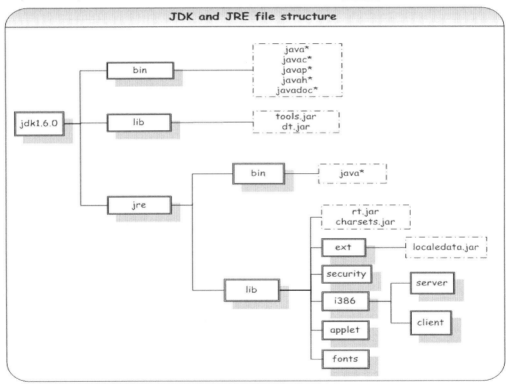

/JDK1.6.0 → The root directory of the JDK software containing license, copyright, and readme files. Also contains **src.zip**, the archive of source code for the Java 2 platform.

/JDK1.6.0/**bin** → The executable files like javac for all the development tools. The PATH environment variable should contain an entry to this directory.

/JDK1.6.0/**lib** → Files used by the development tools. Includes **tools.jar**, which contains non-core classes for support of the tools and utilities in the JDK.

/JDK1.6.0/**jre** → The root directory of the Java runtime environment. This the directory referred by the "**java.home**" system property.

/JDK1.6.0/**jre/bin** →The executable files for tools and libraries used by the Java platform.

/JDK1.6.0/**jre/lib** → Code libraries, property settings, and resource files used by the Java runtime environment. Includes:

- **rt.jar** – the Java platforms core API (the bootstrap classes). The rt most likely stands for RunTime. Some tend to think it stands for **R**oo**T**, since this jar contains the root classes.

- **charsets.jar** – character conversion classes.

/JDK1.6.0/**jre/lib/ext** → This directory is for extensions to the Java platform. The localedata.jar contains locale data for java.text and java.util packages.

/JDK1.6.0/**jre/lib/security** → Contains security policy (java.policy) and security properties (java.security) files.

Q13 What does jar stand for? How does it differ from a zip file? `LF`
A13 The jar stands for **J**ava **AR**chive. A jar file usually has a file name extension .jar. It mainly contains Java class files but any types of files can be included. For example, XML files, properties files, HTML files, image files, binary files, etc. You can use the "jar" application utility bundled inside /JDK1.6.0/jre/bin to create, extract, and view its contents. You can also use any zip file utility program to view its contents. A jar file cannot contain other jar files.

Basically, a jar file is same as a zip file, except that it contains a META-INF directory to store meta data or attributes. The most known file is META-INF/MANIFEST.MF. When you create a JAR file, it automatically receives a default manifest file. There can

29

be only one manifest file in an archive. Most uses of JAR files beyond simple archiving and compression require special information to be in the manifest file. For example,

- If you have an application bundled in a JAR file, you need some way to indicate which class within the JAR file is your application's entry point. The entry point is the class having a method with signature public static void main(String[ ] args). For example,

```
Main-Class: Test.class
```

- A package within a JAR file can be optionally sealed, which means that all classes defined in that package must be archived in the same JAR file. You might want to seal a package, for example, to ensure version consistency among the classes in your software or as a security measure.

```
Name: myCompany/myPackage/
Sealed: true
```

Note: Refer JDK documentation for the manifest format and other options.

Setting up and running Java

Q14 What do you need to develop and run Java programs? How would you go about getting started? `PF`

A14
- Download and install the Java Development Kit (JDK) SE (Standard Edition) for your operating system (e.g. Windows, Linux, etc) and processor (32 bit, 64 bit, etc) .

- Configure your environment. The first environment variable you need to set is the **JAVA_HOME**.

On Windows: use the system environment variables console

```
JAVA_HOME=C:\DEV\java\jdk-1.6.0_11
```

On Linux:

```
export JAVA_HOME=/usr/java/jdk-1.6.0_11
```

This system property will be used by your other command line build tools like ANT and maven.

The second environment variable you need to set is the PATH variable. The PATH variable contains a list of directories that the operating system uses to locate executables to be executed by commands like javac, java, etc typed into the system.

On Windows: use the system environment variables console

```
PATH=%JAVA_HOME%\bin;x:\maven\tools\maven-
2.0.9\bin;C:\bea\weblogic81\server\bin;
```

On Linux:

```
export PATH=$PATH:$JAVA_HOME/bin
```

Verify your configurations with the following commands:

DOS Command:

```
echo %JAVA_HOME%
echo %PATH%
```

UNIX Command:

```
$ echo $JAVA_HOME
$ echo $PATH
```

• Verify your installation with the following commands:

```
$ javac -version
$ java -version
```

If your operating system doesn't recognize these commands, you have not either set up your environment variable correctly or may have to open a new command window for your changes to your environment variables to be detected (especially in windows).

- To list the available options for javac or java just type the command without any arguments.

```
$ javac
$ java
```

Q15 How do you create a class under a package in Java? **LF**

A15 You can create a class under a package as follows with the **package** keyword, which is the first keyword in any Java program followed by the **import** statements. The java.lang package is imported implicitly by default and all the other packages must be explicitly imported. The core Java packages like java.lang.*, java.net.*, java.io*, etc and its class files are distributed in the archive file named rt.jar.

```
package com.xyz.client ;
import java.io.File;
import java.net.URL;
```

Q16 What do you need to do to run a class with a main( ) method in a package? **PF**

For example: Say, you have a class named *Pet* in a project folder *C:\projects\Test\src* and package named *com.xyz.client*, will you be able to compile and run it as it is?

A16 The answer depends on where you run it from. Firstly, the source code *"Pet.java"* is as shown below

```
package com.xyz.client;

public class Pet {
    public static void main(String[ ] args) {
        System.out.println("I am found in the classpath");
    }
}
```

Secondly, this source code can be compiled into byte code i.e. *Pet.class* file as shown below:

C:\projects\Test\src>javac **-d ../bin** com/xyz/client/Pet.java

Note: The compiled byte code file *Pet.class* will be saved in the folder C:\projects\Test\bin\com\xyz\client.

If you run it inside where the *Pet.class* is stored, the answer is yes.

C:\projects\Test\bin>java com/xyz/client/Pet

The output is → I am found in the classpath

The *Pet.class* file will be found since *com.xyz.client.Pet* class file is in the *projects\Test\bin* folder. If you run it in any other folder say c:\

C:\> java com.xyz.client.Pet
                OR
C:\projects\Test\src>java com/xyz/client/Pet

The answer is no, and you will get the following exception: Exception in thread "main" *java.lang.NoClassDefFoundError: com/xyz/client/Pet*. To fix this, you need to tell how to find the *Pet.class* by setting or providing the classpath. How can you do that? One of the following ways:

- Set the operating system CLASSPATH environment variable to have the project folder *c:\projects\Test\bin*.

- Set the operating system CLASSPATH environment variable to have a jar file *c:/projects/Test/pet.jar*, which has the *Pet.class* file in it. You can also specify both the location of the jar file containing the class files for the *Test* project and the location of the folder containing the packages and the class files for the *Test2* project.

  CLASSPATH= c:/projects/Test/pet.jar;C:/projects/Test2/bin

- Run it with -cp or -classpath option as shown below.

  C:\>java **-cp projects\Test\bin** com/xyz/client/Pet

33

Platform Essentials

OR
C:\>java -classpath c:/projects/Test/pet.jar com.xyz.client.Pet
OR
C:\projects\Test\src>java -cp ../bin com/xyz/client/Pet

Important: Two objects loaded by different class loaders are never equal even if they carry the same values. This means a class is uniquely identified in the context of the associated classloader. This applies to singletons too, where each classloader will have its own singleton.

How are your classes loaded?

Q17 Explain Java class loaders? If you have a class in a package, what do you need to do to run it? Explain dynamic class loading? PF FAQ

A17

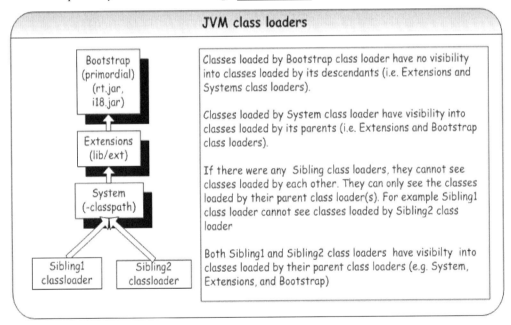

Class loaders are hierarchical. Classes are introduced into the JVM as they are referenced by name in a class that is already running in the JVM. So how is the very first class loaded? The very first class is specially loaded with the help of public static void main(String[ ] args) method declared in your class. All the subsequently loaded classes are loaded by the classes, which are already loaded and running. A classloader creates a name space. A loaded class in a JVM is identified by its fully qualified name and its defining classloader - this is sometimes referred to as the runtime identity of the class. Consequently, each classloader in the JVM can be said to define its own name space. Within a name space, all fully- qualified names are unique. This means class *au.com.Test-Class* defined by classloader A is NOT considered by the JVM to be the same class as class *au.com.TestClass* defined by classloader B.

All JVMs include at least one classloader that is embedded within the JVM called the primordial (or bootstrap) classloader. The JVM has hooks in it to allow user defined class loaders to be used in place of primordial classloader. The following class loaders are created by the JVM.

classloader	Reloadable	Explanation
Bootstrap (primordial)	No	Loads JDK internal classes, java.* packages as defined by the sun.boot.class.path system property. Typically loads the rt.jar and i18n.jar archives.
Extensions	No	Loads jar files from JDK extensions directory as defined by the java.ext.dirs system property. Usually from the lib/ext directory of the JRE.
System	No	Loads classes from the system classpath as defined by the java.class.path property, which is set by the CLASSPATH environment variable or command line options -classpath or -cp as discussed earlier. The developers are responsible for providing the necessary classpath inform-ation.

Class loaders are hierarchical and use a delegation model when loading a class. Class loaders request their parent to load the class first before attempting to load it themselves. When a classloader loads a class, the child class loaders in the hierarchy will never reload the class again. Hence uniqueness is maintained. Classes loaded by a child classloader have visibility into classes loaded by its parents up the hierarchy but the reverse is not true as explained in the above diagram.

Q18 Explain static vs. dynamic class loading? `PF FAQ`

A18 Classes are statically loaded with Java's "new" operator.

```
class MyClass {
    public static void main(String args[ ]) {
        Car c = new Car( );
    }
}
```

A *NoClassDefFoundException* is thrown if a class is referenced with Java's "new" operator (i.e. static loading) but the runtime system cannot find the referenced class.

Dynamic class loading is a technique for programmatically invoking the functions of a classloader at run time. Classes can be loaded dynamically as shown below:

```
Class.forName (className);    //static method which returns a Class
```

The above static method returns the class object associated with the class name. The string *className* can be supplied dynamically at run time. Unlike the static loading, the dynamic loading will decide whether to load the class *Car* or the class *Jeep* at runtime based on a properties file or other runtime conditions. Once the class is dynamically loaded the following method returns an instance of the loaded class. It's just like creating a class object with no arguments.

```
class.newInstance ();              // A non-static method, which creates an
                                   // instance of a class (i.e. creates an object).
```

Example:

```
Jeep myJeep = null ;
//myClassName should be read from a .properties file.
//stay away from hard coding values in your program.
String myClassName = "au.com.Jeep" ;
Class vehicleClass = Class.forName(myClassName) ;
myJeep = (Jeep) vehicleClass.newInstance( );
myJeep.setFuelCapacity(50);
```

A *ClassNotFoundException* is thrown when an application tries to load in a class through its string name using one of the following methods but no definition for the class with the specified name could be found:

- The forName(..) method in class - *Class*.
- The findSystemClass(..) method in class - *ClassLoader*.
- The loadClass(..) method in class - *ClassLoader*.

When you are running within a managed environment like an application server, Servlet engine or EJB Container, you must use the context classloader to retrieve a class as shown below.

```
ClassLoader cl = Thread.currentThread( ).getContextClassLoader( );
if(cl == null) {
    cl = getClass( ).getClassLoader( );
}
Class myClazz = cl.loadClass(className);
```

Q19 What tips would you give to someone who is experiencing a class loading or "Class Not Found" exception? `OEQ`

A19 "Class Not Found" exceptions could be quite tricky to troubleshoot. Firstly, determine the jar file that should contain the class file:

```
$ find . -name "*.jar" -print -exec jar -tf '{}' \; | grep -E "jar$|String\.class"
```

Secondly, check the version of the jar in the manifest file MANIFEST.MF, access rights (e.g. read-only) of the jar file, and any jar corruption by trying to unjar it with *"jar -xvf ..."*. If the class is dynamically loaded, check if you have spelled the class name correctly.

Thirdly, check if the application is running under the right JDK? Check the JAVA_HOME environment property

```
$ echo $JAVA_HOME
```

Finally, you'll need to have a good understanding of your application server's class-loader hierarchy.

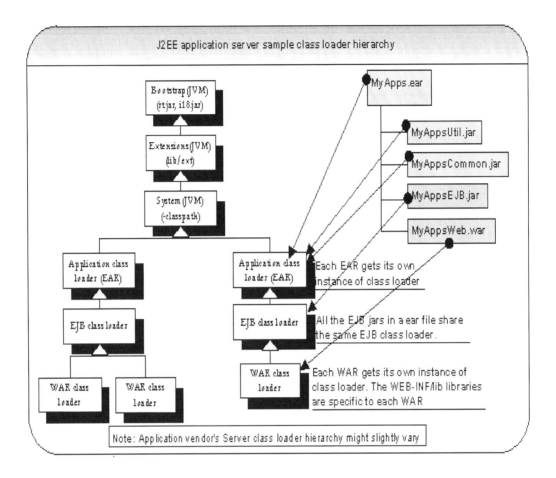

- Is the missing class packaged with the application (e.g., under WEB-INF/lib) and being loaded by one of the parent class-loaders? Most application servers utilize a class-loader hierarchy where WAR file's class-loader is a child of EAR class-loader which in turn is a child of the system (JVM) class-loader. Parent class-loaders can't go down to request a class loaded from a child class-loader. The problem occurs if some jars were moved to a shared library but they still depend on classes packaged with the application.

- Running different versions of the same jar loaded by the different class loaders can cause this issue.

Compile-time versus runtime

Learn to think in terms of compile-time versus runtime to solve issues quickly and identify better solutions to a given problem. Each approach has its pros and cons.

Q20 Explain compile-time versus runtime? `PF FAQ`

A20 **Compile-time** (i.e. static) is when a program text (e.g. *MyProgram.java*) is being read in, analyzed, and translated into byte code version (e.g. *MyProgram.class*) that can be run on the JVM. At compile-time you can get syntactic errors like leaving out a closing bracket or a semicolon, type safety errors like assigning a type long to type int without an explicit casting, etc.

Runtime (i.e. dynamic) is when the generated byte code is executed within the JVM. At runtime you get semantic errors like trying to examine the 4th element of a list that has only 3 elements (e.g. *ArrayIndexOutOfBoundsException*), null reference errors (e.g. *NullPointerException*), attempting to cast an object to a subclass of which it is not an instance (e.g. *ClassCastException*), etc.

Q21 Does this happen during compile-time, runtime, or both? `PF LF FAQ`

A21 **Method overloading**: This happens at compile-time. This is also called compile-time polymorphism because the compiler must decide how to select which method to run based on the data types of the arguments.

```
public class {
    public static void evaluate(String param1);  // method #1
    public static void evaluate(int param1);      // method #2
}
```

If the compiler were to compile the statement:

```
evaluate("My Test Argument passed to param1");
```

it could see that the argument was a string literal, and generate byte code that called method #1.

Method overriding: This happens at runtime. This is also called runtime polymorphism because the compiler does not and cannot know which method to call. Instead, the JVM must make the determination while the code is running.

```
public class A {
  public int compute(int input) {                    //method #3
    return 3 * input;
  }
}
```

```
public class B extends A {
  @Override
  public int compute(int input) {                    //method #4
    return 4 * input;
  }
}
```

The method compute(..) in subclass "B" overrides the method compute(..) in super class "A". If the compiler has to compile the following method,

```
public int evaluate(A reference, int arg2)  {
   int result = reference.compute(arg2);
}
```

The compiler would not know whether the input argument '*reference*' is of type "A" or type "B". This must be determined during runtime whether to call method #3 or method #4 depending on what type of object (i.e. instance of Class A or instance of Class B) is assigned to input variable "*reference*".

Generics (aka type checking): This happens at compile-time. The compiler checks for the type correctness of the program and translates or rewrites the code that uses generics into non-generic code that can be executed in the current JVM. This technique is known as "type erasure". In other words, the compiler erases all generic type information contained within the angle brackets to achieve backward compatibility with JRE 1.4.0 or earlier editions.

```
List<String> myList = new ArrayList<String>(10);
```

after compilation becomes:

```
List myList = new ArrayList(10);
```

Annotations: You can have either run-time or compile-time annotations.

```
public class B extends A {
  @Override
  public int compute(int input){     //method #4
    return 4 * input;
  }
}
```

@*Override* is a simple compile-time annotation to catch little mistakes like typing tostring( ) instead of toString( ) in a subclass. User defined annotations can be processed at compile-time using the Annotation Processing Tool (APT) that comes with Java 5. In Java 6, this is included as part of the compiler itself.

```
public class MyTest{
  @Test
  public void testEmptyness(){
    org.junit.Assert.assertTrue(getList( ).isEmpty( ));
  }

  private List getList( ){
    ...
  }
}
```

@**Test** is an annotation that *JUnit* framework uses at runtime with the help of reflection to determine which method(s) to execute within a test class.

```
@Test(timeout=100)
public void testTimeout( ) {
  while(true);   //infinite loop
}
```

The above test fails if it takes more than 100ms to execute at runtime.

```
@Test (expected=IndexOutOfBoundsException.class)
public void testOutOfBounds( ) {
  new ArrayList<Object>( ).get(1);
}
```

The above code fails if it does not throw "*IndexOutOfBoundsException*" or if it throws a different exception at runtime. User defined annotations can be processed at runtime using the new "*AnnotatedElement*" and "*Annotation*" element interfaces added to the Java reflection API.

Exceptions: You can have either runtime or compile-time exceptions.

RuntimeException is also known as the unchecked exception indicating not required to be checked by the compiler. *RuntimeException* is the superclass of those exceptions that can be thrown during the execution of a program within the JVM. A method is not required to declare in its throws clause any subclasses of *RuntimeException* that might be thrown during the execution of a method but not caught.

Example: *NullPointerException*, *ArrayIndexOutOfBoundsException*, etc

Checked exceptions are verified by the compiler at compile-time that a program contains handlers like throws clause or try{} catch{} blocks for handling the checked exceptions, by analyzing which checked exceptions can result from execution of a method or constructor.

Aspect Oriented Programming (AOP): Aspects can be weaved at compile-time, post-compile time, load-time or runtime.

- **Compile-time:** weaving is the simplest approach. When you have the source code for an application, the AOP compiler (e.g. ajc – AspectJ Compiler) will compile from source and produce woven class files as output. The invocation of the weaver is integral to the AOP compilation process. The aspects themselves may be in source or binary form. If the aspects are required for the affected classes to compile, then you must weave at compile-time.

- **Post-compile:** weaving is also sometimes called binary weaving, and is used to weave existing class files and JAR files. As with compile-time weaving, the aspects used for weaving may be in source or binary form, and may themselves be woven by aspects.

- **Load-time:** weaving is simply binary weaving deferred until the point that a classloader loads a class file and defines the class to the JVM. To support this, one or more "weaving class loaders", either provided explicitly by the run-time environment or enabled through a "weaving agent" are required.

- **Runtime**: weaving of classes that have already been loaded to the JVM.

Inheritance – happens at compile-time.
Delegation or **composition** – happens at runtime.

Q22 Can you differentiate compile-time inheritance and runtime inheritance with examples and specify which Java supports? `PF LF FAQ`

A22 The term "inheritance" refers to a situation where behaviors and attributes are passed on from one object to another. The Java programming language natively only supports compile-time inheritance through subclassing as shown below with the keyword "extends".

```java
public class Parent {
    public String saySomething() {
        return "Parent is called";
    }
}
```

```java
public class Child extends Parent {
    @Override
    public String saySomething() {
        return super.saySomething() + ", Child is called";
    }
}
```

A call to *saySomething( )* method on the class "*Child*" will return "Parent is called, Child is called" because the *Child* class inherits "Parent is called" from the class *Parent*. The keyword "super" is used to call the method on the "*Parent*" class. Runtime inheritance refers to the ability to construct the parent/child hierarchy at runtime. Java does not natively support runtime inheritance, but there is an alternative concept known as "delegation" or "composition", which refers to constructing a hierarchy of object instances at runtime. This allows you to simulate runtime inheritance. In Java, delegation is typically achieved as shown below:

```java
public class Parent {
    public String saySomething() {
        return "Parent is called";
```

```
        }
}
```

```
public class Child {
    public String saySomething( ) {
        return new Parent( ).saySomething( ) + ", Child is called";
    }
}
```

The *Child* class delegates the call to the *Parent* class. Composition can be achieved as follows:

```
public class Child {
    private Parent parent = null;

    public Child( ){
        this.parent = new Parent( );
    }

    public String saySomething( ) {
        return this.parent.saySomething( ) + ", Child is called";
    }
}
```

Q23 Are marker or tag interfaces obsolete with the advent of annotations (i.e. runtime annotations)? **LF**

A23 Everything that can be done with a marker or tag interfaces in earlier versions of Java can now be done with annotations at runtime using reflection. One of the common problems with the marker or tag interfaces like *Serializable*, *Cloneable*, etc is that when a class implements them, all of its subclasses inherit them as well whether you want them to or not. You cannot force your subclasses to unimplement an interface. Annotations can have parameters of various kinds, and they're much more flexible than the marker interfaces. This makes tag or marker interfaces obsolete, except for situations in which empty or tag interfaces can be checked at compile-time using the type-system in the compiler whereas annotation check has to be done at runtime as shown below:

Using an annotation at **runtime**:

```
package annotations1;

public @interface Deletable { }                    // annotation definition
```

```
package annotations1;

@Deletable
public class ClassWithDeletableObjects {           // this class uses the annotation
    //...
}
```

```
package annotations1;

public class Test {

    public void delete(Object obj){
        Deletable ann = obj.getClass( ).getAnnotation(Deletable.class);   // Line A
        if(ann != null) {
            //go ahead and delete
        }
        else {
            throw new RuntimeException("Not a deleteable object");
        }
    }
}
```

Using a tag or marker interface at **compile-time:**

```
package markerinterface;

public interface Deletable { }            // marker  interface definition
```

```
package markerinterface;

public class ClassWithDeletableObjects implements Deletable {
    //....
}
```

```
package markerinterface;
```

```
public class Test {

    // works only with Deletable objects. Compile-time error if a Deletable
    // object is not passed.
    public void delete(Deletable obj){
        // go ahead and delete
    }
}
```

So marker or tag interfaces are only rarely required going forward for situations described below,

- In the very rare event of the profiling indicating that the runtime checks are expensive due to being accessed very frequently, and compile-time checks with interfaces as shown above is preferred.
- In the event of existing marker interfaces like *Serializable, Cloneable,* etc are used or Java 5 or later versions cannot be temporarily used.

BP The best practice going forward is to use an annotation as illustrated above instead of a marker interface since it solves the problem of forcing the subclasses to inherit the interface. For example, since the class *Number* implements *Serializable,* any subclass such as *Integer* or *AtomicInteger* does too. As per the above example using an annotation, if you don't want a particular subclass of *"ClassWithDeletableObjects"* to be deleted, you can achieve it as shown below:

```
package annotations1;

public @interface Deletable {
    boolean value( ) default true;          // by default set to true
}
```

The class that must not be deleted can be defined as shown below,

```
@Deletable(false)
public class NotDeletableObjects extends ClassWithDeletableObjects {
    //...
}
```

The few lines from Line A onwards in the *Test* class needs to be changed from

```
Deletable ann = obj.getClass( ).getAnnotation(Deletable.class);   // Line A
if(ann != null) {
    //go ahead and delete
}
```

to

```
Deletable ann = obj.getClass( ).getAnnotation(Deletable.class);
if(ann != null & ann.value( )) {
    //go ahead and delete
}
```

BP PC The above code checks for the boolean value supplied as well. So the annotations are more explicit and flexible than the marker interfaces. The marker interfaces using *instanceof* operator seems to be a bit faster than the equivalent *Class.isAnnotationPresent* at the time of writing. As mentioned earlier, design principles must not be compromised for gaining smaller performance gains. Premature optimization is bad. If profiling indicates that a particular annotation is adversely impacting performance then look at alternative solutions to address that particular problem.

Q24 What is the difference between line A & line B in the following code snippet? **COQ PC**

```
public class ConstantFolding {
    static final  int number1 = 5;
    static final  int number2 = 6;
    static int number3 = 5;
    static int number4= 6;

    public static void main(String[ ] args) {
        int product1 = number1 * number2;          //line A
        int product2 = number3 * number4;          //line B
    }
}
```

A24 Line A, evaluates the product at compile-time, and Line B evaluates the product at runtime. If you use a Java Decompiler, and decompile the compiled *ConstantFolding.-*

47

class file, you will see why

```
public class ConstantFolding
{
  static final int number1 = 5;
  static final int number2 = 6;
  static int number3 = 5;
  static int number4 = 6;

  public static void main(String[ ] args)
  {
     int product1 = 30;
     int product2 = number3 * number4;
  }
}
```

Constant folding is an optimization technique used by the Java compiler. Since final variables cannot change, they can be optimized. Java Decompiler and **javap** command are handy tool for inspecting the compiled (i.e. byte code) code.

Q. Can you think of other scenarios other than code optimization, where inspecting a compiled code is useful? OEQ

A. Generics in Java are compile-time constructs, and it is very handy to inspect a compiled class file to understand and troubleshoot generics.

Q25 What is a Java debugger? What are the different ways to debug your code? PF
A25 The Java Platform Debugger Architecture (JPDA) consists of three interfaces designed for use by debuggers in development environments for desktop systems.

- The Java Virtual Machine Tools Interface (JVM TI) defines the services a VM must provide for debugging.
- The Java Debug Interface (JDI) defines information and requests at the user code level.
- The Java Debug Wire Protocol (JDWP) defines the format of information and requests transferred between the process being debugged and the debugger front end, which implements the Java Debug Interface (JDI).

The JPDA allows you to peek into your code at runtime, and debug your code. The jdb is an implementation of the Java Debugger Interface. The jdb is a simple command-line debugger for Java classes providing inspection and debugging of a local or remote Java Virtual Machine. JDK ships with jdb. Easier way to debug your code is to use the visual debugging provided by your IDE (e.g. Eclipse, Net Beans, Websphere Application Developer, IntelliJ, etc)

Q. What are the different ways to add break points to your code?
A. You can add break point to any specific line in your code, also you can add break point by exception. This will allow your program to halt at runtime when a particular exception is thrown – like a *NullpointerException*.

Q. Why is remote debugging important and how will you debug a remote Java application?

A. It is increasingly essential with the globalization to be able to debug a Java application that is deployed remotely, in another country or city. You will come across scenarios where an application might be running fine in your sandbox (i.e. local desktop), but might be buggy when running in another environment or country.

Say you want to remotely debug an application called MyApp.jar that is running remotely, you can set up your desktop to be able to debug it by enabling the remote debugging as shown below:

```
java -Xdebug -Xrunjdwp:transport=dt_socket,address=888,server=y -jar MyApp.jar
```

The above command tells the MyApp.jar to start a server socket on port 888, and publish the debugging messages using the jdwp, which stands for **J**ava **D**ebug **W**ire **P**rotocol.

Q. What are some of the challenges you faced in debugging your application? What tips would you give?
A.

* Debugging multi-threaded applications can be tricky because whenever one thread reaches a break-point, all other threads also stopped.

* Intermittent issues arising from improper implementation of *equals( )* or *hashCode( )* methods or data related require a more thorough debugging.

Tips: Carefully analyze the thread stack traces. Use the debugging features like step into, step over, step out, and inspection of the runtime values provided by the visual debugging tools. Where necessary, include adequate debug statements in your code for a more complex situation. Finally, know your Java fundamentals well enough and acquire enough experience to be able to come up with a list of possible causes and narrow it down to the root cause.

Section-3:

Knowing your way around Java

- Judging your exposure to Java through open-ended questions.
- Gauging your exposure to Unix operating systems as most production systems are Unix based.
- Understanding your experience in regards to proper documentation.
- Obtaining a feel for your awareness and attitude towards software quality

This section is mainly for intermediate to senior level. If you are a beginner, skim through this section, and come back to it after reading the other sections. This section is mainly used to judge your experience. So where possible give practical examples by reflecting back on your past experience using the SAR (Situation-Action-Result) technique. The answers provided here are hints only. As an experienced professional, your experience and views may differ. Experienced professionals know what works and what doesn't. They know what tools to use to simplify a task at hand.

Good developers are opinionated based on their past experience. They can handle scenario based questions. They may pause a while to reflect back on their experience, but won't be stumped by the open ended questions. Reflecting back on your past experience and a little preparation prior to your interviews and meetings will really boost your performance.

This is a brush up section that will not only help you sell yourself more effectively, but also will help you reflect back on your past experience and refresh your memory. This section will add value only if you perform well relating to sections 4 – 7 on fundamentals.

This section will also provide valuable insights into getting your job done more effectively, and making yourself heard in team meetings by contributing suggestions or raising opinions. This does not mean that you will have to be inflexible. Most importantly, the good developers get things done by complimenting their technical skills with good soft-skills and right attitude.

Judging Experience

As explained earlier, open ended questions give you a great opportunity to prove your caliber and usefulness to the organization in a well-rounded manner. You have no control over what questions get asked in interviews, but you have control over what messages, skills, experience, and personal attributes you want to nicely get across to your prospective employers or interviewers without bragging, being too critical, or coming across inflexible. The open-ended questions give you the chance to make an impression. A very common open-ended question is – tell me about yourself? `OEQ`

Q1   Can you list some of the Java features you used recently? `LF`

A1   [Hint] JDK 5.0 (external version 5.0 and internal version 1.5.0) is a major feature release that largely centered on <u>enhancing ease-of-development</u>.

Features:

- **Generics**: provides compile-time type safety to operate on objects of various types and collections frameworks. It eliminates the tedious labor of casting. (JSR-14)
- **Enhanced for loop**: eliminates the monotonous labor and error-proneness of iterators and index variables when iterating over collections and arrays. (JSR-201)
- **Autoboxing** and **auto-unboxing**: eliminates the routine work of manual conversion between primitive data types such as int, long, etc and wrapper object types such as *Integer*, *Long*, etc. (JSR-201)
- **Type safe enums**: are flexible object oriented enumerated type facility that allows type safety without the verbosity and error-proneness of the "type safe enum pattern" that existed prior to JDK 5.0. (JSR-201)
- **Varargs**: eliminates the need of manually wrapping up argument list into an array when invoking methods that accept variable-length argument lists. (JSR-201)
- **Static import**: eliminates the need to qualify static members with class names without the shortcomings of the "constant interface" anti-pattern existed prior to JDK 5.0. (JSR-201)
- **Annotations**: let you avoid boilerplate code under many circumstances by enabling tools to generate it from annotations in the source code. This leads to "attribute oriented" (aka declarative) programming. This eliminates the need to maintain "side files" that must be kept up to date with changes in source files.

Instead the information can be maintained in a source file itself. This is also Java's answer to the XDoclet framework used prior to JDK 5.0 (JSR-175). Annotations allow you to add runtime metadata to classes, fields, and methods. Everything that can be done with marker or tag interfaces in earlier versions of Java can now be done with annotations at runtime using reflection.

Libraries:

- The **Collections** framework has been enhanced with support for generics, enhanced for loop, and autoboxing. Three new interfaces named *Queue*, *BlockingQueue*, and *ConcurrentMap* have been added. More efficient copy-on-write *"List"* and *"Set"* implementations have also been added.
- The Java API for XML Processing (**JAXP**) has been included in the JDK so it doesn't need to be downloaded separately. (JSR-206)
- The **concurrency utility** package java.util.concurrent was included as part of the standard edition 5.0, which previously had to be downloaded separately. This package provides a scalable, thread-safe, and high-performance building blocks for developing concurrent applications.

JDK 6.0 (external version 6.0 and internal version 1.6.0) release is centered on being Web Services friendly, mixing of Java with other scripting languages, and general enhancements to existing libraries.

- One of the most significant features of this release is support for the Java API for XML Web Services (JAX-WS), version 2.0. JAX-WS 2.0 includes Java Architecture for XML Binding (JAXB) 2.0 and SOAP with Attachments API for Java (SAAJ) 1.3. So Java SE 6.0 is SOA (Service Oriented Architecture) friendly, and Apache Axis framework is no longer required.
- Java SE 6.0 also includes a new framework and developer APIs to allow mixing of Java technology with scripting languages such as PHP, Python, JavaScript, and Ruby. This is very useful for prototyping, experimentation of an algorithm or function, and one off or ad hoc tasks like transforming a text file into a needed format, looking for a specific item in large log files, getting a subset of data from a database and packing it as a text file, etc. All of the above tasks can be done in a language like Java, but it can be faster and easier to do them in a scripting language like PERL, Ruby, or Python. **BP** It is a best practice to always use the right or best tool for the right job without just being overly passionate about Java alone.

- Full JDBC 4.0 (Java Data Base Connectivity) implementation providing improved XML support for Databases. A free to use Java Database based on Apache Derby is included since JDK SE 5.0 download.
- Improved desktop APIs including newly incorporated "*SwingWorker*" utility to help with multi-threading in GUI applications and much needed "*JTable*" sorting and filtering capabilities. You also have access to new things such as desktop applications through what used to be called the JDesktop Integration Components (JDIC). You can now have the ability to add applications to the system tray. The GUI performance is snappier and integrates well with the native platforms.
- Improved monitoring and management through out of the box on demand support tools and inclusion of Java heap analysis tool (Jhat) for forensic explorations of those core dumps.

Q2 Who are your role models? What books really inspired you? What was the recent Java book you read? What websites do you use to keep your knowledge current? OEQ

A2 [Hint]

Role models:

- Rod Johnson – founder of SpringSource.
- Robert C Martin – author of a number of timeless software books. http://www.objectmentor.com.
- Kathy Sierra – author of popular head first series of books.
- Anyone who worked or working with you.

Books read by the experienced:

- Effective Java by Joshua Bloch.
- Code Complete by Steve McConnell
- The Pragmatic Programmer by Andrew Hunt and David Thomas
- Design Patterns by ErichGamma, RichardHelm, RalphJohnson, and JohnVlis-sides (the GangOfFour).
- Agile Software Development, Principles, Patterns, and Practices by Robert C. Martin
- Clean Code by Robert C. Martin.
- Patterns of Enterprise Application Architecture by Martin Fowler

- Head First Design Patterns by Eric T Freeman, Elisabeth Robson, Bert Bates, Kathy Sierra
- Java Concurrency in Practice by Brian Goetz
- Java Puzzlers by Joshua Bloch and Neal Gafter

Books read by the beginners:
- Thinking in Java by Bruce Eckel
- Head First Java by Bert Bates, Kathy Sierra

Websites:
- http://www.theserverside.com/
- http://java.dzone.com/
- http://www.javaworld.com/
- http://www.infoq.com/

Note: If you get your Java doses more often from blogs and white papers like me than books, elaborate on your favorite online resources.

Q3 Can you list the Java SE features you really love and why? **LF**
A3 [Hint]

Annotations based development relieves Java developers from the pain of cumbersome configuration. Annotations provide declarative style programming where the programmer says what should be done and tools emit the code to do it. This assists rapid application development, easier maintenance, and less likely to be bug-prone. For example, EJB3, Hibernate, and Web Services widely use annotations. You could even write your own service delivery framework making use of annotations whereas the developers concentrate on writing the business logic through business delegates and data access logic through data access objects (DAOs) while the framework takes care of generating the necessary EJB3 and Web Service boiler plate code such as the interfaces, implementations and descriptors based on standard and custom annotations during build time.

Varargs, autoboxing, printf style text formatting, and **for-each loops**: These features make your code more readable by simplifying your code. For example, without varargs and autoboxing one would write:

```
String output = String.format( "%s:%d: %s%n", new Object[ ]
                { inputText, new Integer(inputNumber), inputMessage });
```

With varargs and autoboxing,

```
String output = String.format("%s:%d:%s%n", inputText,
                                inputNumber, inputMessage);
```

new Object[ ] {......} array is not required due to varargs and new Integer(...) is not required due to autoboxing. The enhanced for loop, also known as foreach, is a nice feature that can be used with any of the collection classes in Java 1.5. In addition, Java supplies hooks that allow you to make your own class iterable, so that it can be referenced in a foreach loop.

```
public void write(String[ ] inputs) {
    for (String input: inputs)
        write(input);
}
```

Enums are very powerful. Enums are type safe, readable if proper names are used, can be used in switch statements, self-documents your code, can be compared for equality using "==" identity without requiring to use the equals( ) as they are effectively singletons, and can be used in collections (e.g. as *HashMap* keys). All enum classes inherit the *toString( )*, *hashCode( )*, and *equals( )* methods from the **Enum** class. The *equals( )* and *hashCode( )* methods are marked as final, hence cannot be overridden by your enums. The *toString( )* method can be overridden, as it is not marked final. In short, all of the *Object* class methods in the *Enum* class are marked as final except the *toString( )* method. Refer to the *Enum* class API, as many of the other methods like *name( )*, *compareTo( )*, *ordinate( )*, etc are marked final as well. Enums are *Serializable* and *Comparable* as they implement the relevant interfaces. The enums cannot be cloned as the *Enum* class' clone method throws *CloneNotSupported* exception.

You can add your own field and methods. Each declared field is also an instance of enum. **DP** Hence, you can apply the template method design pattern to create command objects as shown below:

```
public enum EventType {
    ...
    STANDARD() {
```

```java
    @Override public void execute( ) {
        logger.info("Standard Event");
    }
  },

  SPECIAL( ) {
    @Override public void execute( ) {
        logger.info("Special Event");
    }
  };
  ....
  //template method
  public abstract void execute( );
}
```

```java
public class Event {

  private String name;
  private EventType type = null;

  public void getName( ){return this.name;}
  public void getEventType( ){return this.type;}

  public void setName(String name){
    this.name = name;
  }

  public void setEventType(EventType type){
    this.type = type;
  }
  ...
}
```

So instead of writing

```java
if(type == EventType.STANDARD) {
  logger.info("Standard Event");
}else if(type == EventType.SPECIAL) {
  logger.info("Special Event");
```

```
}
...
```

You could write:

```
EventType.STANDARD.execute( );
EventType.SPECIAL.execute( );
```

Even better is to write:

```
getEventType( ).execute( );
```

Q4   Can you list the Java SE features you dislike and why? **LF CO**
A4   [Hint]

Checked exceptions: By removing checked exceptions, one can eliminate the need to implement try/catch clauses that do nothing but log a message, wrap and re-throw as a *RuntimeException*, making the code harder to read with throws clauses all over the place or causing very subtle bugs by sweeping the exceptions under the carpet with empty catch blocks. Nevertheless, when explicitly throwing a *RuntimeException* (i.e an unchecked exception), developers still have the option to catch exceptions that they can actually handle or declare the exceptions in the method signature and Java docs for visibility and explanation. Unchecked exceptions make your code much simpler. For example, the Spring JDBC Template support can shrink your JDBC code enormously by getting rid of those unsightly try, catch, and finally blocks, and cleanly releasing the database resources like connections, statements, etc. Checked exceptions are also the main reason for Java not having closures till JRE 6.0 as it adds to the complexity.

Exception class hierarchy: There are counter arguments in favor of checked exceptions. The development community is divided on this topic.

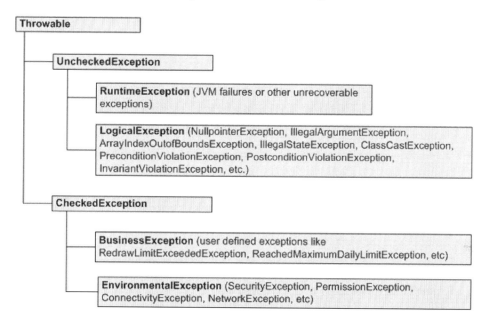

Regardless of this checked versus unchecked exception debate, the exception class hierarchy in general is less intuitive and confusing at times. For example, *SQLException* is used to report both badly constructed SQL code due to programming errors and failure of database connections due to environmental factors. Exception hierarchy could be simplified as shown below.

Checked exceptions denote that an action can be taken to recover from the situation or the situation can be handled more meaningfully. For example, connectivity issues can be recovered from after a few retries. Business exceptions like *ReachedMaximum-DailyLimitException* can be used meaningfully to pass information to the user or to take an alternative course of action like sending an email, writing to the audit tables in the database, and notifying other systems via message queues.

The java.util.Date and **Time** classes in JDK are badly designed and verbose. As discussed later in this section, the third-party library Joda-Time will make your life much easier, especially when complex date related calculations are required. JDK 7 will change the date-time classes significantly with the JSR 310, This will fix the main problem of java.util.Date and java.util.Calendar being mutable objects. The JSR 310 is built around the same basic date/time concepts used in Joda-Time like a discrete timeline, instants, partials, durations, periods, and intervals.

Some of the gotchas and inconsistencies discussed below are caused by some of the bad design decisions like allowing primitive variables in Java, implementation of Java's generics with type erasure, etc.

- **Type erasures in generics**: In the interest of backward compatibility, robustness of generics has been sacrificed through type-erasure. Because of type erasure during compile-time, *List<Integer>* and *List<String>* are the same class, at runtime. They are both just lists. This lack of type information at runtime poses a problem for generic container classes that want to make defensive copies.

```
//constructor attempting a defensive copy using generics
public MyImmute(T param) {
    //compile-error during defensive copy
    this.param = new T(param);
}
```

  As the type information will be erased in the compiled class, the raw type has no way of knowing the type of object you want to construct at runtime. This means that generics in general is a solution for collection classes and seem to only solve the problem of automatically casting in and out of collection classes in addition to improving the readability of your code in collection classes by enclosing the type information in angle brackets.

```
List<String> myList = new ArrayList<String>();
```

- **Autoboxing can cause a mysterious *NullPointerException***: An *Integer* expression can have a null value. If your program tries to auto-unbox a null value, it will throw a *NullPointerException*.

```
public class Unbelievable {
    static Integer i = null;
    public static void main(String[] args) {
        //NullPointerException while auto-unboxing – i.intValue( )
        if (25 == i)
            System.out.println("Unbelievable");
```

```
        }
}
```

Output:

```
Exception in thread "main" java.lang.NullPointerException
                    at Unbelievable.main(Unbelievable.java:5)
```

- **Type-erasure in generics** and **auto-boxing** can cause *NullPointerException* or other mysterious issues:

```java
import java.util.HashMap;
import java.util.Map;

public class Generics1 {
   public static void main(String[ ] args) {
      Map<Long, Long> myMap = new HashMap<Long, Long>();
      myMap.put(3L,4L);              // key & value are auto-boxed to Long
      int key = 3;
      // The key is auto-boxed to type Integer, hence value will be null.
      Long value = myMap.get(key);                          // Line A
      System.out.printf("Result is %1s", Long.toString(value));   // Line B
   }
}
```

Output:

```
Exception in thread "main" java.lang.NullPointerException
                    at Generics1.main(Generics1.java:10)
```

Since generics in Java are compile-time constructs, and are not directly supported by the JVM, the underlying container class *myMap* accepts regular *Object* instances during compile-time check and asserts that it can be safely promoted from *int* to *long* in line A, whereas the actual object passed to the container class "*myMap*" after auto-boxing at runtime is of type *Integer* and not of type *Long*. Since the container doesn't actually have a runtime generics, the collection merely looks up the reference object in the map and fails to find it. This results in *NullPointerException* in line B due to reference *value* being null.

At compile-time, when a generic type is instantiated, all information about the actual parameter type is removed and therefore an instantiation of a type such as List<Integer> and List<String> results at runtime in the same type, that is, its raw type List. Therefore, you can't use the instanceof operator with generics.

```
Collection<String> cs = new ArrayList<String>();
Collection<Integer> cs2 = new ArrayList<Integer>();
if (cs instanceof Collection<String>) {                    // illegal
    // ...
}
```

- **Wild cards in generics** can make your code more complex to use and understand. It is not worth puzzling over complicated generics statements.

```
public static <T extends Comparable<? super T>> void sort(List<T>list) { .
    ...
}
```

In simple cases, generics is clearly a huge improvement in both clarity and safety over just casting all over the place. So understanding how generics works, its pitfalls, and limitations can assist you decide when to use and when to back off, and avoid using it.

Q5   Can you list the Java SE features you like to be added in the future? LF
A5   [Hint]

Closures: are useful for implementing abstractions that involve behavior. A closure is a named or anonymous subroutine. It looks like Java 7 will have closures. Closures can make your life as a developer much easier. Not sure of the actual syntax for Closures at this stage, but it could be something like:

For example, to run a function in a thread pool,

```
myThreadPool.submit(#( ) { for (int i = 1; i < 1000; i++) performTask(i) });
```

```
#() {...} --> is a function (i.e. an  anonymous function)
#() --> empty paranthesis indicate that the function has no arguments.
```

Currently (up to Java 6), custom sorting of objects in a list requires an implementation of a *Comparator* interface. Closure could simplify this as follows to sort strings in a list by its length in an ascending order as shown here:

```
Collections.sort( listStrings, #(String str1, String str2) str1.length( ) - str2.length( ));
```

JavaScript is widely used in web development, and in JavaScript a closure is created every time you create a function within a function. When using a closure, you will have access to all the variables in the enclosing (i.e. the parent) function.

```javascript
var calculate = function(x) {
    var const = 2;
    return function(y) {
        return x + y + const;    // has visibility to parent variable 'const'
    };
}

var plus5 = calculate(5);       //plus5 is now a closure
alert(plus5(3));                //returns 10 i.e. x=5, y=3, const=2
alert(plus5(7));                //returns 14 i.e  x=5, y=7, const=2
alert(plus5(10));               //returns 17 i.e  x=5, y=10, const=2
```

Closures are first class objects in groovy, and in many ways it resembles anonymous inner classes in Java. The above functionality can be implemented in groovy as shown below:

```groovy
def calculate = {x,y -> x + y + 2}  //closure
def plus5 = { calculate.call(5,it)}     //"it" is like "this" in java. Here stands for
                                        //values passed in to plus5 call like 3, 7 or 10

println plus5.call(3)                   //prints 10
println plus5.call(7)                   //prints 14
println plus5.call(10)                  //prints 17
```

Mixins: Java does not support multiple-inheritance, but it is possible to have the concept of "mixins inheritance", which are "partial classes" that you can bolt onto your class, giving you something very much like multiple inheritance. The concept of "mixins inheritances" are great when you want to refactor common functionality from two classes having different super classes. Currently Java does not have "mixins" like

Ruby does. In many languages including Java, you cannot say,

```
class FileTreeNode extends File mixin TreeNode {....}
```

to give you access to all the operations provided by the *File* class to work with files and the *TreeNode* class to arrange files and perform binary searches at the same time. You can achieve mixins in Java with the help of,

- Aspect Oriented Programing (AOP) language like AspectJ. AOP compliments OO.
- Using interfaces and annotations (or reflection, CGLIB, etc) to mix at build time using annotations to generate the mixin code as demonstrated below.

```java
public interface TreeNode {
    TreeNode search(String toSearch);
    // ....other methods
}
```

```java
public class TreeNodeImpl implements TreeNode {
    public TreeNode search(String toSearch) {.... }
    // ....other methods
}
```

```java
@compose ( type = TreeNode.class, field = "tree", implClass=
                                          "TreeNodeImpl.class"
@parentClass (name = "java.io.File")
public FileTreeNode extends FileTreeNodeGenerated implements TreeNode {
    //...
}
```

The *@compose* and *@parentClass* annotations will generate the class *FileTreeNode-Generated* at build time as shown below, which is extended and used by the *FileTreeNode* class.

```java
/**
 *  Generated class that achieves reuse of the File class through
 *  inheritance and the TreeNode class through composition. More
 *  interfaces can be composed if required.
 */
```

```
public class FileTreeNodeGenerated extends File {
    private TreeNode tree;                      //composition

    public FileTreeNodeGenerated(....){
        this.tree = new TreeNodeImpl(...);
    }

    public TreeNode search(String toSearch) {
        tree.search(toSearch);                  //use TreeNode
    }

    //... other methods

}
```

Note: The above example is shown only to demonstrate mixins, and this may not be the ideal solution to a given problem.

You could also fake mixins in Java with the inner classes, but it would be ideal to have true mixins that are easier to use out of the box.

Java Module System: JAR files are hard to distribute, hard to version, and hard to reference in general. Existing JAR format can lead to classpath and class loading problems when:

- a developer or deployer of a Java application has accidentally made two different versions of a library available to the system.

- two different libraries (or a library and the application) require different versions of the same third library. If both versions of the third library use the same class names, there is no way to load both versions of the third library with the same classloader.

- classes loaded by different class loaders may interact in complex ways not fully understood by a developer, leading to inexplicable errors or bugs.

The Java Module System (JSR 277) was initiated to address some of the issues caused by the JAR files. The Java Module System defines a distribution format and a repository for collections of Java code and related resources. It also defines the discovery, loading, and integrity mechanisms at runtime. It looks like Java 7 will have the Java Module System. Until then the OSGi can handle all of these nicely. The OSGi (Open Services Gateway initiative), which is also known as the dynamic module system for Java, defines an architecture for modular application development. The OSGi implementations such as Apache Felix, Equinox, and Knoplerfish allow you to break your application into multiple modules, and thus allow you to better manage the cross dependencies between those modules

Add some of the frequently used third party libraries like "Apache commons collections", "Apache commons lang", and more intuitive and easy to use libraries like "Joda-Time" to the Java core API (Joda-Time may become part of Java SE 7.0).

You may also think of some of the features in other languages that you liked and keen to have those features added to Java if not already present in Java.

For example, multi-line string literal in both Scala and Groovy as shown below is more readable and does not require special escape characters as in Java.

```
String multiLine = """
            Line 1
            Line 2 "no escape"
            Line 3""";
```

The syntax in Java is less readable,

```
String multiLine = "Line 1" +
            "Line 2 \"escape\"" +
            "Line 3";
```

The Java POJOs (Plain Old Java Objects) verbose and less readable with all the getter and setter methods. Groovy comes to the rescue. Groovy makes POGOs (Plain Old Groovy Objects) less verbose and more readable by creating the getters/setters during byte code generation. In a POGO, if you have an access modifier, it will be treated as a property and if you don't specify an access modifier it will be a normal field. The following code shows Groovy and Java code working together by using the -j compiler switch to enable the joint compilation.

The less verbose POGO in Groovy is as shown below:

```
public class Person {

   String name                    //property
   String lastName                //property
   private int id                 //a normal field

   String toString( ) {
      return "I am ${name} ${lastName}."
   }
}
```

The invoking code in Java is as shown below

```
public class Organization {

   public static void main( String args[ ] ) {
      Person person = new Person( ); .
      person.setName( "Peter" );
      person.setLastName( "Smith" );
      System.out.println( person.toString( ) );
   }
}
```

Finally, you may prefer fixing or improving the existing limitations and gotchas in Java before adding any new features as it could make things worse. Most of these pitfalls are brought about by the effort to maintain the backward compatibility.

Note: Being able to compare strengths and weaknesses of Java with other programming and scripting languages will demonstrate some of the recognizable qualities of good programmers. Good programmers get excited chatting about technologies, and are passionate about diversifying on the technology stack. So learn different technologies, frameworks, and tools, and be opinionated about which are better for various scenarios.

Q6   Give me a high level description of your experience with the Java platform? `OEQ`
A6   [Hint]

   •   Working experience with J2SE from 1.3 up to 1.6. Strong experience on J2SE

67

1.5.

- Working experience with J2EE from 1.2 up to 1.5. Recent experience on JEE 1.5 including EJB3 and JAX-WS.

- Working experience with Eclipse, IBM Rational Application Developer, and application servers such as Websphere, JBoss, and Tomcat.

- Special interest and 5+ years of working experience with multi-threaded programming and server side programming.

- Working experience with Web Service technologies and protocols in addition to 3-tier Web applications.

- Strong server side system integration experience using JMS, Web Services (both SOAP & Restful), RMI, and XML technologies like JAXB, XPath, XQuery, XSL, XSD, etc, and middle-ware products like IBM MQSeries, webMethods, Tibco, and Oracle Service Bus.

- Limited client side integration experience by developing Flash widgets, HTML widgets using iframe, and JavaScript widgets. Also, familiar with popular JavaS-cript frameworks like JQuery and Ext JS.

- Working experience with the ETL (Extract, Transform, and Load) batch jobs, using Unix shell scripts, BCP (bulk copy) utility, command line SQL tools like iSQL for Sybase database, SQL*Plus for Oracle database, and SQLCMD for the SQL server, and scheduling tools like Control-M or Unix Cron jobs. jobs.

- Working experience with scripting languages like Javascript, Groovy, Jython, Ruby, Perl, and Unix shell.

- Experience with sought-after technologies & frameworks like Spring, Hibernate, EJB3, JSF, AJAX, and Struts 2.

- Working experience with build and automation systems like ANT, Maven, CruiseControl, Bamboo, IVY, and Hudson.

- Good working knowledge with regular expressions (regex), structured query language (SQL), unified modeling language (UML), and entity relationship diagrams (ERDs).

Note: The above list highlights many of the sought-after technical skills, but streamline your answer based on your experience, the role, job specification, and the briefing you got from your prospective employer.

Q7 What are your favorite areas of the Java APIs and why? `LF CO CC   EH`
A7 [Hint]

java.util.concurrent package is critical to any multi-threaded applications. This concurrency package makes developers' lives easier. Some of the powerful features are,

The **task execution** and **thread pooling** architecture. The "*Executors*" class defines factory methods for obtaining "*ExecutorService*" implementations that use thread pools. The task-execution framework has "*Callable*" and "*Future*" interfaces. Unlike the "*Runnable*" interface, these interfaces can return a result or throw an exception through the "call( )" method. You can also execute a "*Callable*" task asynchronously through the "submit( )" method. The return value of a "submit( )" method is a "*Future*" object, which is used to retrieve the result of your asynchronous task when you are ready through the "get( )" method. If the asynchronous task has completed executing, then "get( )" returns from your method right away. Otherwise, it blocks until the result is ready or interruted.

```java
import java.util.concurrent.Callable;
import java.util.concurrent.ExecutionException;
import java.util.concurrent.ExecutorService;
import java.util.concurrent.Executors;
import java.util.concurrent.Future;

public class Concurrent1 implements Callable<Integer> {

    Integer number;

    public Concurrent1(Integer number) {
        this.number = number;
    }
}
```

```java
public static void main(String[ ] args) {
    ExecutorService pool = Executors.newFixedThreadPool(2);
    // invokes the call( ) method
    Future<Integer> task1 = pool.submit(new Concurrent1(12));
    Future<Integer> task2 = pool.submit(new Concurrent1(8));

    Integer result = null;
    try {
        result = task1.get( ) + task2.get( );
    } catch (ExecutionException ee) {
        ee.printStackTrace( );
        throw new RuntimeException(ee);
    } catch (InterruptedException ie) {
        ie.printStackTrace( );
        throw new RuntimeException(ie);
    } finally {
        pool.shutdown( );
    }

    System.out.printf("The result is = %1s", result);       // result = 100
}

@Override
public Integer call( ) throws Exception {
    return number * 5;
}
}
```

"*CopyOnWriteArrayList*" and "*CopyOnWriteSet*" are very useful in multi-threaded applications in situations where number of traversals greatly outnumber insertions or removals. If you are using a normal "*ArrayList*" in situations where modifications are possible through read and write operations, you are likely to get the "*ConcurrentModificationException*". But using a "*CopyOnWriteArrayList*", the writing task will create a new copy of the data if it needs to add data, thus ensuring that the reader will always have valid data (though potentially stale data) to display without the *ConcurrentModificationException*.

The "*TimeUnit*" enumerated type includes handy time related utilities. For example,

Instead of:

```
Thread.sleep(10000);                    // less readable.  Seconds or milliseconds?
```

Use one of the following forms:

```
Thread.sleep(TimeUnit.MILLISECONDS.convert(10, TimeUnit.SECONDS));

Thread.sleep(TimeUnit.SECONDS.toMillis(10));

TimeUnit.SECONDS.sleep(10);             // easy to read and understand
```

The **Java Collections framework** provides high performance and high-quality implementations of useful data structures and algorithms. In most cases you don't need to create your own data structures and algorithms. It also has several convenience methods for wrapping additional functionality if required. The Java Collections framework is one of the most frequently used Java APIs whether you are using a client side or server side Java development.

The **java.util.regex** is one of the greatest additions to Java 1.4. The addition of *"MatchResult"* to Java 5.0 makes it a lot easier to obtain all of the state as a *"MatchResult"*. The java.util.regex is also one of the popular Java APIs whether you are using a client side or server side Java development.

Example 1:

```java
import java.util.Scanner;
import java.util.regex.MatchResult;

public class Regex1 {

    public static void main(String[ ] args) {
        String input = "1 car 2 cars Red car Blue car";
        Scanner s = new Scanner(input);
        s.findInLine("(\\d+)\\s+car[s]?\\s+(\\d+)\\s+car[s]?\\s+
                                    (\\w+)\\s+car[s]?\\s+(\\w+)");
        MatchResult result = s.match();
        for (int i = 1; i <= result.groupCount(); i++) {
```

```
            System.out.println(result.group(i));
         }
      s.close( );
   }
}
```

Output:

```
1
2
Red
Blue
```

Note: The ones in **(…)** are the groups that get printed. **\\s+** means 1 or more white spaces. **\\d+** means 1 or more digits. **\\w+** means 1 or more words. **[s]?** means 0 or 1s.

Example 2:

```
import java.util.ArrayList;
import java.util.List;
import java.util.regex.MatchResult;
import java.util.regex.Matcher;
import java.util.regex.Pattern;

public class Regex2 {

   public static void main(String[ ] args) {
      String input = "1 car 2 cars Red car Blue car";
      Pattern p = Pattern
            .compile("car[s]?");
      Matcher m = p.matcher(input);
      List<MatchResult> list = new ArrayList<MatchResult>(10);
      while (m.find( )) {
         list.add(m.toMatchResult( ));
      }
      for (MatchResult result : list) {
         System.out.printf("Found '%s' at (%d,%d) %n" , result.group( ),
                                   result.start( ), result.end( ));
```

```
      }
   .}
}
```

Output:

```
Found 'car' at (2,5)
Found 'cars' at (8,12)
Found 'car' at (17,20)
Found 'car' at (26,29)
```

Q8 What are some of the very common runtime (or unchecked) exceptions you have come across in Java? When is a *ConcurrentModificationException* thrown? **LF**

A8 *NullPointerException, ClassCastException* (very common prior to JDK 5), *ArrayIndexOutOfBoundsException, StringIndexOutOfBoundsException,* and *ConcurrentModificationException*. The *ArrayLists* can throw "*ConcurrentModificationException*":

```
import java.util.ArrayList;
import java.util.Iterator;
import java.util.List;

//throws java.util.ConcurrentModificationException
public class Concurrent2 {

   public final static void main(String args[ ]) {
      List<String> list = new ArrayList<String>();
      list.add("A");
      list.add("B");
      Iterator<String> i = list.iterator( );
      while (i.hasNext()) {
         System.out.println(i.next( ));         // exception after adding "C"
         list.add("C");
      }
      System.out.println("After: " + list);
   }
}
```

Output:

AException in thread "main" java.util.ConcurrentModificationException
at java.util.AbstractList$Itr.checkForComodification(Unknown Source)
        at java.util.AbstractList$Itr.next(Unknown Source)
        at Concurrent2.main(Concurrent2.java:14)

CopyOnWriteArrayList to the rescue:

```
import java.util.Iterator;
import java.util.List;
import java.util.concurrent.CopyOnWriteArrayList;

//No exception
public class Concurrent3 {

    public final static void main(String args[ ]) {
        List<String> list = new CopyOnWriteArrayList<String>( );
        list.add("A");
        list.add("B");
        Iterator<String> i = list.iterator( );
        while (i.hasNext( )) {
            System.out.println(i.next( ));
            list.add("C");
        }
        System.out.println("After: " + list);
    }
}
```

Output:

```
A
B
After: [A, B, C, C]
```

Q9 Can you explain thread-safety and atomicity with an example? What do you understand by optimistic versus pessimistic locking? **LF CC**

A9 The "***ConcurrentHashMap***" is a thread-safe implementation of a *Map* that offers far better scalability than a "*Collections.synchronizedMap(..)*". Multiple reads can almost always execute concurrently, simultaneous reads and writes can usually execute concurrently, and multiple simultaneous writes can often execute concurrently. Iterators returned by

ConcurrentHashMap.iterator( ) will return each element once at most and will not ever throw a "*ConcurrentModificationException*", but may or may not reflect stale data due to insertions or removals that occurred since the iterator was constructed.

```java
import java.util.Collections;
import java.util.HashMap;
import java.util.Map;
import java.util.concurrent.ConcurrentHashMap;
import java.util.concurrent.ConcurrentMap;
import java.util.concurrent.ExecutorService;
import java.util.concurrent.Executors;

public class Concurrent6 implements Runnable {

    private ConcurrentMap<String, Integer> counts =
                    new ConcurrentHashMap<String, Integer>(10);

    private static final String KEY = "key";

    public static void main(String[ ] args) {
        ExecutorService pool = Executors.newFixedThreadPool(10);
        try {
            Concurrent6 concur = new Concurrent6( );
            int totalRuns = 20;
            int i = 0;
            while (i < totalRuns) {
                pool.execute(concur);                         // invokes run( )
                i++;
            }
        } finally {
            pool.shutdown( );
        }
    }

    //This method is thread-safe, but not atomic.
    private void count( ) {
        Integer cnt = counts.get(KEY);
        cnt = (cnt == null) ? 1 : (cnt + 1);
        counts.put(KEY, cnt);
```

```
    System.out.printf("Count for %1s is %2s \n",
                Thread.currentThread().getName(), cnt);
}

@Override
public void run() {
    count();
}
}
```

Output:

```
Count for pool-1-thread-1 is  1
Count for pool-1-thread-1 is  9
Count for pool-1-thread-1 is 10
Count for pool-1-thread-1 is 11
Count for pool-1-thread-1 is 12
Count for pool-1-thread-1 is 13
Count for pool-1-thread-1 is 14
Count for pool-1-thread-1 is 15
Count for pool-1-thread-1 is 16
Count for pool-1-thread-9 is  8
Count for pool-1-thread-9 is 18
Count for pool-1-thread-1 is 17
Count for pool-1-thread-7 is  7
Count for pool-1-thread-3 is  6
Count for pool-1-thread-5 is  5
Count for pool-1-thread-10 is  4
Count for pool-1-thread-8 is  3
Count for pool-1-thread-6 is  2
Count for pool-1-thread-4 is  1
Count for pool-1-thread-2 is  1
```

The above code is safe enough to leave the map in a consistent state without any data corruption due to concurrent access. But it does not make the *count()* method **atomic**. For example, two or more threads can concurrently access the count method and read a current value of say 0, and both will independently increment the count to 1. This results in value of 1 being printed 3 times as shown above. This behavior of skipping or missing a count is not desired in some scenarios. You can fix this situation by using synchronization as shown below:

```
private void count( ) {
    //pessimistic locking locks every time
    synchronized (counts) {
        Integer cnt = counts.get(KEY);
        cnt = (cnt == null) ? 1 : (cnt + 1);
        counts.put(KEY, cnt);
        System.out.printf("Count for %1s is %2s \n",
                            Thread.currentThread( ).getName( ), cnt);
    }
}
```

The above code provides an atomic update, but the *"ConcurrentMap"* interface provides a more efficient way to handle truly atomic updates with the following interface methods:

```
public interface ConcurrentMap<K, V> extends Map<K, V> {
    V putIfAbsent(K key, V value);
    boolean remove(Object key, Object value);
    boolean replace(K key, V oldValue, V newValue);
    V replace(K key, V value);
}
```

PC   Check the *"ConcurrentMap"* API document for more details. Also, check the *"AtomicInteger"* and *"AtomicLong"* APIs. Now, you can rewrite the count( ) method as follows:

```
//optimistic locking assumes concurrent update is rare and deals
// with it only when it happens by looping again & retrying
private void count( ) {
    Integer oldCnt, newCnt;
    do {
        oldCnt = counts.get(KEY);
        newCnt = (oldCnt == null) ? 1 : (oldCnt + 1);
    } while (!counts.replace(KEY, oldCnt, newCnt));

    System.out.printf("Count for %1s is %2s \n",
```

```
        Thread.currentThread( ).getName( ), newCnt);
}
```

Output:

```
Count for pool-1-thread-1 is  1
Count for pool-1-thread-1 is 11
Count for pool-1-thread-9 is 10
Count for pool-1-thread-9 is 13
Count for pool-1-thread-9 is 14
Count for pool-1-thread-7 is  9
Count for pool-1-thread-7 is 16
Count for pool-1-thread-7 is 17
Count for pool-1-thread-7 is 18
Count for pool-1-thread-7 is 19
Count for pool-1-thread-7 is 20
Count for pool-1-thread-5 is  8
Count for pool-1-thread-10 is  7
Count for pool-1-thread-3 is  6
Count for pool-1-thread-6 is  5
Count for pool-1-thread-8 is  4
Count for pool-1-thread-4 is  3
Count for pool-1-thread-2 is  2
Count for pool-1-thread-9 is 15
Count for pool-1-thread-1 is 12
```

This is more efficient compared to synchronizing the whole "counts" every time because we rarely expect another thread to sneak in to read the same count. If this situation does happen, the above code simply loops and tries again.

Q10 What open source libraries/frameworks do you have experience with? `LF OEQ`
A10 [Hint]

- **Apache commons libraries**: Apache commons collections, Apache commons lang, etc. For example,

  ```
  StringUtils.isEmpty(inputString);
  StringUtils.isBlank(inputString);
  ```

```
CollectionUtils.isEmpty(myList);
CollectionUtils.containsInstance(myList, myObject);
```

```
ArrayUtils.isEmpty(myArray);
```

```
return new HashCodeBuilder(17,
                  37).append(name).append(age).toHashCode( );
```

```
return new EqualsBuilder( ).appendSuper(super.equals(obj))
        .append(name, rhs.name)
        .append(age, rhs.age)
        .isEquals( );
```

Note: Google Collections library from Google Core Libraries (for Java 1.6 aka Guava) can be an alternative to Apache commons collection library.

- **Joda-Time**: has been created to radically change date and time handling in Java. The JDK classes Date and Calendar are very badly designed and not intuitive. Joda classes are immutable (hence thread-safe) and more intuitive. For example, to represent 1st of January 2009 midnight:

```java
import java.text.SimpleDateFormat;
import java.util.Calendar;
import java.util.GregorianCalendar;
import static java.lang.System.out;

import org.joda.time.DateTime;

public class Calendar1 {

    private static final String FORMAT = "yyyy/MMM/dd HH:mm:ss";

    public static void main(String[ ] args) {
        Calendar cal = GregorianCalendar.getInstance( );
        // define it locally as this class is not thread-safe
        SimpleDateFormat sdf = new SimpleDateFormat(FORMAT);

        // You may think it is midnight 1st of Jan 2009
        cal.set(2009, 1, 1, 0, 0, 0);
```

```
        out.println("Bad=" + sdf.format(cal.getTime( )));

        // fix it by
        cal.set(2009, 0, 1, 0, 0, 0);
        out.println("Good=" + sdf.format(cal.getTime( )));

        // or better fix
        cal.set(2009, Calendar.JANUARY, 1, 0, 0, 0);
        out.println("better=" + sdf.format(cal.getTime( )));

        out.println("===== zero and one index based gotchas =======");
        out.println("Day Of The Month="
            + cal.get(Calendar.DAY_OF_MONTH));
        out.println("Month=" + cal.get(Calendar.MONTH));

        out.println("===== Joda to the rescue =======");
        // best - intuitive and immutable(hence thread-safe)
        DateTime dateTime = new DateTime(2009, 1, 1, 0, 0, 0, 0);
        System.out.println("bestWithJoda="
                    + dateTime.toString(FORMAT));
    }
}
```

Output:

```
Bad=2009/Feb/01 00:00:00
Good=2009/Jan/01 00:00:00
better=2009/Jan/01 00:00:00
===== zero and one index based gotchas =======
Day Of The Month=1
Month=0
===== Joda to the rescue =======
bestWithJoda=2009/Jan/01 00:00:00
```

To add 60 days to this date and print using the JDK Calendar:

```
cal.add(Calendar.DAY_OF_MONTH, 60);
System.out.println(sdf.format(cal.getTime( )));
```

To add 60 days to this date and print using Joda:

```
System.out.println(dateTime.plusDays(60).toString(FORMAT));
```

As you can see one line of more readable code for Joda versus two lines for the JDK. As the calculation gets more complex, the gap widens. To represent last day of the week after 1 month and 20 days Joda way:

```
System.out.println(dateTime.plusDays(20).plusMonths(1).
    dayOfWeek( ).withMaximumValue( ).toString(FORMAT));
```

Try the above code using the Calendar class from JDK to appreciate Joda-Time library. Most business applications require date manipulation. If you are looking for an easy-to-use and more intuitive replacement for JDK (up to SE 6.0) class based date processing, then you really should consider Joda. Joda is interoperable with your JDK *Date* class and this lets you keep your existing JDK dependent code, but use Joda to do the heavy lifting when it comes to date/time calculations.

- **Dozer** is a JavaBean to JavaBean mapper that recursively copies data from one object to another. Typically, these Java beans will be of different complex types. It also makes your code more readable without the nested loops and null reference checks.

- **JasperReports**: is a Java reporting tool that can write to screen, to a printer or into PDF, HTML, Microsoft Excel, RTF, ODT, CSV and XML files.

- **Quartz**: is a full-featured, open source job scheduling service that can be integrated with, or used along side virtually any Java EE or Java SE application - from the smallest stand-alone application to the largest e-commerce system.

- **Apache MINA**: is a network application framework which helps users develop high performance and high scalability network applications easily. It provides an abstract event-driven and asynchronous API over various transports such as TCP/IP and UDP/IP via the Java NIO API.

- **Spring**: utility APIs like org.springframework.util.*Assert* help you write fail-fast code by validating arguments. Useful for identifying programmer errors early and clearly at runtime. For example, if the contract of a public method states it does not allow null arguments, Assert can be used to validate that contract. Doing this clearly indicates a contract violation when it occurs and protects the class' invariants.

```
Assert.notNull(employee, "The employee must not be null");
Assert.isTrue(employees.size( ) > 0,
              "The no. of employees must be greater than zero");
```

Other useful utility classes under org.springframework.util package are *StringUtils*, *FileCopyUtils*, *CollectionUtils*, *ClassUtils*, etc.

- Many other frameworks like Hibernate, Struts, Tiles, Maven, ANT, IVY, Terracotta, OSCache, Log4J, etc.

Q11 In your experience, what are some of the most common errors Java programmers make? `LF CO CC EH`

A11

- Not being aware of data over flows, using "==" with float or double comparisons, and storing money in floating point variables.

- Comparing two objects using "==" instead of *.equals( )*. When you use "==", you are actually comparing two object references, to see if they point to the same object. For example:

```
public class StringEquals {

    public static void main(String[ ] args) {
        String s1 = "Hello";
        String s2 = new String(s1);
        String s3 = "Hello";
        System.out.println(s1 + " equals " + s2 + " -> " +
                                        s1.equals(s2));        //true
        System.out.println(s1 + " == " + s2 + " -> " + (s1 == s2));   //false
        System.out.println(s1 + " == " + s3+ " -> " + (s1 == s3));   //true
    }
}
```

82

The variable s1 refers to the *String* instance created by "Hello". The object referred to by s2 is created with s1 as an initializer,. thus the contents of the two *String* objects are identical, but they are distinct objects. This means that s1 and s2 do not refer to the same object and are, therefore, not ==, but *equals( )* as they have the same value "Hello". The *s1 == s3* is true, as they both point to the same object due to internal caching.

- Mistyping the name or getting the signature wrong of an overridden method. If you mistype the name, you are no longer overriding a method, and you are creating a new method. This issue can be easily picked up in JDK 1.5 or greater versions by annotating an overridden method with @Override annotation. The other benefit of the @Override annotation is that if the parent class changes, the compiler will make sure that the child classes have been updated as well. Typical methods like *hashCode( )*, *equals( )*, *toString( )*, *compare( )*, *run( )*, etc are meant to be properly overridden.

- Failing to override *hashCode( )* and *equals( )* methods or breaking the *hashCode( )* and *equals( )* contract through incorrect implementation by violating the contract.

  - if a class overrides the *equals( )* method, it must also override the *hashCode( )* method.
  - if two objects are equal, then their *hashCode( )* values must be same as well. But the reverse is not always true. If two objects have the same *hashCode( )* does not mean that they are equal as well.

If you plan to add objects of your own class to sets or maps, your class should override *hashCode( )* and *equals( )* methods. If a class implements a Comparable interface, the *compareTo(..)* must return zero, if and only if the *equals(..)* method returns true for the same non-null argument, and vice versa. Violating these contracts may cause unexpected results.

- Sweeping exceptions under a carpet by writing blank exception handlers and just ignoring all the exceptions. If you run into problems, and have not written any error messages, it becomes almost impossible to find out the cause of the error. For example:

// Don't do this

```
try {
    // some code that can throw exceptions
}
catch(Exception ex) {
    //do nothing
}
```

```
// Do something like this
try {
    // some code that can throw exceptions
}
catch(Exception ex) {
    logger.error(ex);                         //optional
    throw new RuntimeException(ex);
}
```

- Not thinking about immutability, thread safety, and atomicity every time designing a Java class. To be more specific, not using proper synchronization or immutable objects. Given the architecture of the JVM, you need to only be concerned with instance and class variables when you worry about thread safety. Because all threads share the same heap, and the heap is where all instance variables are stored, and multiple threads can attempt to use the same object's instance variables concurrently. You needn't worry about multi-threaded access to local variables, method parameters, and return values, because these variables reside on the Java stack. In the JVM, each thread is awarded its own Java stack. No thread can see or use any local variables, return values, or parameters belonging to another thread.

- Using floating point to try to represent exact quantities like monetary amounts. Double or float are not recommended for monetary calculations, since they always carry small rounding differences. Either use *BigDecimal* or represent them with smallest possible units without the decimals like in cents using int or long. For example,

```
import java.math.BigDecimal;

// $2.00 - $1.10
public class FloatingPoint {
```

```java
public static void main(String[] args) {
    // Don't: inaccurate and unpredictable monetary result
    double result1 = 2.00 - 1.10;
    System.out.println("Result1 = " + result1); //0.8999999999999999 Bad

    // predictable and efficient – int or long fix
    int result2 = 200 - 110;
    System.out.println("Result2 = " + result2 + " cents");      //90 cents

    // predictable BigDecimal fix
    BigDecimal result3 = new BigDecimal("2.00").subtract(
                new BigDecimal("1.10"));
    System.out.println("Result3 = " + result3);                //0.90
    }
}
```

It is preferable to use the "ROUND_HALF_EVEN" style rounding mechanism as it has the least bias. It is also known as the bankers' rounding or round-to-even.

- Use of *Integer* (immutable wrapper object) vs int (primitive), and this goes for any primitive version of an object. This is specifically an annoyance caused by not thinking of *Integer* as different from int since you can treat them the same much of the time due to auto-boxing.

```java
public class AutoBoxing2 {
    public static void main(String[] args) {
        int p1 = 6;
        int p2 = 6;

        Integer o1 = new Integer(6);
        Integer o2 = new Integer(6);

        Integer o3 = Integer.valueOf(6);
        Integer o4 = Integer.valueOf(6);

        System.out.println(6 == p1);        // Prints true
        System.out.println(p1 == p2);       // Prints true
        System.out.println(p1 == o1);       // Prints true
```

```
                                          // auto-unboxing o1.intValue( )
    System.out.println(6 == o1);          // Prints true
                                          // auto-unboxing o1.intValue( )
    System.out.println(o1 == o2);         // Prints false
                                          // points to 2 different objects
    System.out.println(o3 == o4);         // Prints true
                                          // Points to the same object
    System.out.println(o1.equals(o2));    //Prints true
  }
 }
}
```

Note: o3 and o4 points to the same object as the same instance is returned due to caching when *valueOf( )* method is used.

• Relying on the default TimeZone.

```
Calendar cal = new GregorianCalendar( );
```

The code above uses the default TimeZone. This might lead to incorrect date/time in your server application. The 0h00 in Sydney is different to moment in London. Make sure that the JVMs default TimeZone is suitable for your locale.

```
java -Duser.timezone=Australia/Sydney
```

You can also set the user.timezone property by using the java.lang.System class's setProperty method:

```
System.setProperty("user.timezone" , "Australia/Sydney");
```

Use the correct TimeZone.

```
Calendar cal = new GregorianCalendar(user.getTimeZone( ));
```

• Using a *java.util.LinkedList* for random access. The *LinkedLists* are designed for sequential access. The stacks and queues are designed for sequential access as well. Using these collection classes for random access (e.g. get(i)) has the complexity of O(n). For random access, use a List – if duplicates are allowed, use a Set – if duplicates are not allowed, and use an array – if the size is known and duplicates are allowed, as the arrays are more efficient than Lists.

- Other nuances and gotchas like:

    - Calendar.get(Calendar.**DAY_OF_MONTH**) is 1 based and Calendar.get(Calendar.**MONTH)** is 0 based.

    - The classes *SimpleDateFormat,* **NumberFormat**, and its subclass **DecimalFormat** are not thread-safe.

    - Manipulating Swing components from outside the event dispatcher thread can cause undesirable issues. Swing components can be accessed by only one thread at a time, and generally, this thread is the event-dispatching thread. You can handle I/O bound or computationally expensive tasks using *SwingWorker* or *Timer* utility classes. When you need access to the UI from outside event-handling or drawing code, then you can use the *SwingUtilities invokeLater( )* or *invokeAndWait( )* method.

    - *Integer* division 1/2 returns 0, not 0.5. Use ((float)1/2) or (1/(float)2) that returns 0.5.

    - *ConcurrentModificationException* when removing an object from a list that you were iterating.

    - Using static variables in a clustered environment. Static variables are scoped to the class in which they are defined. So in a clustered environment, if you change one in the first JVM, the other JVMs are not going to know about the change. Strictly speaking, it is also possible to have multiple copies of the same class, if it is loaded by more than one class-loader within the same JVM.

Note: Even if you are not an experienced professional, you can proactively learn the potential pitfalls and avoid them. You can also use this to your advantage to prove your technical capabilities at job interviews, team meetings, and code review sessions. You must learn from others' mistakes and experience rather than waiting to experience it yourself. This is where good books and tapping into the amazing online resources come in handy. This will also help you progress in your career a lot quicker.

Gauging Your Experience with UNIX

Most production systems are run in a Unix environment. The Unix environment is very robust, and offers powerful tools to automate tasks. You might be asked a scenario based question as shown below:

Q. How would you go about replacing a piece of a text or a phrase from 20,000+ web templates residing on a Unix file system? `SBQ`

Even some candidates with 5+ years of experience will be tempted to spend a day or two to write 200+ lines of code to achieve the above requirement, when it can be achieved in 5 minutes with a simple Unix command. Some of the Unix commands like grep, find, awk, sed, etc along with the power of regular expressions can make you more productive.

Q12 Can you list some of the "UNIX" commands Java developers use very frequently? `PF`

A12 Find command: allows a Unix user to process a set of files and/or directories in a file sub tree. Examples,

- Recursively delete .svn directories: Subversion is a widely used open-source revision control application. Every copy of source code received from subversion repository has .svn folders, which store metadata. However, if you want to use or distribute source code, these .svn folders are often not necessary. When creating a new subversion project (or folder) based on an existing subversion project, it is imperative that the .svn folders are deleted before checking in the copied and subsequently modified project. Otherwise you run the risk of corrupting the original subversion project with the newly copied and modified project.

```
rm -rf `find . -type d -name .svn`
```

- Search for a file with a specific name in a set of files in the current (i.e. ".")

directory.

```
find . -name "rc.conf" -print
```

- Search for "*.java" files that are using "java.util.concurrent" classes.

```
find . -type f -name "*.java" -exec grep "java.util.concurrent" {} \; -print
find . -type f -name "*.java" | xargs -n1 grep "java.util.concurrent"
```

- Searching for old files. Finding files that are 7 days old or finding a file that has not been accessed for 30 days more, and files that are larger than 100k:

```
find . -mtime 7 -print
find . -type f -atime +30 -print
find . -type f -size +100k -ls
```

The grep and egrep commands are very handy for tearing through text files and finding exactly what you want very quickly.

- Search the log files to see if a particular user logged in.

```
cat /var/log/server.log | grep "login.jsp" | grep "userid"
```

- List all the log files that have a particular search text.

```
grep -l "Missing Characteristic Value" *.log*
```

- You can use regular expression patterns to search.

```
grep -e '^import.*util.regex' *.java
```

- Find all occurrences of util.* packages except the util.regex package.

```
grep -e '^import.*util' *.java | grep -v 'regex'
```

Tip: The Java *LinkageError* is tricky to resolve and it indicates that a class has some dependency on another class; however, the latter class has incompatibly changed after the compilation of the former class. Since plethora of third party jar files are used in commercial applications, it is not uncommon to get an error like,

```
java.lang.LinkageError: Class javax/xml/namespace/QNAme violates loader
constraints
```

This means the class *javax.xml.namespace.QName* is loaded by two or more different class loaders, and the versions are not compatible. For example, one might be under WEB-INF/lib, another might be loaded through an EJB or from a server lib folder. The "find" and "grep" Unix command can come to the rescue to identify the offending jars as shown below:

```
$ find . -name "*.jar" -print | -exec jar tvf {} \; |
              grep -E "jar$|javax/xml/namespace/QName\.class"
```

Q. What is the difference between the following 2 commands?

```
a) find . | grep mortgageonline
b) find . | xargs grep mortgageonline
```

A. The command (a) finds all the files containing the text "mortgageonline" in their file names. The command (b) recursively executes the grep command for each file, and displays the file contents that have the text "mortgageonline". This is equivalent to the command:

```
grep mortgageonline `find .`
```

Tip: The above commands are handy if you are modeling a new project based on an existing project where you need to change some file names and file contents.

To set **PATH** and **CLASSPATH**:

- export JAVA_HOME=/usr/java/jdk1.5.0_09
- export PATH=$PATH:${JAVA_HOME}/bin
- export CLASSPATH=./:${JAVA_HOME}/lib/rt.jar

Working with the Java processes and checking your network configurations. These are useful tools for monitoring processes, connections, and diagnosing problems.

- List all Java processes running on a box.

```
ps -def | grep java
/usr/ucb/ps -auxwww | grep java
```

Note: The /user/ucb/ps gives you the complete list of the JVM arguments.

- List all the processes except the root process.

```
ps auxwww | grep -v root
```

- Kill a particular Java process.

```
kill -9 <process-id>
```

- Get a thread dump.

```
kill -3 <process-id>
```

- Check for bound host-name or port number.

```
netstat -a | grep hostname
netstat -na | grep 80
```

Tip: There are times where an application server might be stopped, but either the address or port might still be bound. When this happens, the process id that is bound to either the port or address needs to be forcefully ended (i.e. end process on Windows task manager) or killed (in Unix).The following netstat command with the option "o" will display the process id.

```
netstat -ano | grep 1099
```

Output: 4784 is the process id that needs to be forcefully ended or killed.

```
127.0.0.1:1099      0.0.0.0:0        LISTENING    4784
```

- Check for cpu or memory usage.

```
top
```

```
vmstat
```

Testing whether a host or URL is reachable across the network.

- **ping** <hostname>
- **telnet** <hostname> <port-no>
- ping   www.example.com
- telnet www.example.com 80
- **wget** <URL>
- wget http://www.example.com/
- wget ftp://ftp.example.com/.sample.tar.gz
- **nslookup** www.example.com

The sudo command stands for "superuser do". It prompts you for your personal password and confirms your request to execute a command by checking a file, called "sudoers", which the system administrator configures. Using the "sudoers" file, system administrators can give certain users or groups access to some or all commands without those users having to know the root password. It also logs all commands and arguments so there is a record of who used it for what, and when.

- sudo -u jboss_user /etc/init.d/jboss-server status
- sudo rpm /tmp/rpms/charging-services.rpm

Working with the archive files:

- tar -cvf MyArchive.tar /home   (creating a tar file)
- tar -xvf MyArchive.tar   (extracting)
- gzip MyArchive.tar
- gunzip -f MyArchive.tar.gz

Accessing previous Unix commands you have entered.

- history   (display all recent commands)
- history | grep ps   (display ps related commands)
- !!   (repeat the previous command)
- !45   (!n –> 45 is the number from history list. Repeat this command)

- !sudo   (!string –> repeat the most recent sudo command)

Note: If you are running on Windows, install Cygwin or MSYS, which gives you a Unix like environment for Windows to practice on.

Q13 Can you give some examples of where you used "sed" and "awk" utilities? PF

A13 **Note**: find, grep, sed, and awk are cornerstones of shell programming. The last question covered some practical examples of "find" and "grep". The awk and sed commands are discussed below.

Awk is used for processing text based data, either in data streams or files. It extensively uses regular expressions. Here is a stream based example, using space as the default delimiter.

```
$ date "+%Y %m %d"
```

outputs: 2011 01 31, if you want to extract only year

```
$ date "+%Y %m %d" | awk '{print $1}'
```

outputs: 2011, and if you want to extract date/month

```
$ date "+%Y %m %d" | awk '{print $3 "/" $2}'
```

outputs: 31/01.

Another typical example would be to extract the shell script name as shown below:

```
#!/bin/sh
#This is a comment

echo $0
echo `basename $0`

SCRIPTNAME=`basename $0 | awk -F. '{print $1}'`
echo "script names is $SCRIPTNAME"

EXTENSION=`basename $0 | awk -F. '{print $2}'`
echo "extension is $EXTENSION"
```

93

The above script is stored under /Temp, and executed as shown below

```
$ sh ./Temp/EchoScriptName.sh
```

The output is:

```
./Temp/EchoScriptName.sh
EchoScriptName.sh
script names is EchoScriptName
extension is sh
```

The awk uses the "." as the field for delimiter to break the output into SCRIPTNAME and EXTENSION. The SCRIPTNAME can be used for logging as shown below:

```
LOG=/logs/${SCRIPTNAME}-`date +%Y%m%d-%H%M%S`.log
date +"`basename $0`: Started at %c" >> $LOG
```

If you want to extract the number of lines, you could do as follows

```
$ wc -l "./Temp/EchoScriptName.sh" | awk '{print $1}'
```

The $ wc -l "./Temp/EchoScriptName.sh" command outputs

```
10 ./Temp/EchoScriptName.sh
```

where 10 is the number of lines, and the awk '{print $1}' outputs just

```
10
```

The above command is quite handy in ETL (Extract Transform and Load) jobs to compare the number of lines in the data extract or feed against the number of records actually loaded into a staging table.

Sed is a powerful tool to make changes in a file or data streams. Sed has 4 spaces -- **input stream, output stream, pattern space,** and **hold buffer**. Sed operates on input stream and produces an output stream. The lines from input stream are placed into the pattern space where they are modified. The hold buffer can be used for temporary storage. In the following simple example, "day" can be replaced with "night" as shown below:

Note: The commands s (substitute), d (delete) , p (print), etc work on the pattern space.

```
$ echo day market | sed -e s/day/night/
```

The above "s" command substitutes first occurrence of "day" with "night". The out put is:

```
night market
```

the "**s**" in **s**/day/night/ stands for substitute or replace.

```
$ echo day market, day job | sed -e s/day/night/g
```

The output is:

```
night market, night job
```

The "g" in s/day/night/g stands for global replacement. i.e. replace every occurrence of "day" with night.

In real life examples, the ETL jobs uses shell scripts to validate and load data from feed files that look as shown below (e.g. MyFeedFile):

```
#SourceSystem:MortgageCustomers
#TERM.DEPOSIT.ACCOUNTS.20100603.01:45
2083490~MRS Liz RICHES~1055.43~2008/06/06 00:00:00~2009/09/04
2083491~MRS Liz Jones~1055.43~2008/06/06 00:00:00~2009/09/04
#END
```

The records starting with # are the header records and ending with # is the trailer record. The detailed records are delimited by "~". Often, the header and trailer records need to be removed before passing to a bulk copy utility like bcp to load the data in to a database.

```
$ `sed -e '1d;2d;$d' MyFeedFile > TEMP_MyFeedFile`
```

The above command uses the sed command to delete the first, second, and last lines of the feed file, and outputs the resulting detail records alone to a new temporary file. The "d" '1d;2d;$d' stands for delete. 1d, deletes the first line, 2d deletes the second line, and the $d delete the last line. The TEMP_MyFeedFile will look as shown below:

```
2083490~MRS Liz RICHES~1055.43~2008/06/06 00:00:00~2009/09/04
2083491~MRS Liz Jones~1055.43~2008/06/06 00:00:00~2009/09/04
```

Alternatively, you can use the following command with the help of regular expressions to delete comment lines (i.e. lines starting with #) and blank lines as shown below:

```
$ sed -e 's/#.*//' -e '/^$/ d' MyFeedFile > TEMP_MyFeedFile2.txt
```

The "s" is for substitute and 'd' is for delete. The "#.*" is the regular expression to match any line starting with a "#" followed by any character (i.e. ".") any number of times (i.e. "*"). The "^$" is the regular expression for blank lines. "^" means beginning with and "$" means ending with.

if you want to output just the first two fields, which are account number and account name using "|" as the delimiter, you could do it as shown below

```
$ awk -F~ '{ print $1 "|" $2 }' ./Temp/Temp_MyFeedFile.txt
```

The output is:

```
2083490|MRS Liz RICHES
2083491|MRS Liz Jones
```

If you want to replace all occurrences of "MRS" with "MS", you could do it as shown below:

```
$ sed -e 's/MRS/MS/g' ./Temp/Temp_MyFeedFile.txt
```

The output is:

```
2083490~MS Liz RICHES~1055.43~2008/06/06 00:00:00~2009/09/04
2083491~MS Liz Jones~1055.43~2008/06/06 00:00:00~2009/09/04
```

The command that was discussed earlier to resolve *LinkageError*

```
$ find . -name "*.jar" -print -exec jar tvf {} \; | grep -E "jar$|
          javax/xml/namespace/QName\.class"
```

produces the following output:

```
./deploy/MyApp/WEB-INF/stax-api.jar
  2254 Thu May 06 15:35:48 EST 2010 javax/xml/namespace/QName.class
./deploy/MyApp/WEB-INF/xalan.jar
./deploy/MyApp/WEB-INF/xercesImpl.jar
./deploy/MyApp/WEB-INF/xpp3_min-1.1.3.4.O.jar
./deploy/MyApp/WEB-INF/xstream-1.3.1.jar
./lib/stax-api.jar
  2254 Thu May 06 15:35:48 EST 2010 javax/xml/namespace/QName.class
```

This can be further extended using "sed" to print only the offending jar file as shown below. The command shown below

```
$ find . -name "*.jar" -print -exec jar tvf {} \; | grep -E "jar$|
   javax/xml/namespace/QName\.class" |
   sed -nre "/jar$/ { x; d; }; /class$/ { x; p; }"
```

outputs:

```
./deploy/MyApp/WEB-INF/stax-api.jar
./lib/stax-api.jar
```

Note: Only three commands 'h', 'H' and 'x' modify hold buffer.

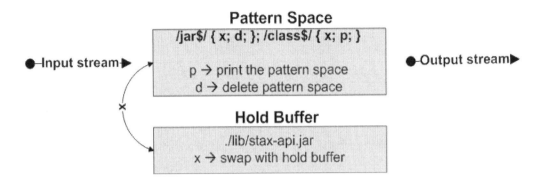

x → exchanges the hold buffer with the pattern buffer, p → prints out the pattern space. d → deletes the current pattern space.

**/jar$/{x;d;};** → Applies the regular expression jar$ that matches lines ending with "jar" like ./deploy/MyApp/WEB-INF/stax-api.jar. It swaps this value with the hold buffer, and deletes pattern space. Initially the hold buffer will be empty. The line ending with "jar" will be moved to the hold buffer as shown in the diagram.

**/class$/ {x; p;}** → Applies the regular expression class$ that matches text ending with "class" like "2254 Thu May 06 15:35:48 EST 2010 javax/xml/namespace/QName.class". It swaps the hold buffer with the pattern space, and then prints the pattern space. For example, the line ending with "jar" residing in the hold buffer will be moved to the pattern space and printed. The lines ending with "class" will be moved to the hold buffer.

Note: The above examples have only scratched the surface of the awk and sed utilities. There are plethora of online resources to expand your experience and knowledge on these utilities. Reference: http://www.catonmat.net/blog/sed-one-liners-explained-part-one.

Q14 Can you answer the following Unix questions? PF

Q. Can you explain the following Unix command?

```
$ date ; ps -ef | awk '{print $1}' | sed -e '1d'| sort | uniq | wc -l >> activity.log
```

A. The "date" prints the date and time. The "ps -ef" outputs all the running processes with the UID (user ids) as shown below:

```
  UID    PID   PPID TTY    STIME COMMAND
AKumara1   1120     1 con  11:25:36 /usr/bin/rxvt
AKumara1   3280  1120  0 11:25:37 /usr/bin/sh
AKumara1   5884  3280  0 13:05:02 /usr/bin/ps
```

The "awk '{ print $1}' " extracts out only the UID column. The "sed -e '1d' " deletes the first line of the above output, which is the column name UID. The "sort" and "uniq", sort the results and remove the duplicates respectively. The "wc -l" counts the number of lines. Hence, the above program appends (i.e. >>) the date and the number of unique UIDs to the file named *activity.log*. The actual output written to the file looks as shown below, where 1 is the unique row count.

```
Tue Feb  1 13:14:53 AUSEDT 2011  1
```

Q. How will you list the top 5 largest files or directories?
A. The "du" is the disk usage utility. The "head -5" returns the top 5 results.

```
$ du -sk * | sort -nr | head -5
```

Note: To get a better understanding of the command options like "-sk" or "-nr", refer to the Unix manual by typing the following command:

```
$ man <command-name>
$ man du
$ man sort | more
```

Q. How will you find out the disk free space?
A.
```
   $ df -k
   $ df -h
```

Q. How will you display all the processes running under your name?
A.
```
$ ps -aef | grep "AKumara1"
```

Q. What is NFS? What is its job?
A. NFS stands for Network File System. It enables a file system physically residing on another computer in the network, to appear on your computer just as another local

disk.

mount -F nfs nfs_server_name:/remote_filesystem /local_filesystem

Q. How do you change file access permissions in Unix?
A.
$ **chmod** 754 file

```
u   g   o
7   5   4
```

u → user, g--> group, o → others
'r w x -r w x- r w x' --> r-read, w-write, x-execute

```
r   w   x
4   2   1
```

7 → means the user can read, write, and execute (i.e. 4+2+1). Same as chmod u+rwx file
 5 → means the group can read and execute (i.e. 4+1). Same as chmod g+rx file
 4 → means others can only read (i.e. 4). Same as chmod g+r file

Q. How will you remove execute access to the group in the above example?
A. One of the the following 2 ways

```
$ chmod g-x file          #line1
$ chmod 744 file          #line2
```

Note: In line1, you can use "+" to add a permission and "-" to remove a permission. A "-" is used here because you are removing the execute permission from the group.

Note: Every user has a default set of permissions which apply to all files created by that user, unless the software explicitly sets something else. This is often called the **'umask'**. It is either inherited from the login process, or set in the .cshrc or .login file which configures an individual account, or it can be run manually.

Q. How do you create a new file in Unix?
A. $ **touch** MyFile.txt

Q. What are ex and vi?
A. ex is Unix line editor and vi is the standard Unix screen editor.

Q. Can you explain "$#" and "$?" with example?
A. $# → means the total number of command-line arguments supplied to the shell script. For example:

```
$ myscript.sh mynew.profile
```

The $# value is 1 here, as it has only one argument of *"mynew.profile"*. The $# can be used in your shell script as follows. The $1 value is *"mynew.profile"*. If you had supplied 2 command-line arguments, then the second argument will be stored in variable $2, and so on.

```
if [ $# -eq 0 ]; then
        CONFIGFILE=${SDROOT}/scripts_sh/myapp/myapp.profile
else
    CONFIGFILE=${SDROOT}/scripts_sh/myapp/$1
fi
```

$? → is the return code from a previous command or function in Unix, 0 is the standard return code for a successful completion. Any other codes indicate there has been an error. For example, the code below validates a header record and mails an error if there is an error.

```
echo $HEADER | awk '{

        #header line 1 #PIVOT
        if($1 !~ /^#[Pp][Ii][Vv][Oo][Tt]/){
            print "INVALID - HEADER first line must be PIVOT"
                exit 1
        }
    }'

if [ $? -ne 0 ] ; then
        echo "awk exited with status code of $?"                    # $? is 1
        ${MAIL} -s "Error in ${SCRIPTNAME}" ${FUND_EMAIL} < ${LOG}

        exit 1
```

```
fi
```

Note: Just "#" followed by some text indicates comments.

Q15 Can you brief on a shell script that you had worked on? OEQ
A15 [Hint]

A term deposit application loads the fund rates extracted out from another application named funds. The funds application extracts out the fund rates to a CSV file, and sends it over to the term deposit application via sftp (Secured File Transfer Protocol). A batch process was written using a shell script for the term deposit application to load the data from CSV extract into its database. This shell script was scheduled to run at midnight on week days. The shell scripts perform the following tasks:

- Validates the extract file to ensure that it has the right header and trailer records.
- Counts the number of detail records.
- Uses a command-line utility known as bcp (bulk copy) to load the data from the csv extract file into a staging table in the database.

```
${BCP} staging_fund in fund_extract_file.csv -U user1 -S fund_server -P
                    pwd -e   $ERRLOG -t\, -c
```

Note that the -t\, indicate that the extract file "*fund_extract_file.csv*" is comma delimited, and the data will be loaded in to a staging table named "*staging_fund*" running on a database server named "fund_server". The credentials to log in are user1/pwd.

- Uses an interactive command-line SQL tool like iSQL (i.e. for the Sybase database) or SQL*Plus (i.e. for the Oracle database) to execute a database stored procedure that will move the fund rates data from the de-normalized staging table to a number of other normalized tables used by the term deposit application.

```
${ISQL} -U $user1 -S $fund_server -D fund_database -P pwd -o
$TEMP_ROWCOUNT<<
```

```
EOF
declare @rowcount int
SELECT @rowcount = COUNT(*) FROM staging_fund
SELECT "ROWCOUNT=" + convert(varchar, @rowcount)
go
EOF
```

- Compares the number of records loaded into the staging table against the record count that was performed in the earlier step.

- If the count matches return the batch process as a success. Otherwise, mark it as a failure with an exit code of 2, and email the error message.

```
TEMPTABLE_ROWCOUNT=`grep ROWCOUNT $TEMP_ROWCOUNT
| cut -d= -f2`
#forced conversion into numeric
TEMPTABLE_ROWCOUNT=`expr $TEMPTABLE_ROWCOUNT + 0`

if [ $TEMPTABLE_ROWCOUNT -ne $ROWCOUNT ] ; then
   echo "failed to fully load into database" >> $LOG
   ${MAIL} -s "Error Loading Funds" ${FUND_EMAIL} < ${LOG}
   exit 2
fi
```

Exposure to tools, technologies, and frameworks

Using the right tools, technologies, and frameworks for the right job can not only make developers more productive, but also can significantly increase the robustness and quality of the applications built. There are so many free online resources to master the tools if you know what tools to use and when to use them. Tools will not only help you become more productive, but also enable you to impress your superiors and peers by delivering your work on time without compromising on the quality.

Q16 Can you name some tools, technologies, or frameworks you had to use in Java for source code generation, byte code manipulation, or assembling code at runtime? **PF**

A16 The tools and libraries discussed here are very powerful and can improve productivity, but can be complex, expensive to create and maintain, and requires expertise. So

103

should not use these unless you have a very good reason to do so. Even if you don't use these tools directly, you will be using them indirectly by making use of third-party libraries and frameworks, and worth knowing the options available.

Reflection: is a powerful tool that lets you build flexible code that can be assembled at runtime without requiring source code links between components. But care must be taken as this flexibility may come at other potential expenses like slow performance and security risks. Even though there is a clear speed disadvantage (i.e. roughly 2 times slower) to using reflection, for most use cases it does not matter. For it to matter, these operations have to be done in significant numbers, and for an on-going period (e.g. handling a heavy load of a web service). Reflection is often used in frameworks. It does also come in very handy in applying the DRY (Don't Repeat Yourself) principle. As duplication of code is very bad in terms of maintainability and often you can refactor the code to remove duplication. If you can see that you would be able to refactor the code but there are just two to three lines of code that is causing trouble in each method, you may be able to benefit from reflection.

Parser generator or **lexical analysis** tools. Parsing is the division of text into a set of discrete parts, or tokens, which in a certain sequence can convey a semantic meaning. If your requirements are very basic then regular expressions should be sufficient to parse your input text. However, if your requirements are more complex then a tool like JavaCC or ANTLR comes in very handy in automatically generating the parser source files from a grammar definition file written by you.

For example, if you would like to create a simple "online user query language" (i.e. like SQL but simpler to use by non-technical users) for your end users to use to query your back end database.

- Firstly, you will be defining a simple online query language for the end users to use. For example,

  ```
  display inactive users;
  display new users;
  ```

- Secondly, you will be writing a grammar or definition file for the query language you just created to validate and parse the entries. Parser generation tools like JavaCC, ANTLR, etc take this grammar definition file as input to automatically generate a number of .java source files containing complex logic to parse user input.

- Finally, you will use these auto-generated parser source files in your application code to validate and tokenize a stream of input characters from the "online user query language" into tokens. These tokens can be used to programmatically generate an SQL statement to retrieve relevant data from the database and passed back to the user.

Annotation Processing Tool (APT) was introduced in JRE 1.5 along with annotations. This very powerful tool enables you to generate new derived source files, class files, deployment descriptors, etc from a number of base files (i.e. java source code files) and annotations. To use APT, you need to have tools.jar in your classpath.

APT determines what annotations are present on the source code being operated on. Next, APT looks for annotation processor factories you've written. The tool asks the factories what annotations they process. Then APT asks a factory to provide an annotation processor if the factory processes an annotation present in source files being operated on. Next, the annotation processors are run. If the processors have generated new source files, APT will repeat this process until no new source files are generated.

Example: Generate a simple Java source file named "*ClassPrinter.java*" in a package named "annotation.example" that simply prints the class names of all supplied source files.

```
package annotation.example;

import java.io.IOException;
import java.io.PrintWriter;
import java.util.Arrays;
import java.util.Collection;
import java.util.Collections;
import java.util.Set;

import com.sun.mirror.apt.AnnotationProcessor;
import com.sun.mirror.apt.AnnotationProcessorEnvironment;
import com.sun.mirror.apt.AnnotationProcessorFactory;
import com.sun.mirror.declaration.AnnotationTypeDeclaration;
import com.sun.mirror.declaration.TypeDeclaration;
```

```java
public class ClassPrinterAnnotationProcessorFactory implements
    AnnotationProcessorFactory {

  private static final Collection<String> supportedAnnotations = Collections
      .unmodifiableCollection(Arrays.asList("*"));

  //prevent recursing
  private static boolean processedOnce = false;

  public Collection<String> supportedOptions() {
    return Collections.emptyList();
  }

  public Collection<String> supportedAnnotationTypes() {
    return supportedAnnotations;
  }

  public AnnotationProcessor getProcessorFor(
      Set<AnnotationTypeDeclaration> atds,
      AnnotationProcessorEnvironment env) {
    return new ClassPrinterAnnotationProcessor(env);
  }

  //inner class
  private class ClassPrinterAnnotationProcessor implements
      AnnotationProcessor {

    AnnotationProcessorEnvironment env;

    public ClassPrinterAnnotationProcessor(
        AnnotationProcessorEnvironment env) {
      this.env = env;
    }

    public void process() {
      PrintWriter writer = null;
      try {
        System.out.println("process() method is called processedOnce="
```

```
                                          + processedOnce );
        if(processedOnce) {
          return;
        }

        writer = env.getFiler( ).createSourceFile(
            "annotation.example.ClassPrinter");
        writer.println("package annotation.example;");
        writer.println( );
        writer.println("public class ClassPrinter {");
        writer.println( );
        writer.println("  public static void main(String[ ] args) {");
        for (TypeDeclaration typeDeclaration : env
            .getTypeDeclarations( )) {
          writer.println(String.format(
              "    System.out.println(\"Class: %s\");",
              typeDeclaration.getQualifiedName( )));
        }
        writer.println("  }");
        writer.println( );
        writer.println("}");
        processedOnce = true;

      } catch (IOException e) {
        throw new RuntimeException(e);
      }
    }
  }
}
```

To run the apt:

```
apt -cp ./bin -s ./gen-src -factory
    annotation.example.ClassPrinterAnnotationProcessorFactory  src/*.java
```

-cp :   where to find class files and annotation processor factories.
-s :   where to place source files generated by the annotation processor
        "ClassPrinterAnnotationProcessor".
-factory: Name of AnnotationProcessorFactory to use

There are a number of libraries available like Javassist, BCEL, ASM, etc to manipulate byte code. Even if you are not using it directly, today's applications will most probably rely on byte code manipulation at least indirectly through the other tools and frameworks used by your application. Byte code manipulation has become increasingly popular over the years, and it is used by application servers (e.g. JBoss), AOP libraries, web frameworks, JPA implementations (e.g. Hibernate), monitoring systems, profilers, clustering solutions, scripting languages, work-flow engines, and much more. Care should be taken in using these code generation tools directly as these can adversely impact maintainability and readability while providing benefits like better performance and flexibility. You need to have the right expertise and reason to use these powerful code generation and manipulation tools.

Q17 What tools do you generally need to get your job done? **OEQ FAQ**
A17

- **Integrated Development Environments (IDE)** like Eclipse, NetBeans, IntelliJ, etc to increase developer productivity in writing and debugging code. The right IDE for you is the one you are efficient with. The IDEs help you with quick navigation, interactive debugging, refactoring, auto-completion, organizing imports, warnings as you type, hovering over to get API assistance, etc.

- Hot deployment tools like **JRebel**, improves developer productivity by skipping the build and redeploy phases in your sandbox. JRebel is a JVM agent, which instantly reloads your code upon change without having to restart your application server or redeploy the application. It integrates into your JVM as a classloader extension and enables reloading of classes without requiring to create a new classloader, which is usually the case when redeploying or restarting application servers.

- **Cygwin** or **MSYS** to emulate Unix like environment for Windows. Many production systems are Unix/Linux based, and having a Unix/Linux environment on your local environment can make you more productive across other environments like System Testing, User Acceptance Testing (UAT), Business Acceptance Testing (BAT), Staging, and production.

- **Beyond Compare** for comparing both ASCII and binary files and directories. This is a very handy utility, if you want to compare different versions of the same ASCII file to understand what has changed or to compare two archive files to ascertain what new files have been added or deleted. Very handy especially during the build and release phases of the software development life cycle (SDLC).

- **Notepad++** for editing and viewing text files and log files. It has powerful editing features, uses less CPU, and opens larger files.

- **WinZip** or **7-zip** for working with the archived files (e.g. .zip files).

- **PuTTY** for SSH and Telnet implementation on Windows. You can connect to other Unix/Linux environments using SSH or Telnet. This tool also allows you to perform SSH tunneling or also known as port forwarding to bypass firewalls where certain ports are blocked. Common ports for example POP3,SMTP,HTTP and FTP can be easily tunneled using SSH.

- **FileZilla** or **WinSCP** to transfer files using FTP or SCP respectively. Log files or database extract files can be transferred from a Unix machine to your sandbox (i.e. local machine) using these utilities, and explored further using Notepad++ as it highlights search text or database extracts can be executed against a database.

- **Ethereal** or **Wireshark** for analyzing the network protocols & issues. Developing applications that interact with web services presents a unique set of problems like not knowing exactly what message was sent to the server, or what response was received. Some of the most difficult bugs to track down are caused by a disconnect between what you think you are sending to the server, and what is actually going across the wire. These tools are commonly called "packet sniffers" and capture all network packets that move across your network interface. Examining the contents of these packets and the order in which they were sent and received can be a useful debugging technique.

- **Tigris.org** provides a stack of tools that can enhance efficiency in various phases of the SDLC like analysis, construction, deployment, design, testing, issue tracking, requirements management, and source control management. For example, source control management (SCM) tools like Subversion, Subclipse, TortoiseSVN, & RapidSVN; design tools like ArgoUML to name a few popular ones.

- **Atlassian.com** software development and collaboration tools like **JIRA** for issue tracking, **Confluence** to share information, **Bamboo** for continuous integration server that automates the building and testing of your software, **FishEye** for real time notifications of code changes and web based reporting, and **Crucible** for constant code reviews to name a few popular tools.

- **JMeter** for performance testing. **Badboy** can be used to record your scripts during functional testing, and then save the same script as a JMeter file to do performance testing using JMeter. There are other commercial performance testing tools like **HP Load Runner**.

- Database administration and SQL execution tools such as **db-visualizer, SQuirreL SQL, SQL Developer, DBArtisan**, and Toad.

- Web service execution and testing tools like **SoapUI**, **PushToTest, TestMaker**, and **WebInject**.

- XML editors like **XMLSpy** and **Oxygen** to work with XML related technologies like XSDs, XSLs, WSDLs, XQuery, XPath, etc.

- Client side debugging tools like **FireBug** for FireFox and **Fiddler** to debug HTML, JavaScript, CSS, and Ajax requests/responses. There are many other handy FireFox plugins like "Modify Headers", "Live HTTP headers", and "Tamper Data" to test and debug client side.

Static analysis tools: Static analysis tools are used to find out programming errors in the code by analyzing their byte code.

- **CheckStyle** is a development tool to help programmers write Java code that adheres to a coding standard

- **FindBugs** is a program which uses static analysis to look for bugs in Java code.

- **PMD** scans Java source code and looks for potential problems like unused code, duplicate code, overcomplicated expressions, suboptimal code, etc.

- **CheckThread** for catching Java concurrency bugs.

Any good software development should have good documentation. This includes technical specifications, user manuals, support documentations, etc. These documents are generally produced using either Microsoft Word application or Oracle's Open Office writer. A good documentation must be concise with adequate diagrams, proper versions and access control. The following tools come in very handy.

- **ScreenHunter** or any other screen capturing tools to capture screen shots.
- **Visio** or **argouml** for solution design and UML diagrams.
- **Microsoft SharePoint** or any other document management software/repository to manage documents.
- **Wiki** or **Confluence** for team communication and knowledge sharing by providing adequate information for developers to share knowledge. For example, high level solution design, how to guides (e.g. How to set up your environment, application, etc), quick start guides, information on environments like database servers, application servers, etc across various environments like development, system testing, user acceptance testing, staging, and production.

Q. What tools have you used for the build and release processes? Can you also discuss some of the benefits of using those tools? **SD**
A.

- Maven and/or Ant with IVY to build and package the relevant artifacts.
- Bamboo, Continuum, CruiseControl, Hudson (more poplar), etc for continuous build and integration.
- Unix based package management tool like RPM for release and installation.

Use tools like Maven or Ant with Ivy for build & dependency management:

- In a nutshell, Maven manages your build, reporting, and documentation from a central piece of information you provide via the pom.xml file. It automates your dependency management, build, and deployment tasks.
- Once you describe what your dependencies are, Maven or Ant/Ivy will pretty much automatically build and test your code by downloading all the dependency jar files from various repositories.
- Maven automate all your common build tasks and also allow you to customize any tasks through prebuilt Maven or Ant plugins/wizards.

Continuous integration and build tools like **Hudson**:

- Monitor build results by e-mail or RSS to send real-time notifications on failure.
- Detect new failing unit tests while build and send notifications when first test in build fails. Also, produces a JUnit/TestNG unit testing framework test reports.
- Can distribute build/test loads to multiple computers.
- Keeps track of which builds produced which jars, and which build is using which version, etc.
- Provides a dashboard to view all the projects and its subgroups.

RPM offers a number of benefits like:

- Ability to upgrade individual components of your application without completely reinstalling.
- It provides powerful querying options. You can search for what package a file belongs to and from where the package came.
- You can also identify changes made to your artifacts since the last release.
- Support for automatic rollback.
- It provides extensive history and version information on installed packages.

Q18 What other languages have you used? `LF`

A18 [Hint] Perl, Python, Jython, Scala, Smalltalk, Ruby, JRuby, Groovy, Clojure, C++, C#, VisualBasic, **Java Script, Unix Shell scripting**, etc.

No more Java purism. Some of the scripting languages can make you more productive with features like fewer key strokes, easy to read, good libraries, and quick write/compile/run life cycle. Learning additional languages will also increase your understanding of programming in general, and more importantly it adds another tool to your tool box. Different languages use different programming paradigms, and get you to not only think differently and open your mind, but also make you conscious of their respective strengths and weaknesses. For example, another JVM language like Groovy can make developers more productive as the Groovy code is often easier and faster to write than a Java code, which makes it a worthwhile addition to your development toolkit. It is also important to understand that Groovy isn't a replacement for

Java, but compliments it with simpler syntax, dynamic typing, and features like closures and builders. In some cases, it makes more sense to use Groovy over Java. For example,

- You can do all the same things with JUnit in Groovy that you can do in the Java language with far fewer keystrokes. The JUnit run time is built into the Groovy runtime, and Groovy unit tests are easily scriptable with build tools like ANT, and provides many additional JUnit assertion statements and you can mock with Groovy Mocks. For example, to test for three persons with names "Peter", "Jason", and "Tom" in Java

```
List<Person> persons = s.getPeople( );
assertEquals(3, persons.getSize( ));
assertEquals("Peter", persons.get(0).getName( ));
assertEquals("Jason", persons.get(1).getName( ));
assertEquals("Tom", persons.get(2).getName( ));
```

Same results can be achieved in Groovy with a single line as shown below.

```
assertEquals(['Peter', 'Jason', 'Tom'], s.persons.collect {it.name})
```

Note: "it" means "this" person. It compares each person object for his/her name, and compares it with the supplied names. You can do more with less code in groovy.

- You can write a generic online forms engine in Java/JEE, and customize its behavior with simple Groovy driven scripts for specific online form applications like term deposit forms, cash management account forms, etc..

- You can use Java with Groovy or Jython for rapid prototyping. For example, you can build web applications using the *GroovyServlet*. Groovy has a concept that lets you write Java servlets in Groovy called Groovelets. Even the JDK is boosted with some nice features from Groovy to work with Files and mark up languages like XML, HTML, etc.

Some of the other scripting languages like JavaScript and Unix shell scripting are kind of must know scripting languages to be a well rounded developer, as many applications are Web based and run on Unix machines. JavaScript is really unavoidable these days. When people talk about HTML 5, they are mostly talking about JavaScript. JavaScript is used by many organizations including Microsoft, Amazon, Google, Apple and Facebook to provide a much richer user experience. The Java Script frameworks like JQuery can simplify coding.

Q. What tools or languages do you use for rapid prototyping?
A.

- Using HTML with CSS, Flash, JavaScript, and frameworks like JQuery.
- Using Python or Ruby
- Using Java with Groovy or Jython.
- Using wireframe and prototyping tools like Axure, MockupScreens, MindManager, etc.

The best tool is the one you are most comfortable with to get the job done at hand.

Note: Before you choose a main stream language refer to the TIOBE Programming Community Index at
http://www.tiobe.com/index.php/content/paperinfo/tpci/index.html.

Q19 How would you go about......? questions like

- How would you go about performance tuning an application?
- How would you go about identifying memory leaks or thread safety issues in an application?
- How would you go about gathering requirements, designing, and documenting your applications?
- How would you go about identifying and fixing any potential transactional issues in your application?
- How would you go about determining the security requirements for your application?
- How would you go about describing the software development process you are familiar with?

A19 These questions have been addressed in the "Java/J2EE Job Interview Companion (400+ Q&A)".

Documenting your Java applications

Good documentation is vital to any software project. As your documentation will be reviewed by your superiors and peers, a good documentation will also make a good impression and can surely help you progress in your career or get your contracts extended.

Q20 What are the different types of documents you refer to while designing or coding your system? `DC OEQ FAQ`

A20 **High Level Business Requirements document,** which contains the basic requirements that are to be developed as a software project. These are the "why" and "what" in business language.

Detailed Business Requirements document is more detailed than a high level business requirements document. It contains the information and data needed to design the application. These are the "how" in the business language. These documents address each functional requirements. Use case diagrams are often used to communicate the intended behavior of the system.

Non-functional requirements document is used for addressing non-functional requirements like how long transactional data should be kept for before archiving, volume of expected data and its growth over a period of time, estimated number of concurrent users or requests, auditing, logging and alarming requirements for ongoing customer support, process monitoring, metrics evaluation, disaster recovery strategy, and service level agreements (SLA) to define the system's mission criticality, availability and performance requirements. At times, non-functional requirements are included within detailed business requirements document itself.

Software architecture documents describing conceptual architecture (abstract), logical architecture (detailed), and execution architecture (deployment). These documents provide both structural and behavioral view of the system.

High level design documents provide an abstract (coarse-grained) view of the system based on the above mentioned documents. Details required to write the code are not shown. High level documents can have class and sequence diagrams at a conceptual level without defining operations in detail.

Low level design documents provide a detailed view of the system. These documents can include class diagrams, sequence diagrams, and entity-relation ship diagrams among many other details and diagrams to communicate the implementation level details.

Other relevant documents highlighting coding standards, development processes, deployment procedures, platform specifications, etc. These are usually accomplished via team based wiki sites.

The distinction between the above mentioned documents are not always very clear. For example, high level and detailed design documents can be combined into one at times. These documents are mainly written with the **target audience** in mind. So when writing these documents, one needs to ask the following questions –

Who's reading it? What do they want to know? And Why?

If you are writing a technical specification, it should have enough details so that you can give it to any developer and he or she should be able to start coding based on it. If you are writing a design document, it should answer all the questions an architect or a developer will be interested in understanding the system on a much higher level. So a design documentation should entail high level diagrams depicting the overall architecture, design alternatives, pros and cons of each alternative, why a particular alternative was recommended?, potentials risks, likelihood of those risks and the impacts of those risks to the business, etc. In general, these documents must also spell out any inclusions, exclusions, and most importantly map to relevant business and functional requirements.

Java reference Documentation

- JDK 6 Documentation --> http://java.sun.com/javase/6/docs/

Java Platform API Specification for Java core APIs and third party library APIs.

- Java 6 API → http://java.sun.com/javase/6/docs/api/index.html

Java Language Specification (JLS) is worth reading a bit at a time. For example, section 3.8 covers the "Identifiers" and 3.9 covers the "Keywords".

- JLS --> http://java.sun.com/docs/books/jls/third_edition/html/j3TOC.html

JDK Tools and Utilities reference documentation covers the tools you use to create, build, and run applications.

- tools doc → http://java.sun.com/j2se/1.5.0/docs/tooldocs/index.html

Q21 In your experience, why is it important to have relevant APIs handy while coding? `LF` `COQ`

A21

- It is a best practice to reuse proven, well-tested, and robust APIs as opposed to reinventing the wheel or writing sub-standard functions. Writing APIs is not a trivial task.

- These APIs and methods make your code more readable and maintainable. It can not only help you write one liner code, but also can warn you of some hidden dangers like if a particular class is thread-safe, if a particular method is deprecated and relevant replacement for a deprecated method, and other recommendations you can find like the one under *java.lang.Object* class' *equals( )* method details as described below:

  "Note that it is generally necessary to override the *hashCode( )* method whenever this method is overridden, so as to maintain the general contract for the *hashCode( )* method, which states that equal objects must have equal hash codes."

  Lets look at this with some interesting examples.

  Example1: The *BigDecimal* API clearly states that the *BigDecimal(double)* constructor is not recommended as it is unpredictable and *BigDecimal(String)* must be used instead. Try running the following code?

```java
import java.math.BigDecimal;

//$2.00 - $1.10
public class JavaAPI {

    public static void main(String[] args) {
        //Don't: unpredictable and not recommended
```

117

```
    BigDecimal result = new BigDecimal(2.00).subtract(new
                                        BigDecimal(1.10));
    System.out.println("Result = " + result);

    //predictable based on API recommendation
    BigDecimal result2 = new BigDecimal("2.00").subtract(new
                                        BigDecimal("1.10"));
    System.out.println("Result2 = " + result2);
  }
}
```

Output:

```
Result4 = 0.899999999999999991118215802998747676610946665527
Result3 = 0.90
```

If you really want to use a double value, then do the following with the *valueOf(...)* methods in the *String* class that can represent any primitive value as a string.

```
BigDecimal result3 = new
                BigDecimal(String.valueOf(2.00)).subtract(new
                                BigDecimal(String.valueOf(1.10)))
```

This shows that you need to take notice of the warnings and recommendations in the API documentation.

Example2: The Java API for JRE 5 and 6 clearly states that the class *String-Tokenizer* should not be used from JRE 1.4 onwards. This is what you can find in the API documentation:

"*StringTokenizer* is a legacy class that is retained for compatibility reasons although its use is discouraged in new code. It is recommended that anyone seeking this functionality use the split method of *String* or the *java.util.regex* package instead. "

The following sample code demonstrates that *String.split(regex)* and *Arrays.deep-ToString(myArray)* are one liners that improve readability of your code.

```java
import java.util.ArrayList;
import java.util.Arrays;
import java.util.List;
import java.util.StringTokenizer;

public class OneLiner {

    private static final String FRUITS = "Apple, Mango, Orange,   Grapes";

    public static void main(String[] args) {
        // No need to do this
        StringTokenizer st = new StringTokenizer(FRUITS, ",");
        List<String> listFruits = new ArrayList<String>();
        while (st.hasMoreTokens()) {
            listFruits.add(st.nextToken());
        }

        String[] fruits1 = new String[listFruits.size()];
        fruits1 = listFruits.toArray(fruits1);
        System.out.println(Arrays.deepToString(fruits1));

        // Do this instead
        // one liner tokenizing using Regex
        String[] fruits2 = FRUITS.split(",\\s*");

        // prints only the reference
        System.out.println("reference only --> " + fruits2);

        // No need to do this
        int count = 0;
        for (String fruit : fruits2) {
            ++count;
            System.out.print(fruit);
            if (count <= fruits2.length - 1) {
                System.out.print(", ");
            }
            else {
                System.out.print("\n");
            }
        }
```

```
        }

        //one liner deepToString method
        System.out.println(Arrays.deepToString(fruits2));
    }
}
```

Output:

```
[Apple, Mango, Orange, Grapes]
reference only --> [Ljava.lang.String;@7c6768
Apple, Mango, Orange, Grapes
[Apple, Mango, Orange, Grapes]
```

Note on regular expression: ",\\s*" means, a comma followed by white space characters repeated zero or more times.

- "," → a comma <u>followed by</u>,
- \\s → white space character in regular expression pattern is denoted as "\s", and since "\" has a special meaning as an escape character in Java, you need to escape the backslash in "\s" with another backslash, which results in "\\s") <u>repeated</u>,
- * → zero or more times. Note that *, + & ? are NOT wild card characters. ***** → **repeated** zero or more times, **+** → **repeated** 1 or more times, and **?** → **repeated** 0 or 1 time).

Refer to *java.util.regex.Pattern* API for the regular expression syntax.

Q22 What do you expect to see in a high level or detailed technical specification document? `DC OEQ`

A22

- **Objective** and **brief description** of the project.
- **Inclusions, exclusions**, and **assumptions** to clearly spell out what is in scope, what is out of scope, and the assumptions made.
- **Risks** highlighted with brief description, likelihood, impact, and mitigation strategy.
- High level and detailed **solution diagrams** to provide a quick overview.
- **Matrices** to map key business requirements with the technical solutions.

- The design alternatives addressed with pros, cons, and recommendations.
- Any relevant pre-conditions, post-conditions, and alternative flow paths.
- Other relevant **UML diagrams** like class diagrams, sequence diagrams, package diagrams, state chart diagrams, etc.
- **ER (Entity Relationship) diagrams** to represent database schema and relationships.
- The non-functional requirements like disaster recovery, security, response times, performance metrics, system monitoring, scalability, high availability, look and feel, etc addressed.
- Revision history to track changes, references to business requirements documents, and a list of reviewers and approvers of the document.

Q23 What do you expect to see in a high level or detailed business requirements document? OEQ

A23
- Purpose, constraints, scope inclusions, scope exclusions, etc to give an introduction to the project.
- Business objectives clearly defined, so that the design alternatives can be appropriately evaluated. For example,

    - **Objective 1:** Improve customer satisfaction by reporting sales information online.
    - **Objective 2:** Keep investment to <$250K whilst still delivering the service
    - **Objective 3:** Reduce the risk of operator errors.

- Business requirements with relevant use case diagrams, pre-conditions, alternative flows, post-conditions, expected results, etc so that the technical design specifications can be produced.
- Requirements should also address typical business scenarios so that the test cases can be easily written. For example

    - What if the rebate elections are made after the monthly process is started?
    - What if the accounts are moved from one adviser to another adviser?

- Non functional requirements like 24 x7 availability, average response times, usage patterns and forecasts, etc.

- Revision history to track changes and a list of reviewers and approvers of the document.

Q24 What tips do you give to someone who wants to write a technical documentation?

A24
- Be clear about why you are creating this documentation and who will be reading it. Put yourself in their shoes.

- Gather information in the domains where you are not the subject matter expert.

- Organize and outline information. Fill the information you already have and leave areas blank where you need to gather more information.

- Identify gaps in the requirements, get it clarified, and updated.

Ensuring code quality.

As a software engineer, you should ensure how your users will a have quality experience with the system you build. You must learn not only to think from a technology perspective, but also from a user experience and business objective perspective. No point in building something with a bleeding edge technology, if it does not add real value to your business and their users. QOS

Q25 Do you use test driven development? Why / Why not? COQ SP

A25 [Hint:] Yes.

- Gives you a better understanding of what you're going to write. Gets you to clearly think what the inputs are and what the output is. Helps you separate the concerns by getting you to think about the single responsibility principle (SRP).

- Enforces a better test coverage. This gives you the confidence to refactor your code in the future, since you have a good coverage.

- You won't waste time writing features you don't need.

Q26 What tips do you give someone who is writing the unit testing? COQ SP

- **Write unit tests and re-factor your code where necessary** to make it more maintainable and readable. **BP** It is a best practice to write your unit tests first along with an empty implementation of your functionality For example, a function that just returns false or null so that your tests fail. Then fill the empty functions with proper implementations to pass your tests.

- Tests should not depend on other tests. Use mock objects where appropriate to ensure that the tests are re runnable without the fear of having the right data in the database. Alternatively, the *dbUnit* framework allows you to create a data set, which is automatically created into the real database before running the test code and can clean up its mess at the end if necessary.

- **Think of all possible inputs your test should pass** for it to be correct. For example, can you think of all possible input values you need to test for the following method?

```
public class isOdd {
    public static boolean isOdd (int i) {
        return i % 2 == 1;                    // buggy
    }
}
```

You need to test with an odd number (e.g. 3), even number (e.g. 4), zero (e.g 0), and a negative number (e.g. -3). If you closely pay attention, you will notice that the above code will fail for negative odd numbers. Say i = -3;

```
-3 % 2 returns -1;
-1 == 1 returns false. This should actually be true since -1 is an odd number.
```

If tested for all possible conditions, this error can be picked up during testing and rectified as follows,

```
public class isOdd {
    public static boolean isOdd (int i) {
        return i % 2 != 0;                    //fixed
    }
}
```

- **Include negative test cases** in your test plan. Under ideal testing conditions, network timeouts don't occur. it is critical that attention is given to the problem of network timeouts during application development, for both network clients and network servers. Infinite timeouts can cause your application to hang for ever.

```
socket.connect(remote, 30000);              // timeout after 30s
java.net.Socket.setSoTimeout(30000) ;       // timeout after 30s
```

- **Write your code for better testability**. The key to any unit testing, as the term unit implies, being able to instantiate and test a small portion of the application and asserting that it does something correctly with both positive and negative test cases. If you can only instantiate a large portion or the whole application, then you cannot have a small unit test. So always look for signs that can make your code harder to unit test while writing your code. Please refer to Misko Hevery's thought provoking online articles for writing better testable code at http://misko.hevery.com/.

  ✔ Avoid constructing complex object graphs in your constructor. Use a factory or builder class to construct complex objects.

  ✔ Use **dependency injection** to more loosely couple your callee from the caller. The dependency injection frameworks (aka **Inversion of Control** (IoC) containers) like Guice, Spring, HiveMind, etc make your code more testable, maintainable, and flexible through looser coupling.

  ✔ Judiciously apply the "**Law of Demeter**" to minimize coupling and improve testability. The Law of Demeter was originally formulated as a style rule for designing OO systems by only talking to your immediate object. For example. Prefer writing,

  ```
  customer.getName( );
  ```

  to a longer version shown below:

  ```
  order.getContact( ).getCustomer( ).getName( );
  ```

124

By allowing access to the extra depth into nested lists or objects, coupling is increased. Increased coupling makes your code harder to test or change. It's usually a trade off between increased coupling between the code and the data and the increased performance.

Some of the signs that your code is bad are:

- Classes with too many instance variables, methods and code or too little instance variables and methods (i.e. anaemic domain model).
- Large methods performing too many things. A method should only perform one specific task.
- Excessive comments to explain the code. Code should be able to explain itself with meaningful names, smaller methods, and logical steps.
- Repeated use of switch/case and if/else statements. Replace this with polymorphism.
- Same logic is copied and pasted in multiple places. Refactor the shared code to a helper class or method and reuse it.
- Deeply nested for loops and "goto" statements producing a spaghetti code that is hard to understand and maintain. Replace multilevel nested loops with recursive method calls or use divide and conquer approach with more meaningful methods.
- Use of too many design patterns in a small space.
- Over use of implementation inheritance.

Q. Is there any downsides to writing unit tests?
A. Yes. Writing too many unit tests can make your code more fragile. Any valid change to your code will make a number of unit tests to fail. So, strike a good balance.

Q27 How will you ensure quality of your design and code? **COQ BP DC DP**
A27

- Make your code more maintainable by applying the **DRY** (Don't Repeat Yourself) principle.

- Apply the **fail fast principle** (aka design by contract). A fail-fast code will immediately report any failure or conditions attempting to continue a possibly-flawed process. Firstly, define your **preconditions** which check if the object is in a valid state or the parameters are valid. For example, check your input for null or empty values before start using them. Also, check your post conditions where required. Reduce preconditions in your code. Code that is very tedious about how it's invoked can make everything else harder to maintain.

```java
public class EmployeeAge {

    int age;
    ..
    public void setAge(int age) {

        //check preconditions and fail fast
        if (age < 0) {
            throw new IllegalArgumentException("Invalid age");
        }

        // check business pre-conditions and fail fast
        if (age >= 0 && age < 16) {
            throw new IllegalArgumentException("Outside eligible age range");
        }

        this.age = age;
    }
    ..
}
```

- **Business logic must be written in a protocol agnostic manner**. This improves code maintainability and reuse by centralizing the business logic in one place, and enabling access to it by various protocols like HTTP, TCP, HTTP over SOAP, RMI, etc.

- **Know your OO concepts and apply them**. For example, use of encapsulation lets you create well-defined boundaries which are only connected by narrow bridges. Another example would be to prefer interface-inheritance with composition to implementation inheritance for loose coupling and better flexibility.

- **Be aware of the design principles** that allow your code to be more flexible to extend, reuse, and understand. **DC DP**

126

✔ **Open Closed Principle** (OCP), which states that a software module should be closed for modification, but open for extension. Promotes looser coupling through coding against an interface as opposed to an implementation.

✔ **Liskov's Substitution Principle** (LSP), in a simpler term states that if a program module is using the reference of a base class say *Base*, then it should be able to replace the base class with a derived class say *Derived* without affecting the functioning of the program module. For example, a *Rectangle* is not a *Square* as per this principle. Mathematically, a square is a rectangle where the length is equal to the width. But functionally or behaviorally, a square is different from a rectangle. A rectangle must define both length and width. A square must define only width.

✔ **Dependency Inversion Principle** (DIP), which states that high-level modules should not depend upon low-level modules. Both should depend upon abstractions. Abstractions should not depend upon details. Details should depend upon abstractions. This principle helps your design to be Open Close Principle (OCP) compliant. why is it called Dependency Inversion Principle? The answer is again in how you think about building your modules. In the traditional approach, you start thinking from the high-level modules and cascade down to the lower levels. In Dependency Inversion Principle, you start thinking from the low-level modules. You start by writing lower level abstractions for example a *Writer*, which may have a number of concrete implementations like *DatabaseWriter*, *FileWriter*, *LdapWriter*, etc. Then you start associating this abstraction to higher level modules like *DataCollectors*, *DataProcessors*, etc. Design is always about trade-offs, and designing with too many levels of abstractions can be an over kill and time consuming. In many cases the requirements are rigid and unlikely to change too often. Designing is all about finding the right balance between flexibility based on the requirements and letting the project get on without over complicating things.

✔ **Composite Reuse Principle** (CRP), which favors **composition** with **interface inheritance** over **implementation inheritance** to achieve polymorphism. Think twice before just inheriting functionality. There are times when it is a good idea to use implementation inheritance such as when there is a <u>logical default behavior</u> and only some child classes need to over-ride it, for example the **template method** and **composite** design patterns. But, if the intent is to utilize the functionality rather than expose it to child class callers, composition with interface inheritance is almost always the right decision. For example, **strategy**, **decorator**, and **proxy** design patterns use interface inheritance. Some of the reasons to favor composition over implementation inheritance are:

◆ Inheritance can easily be used improperly. Some designs look like "is-a" situation, but aren't really. For example, A *Square* is not a *Rectangle* in terms of behavior.

◆ As the number of classes increases the complexity of the code base increases.

◆ Inheritance happens at compile-time, hence is static and composition is dynamic as it happens at runtime. Hence composition is more flexible.

◆ Implementation inheritance tends to create more strongly coupled classes that are more fragile and can be harder to test in isolation.

✔ **Interface Segregation Principle** (ISP), which states that many specific interfaces are better than one combined general interface. The intent of this principle is that the clients should not be forced to implement interfaces they don't use.

✔ **Single Responsibility Principle** (SRP), which states that there should never be more than one reason for a class to change. This principle represents a good way of identifying classes during the design phase of an application and it reminds you to think of all the ways a class can evolve. If you have 2 reasons to change a class, you will have to split the functionality into two classes. Each class will handle only one responsibility, and in the future if you need to make one change, you will be making it in the class which is responsible for handling it. For example, business logic and data access logic are segregated into their own classes.

- **Apply well proven design patterns** like Gang of Four (GoF) design patterns that help you solve recurring problems in software development. Based on the GoF authors' experience, a good software design should "Program to an interface, not an implementation" and "object composition" should be favored over "class inheritance" (aka implementation inheritance).

- One major factor of the maintainability of software systems is the control of dependencies. Using open source tools like *Sonar* for reporting design/code tangles and other code quality metrics like check style reports and code duplication can improve the overall software quality. There are other open source tools like *JLayerCheck* and *Macker* with IDE (e.g. eclipse) plugins to identify and remove tangles in your design.

Q28 Can you list some of the key aspects you keep in mind while coding to ensure quality & robustness? **COQ BP DC DP**

A28

- **Use the right tool to get the job done.** For example, don't use String operations to parse or write XML documents. There are a number of considerations to look out for like:

  - Escaping reserved characters like '<', '>', '&', etc,
  - Handling XML name-spaces and encoding correctly.
  - Using the memory efficiently.

  Use an appropriate XML library like Xerces, JDom, StAX, JiBX, etc to get the job done correctly and efficiently.

- When coding, think about **thread-safety** and **atomicity**. Issues arising from these are harder to detect and test.

- Always write **readable** code. Don't rely too much on comments. Make your code self-explanatory with meaningful variable, method and class names.

  "Any fool can write code that a computer can understand.

Knowing your way around Java

Good programmers write code that humans can understand."
—   by Martin Fowler

Instead of writing:

```
int a;
```

Use:

```
int maxAge;
```

If you have meaningful variable and method names, you don't have to clutter your code with comments. Books like "Clean Code: A Handbook of Agile Software Craftsmanship" by Robert C. Martin will be a good start to write clean code.

- **Handle exceptions properly.** Don't sweep them under a carpet.

- **Reduce state** with local variables or make your code inherently thread-safe with immutable objects where possible.

- Where possible **reuse well proven and tested API methods** from the Java code libraries and open-source libraries without having to write your own.

- **Be aware of the common gotchas, pitfalls, anti patterns, or caveats** of the Java language discussed throughout this book. Some of these are highlighted in the Java API documentation. Always have the API document-ation handy and refer to it. For example, the *SimpleDateFormat* API document-ation states that,

  "Date formats are not synchronized. It is recommended to create separate format instances for each thread. If multiple threads access a format concur-rently, it must be synchronized externally."

- **System resources are finite and manage them properly**. The non-memory resources like file handles, sockets, database connections, LDAP connections, etc need to be closed properly in a finally block once finished with them. Don't rely on the finalize( ) method to close these finite resources as you can't know when a finalize( ) method will be invoked by the garbage collector. It may take hours for the garbage collector to invoke a finalize( ) method. Creating and destroying some of these resources like threads and connections frequently can be expensive. Hence, maintain a pool of these resources and return them to the pool to be reused. Use proper time out values for the network connections, to prevent a thread being blocked infinitely. The heap memory is finite and use proper object reuse (e.g. immutable objects) strategies. Don't assume that generating a file is small enough to fit into the available heap memory as shown below:

```
byte[ ] readFile = generatePDF(...);
```

The above code is vulnerable to memory issues if accessed concurrently by multiple threads. Don't use byte arrays for bulk data. Use streams to write the data to a file or database. Make it a point to buffer your streams to minimize the number of read/write call to the native system.

```
InputStream in = new BufferedInputStream(new
                              FileInputStream(myFile));
```

Q29 What are mock objects and when do you use them? **COQ**

A29 Mock objects are simulated objects that mimic the behavior of real objects in controlled ways. Mock objects can be used in unit tests and other parts of your code to simulate interactions with resources that are

- harder to set up. For example, complex database set up is required.
- Real object is not yet ready or a separate team is responsible for providing the real objects.
- The real object may be too slow.
- The real object may have a non-deterministic behavior like not running immediately as it logs the request and only runs after midnight or kicked off only when the temperature reaches above 40 degrees centigrade.

Some of the frameworks used in Java for creating mock objects are *EasyMock*, *Mockito*, *PowerMock*, and jM*ock*. The *Mockito* framework is quite easy to learn, and the *PowerMock* extends *Mockito* and *EasyMock* to provide support for private and static methods. The *PowerMock* also contains other useful features such as suppressing static initializers and constructors.

Q30 What development methodologies are you comfortable with? SP

A30 [Hint:] Experienced in both waterfall and agile development practices. Strictly speaking, waterfall is a methodology, and "Agile" is a set of principles. Scrum and XP (eXtreme Programming) are methodologies that use these agile principles. Agile came about because methods like waterfall didn't allow for a high level of customer involvement, or change. Many companies adopt a hybrid approach where a waterfall approach is followed with good documentation and agile principles like:

- Daily stand-up meetings.
- Iterative development.
- Test driven development
- Better customer/user engagement

At the end of the day, Information Technology exists for the business. Business must be able to respond to changing customer needs and wants very quickly. So take the best parts of the tool kits and attack projects in a way that makes sense for that project. It is also at times required to resort to tactical or hybrid solutions as opposed to strategical or cleaner solution, to meet the business objectives. A typical example would be that a business might be structured and operates in a certain way, for example by products or services. A good developer will look at things from both business and technology perspective. This is why in real life, you will often end up having hybrid solutions to get the best of both worlds as opposed to religiously following what the proponents say.

**"In theory there is no difference between theory and practice.
In practice there is."**

– YogiBerra

Section-4:

Language Essentials

- Valid identifiers and reserved keywords
- Choosing the right data types
- Widening versus narrowing conversions
- Understanding the operator precedence
- Thinking in binary and bitwise operations
- Initializing your data correctly
- Packaging your classes to avoid conflicts
- Constants and static imports
- Modifiers and where are they applicable?
- Methods and constructors
- Recursive functions
- It is always pass-by-value in Java
- Class, instance, and local variables

This section is mainly for beginner to intermediate level. It also contains useful information for senior level candidates, and worth having a quick browse through, especially if you are required to sit for a basic Java technical test. Even among experienced professionals, there are a breed of developers who know how to get things done by using various frameworks, tools, and googling without fully understanding the fundamentals. Understanding the core Java fundamentals are essential not only from the point of view of passing the technical tests used for screening potential candidates and to perform well in technical job interviews, but also from the point of view of showing off your technical capabilities within limits to your peers and superiors during code review sessions, team meetings, and situations where you were able to resolve an intermittent, critical, or obscure problem more quickly than others as you understand the nitty-gritty details.

It's important to let others know about the good things you are accomplishing. Don't think that by just working hard that you'll get noticed. You need to let people know, especially your leaders like to know these things because they can't know everything that is going on, so speak up when required to. A little preparation prior to a code review session or an important team meeting that was going to discuss "a class loading issue" can make a huge difference in making an impact. All you have to do is refresh your memory on the basics.

Valid identifiers and reserved keywords

Q1   What are identifiers in Java? What does the following code do? Can you talk us through the code highlighting some of the key language and design features? **COQ**
LF BP

```
package chapter2.com;

import java.util.Arrays;
import java.util.HashSet;
import java.util.List;
import java.util.Set;

public final class ValidIdentifiers {

    private enum Validity {
        Valid, InvalidIdentifierStart, InvalidIdentierPart, ReservedKeyWord,
                                        ReservedLiteral
    };

    private static final String[ ] RESERVED_KEYWORDS = { "abstract",
        "continue", "for", "new", "switch", "assert", "default",
        "if", "package", "synchronized", "boolean", "do", "goto",
        "private", "this", "break", "double", "implements",
        "protected", "throw", "byte", "else", "import", "public",
        "throws", "case", "enum", "instanceof", "return",
        "transient", "catch", "extends", "int", "short", "try",
        "char", "final", "interface", "static", "void", "class",
        "finally", "long", "strictfp", "volatile", "const",
        "float", "native", "super", "while" };

    private static final String[ ] RESERVED_LITERALS = {"true", "false", "null"};

    private static Set<String> KEYWORDS = new HashSet<String>(
        (int)(RESERVED_KEYWORDS.length/0.75));

    private static Set<String> LITERALS = new HashSet<String>(
        (int)(RESERVED_LITERALS.length/0.75));
```

```
static {
   List<String> list = Arrays.asList(RESERVED_KEYWORDS);
   KEYWORDS = new HashSet<String>(list);

   List<String> listLit = Arrays.asList(RESERVED_LITERALS);
   LITERALS = new HashSet<String>(listLit);
}

public static final Validity valid(String input) {
   if (input.length() == 0
         || !Character.isJavaIdentifierStart(input.charAt(0))) {
      return Validity.InvalidIdentifierStart;
   }

   for (int i = 1; i < input.length(); i++) {
      if (!Character.isJavaIdentifierPart(input.charAt(i))) {
         return Validity.InvalidIdentierPart;
      }
   }

   if (KEYWORDS.contains(input)) {
      return Validity.ReservedKeyWord;
   }

   if (LITERALS.contains(input)) {
      return Validity.ReservedLiteral;
   }
   return Validity.Valid;
}
}
```

A1   Identifiers are names you give to your variables, constants, classes, interfaces and methods.

The above code verifies if a given input is a valid identifier, complying with the following rules:

- The first character of an identifier must be a letter, an underscore(_), or a currency sign(e.g. $).

- The rest of the characters in the identifier can be a letter, underscore, currency sign, or digit. Note that spaces are NOT allowed in identifiers.
- Identifiers are case-sensitive. This means that *age* and *Age* are considered as different identifiers.
- Identifiers cannot match any of Java's reserved words like for, int, etc or literals like null, true, and false..

Note: `true`, `false`, and `null` might seem like keywords, but they are actually literals; you cannot use them as identifiers in your programs.

Note: *const* and *goto* are reserved, but not currently used. *enum* was added in Java 5. *strictfp* allows you to have more predictable control over floating-point arithmetic.

Q. Can you talk us through the code highlighting some of the key language and design features?
A.

- Use of enums and generics indicates that this code must be using JDK version 1.5 or greater.

- **LF** Private access modifiers are used where required to encapsulate the internal details.

- **LF** The class is marked final so that it cannot be extended.

- **DC** It follows the "**code to interface**" design principle. For example, the Set, List, etc shown below are interfaces.

```
private static Set<String> KEYWORDS = new HashSet<String>(
        (int)(RESERVED_KEYWORDS.length/0.75));
//...
List<String> list = Arrays.asList(RESERVED_KEYWORDS);
```

- **BP** Making use of the Java API methods where possible. For example, the methods shown below from the *Character* and *Arrays* classes, simplify your code. So don't memorize the Java API, but keep it handy and constantly refer to it.

137

```
Character.isJavaIdentifierStart(input.charAt(0))
Character.isJavaIdentifierPart(input.charAt(i))
List<String> list = Arrays.asList(RESERVED_KEYWORDS);
```

- **BP** If a size of a collection is known in advance, it is a best practice to set its initial size appropriately to prevent any resizing. Implementing the code as shown below would not quite work.

```
private static Set<String> KEYWORDS = new HashSet<String>(
                    RESERVED_KEYWORDS.length);
```

The internal threshold for *HashSets* and *HashMaps* are calculated as (int) (capacity * loadFactor). The default loadFactor is 0.75. This means the *HashSet* will resize after 75% of its capacity has been reached. The resizing and rehashing of the set can be prevented as follows,

```
private static Set<String> KEYWORDS = new HashSet<String>(
                    (int)(RESERVED_KEYWORDS.length/0.75));
```

- **BP**: Checking for null and empty string as a **precondition** in the beginning of the *valid(String input)* method.

```
if (input == null || input.length() == 0 ...)
```

The above code snippet is a slight deviation of the fail fast principle, which states that check and report any possible failures as soon as possible. Testing your code for failure points will lead to better, safer, and more reliable code.

Q. Do you have any recommendations to further improve the code? **OEQ**
A. Yes.

- The Apache commons library class *StringUtils* can be introduced here. The method *isEmpty (String input)* can be used to check for both null and empty string. This library does have other useful methods that can be used elsewhere in the application code to enforce the fail fast principle.

```
StringUtils.isEmpty(input)
```

138

- The RESERVED_KEYWORDS and RESERVED_LITERALS constants may be loaded from a configuration file. This will ensure that if new keywords or literals are added to Java in the future, it will require only a configuration change.

Note: Even though the above recommendations are debatable depending on various other factors, it is better to know the possible options to demonstrate your experience than to have no ideas at all.

Q2   Which of these are legal Identifiers? **LF**

    a) $Ident1
    b)   _Ident1
    c)   -Ident1
    d)   2Ident1
    e)   private
    f)   private1
    g)   null
    h)   Ident-1
    i)   Ident$1
    j)   \u00A3Ident1
    k)   \u00A5Ident1

A2   The legal identifiers are a,b, f, i, j, and k. Let's make use of the class "*ValidIdentifiers*" shown in Q1, to test the identifiers.

```
package chapter2.com;

//using JDK 1.5 static import
import static chapter2.com.ValidIdentifiers.valid;
import static java.lang.System.out;

public class ValidIdentifiersExample {

    public static void main(String[ ] args) {
    /**
     * A valid identifier start consists of letters (e.g.
     * a-zA-Z), digits(0-9),underscores (_) and currency symbols
     * ($,\u00A3(Pound),etc),But cannot start with a digit.
```

```
  */

    out.println("a) $Ident1=" + valid("$Ident1"));        //Valid
    out.println("b) _Ident1=" + valid("_Ident1"));        //Valid
    out.println("c) -Ident1=" + valid("-Ident1"));        //InvalidIdentifierStart
    out.println("d) 2Ident1=" + valid("2Ident1"));        //InvalidIdentifierStart


    /**
     * an identifier cannot have the same spelling as one of
     * Java's reserved words like final, synchronized, etc or
     * a reserved literal
     */

    out.println("e) private=" + valid("private"));        //ReservedKeyWord
    out.println("f) private1=" + valid("private1"));      //Valid
    out.println("g) null=" + valid("null"));              //ReservedLiteral


    /**
     * Cannot use anything other than letters,digits, under-scores and
     * currency symbols in part of the identifier
     */

    out.println("h) Ident-1=" + valid("Ident-1"));        //InvalidIdentierPart
    out.println("i) Ident$1=" + valid("Ident$1"));        //Valid

    //Pound & Yen
    out.println("j) \u00A3Ident1=" + valid("\u00A3Ident1"));      //Valid
    out.println("k) \u00A5Ident1=" + valid("\u00A5Ident1"));      //Valid

  }
}
```

Q. What is an escape character? Can you list some character escape codes in Java? What are the differences between decimal, octal, and hexadecimal literals?

A. The escape character, the back slash \, is the character that signals the following character is not what it normally means. Java provides escape sequences for several non-graphical characters. All characters can be specified as a hexadecimal Unicode character (\udddd) with some as an octal character (\ddd where the first d is limited to 0-3, and the others 0-7). **Refer:** http://www.ascii-code.com/

```java
import static java.lang.System.out;

public class EscapeCharacters2 {

    public static void main(String[] args) {
        char c1 = 'A';                      //Decimal value of 65
        char c2 = '\n';                     //new line character
        char c3 = '\u0041';                 //Hexadecimal character = Decimal value of 65
        char c4 = 65;

        out.println(c1 + "\t" + c3 ); //prints 'A <tab> A'
        out.print(c2);                  //prints a 'new line'
        out.println(c4);                //Decimal value of 65, which prints letter 'A'
        out.println("\\ ");             //prints back slash
        out.println("\' \" ");          //prints a single quote followed by a double quote
        out.println("\f");              //prints a form feed
        out.println("\101");            //Octal value, representing a decimal value of 65
                                        // 1x8^2 + 0x8^1 + 1x8^0 = 65. Prints letter 'A'
        out.println("\377");            //Max Octal value -- Decimal value 255
                                        // 3x8^2 + 7x8^1 + 7x8^0 = 255.
                                        //prints a symbol 'ÿ', according to ASCII table
                                        // value of 255

        out.print("\r");                //prints a Carriage Return
        out.println("\u0041");          //Hexadecimal value, representing a decimal
                                        //value of  65
                                        // 0x16^3 + 0x16^2 + 4x16^1 + 1x16^0 = 65.
                                        // Prints letter 'A'
        out.print("\uFFFF");            //max Hexadecimal value -- Decimal value 65,535
                                        //15x16^3 + 15x16^2 + 15x16^1 + 15x16^0 = 65535
                                        //0-9 and A - F to represent values 10 to15. F=15.
                                        //prints unicode value 65535, which is a symbol '?'
                                        //according to unicode table at
                                        //http://unicode.coeurlumiere.com/?n=61440
    }
}
```

Q. How does Java treat Unicode escapes within string literals?
A. The compiler translates Unicode escapes into the characters they represent before parsing into tokens, such as string literals.

```
public class UnicodeRepresentation {

  public static void main(String[ ] args) {
    System.out.println("\u00A3-Pound, \u00A5-Yen");
  }
}
```

Ouput:

£-Pound, ¥-Yen

Q3 Which of the following are keywords in Java? **LF**

   a) friend
   b) NULL
   c) implement
   d) synchronized
   e) throws
   f) implements
   g) synchronize
   h) volatile
   i) transient
   j) native
   k) interface
   l) TRUE
   m) new
   n) true
   o) strictfp
   p) instanceof
   q) then
   r) throw
   s) this

A3 The keywords are: d, e, f, h, i, j, m, o, p, r, s.

Note: *true* is a reserved literal not a reserved keyword. Also, take care with the spelling. *implements* ending with an 's' is a keyword, but *implement* is not. *synchronized* ending with 'ed' is a keyword, but *synchronize* is not. Unlike other languages, *then* is not a keyword. You only have *if* and *else* in Java. Both *throw* and *throws* are keywords.

Q4 Why is it a best practice to adhere to naming conventions and what are they? **BP**

A4 Naming conventions make programs more understandable by making them easier to read. They can also give information about the function of the identifier. For example, whether it's a constant, package, or class. The conventions really depend on the individual place you're coding for. In general,

- For classes and interfaces, use UpperCamelCase.
- For class members and local variables use lowerCamelCase
- For packages, use reverse URI, e.g. org.project.subsystem
- For constants, use ALL_CAPS.

If you really want to begin a variable name with a digit, prefix the name you'd like to have (e.g. *9pins*) with an underscore, e.g. *_9pins*. Otherwise use something like *ninePins*.

Some try to differentiate between member variables, local variables, and arguments with different patterns. For example,

- field (aka instance or member variable): _name or **this**.name. "this" is a reserved keyword in Java referring to the current object.
- argument : aName
- parameter : pName
- local variable : _name

Coding standards are a key best practice in many development processes, especially in agile development. Some recommendations simply define a standard way to layout code or to name classes or variables, while others are designed to make code more reliable or better performing. There is no real objective reason to prefer one style over the other as long as it is consistent across the team or organization. *Checkstyle* is an open-source tool that can help enforce coding standards and best practices.

Choosing the right data types

Some simple mistakes like having an integer overflow can bring an application down and cost companies in thousands.

Q5   How would you go about choosing the right data types for your application? What are wrapper classes, and why do you need them? **LF BP FAQ**

A5   Java is what is known as a strongly typed language. This means Java only accepts specific values within specific variables or parameters. Some languages, such as JavaScript, PHP, and Perl are weakly typed languages.

1. Know the data limits to prevent any data overflow

Choose the most appropriate data type based on the minimum and maximum limit. If you are not too sure, select a larger value to avoid any **data overflow**. For example,

```
...
public class OverFlow {

    public static void main(String[ ] args) {
        // 1 byte - 8 bits -2^7 to 2^7-1
        out.println("Min byte:" + Byte.MIN_VALUE);          // -128
        out.println("Max byte:" + Byte.MAX_VALUE);          // 127

        // 2 bytes - 16 bits -2^15 to 2^15-1
        out.println("Min short:" + Short.MIN_VALUE);        // -32768
        out.println("Max short:" + Short.MAX_VALUE);        // 32767

        // 2 bytes - 16 bits -- unsigned
        out.println("Min char:" + (int) Character.MIN_VALUE);   // 0
        out.println("Max char:" + (int) Character.MAX_VALUE);   // 65535

        // 4 bytes - 32 bit signed integer (int): -2^31 to +2^31-1
        out.println("Min int:" + Integer.MIN_VALUE);        // -2147483648
        out.println("Max int:" + Integer.MAX_VALUE);        // 2147483647
```

```java
    // 8 bytes - 64 bit signed integer (long): -2^63 to +2^63-1
    out.println("Min long:" + Long.MIN_VALUE);      // -9223372036854775808
    out.println("Max long:" + Long.MAX_VALUE);      // 9223372036854775807

    // 4 bytes - 32 bit -- single precision
    out.println("Min float:" + Float.MIN_VALUE);     // 1.4E-45
    out.println("Max float:" + Float.MAX_VALUE);     // 3.4028235E38

    // 8 bytes - 64 bit -- double precision
    out.println("Min double:" + Double.MIN_VALUE);  //4.9E-324
    //1.7976931348623157E308
    out.println("Max double:" +  Double.MAX_VALUE);


    // boolean has either true or false

    int bad = 2100000000;                           // Close to int max value.
    out.println("bad + 7 = " + (bad + 7));          // 2100000007
    out.println("bad * 3 = " + (bad * 2));          // -94967296 – data over flow

    long good = 2100000000L;
    out.println("good + 7= " + (good + 7));     // 2100000007
    out.println("good * 2 = " + (good * 2));    // 4200000000

    long badAgain = 9000000000000000000L;   // Close to long max value
    out.println("badAgain + 7 = " + (badAgain + 7)); // 9000000000000000007
    out.println("badAgain * 2 = " + (badAgain * 2));   // -446744073709551616
                                                       // data over flow

    BigInteger goodAgain = BigInteger .valueOf(9000000000000000000L);
    out.println("goodAgain + 7 = "
        + (goodAgain.add(BigInteger.valueOf(7)))); // 9000000000000000007

    // 18000000000000000000
    out.println("goodAgain * 2 = " + (goodAgain.multiply(BigInteger.valueOf(2))));
  }
}
```

2. Prefer immutable wrapper objects to primitives.

Each primitive data type has a corresponding wrapper class like *Integer*, *Long*, *Character*, *Float*, *Double*, etc. There are 8 primitive variables and as many wrapper objects. In Java 5, additional wrapper classes like *AtomicInteger*, *AtomicLong*, *AtomicBoolean* and *Atomic-Reference*<V> were introduced to provide **atomic operations** for addition, increment, and assignment. These additional classes are mutable and cannot be used as a replacement for regular immutable wrapper classes.

Why prefer wrapper objects to primitives? Wrapper objects can be initialized to null. This can't be done with primitives. Many programmers initialize numbers to 0 or -1 to signify default values, but depending on the scenario, this may be incorrect or misleading. Wrapper objects are very useful for optional data. Databases almost always have a significant fraction of their fields as optional (that is, as possibly NULL). In addition, the forms submitted in Web applications can contain optional parameters. Both NULL database fields and missing request parameters naturally map to null object references. With primitives, there is no such natural mapping.

BP Wrapper objects will also set the scene for a *NullPointerException* when something is being used incorrectly, which is much more programmer-friendly as it **fails fast** than some arbitrary exception buried down the line. Preferably, check for null early on in the method and report it immediately where applicable to adhere to the fail fast principle.

CC The wrapper objects are immutable, hence inherently thread-safe. Other threads can only read the values set by the thread that initialized this object.

PC When you create wrapper objects, use the *valueOf( )* static factory method for efficiency.

```
Integer i2 = new Integer(5);        //first approach is okay
Integer i1 = Integer.valueOf(5);    //2nd approach is more efficient
```

DP The second approach is in fact an implementation of the flyweight design pattern. When auto-boxing occurs for a well-known value, instead of creating a new wrapper instance, a pre-created instance is fetched from a pool and returned.

Q. When to prefer primitives?
A. Primitives are faster to create and use than wrapper objects. Wrapper objects need

to be auto-unboxed before use. Thus there is an extra step for the JVM to perform. For example, in order to perform arithmetic on an *Integer*, it must first be converted to an int before the arithmetic can be performed. In many business applications this rarely matters unless you were writing something very number-crunching or profiling indicates that the auto-boxing is a performance or memory issue in a particular part of your code as it is executed very frequently.

Anti-pattern: Watch out for premature-optimization anti-pattern where you are tempted to code for a perceived (whether rightly-or-wrongly) performance gain and sacrificing good design and maintainability.

Q6 When working with floating-point data types, what are some of the key considerations? **LF BP COQ FAQ**

A6 **1. Never compare float or double with "==" or != operator**

```
package chapter2.com;

public class FloatingPointEquality {

    public static void main(String[] args) {
        //use "<" or " >"
        for (float f = 5f; f < 10.0; f += 0.1) {
            System.out.println(f);
        }

        //endless loop -- don't compare float or double for == or !=
        for (float f = 5f; f != 10.0; f += 0.1) {
            System.out.println(f);
        }
    }
}
```

Floating point numbers are represented (using IEEE 754) as base 2 decimal numbers in scientific notation. An IEEE floating point number dedicates 1 bit to the sign of the number, 8 bits to the exponent, and 23 bits to the mantissa part. The double-precision floating point dedicates, 1 bit to the sign of the number, 11 bits to the exponent and 52 bits to the mantissa part. The sign is either a 1 or -1. The mantissa, always a positive number, holds the significant digits of the floating-point number. The exponent indicates the positive or negative power of the radix that the mantissa and sign should be multiplied by. The four components are combined as follows to get the floating-point value:

$$sign * mantissa * radix^{exponent}$$

Floating-point numbers in the JVM use a radix of two as computers only understand binary. **Refer**: http://www.h-schmidt.net/FloatApplet/IEEE754.html

$$sign * mantissa * 2^{exponent}$$

This means:

```
0.5    is represented as 1 * 1.0 * 2⁻¹
-0.25  is represented as -1 * 1.0 * 2⁻²
0.1  is represented as 1 * 1.6 * 2⁻⁴
```

Floating point arithmetic is rarely exact. While some numbers, such as 0.5, can be exactly represented as a binary (base 2) decimal (since 0.5 equals $2^{-1)}$, other numbers, such as 0.1, cannot be. As a result, floating point operations may result in **rounding errors**, yielding a result that is close to, but not equal to the result you might expect. In the above *FloatingPointEquality* example, "f" will never be exactly 10.0. Use greater than or less than operators instead.

2. Use long, int, or *BigDecimal* for storing money, and performing monetary calculations.

As discussed earlier, floating point data types like float, double, *Float*, or *Double* can have strange results as shown below, and use either the *BigDecimal* or int/long representing the value in its lowest units like cents..

```
import java.math.BigDecimal;
import java.math.RoundingMode;

public class FloatingPoint2 {

    public static void main(String[] args) {
        int itemCount = 100;
        float unitCost = 0.30f;
```

```java
    int unitCostInCents = 30;

    FloatingPoint2 fp = new FloatingPoint2( );
    fp.calculateTotalInaccurately1(unitCost, itemCount);
    fp.calculateTotalInaccurately2(unitCost, itemCount);
    fp.calculateTotalAccurately1(unitCost, itemCount);
    fp.calculateTotalAccurately1(unitCostInCents, itemCount);
}

//using a float
private void calculateTotalInaccurately1(float unitCost, int itemCount){
    float total = unitCost * itemCount;
    System.out.println("Total1 --> " + total);        // 30.000002 – Bad
}

//using a double
private void calculateTotalInaccurately2(float unitCost, int itemCount){
    double total = unitCost * itemCount;
    System.out.println("Total2 --> " + total);        // 30.000001907348633 – Bad
}

//using a BigDecimal
private void calculateTotalAccurately1(float unitCost, int itemCount){
    BigDecimal total = BigDecimal.ZERO;
    //use the right constructor
    BigDecimal uc = new BigDecimal(String.valueOf(unitCost));
    BigDecimal ic= new BigDecimal(String.valueOf(itemCount));
    total = uc.multiply(ic);

    total = total.setScale(2, RoundingMode.HALF_EVEN);
    System.out.println("Total3 --> " + total);        // 30.00 – good
}

//using an int or long
private void calculateTotalAccurately1(int unitCost, int itemCount){
    long total = unitCost * itemCount;
    System.out.println("Total4 in cents --> " + total);     // 3000 – good
}
}
```

Widening versus narrowing conversions

Q7   What is your understanding of widening versus narrowing conversions of primitive data types? Can you explain explicit and implicit casting? **LF COQ FAQ**

A7

$$\textbf{byte} \rightarrow \textbf{short} \rightarrow \textbf{char} \rightarrow \textbf{int} \rightarrow \textbf{long} \rightarrow \textbf{float} \rightarrow \textbf{double}$$
(1 byte)   (2 bytes)   (2 bytes)   (4 bytes) (8 bytes) (4 bytes)   (8 bytes)

Left to right (e.g. byte to short) is a <u>widening conversion</u> and considered safe because there is no chance for data loss. For example, byte has a range between -128 and 127 and short has a wider range between -32768 and 32767. So when you go from left to right, the data types are <u>implicitly cast</u> by the compiler since it is safe to do so.

Right to left (e.g. short to byte) is a <u>narrowing conversion</u> and considered unsafe because there is a chance for data loss. So when you go from right to left, the compiler expects you to <u>explicitly cast</u> the data to clearly state that it is safe to do so. If you do not cast explicitly, you will get a compile-time error. For example,

```
package chapter2.com;

public class DataTypes1 {

   /**
    * Think about the resulting data type
    * if you type a numeric value of 5 means of type int.
    * if you type a numeric value of 5L or 5l means of type long.
    * if you type a decimal value of 5.0f or 5.0F means of type float
    * if you type a decimal value of 5.0, 5.0D, or 5.0d means of type double
    */

   public static void main(String[ ] args) {

      /**
       * signed default values. Anything outside the valid range will cause a
       * compile-time error requiring either explicit cast or use of a wider
       * data type to fix it. Implicit cast is applied automatically when
```

```java
 * within the Min and Max range.
 */

byte b = 0;              // valid values are -128 to 127
short s = 0;             // valid values are -32768 to 32767
int i = 0;               // valid values are -2147483648 to 2147483647.
long l = 0L;             // valid values are  -9223372036854775808
                         //            to  9223372036854775807
float f = 0.0F;          // valid values are 1.4E-45 to 3.4028235E38
double d = 0.0;          //  valid values are 4.9E-324 to
                         //                1.7976931348623157E308

b = 30;      // okay (30 is of type int, but within the byte range)
b = 128;     // Not okay (128 is of type int, but is outside the byte range)

/**
 * unsigned default value
 */
char c = '\u0000';           // valid values are 0 to 65535
boolean bool = false;        // valid values are true or false

/**
 * left to right widening assignment is generally okay. Implicitly cast
 * to the right type. Exception being assigning a byte or short to a
 * char.
 */

s = b;                   // okay: short  is wider than byte.
i = s;                   // okay: int is wider than short.
l = i;                   // okay: long is wider than int.
f = l;                   // okay: float is wider than long.
d = f;                   //okay: double is wider than float.

i = c;                   //okay: int is wider than char.
l = c;                   //okay: long is wider than char.
d = s;                   //okay: double is wider than short.

/**
```

```
 * compile-time error. Can't do this
 */
c = s;                    //Not okay: type char is unsigned & type short is signed.

/**
 * right to left narrowing assignment causes compile-time error if
 * not explicitly cast to the right type. Even though the values assigned like i, l,
 * f, and d are either 0 or 0.0, the actual values can only be evaluated at run
 * time. At compile-time only the "type" of the data is known, and its actual
 * value gets evaluated only at run-time. It is okay to say b = 0; as it is evaluated
 * at compile-time.
 */

b = i;                    // Not okay: type int is wider than byte
i = l;                    // Not okay: type long is wider than int
l = f;                    // Not okay: type float is wider than long
f = d;                    // Not okay: type double is wider than float

/**
 * fix above compile-time errors with explicit casting.
 **/

c = (char)s;              // see explanation below

b = (byte) i;
i = (int) l;
l = (long) f;
f = (float) d;

    }
}
```

Note: byte and short are signed data types and they cannot be implicitly cast to unsigned char data type even though it is a widening conversion. As per the code in the above example, the short "s" is first converted to an int using a widening conversion and then casts it to a char using a narrowing conversion.

Short (s) –widening→ **Int** --narrowing→ **Char** (c)

Q8   What are the dangers of explicit casting? **LF COQ FAQ**

A8   Not knowing the MIN and MAX values can result in unexpected results due to loss of
data during **narrowing**.

```
package chapter2.com;

public class DataTypes2 {
    /**
     * Trap #1 Be careful when casting explicitly.
     *
     * Not knowing the correct range (i.e Min and Max) can cause
     * unexpected results as illustrated
     */
    public static void main(String[] args) {
        int iWithinByteRange = 125;
        int iOutsideByteRangeMax = 129;
        int iOutsideByteRangeMin = -129;

        byte bGood = (byte) iWithinByteRange;
        System.out.println("bOkay=" + bGood);            // 125 – good

        byte bBad = (byte) iOutsideByteRangeMax;
        System.out.println("Trap #1 - bBad=" + bBad);    // -127 – bad

        byte bBadAgain = (byte) iOutsideByteRangeMin;
        System.out.println("Trap #1 - bBadAgain=" + bBad); // -127 – bad
    }
}
```

Q9   Can you explain why the code snippet under (a) gives a compile-time error and code
snippet under (b) compiles and runs with an output of 20? **COQ LF**

a)

```
byte b = 10;          // line 1
b = b + 10;           // line 2
```

b)

```
byte b = 10;                    //line 1
b+=10;                          //line 2
```

A9 **If you take (a):**

Line 1 is valid as long as the value is between the valid range for byte. This is -2^7 to 2^7-1 or -128 to +127. Same principle is applicable to other data types as well. if you assign 128 to the variable b, you will get a compile-time error "cannot convert from int to byte". Since 10 is within the range, you will not get a compile-time exception.

Line 2 throws a compile time error because b+10 evaluates to an int. You need an explicit cast to convert an int to byte as it is a **narrowing conversion**. As per the last principle, you may think that 10 + 10 = 20 is well within the byte range and should not give any compile-time error. This assumption is incorrect.

- Firstly, "b" is a variable and its value would not be known at compile-time. Its value will be evaluated only at **runtime**. Adding 10 to the variable "b" might push it outside the byte range as <u>it is not known at compile-time</u>.

- Secondly and most importantly, there is a different principle known as "**binary numeric promotions**" when performing a binary operation (an operation requiring two operands). The binary **numeric promotion** automatically casts each operand to the size of the larger operand type. If neither operand is larger, then both are cast to the same type. In b = b + 10, the value 10 is of type int and is the larger operand type compared to b, which is of type byte, hence will be evaluated as follows:

```
b = (int)b + (int)10;
```

An explicit cast is required to avoid compile-time error:

```
b = (byte)(b + 10);
```

This is what really happens:

```
b = (byte) ((int)b + (int)10 ) ;
```

154

If you take (b):

Line1 is same as above.

Line 2 is performing a **compound assignment operation** (e.g. +=, -=, *=, etc). You may be thinking that b+=10 will be expanded as b = b + 10. But it is really not correct. This is because the compound operations will have an **explicit cast** even though it is not shown in the code. So the line 2 will be evaluated as follows,

```
b = (byte) (b + 10);
```

This has the hidden danger of data loss. The following example highlights what had been discussed here.

```
package chapter2.com;

public class DataTypes3 {

    /**
     * Simple versus compound assignment operators.
     *
     * Think about the resulting data type after an operation
     * like +, -, *, /  etc.
     *
     * Keep operator priorities in mind. Casting takes precedence
     * over + and -.
     */
    public static void main(String[ ] args) {

        byte b = 0;          // valid values are -128 to 127
        short s = 0;         // valid values are -32768 to 32767
        int i = 10;          // valid values are -2147483648 to 2147483647.

        long l = 0L;         // valid values are  -9223372036854775808 to
                             //                   9223372036854775807
        float f = 0.0F;      // valid values are 1.4E-45 to 3.4028235E38
        double d = 0.0;      // valid values are   4.9E-324 to
                             //                   1.7976931348623157E308
```

```
/**
 * ### Simple operations using 'binary numeric promotions'  ###
 *  explicit cast is required to fix compile-time errors
 */

b = b + 10;            // evaluates to an int – compile-time error
                       // fix: b = (byte) (b+10);

i = i + 20;            // evaluates to an int – good

s = s + 5;             // evaluates to an int –  compile-time error
                       // fix: s = (short) (s + 5);

l = l + 5;             // evaluates to a long – good

i = l + 5;             // evaluates to a long – compile-time error
                       // fix-1:  i = (int)(l + 5);  or
                       // casting takes precedence over "+" so
                       // fix-2:  i = (int)l + 5;

i = i + 3.0f;          // evaluates to a float – compile-time error
i = i + 3.0;           // evaluates to a double – compile-time error

d = d + 20;            // evaluates to a double – good
f = f + 20;            // evaluates to a float  – good
f = d + 20;            // evaluates to a double – compile-time error

f = f + 20.0f;         // evaluates to float  – good
d= d + 20.0;           // evaluates to double – good

/**
 * Compound Operators, such as +=, -=, *= all contain
 * an explicit cast, even though it's not shown.
 *
 * b+=250; expands to b = (byte) (b + 250); so no compile-time error.
 * This can cause unexpected results as shown below due to
 * loss of data discussed earlier.
 */
```

```
    System.out.println("b=" + b + ",i=" + i);      // b=0, i=30

    b += 250;                                 // evaluates to --> b = (byte) (b + 250)
    System.out.println("b=" + b);             // evaluates to 44 – bad

    i *= 2147483647;                          // evaluates to → i = (int) (i * 2147483647)
    System.out.println("i=" + i);             // evaluates to -30 – bad
  }
}
```

Q10 What is wrong with the following code, and how will you fix it? **LF COQ**

```
package chapter2.com;

public class IntegerMaxValue {

    public int addFive(int input) {
        if (input + 5 > Integer.MAX_VALUE) {
            throw new IllegalArgumentException("Invalid input: " + input);
        }
        return input + 5;
    }


    public static void main(String[] args) {
        IntegerMaxValue imv = new IntegerMaxValue();
        System.out.println("value = " + imv.addFive(5));
    }
}
```

A10 As the integer will never exceed Intger.MAX_VALUE, the *IllegalArgumentException* will never be thrown. If you try and invoke the method with an integer value within 5 short of its maximum value, data overflow takes place after (input + 5) is evaluated, resulting in incorrect result, but an exception will never be thrown. The corrected method *addFiveCorrected(..)* is added below:

```
package chapter2.com;

public class IntegerMaxValue {
```

```
//..
public int addFiveCorrected(long input) {
   if (input + 5> Integer.MAX_VALUE) {
      throw new IllegalArgumentException(
            "addFiveCorrected() -- Invlid input: " + input);      // fail fast
   }

   /**
      * (long+int) is implicitly cast to a long due to numeric promotion
      * explicit casting is required to convert implicitly cast long to an int
   **/

   return (int) (input + 5);
}

public static void main(String[ ] args) {
   IntegerMaxValue imv = new IntegerMaxValue( );
   //...
   System.out.println("addFiveCorrected( ) call value = " +
                                     imv.addFiveCorrected(5));

   System.out.println("addFiveCorrected( ) call value = "
                        + imv.addFiveCorrected(Integer.MAX_VALUE + 1L));
   }
}
```

Output:

```
addFiveCorrected( ) call value = 10
Exception in thread "main" java.lang.IllegalArgumentException:
                addFiveCorrected( ) -- Invlid input: 2147483648
      at chapter2.com.IntegerMaxValue.addFiveCorrected(IntegerMaxValue.java:18)
      at chapter2.com.IntegerMaxValue.main(IntegerMaxValue.java:33)
```

Hence, be aware of the data types and its valid ranges when used in conditional checks.

Understanding the operator precedence

Q11 What do you understand by operator precedence in Java? **LF**

A11 In Mathematics, multiplication and division are done before addition and subtraction. Programming languages also dictate that some operations are done before others. For example, a+b*c is evaluated as

```
a+(b*c)
```

and NOT as

```
(a+b)*c.
```

This is because multiplication (*) has higher precedence than addition (+). The precedence determines which operation will be performed first. Also, as discussed earlier, casting has precedence over + or – operator. Don't memorize the operator precedence table, but be aware of it as to how it can change the results and refer to it http://www.difranco.net/cop2551/java_op-prec.htm, when required.

Q12 Do you think the following code will throw a compile-time exception? If yes, how will you fix it? **LF**

```
float myVal = (float)3.0/2.0;
```

A12 Yes. It is cast first and then divided as casting operator has precedence over division operator as per the precedence table. So the above code is equivalent to

```
float myVal = 3.0f/2.0;   // float divided by double returns a double
                          //as per the binary numeric promotion principle
```

To fix it, you need to get the division operator to evaluate prior to casting. You can achieve this by introducing a parenthesis around the division as parenthesis has higher precedence (in fact highest) than casting as per the precedence table.

```
float myVal = (float)(3.0/2.0);      // double divided by double returns a
                                     // double and it is then explicitly
                                     // cast to float to return a float value.
```

Q13 What is the output of the following code snippet? **LF COQ**

```
package chapter2.com;

public class PrePostOperators {

    public static void main(String[ ] args) {
        int x = 5;                                        // line 1
        int y = ++x;                                      // line 2
        int z = y++;                                      // line 3

        System.out.println("x=" + x + ", y=" + y + ", z=" + z);
    }
}
```

A13 x=6, y=7, z=6

```
line 1: x=5, y=0, z=0
line 2: x=6, y=6,z=0;
line 3 x=6, y=7, z=6
```

You need to understand the pre and post increment operators to get this right. ++x is a pre-increment and x++ is a post increment. ++x means x is incremented before being used and x++ means x is incremented after being used. So line2 increments x by one and then assign it to y. Whereas in line 3, z is assigned the old y value (i.e. prior to incrementing) of 6 and then y value is incremented to 7.

As you may rightly ask that as per the precedence table, both pre-increment (i.e. ++expr) and post-increment (i.e. expr++) operators do have precedence over the assignment operator (i.e "="). The line 3 int z = y++; is roughly evaluated as follows:

```
int oldY = 6;        // current value of y is used by storing it to a variable
y = y+ 1;            // increment y by 1 to 7
z = oldY;            // z is set to the stored oldY value of 6
```

it is a common gotcha that the increment is happening last. The increment is executed immediately when the expression gets evaluated, and the value before the increment is remembered for future use inside the same statement. So if you want z to be 7, you could do either

```
int z = ++y;              // line 3
        or
y++;                      // added line
int z = y;                // line 3
```

Note: This is a common mistake beginners make, especially x=x++ and just x++ do have different meanings. For example,

```
int x= 0;
x=x++;
System.out.println(x);
```

The value of "x" printed above is 0. This is because the evaluation takes place as shown below:

```
int oldX = 0;      // store the current value of x for later use.
x= x+1;            // x is incremented by 1 as "+" takes precedence over "="
x = oldX;          // x is set to the stored oldX value of 0
```

If you were expecting to get 1, you can fix this by changing the code as follows,

```
int x = 0;
x++;
System.out.println(x);
        or
int x = 0;
System.out.println(++x);
```

A post-increment (i.e. i++) or pre-increment (++i) in a loop generally makes no difference. The latter is preferable as it is sometimes more efficient.

Q14   What is the output of the following code snippet? **LF**

```
package chapter2.com;

public class NaN {
   public static void main(String[ ] args) {
```

```
System.out.println("Output=" + 2.0/0.0);    //floating-point division by zero
System.out.println("Output=" + -2.0/0.0);   //floating-point division by zero
System.out.println("Output=" + 2 /0);       //integer division by zero
    }
}
```

A14 Floating point division by 0.0 returns a NaN (Not a Number) and integer divisions by 0 returns a runtime exception.

Output:

```
Output=Infinity
Output=-Infinity
Exception in thread "main" java.lang.ArithmeticException: / by zero
        at chapter2.com.NaN.main(NaN.java:7)
```

Q15 What will be the output of following operations? **LF**

```
int i = 10 / 3;
int r = 10 % 3;
```

A15 The integer division results in dropping the remainder of the operation

```
int i = 10 /3;              // i = 3
```

Java provides a mechanism to get the remainder of a division operation through the **modulus** (aka remainder) operator, denoted by the percent character (%).

```
int r = 10 % 3;             // r = 1
```

Thinking in binary and bitwise operations

Even though there is rarely a time bitwise operations seem directly necessary, the standard library uses bitwise operations indirectly for efficient processing. For example, the *StringBuffer.reverse( )*, *Integer.toString( )*, *BigDecimal* and *BigInteger* classes to name a few. There are number of practical examples listed where bitwise operations are very handy. Some interviewers prefer asking questions on this topic or including it in the written test to determine how technical you are. If pressed for time, either scan through or skip this topic.

Q16 Can you convert the decimal value of 127 to binary, octal, and hexadecimal values? **LF**

A16 **Binary:**

Bit number	8	7	6	5	4	3	2	1
Binary has 2 possible values 0 (off) and 1(on).	2^7	2^6	2^5	2^4	2^3	2^2	2^1	2^0
Expanded	128	64	32	16	8	4	2	1
Bits that need to be on (i.e. 1) to add up to 127 are	0	1	1	1	1	1	1	1

$64 + 32 + 16 + 8 + 4 + 2 + 1 = 127$. Hence the binary value is **0111 1111**.

Octal:

Binary value for 127 is	0	1	1	1	1	1	1	1
Octal has 8 possible values 0, 1, 2, 3, 4, 5, 6, 7	8^2			8^1			8^0	
Represent the octal values in binary	2^1	2^0	2^2	2^1	2^0	2^2	2^1	2^0
Expanded, and the bits that are "turned on" (i.e. 1's) highlighted. Shaded values add up to the octal values shown below.	2	1	4	2	1	4	2	1
Octal representation of 127.	1			7			7	

The octal value is 0177. (First zero denotes octal representation). You can verify your result by converting this back to decimal as follows:

$1 \times 8^2 + 7 \times 8^1 + 7 \times 8^0 = 64 + 56 + 7 = 127.$

Hexadecimal:

Binary value for 127 is	0	1	1	1	1	1	1	1

Hexadecimal has 16 possible values from 0 to 15 denoted by 0,1, 2, 3, 4, 5, 6, 7, 8, 9, A, B, C, D, E, F (i.e. A is 10, B is 11 … and F is 15)	16^1				16^0			
Represent the hexadecimal values in binary	2^3	2^2	2^1	2^0	2^3	2^2	2^1	2^0
Expanded, and the bits that are "turned on" (i.e. 1's) highlighted. Shaded values add up to the hexadecimal values shown below.	8	4	2	1	8	4	2	1
Hexadecimal representation of 127.	7				F			

The hexadecimal value is 0x7F. (0x denotes hexadecimal). You can verify your result by converting this back to decimal as follows:

$$7 \times 16^1 + 15 \times 16^0 = 112 + 15 = 127.$$

Q. How will you convert 0x7F back to binary? `LF`

Hexadecimal value	7				F			
Value	7				15			
Shaded values add up to the value above	8	4	2	1	8	4	2	1
	2^3	2^2	2^1	2^0	2^3	2^2	2^1	2^0
	0	1	1	1	1	1	1	1

The binary value for 0x7F is **0111 111**. Here is a sample Java program.

```
package chapter2.com;

public class Binary1 {

    public static void main(String[] args) {
```

```
Byte bOctal = 0177;                          // decimal value 127
Byte bHexaDecimal = 0x7F;                     // decimal value 127

System.out.println("decimal value of bOctal = "
                + bOctal.intValue( ));               //127
System.out.println("decimal value of bHexaDecimal = "
                + bHexaDecimal.intValue( ));         // 127

System.out.println("binary value of bOctal = " +
                Integer.toBinaryString(bOctal));     //1111111
System.out.println("binary value of bHexaDecimal ="
                + Integer.toBinaryString(bHexaDecimal)); //1111111
    }
}
```

Q17 How do you represent negative numbers in Java? What is the negative binary value for the number 37? **LF**

A17 Negative numbers use 2's complement notation. In order to get 2's complement:

Step 1: take the bit pattern for the equivalent positive number and invert all bits. All 1's to → 0's, and all 0's to 1's. This is 1's complement achieved with the Java's unary operator ~. Unary is a single operand. For example, 5 is 00000101 and ~5 is 11111010.

Step 2: add 1 to the above result. -5 is 11111010 + 000000001 = 11111011.

To evaluate -37:

	2^7	2^6	2^5	2^4	2^3	2^2	2^1	2^0
	128	64	32	16	8	4	2	1
37 in binary is (32 + 4 + 1)	0	0	1	0	0	1	0	1
~37 (complement of 1's)	1	1	0	1	1	0	1	0
1 in binary =	0	0	0	0	0	0	0	1
Add 1 to ~37 to get -37.	1	1	0	1	1	0	1	1

-37 = 128 + 64 + 16 + 8 + 2 + 1 = 219.

Note: For signed bits, the most significant bit (i.e. left most bit) represents the sign. 0 means a positive number and 1 means a negative number. In order to put things into perspective, some byte values in the range of -128 to 127 are:

-1	-2	-5	-9	-20	-37	-127	-128	127	37	30	5	1	0
255	254	251	247	236	219	129	128	127	37	30	5	1	0

To verify the answer: 37 + -37 should be equal to 0.

37 in binary	0	0	1	0	0	1	0	1
-37 in binary	1	1	0	1	1	0	1	1
37 + -37 =	0	0	0	0	0	0	0	0

Note: The possible values for binary are 0 and 1. Similar to decimal addition, when you add 1 and 1, you get 0 and 1 carried over to the left. For example,

```
0 + 0 = 0;
1 + 0 = 1;
0 + 1 = 1;
1 + 1 = 0; (and 1 is carried over to the left).
```

Q18 What are the common bitwise operations? **LF**

A18

b1	b2	Operations			
		b1 | b2 (inclusive OR)	b1 & b2 (AND)	b1 ^ b2 (exclusive XOR)	~ b1 (NOT)
0	0	0	0	0	1
1	0	1	0	1	0
0	1	1	0	1	1
1	1	1	1	0	0

The other operations are

>> → signed right shift

$>> 2$, slide to right 2 bit places, dropping lower order bits filling on left with the **sign bit**. Shifting right by 1 bit is equivalent to dividing by 2 with the following exception that $-1 >> 1 = -1$ because of sign extension. $-1/2$ should be 0. Other negative numbers will work fine. So $x >> n$ is equivalent to $x / 2^n$. $36 >> 2$ is $36 / 2^2 = 9$.

	128	64	32	16	8	4	2	1
36 in binary is → (The significant bit is 0 in bold face). Shaded area is shifted out.	**0**	0	1	0	0	1	0	0
36 >> 2	0	0	0	0	1	0	0	1
	$8 + 1 = 9$							

Note: $36 >> 1 = 18$ and $36 >> 2 = 9$. The sign bit 0 means a positive number, and 1 means a negative number. The significant bit is the left most bit.

	128	64	32	16	8	4	2	1
-36 in binary → (The significant bit is 1 in bold face). Shaded area is shifted out	**1**	1	0	1	1	1	0	0
-36 >> 2 (Highlighted area is inserted)	1	1	1	1	0	1	1	1
	$128 + 64 + 32 + 16 + 4 + 2 + 1 = 247$, which is -9							

<< → signed left shift

$<< 3$, slide to left 3 bit places, dropping higher order bits filling on right with 0's. Shifting left by 1 bit is equivalent to multiplying by 2 . You calculate 2 to the nth power with $x << n$. if $x = 5$, then $x << 3$ is equivalent to $5 * 2^3 = 40$ where n is 3.

	128	64	32	16	8	4	2	1

5 in binary is → (The significant bit is 0 in bold face). Shaded area is shifted out.	**0**	**0**	**0**	0	0	1	0	1
5 << 3 ((Highlighted area is inserted))	0	0	1	0	1	0	0	0
					32 + 8 = 40			

>>> → unsigned right shift

>>> 2 , slide to right 2 bit places, dropping lower order bits and filling on left with the 0 bit. Shifting right by 1 bit is equivalent to dividing by 2, but this won't work for negative numbers because the sign bit gets converted to 0 with an unsigned shift.

The "**&**" bitwise operator is used for **masking** and "**|**" bitwise operator is used for **combining**. Often bit manipulations are used for **packing** several fields into a single int and then **unpacking** them again. You can achieve this with >>>, <<, &, | and ~ bitwise operators. Rarely you might use the signed right shift operator >>.

Example 1: Extract **low order three bits** from x, where x = 37.

The operation can be written as **x & 0x07** where 0x07 is equivalent to the masking bits 00000111.

Binary	0	0	0	0	0	1	1	1
	8	4	2	1	8	4	2	1
Hexadecimal 0x			0				7	

	2^7	2^6	2^5	2^4	2^3	2^2	2^1	2^0
	128	64	32	16	8	4	2	1
x in binary (32 + 4 + 1)	0	0	1	0	0	1	0	1
Masking bits to extract low order 3 bits (**0x07**)	0	0	0	0	0	1	1	1

x & 0x07	0	0	0	0	0	1	0	1

The resulting value is 5 (i.e. $1 \times 2^2 + 0 \times 2^1 + 1 \times 2^0 = 4 + 0 + 1$).

```
package chapter2.com;

public class Binary2 {

  public static void main(String[ ] args) {
    byte x = 37;
    byte result = (byte)(x & 0x07);
    System.out.println("Low order 3 bits for x = "+ Integer.toBinaryString(result));
    System.out.println("Numeric value of the result = " + result);
  }
}
```

Output:

```
Low order 3 bits for x = 101
Numeric value of the result = 5
```

Example 2: Extract **bits 5 & 6** from x, where x = 37.

Bits 5 and 6 are highlighted.	8	7	6	5	4	3	2	1
	2^7	2^6	2^5	2^4	2^3	2^2	2^1	2^0
	128	64	32	16	8	4	2	1
x in binary (32 + 4 + 1)	0	0	1	0	0	1	0	1
x >>> 4. Shaded area above (4 bits) is shifted out and highlighted values on the left are moved to the right, and the left is filled with 0's	0	0	0	0	0	0	1	0
Masking bits to extract low order 2 bits (**0x03**)	0	0	0	0	0	0	1	1
x >>> 4 & 0x03	0	0	0	0	0	0	1	0

169

Hence the 5th and 6th bits of the value x are 0 and 1.

```
package chapter2.com;

public class Binary3 {

    public static void main(String[ ] args) {
        Byte x = 37;
        Byte result = (byte) (x >>> 4 & 0x03);
        System.out.println("Extract 5th and 6th bits of x = " +
                                Integer.toBinaryString(result));
        System.out.println("Numeric value of result = " + result);
    }
}
```

Output:

Extract 5th and 6th bits of x = 10
Numeric value of result = 2

Example 3: Say value of x=37, and value of y=7. You can now **combine** the 2 low order bits of x into bit positions 5 & 6 with the 3 low order bits of y (i.e. bit positions 1, 2, and 3).

Bits	8	7	6	5	4	3	2	1
	128	64	32	16	8	4	2	1
x in binary (32 + 4 + 1)	0	0	1	0	0	1	0	1
x << 4 (highlighted bits are shifted to the left by 4 bits, and the shaded area is shifted out.). This enables the 2 low order bits of x to be in position 5 & 6.	0	1	0	1	0	0	0	0
y in binary (4+2+1)	0	0	0	0	0	1	1	1

x << 4 | y (combines 5th & 6th position of x with y).	0	1	0	1	0	1	1	1

```
package chapter2.com;

public class Binary4 {

    public static void main(String[ ] args) {
        Byte x = 37;
        Byte y = 7;
        byte result = (byte)(x << 4 | y);
        System.out.println("Combined result = "  + Integer.toBinaryString(result));
        System.out.println("Numeric value of result = " + result);
    }
}
```

Output:

```
Combined result = 1010111
Numeric value of result = 87
```

Q19 Can you list some practical applications where the bitwise operations can be applied?
LF   COQ

A19 **Example 1**: To **pack** and **unpack** values. For example, to represent

- age of a person in the range of 0 to 127. Use **7 bits.**
- gender of a person 0 or 1 (0 – female and 1 – male). Use **1 bit.**
- height of a person in the range of 0 to 255. Use **8 bits**.

To pack this info: (((age << 1) | gender) << 8) | height.   For example, age = 25, gender = 1, and height = 255cm. **Shift** the age by 1 bit, and **combine** it with gender, and then **shift** the age and gender by 8 bits and **combine** it with the height.

Packing

	Age	Ge nde r	Height

Bits	16	15	14	13	12	11	10	9	8	7	6	5	4	3	2	1
age (25 years) using 7 bits	0	0	0	0	0	0	0	0	0	0	0	1	1	0	0	1
Age << 1 (Shift age by 1 bit)	0	0	0	0	0	0	0	0	0	0	1	1	0	0	1	0
Gender (1 – male) using 1 bit	0	0	0	0	0	0	0	0	0	0	0	0	0	0	0	1
Combine age with gender: (age << 1) | gender	0	0	0	0	0	0	0	0	0	0	1	1	0	0	1	1
((age << 1) | gender) << 8), shift age and gender by 8 bits.	0	0	1	1	0	0	1	1	0	0	0	0	0	0	0	0
Height (255 cm) using 8 bits.	0	0	0	0	0	0	0	0	1	1	1	1	1	1	1	1
Combine height with age and gender: **val** = (((age << 1) | gender) << 8) | height	0	0	1	1	0	0	1	1	1	1	1	1	1	1	1	1
	Age range 16 + 8 + 1 = 25							Ge nd er = 1	Height range 128 + 64 + 32 + 16 + 8 + 4 + 2 + 1 = 255.						

package chapter2.com;

public class Binary5 {

```java
public static void main(String[] args) {

    //packing
    int val = ((((25 << 1) | 1) << 8) | 255);
    System.out.println("packed=" + val);
    System.out.println("packed binary="
                + Integer.toBinaryString(val));        //0011001111111111

    //unpacking
    System.out.println("height=" + (val & 0xff));        //extract last 8 bits.
    System.out.println("gender=" + ((val >>> 8) & 1));   //extract bit 9
    System.out.println("age=" + ((val >>> 9)));          //extract bits 10 – 16.

    }
}
```

Output:

```
packed=13311
packed binary=11001111111111
height=255
gender=1
age=25
```

Unpacking (or extracting) height: Extract the low order 8 bits.

packed **value:**	0	0	1	1	0	0	1	1	1	1	1	1	1	1	1	1
Masking: 0xFF	0	0	0	0	0	0	0	0	1	1	1	1	1	1	1	1
Extract height = value **&** 0xFF:	0	0	0	0	0	0	0	0	1	1	1	1	1	1	1	1
									2^7	2^6	2^5	2^4	2^3	2^2	2^1	2^0
height:									128 + 64 + 32 + 16 + 8 + 4 + 2 + 1 = **255**							

Unpacking (or extracting) gender: Extract bit 9.

packed **value:**	0	0	1	1	0	0	1	1	1	1	1	1	1	1	1	1

8 lower order bits (i.e. shaded area) are shifted out. value >>> 8	0	0	0	0	0	0	0	0	0	0	1	1	0	0	1	1
Masking: 1	0	0	0	0	0	0	0	0	0	0	0	0	0	0	0	1
Extract gender = (value >>> 8) **&** 1:	0	0	0	0	0	0	0	0	0	0	0	0	0	0	0	1
																2^0
gender:																**1**

Unpacking (or extracting) age: Extract bits 10 – 16 (i.e. higher order bits).

packed **value**:	0	0	1	1	0	0	1	1	1	1	1	1	1	1	1	1
Extract age = value >>> 9:	0	0	0	0	0	0	0	0	0	0	0	1	1	0	0	1
										2^6	2^5	2^4	2^3	2^2	2^1	2^0
age:										$2^4 + 2^3 + 2^0 =$ $16 + 8 + 1 =$ **25**						

Example 2: To compactly represent a number of attributes like being bold, italics, etc of a character in a text editor. This is a more practical example.

shadow	blink	subscript	superscript	strikethrough	underline	italics	bold
0	1	0	1	0	0	0	1

```
package chapter2.com;
import java.util.Arrays;

public class Binary6 {
    public static void main(String[ ] args) {
        byte[ ] vals = { 0, 1, 0, 1, 0, 0, 0, 1 };

        byte value = pack(vals);
        System.out.println("packedValue=" + value);     // 81
```

```java
        System.out.println("unpackedValues="
            + Arrays.toString(unpack(value)));          // [0, 1, 0, 1, 0, 0, 0, 1]
    }

    public static byte pack(byte[ ] vals) {
        byte result = 0;
        for (byte bit : vals) {
            result = (byte) ((result << 1) | (bit & 1));
        }
        return result;
    }

    public static byte[ ] unpack(byte val) {
        byte[ ] result = new byte[8];
        for (int i = 0; i < 8; i++) {
            result[i] = (byte) ((val >> (7 - i)) & 1);
        }
        return result;
    }
}
```

Example 3: If you can think of anything as slots or switches that need to be flagged on or off, you can think of bitwise operators. For example, if you want to mark some events on a calendar.

6	5	4	3	2	1	0
Saturday	Friday	Thursday	Wednesday	Tuesday	Monday	Sunday

Example 4: To multiply or divide by 2^n.

```java
public class ShiftOperator {

    //multiply by 2 power n. n = 6
    private static final int  MULTIPLY = 10 << 6;
    //Divide by 2 power n where n = 6.
    private static final int  DIVIDE = 640 >> 6;
```

```
public static void main(String[ ] args) {
    System.out.println(MULTIPLY);            // 640
    System.out.println(DIVIDE);              // 10
}
}
```

Initializing your data correctly

Q20 What would happen when the following code is compiled and run? **LF COQ**

```
package chapter2.com;

public class VariableInitialization2 {

    public static void main(String[ ] args) {
        int x = 10, y;
        if (x < 10) {
            y = 1;
        }
        if (x >= 10) {
            y = 2;
        }
        System.out.println("y is " + y);
    }
}
```

A20 The above program won't compile. It will be complaining about "y" not being initialized. Even though you know that one of the if conditions will be satisfied, the "if" conditions will not be evaluated until runtime. As far as the compiler is concerned, they are two conditional statements that may or may not be reached.

Proper initialization of variables is an important aspect of programming. In Java, instance and static (i.e. class) variables have default values: null for all object types, false for boolean primitive type and 0 for numeric primitive types. But local variables inside a method (either static or non-static method) have no defaults.

Local variables in Java <u>must be initialized before they are first read</u>. So it's perfectly OK to first declare a local variable without initializing it, and initialize it later down the code, and then use it. But if you try to use it without initializing it anywhere at all or if your initialization takes place within a conditional block and you try to use it outside the conditional blocks as in the above sample code, you will get a compile-time error when you try to use it.

You can fix the above code as follows:

```java
package chapter2.com;

public class VariableInitialization2 {

    public static void main(String[ ] args) {
        int x = 10, y;                          // y is declared but not initialized
        if (x < 10) {
            y = 1;                              // y is initialized
            System.out.println("y is " + y);    // y is used
        }
        if (x >= 10) {
            y = 2;                              // y is initialized
            System.out.println("y is " + y);    // y is used
        }
    }
}
```

or by initializing it prior to using it.

```java
package chapter2.com;

public class VariableInitialization2 {

    public static void main(String[ ] args) {
        int x = 10, y;                          // y is declared but not initialized
        y=0;                                    // y is initialized
        if (x < 10) {
            y = 1;
        }
```

```
    if (x >= 10) {
        y = 2;
    }
    System.out.println("y is " + y);        // y is used
    }
}
```

It can also be fixed by changing the second "if" condition to an "else" condition so that the compiler knows for sure that one of the two conditions will be reached.

```
package chapter2.com;

public class VariableInitialization4 {

    public static void main(String[ ] args) {
        int x = 10, y;
        if (x < 10) {                    // Either the if or else will be  executed
            y = 1;                       // y would be initialized to 1
        }
        else {
            y = 2;                       // y would be initialized to 2
        }
        System.out.println("y is " + y);
    }
}
```

The instance and static variables don't require to be explicitly initialized at all before using them. They are automatically initialized with appropriate default values.

```
package chapter2.com;

import static java.lang.System.out;

public class VariableInitialization {

    //instance & static variables are initialized by default
    private int iInstance;
    private static String sStaticInstance;
```

```
public static void main(String[ ] args) {
    VariableInitialization vi = new VariableInitialization( );
    int iLocal;
    out.println(iLocal);                            //compile-error - iLocal is not initialized

    int iLocal2 = 1, iLocal3, iLocal4;      // iLocal2 is initialized
    iLocal3 = iLocal2;                           // iLocal3 is initialized
    iLocal4 = iLocal3;                           // iLocal4 is initialized

    // instance variable - default initialization to 0
    out.println("iInstance=" + vi.iInstance);                // 0
    // static variable - default initialization to null
    out.println("sStaticInstance=" + sStaticInstance);       // null
    }
}
```

Q21 Can you tell me what is the use of a static block in a class with an example? Is it a good practice to use static blocks? **LF BP COQ**

A21 When a class is loaded, all blocks that are declared static and don't have function name (i.e. static initializers) are executed even **before the constructors are executed**. As the name suggests, they are typically used to initialize static fields. If you need to do computation (e.g. for loop to fill an array, determine the value based on a conditional logic, date computation using a calendar, etc) in order to initialize your static variables, you can declare a static block which gets executed exactly once, when the class is first loaded. It's a normal block of code enclosed within a pair of braces and preceded by a 'static' keyword. These blocks can be anywhere in the class definition where you can have a field or a method. The Java runtime guarantees that all the static initialization blocks are called in the order in which they appear in the source code and this happens while loading of the class in the memory.

```
package chapter2.com;

public class StaticInitilization {

    private static int[ ] square;
    private static final  int MAX = 10;

    static {
        square = new int[MAX+1];
```

```
    for (int i = 0; i <= MAX; i++) {
      square[i] = i * i;
    }
  }

  public static void main(String[ ] args) {
    System.out.println("Square of 7 = " + square[7]);    // evaluates to 49
    System.out.println("Square of 9 = " + square[9]);    // evaluates to 81
  }
}
```

BP A private static method is a suitable alternative to static initialization blocks. In fact, it has advantages over static initialization blocks, as you can re-use a private static method to re-initialize static fields. Static blocks are also harder to unit test. So use static blocks judiciously. If you have to use it, move the body of the static block into a private static method, and call this static method from your static block as shown below.

```
package chapter2.com;

public class StaticInitilization {

  private static int[ ] square;
  private static final  int MAX = 10;

  static {
    initilizeSquares(MAX);
  }

  private static final void initilizeSquares(int max) {
    square = new int[max];
    for (int i = 0; i < max; i++) {
      square[i] = i * i;
    }
  }

  public static void main(String[ ] args) {
    System.out.println("Square of 7 = " + square[7]);    // evaluates to 49
    System.out.println("Square of 9 = " + square[9]);    // evaluates to 81
```

```
        //initialize it again on demand
        initilizeSquares(100);
        System.out.println("Square of 40 = " + square[40]);        // evaluates to 1600
    }
}
```

Q22 How will you provide a member variable named *dueDate* with an initial default value
      set to first day of the following month? **LF COQ**

A22 Like static initializers, you can use an initializer block for instance variables. Initializer
      blocks for instance variables look just like static initializer blocks, but without the
      'static' keyword.

```
package chapter2.com;

import java.util.Calendar;
import java.util.Date;
import java.util.GregorianCalendar;

public class Initilization2 {

    private Date dueDate;

    //initializer block
    {
        Calendar cal = GregorianCalendar.getInstance();
        cal.add(Calendar.MONTH, 1);
        cal.set(Calendar.DAY_OF_MONTH, 1);
        dueDate = cal.getTime();        //dueDate defaults to first day of next month
    }

    //...

    public static void main(String[] args) {
        Initilization2 init = new Initilization2();
        System.out.println("dueDate = " + init.dueDate);  // first day of next month
    }
}
```

Q23 Is there anything wrong with the following code snippet? **COQ**

```
package chapter2.com;

public class VariableInitialization3 {

    private static final String CONSTANT_VALUE = null;          // line A

    static {
        // ... load values based on some condition or .properties file.
        CONSTANT_VALUE = "loaded";                              // line B
    }
}
```

A23 Yes. Compile-time error at line B.

```
CONSTANT_VALUE = "loaded";
```

indicating that the final field VariableInitialization3.CONSTANT_VALUE cannot be assigned.

Q. How will you fix it?
A. Remove the initial null assignment in line A. <u>Final variables can only be assigned once</u>.

```
private static final String CONSTANT_VALUE;          // fixed
```

Constants and static imports

Q25 What is a constant interface anti-pattern? How will you avoid it? **DP**
A25 The following code snippet demonstrates the constant interface anti-pattern described by Joshua Bloch in his book "Effective Java".

```
package chapter2.com;

public interface Constants {

    public static final double TRIANGLE_AREA_PREFIX = 1.0 / 2.0;
```

```java
public static final double SPHERE_VOLUME_PREFIX = 4.0 / 3.0;

//assume that there are 98 other constants defined here
}
```

The inheriting class:

```java
package chapter2.com;

import java.text.DecimalFormat;

public class ConstantsInterfaceAntiPattern implements Constants {

public static void main(String[] args) {

  double radius = 3.0;
  double base = 2.0;
  double height = 1.5;

  // declared as local since class DecimalFormat is not thread-safe.
  DecimalFormat df = new DecimalFormat("#,###,###,##0.00");

  /**
   * Since Constants interface is inherited No need to write it as
   * Constants.TRIANGLE_AREA_PREFIX
   */
  double triangleArea = TRIANGLE_AREA_PREFIX * base * height;
  double sphereVolume = SPHERE_VOLUME_PREFIX * Math.PI *
                                      Math.pow(radius, 3);


  System.out.println("Area of the triangle = " + df.format(triangleArea));
  System.out.println("Area of the sphere = "  + df.format(sphereVolume));

  // assume that TRIANGLE_AREA_PREFIX & SPHERE_VOLUME_PREFIX
  // get used  many more times throughout this class.
}
}
```

As per the above example, the class "ConstantsInterfaceAntiPattern" only requires 2 constants (i.e. TRIANGLE_AREA_PREFIX and SPHERE_-VOLUME_PREFIX) from the interface "Constants", which has 98 other constants not relevant to the "ConstantsInterfaceAntiPattern" class. The problem is that by implementing the "Constants" interface for convenience reason, all the 100 constants from the interface "Constants" end up being a part of the public API of the client class "ConstantsInterfaceAntiPattern". This not only breaks inheritance, but also the 100 constants will end up in your JavaDoc for "ConstantsInterfaceAntiPattern" class. A better approach would be to use a constants class say "MyConsts" to only define the relevant constants.

```
package chapter2.com;

public final class MyConsts {

    //Marked private so that this class can never be instantiated from outside
    private MyConsts( ) {
        //to prevent the native (i.e. from within) class from calling it
        throw new AssertionError( );
    };

    public static final double TRIANGLE_AREA_PREFIX = 1.0/2.0;
    public static final double SPHERE_VOLUME_PREFIX = 4.0/3.0;
}
```

If you are using a J2SE version prior to 1.5, then it is necessary to fully qualify the constant with the class name as shown below:

```
MyConsts.TRIANGLE_AREA_PREFIX
MyConsts.SPHERE_VOLUME_PREFIX
```

If you are using a J2SE version 1.5 or later, static imports can be used as shown below:

```
package chapter2.com;

// static imports from Java 5
import static chapter2.com.MyConsts.*;
import static java.lang.Math.PI;
```

```java
import static java.lang.Math.pow;

import java.text.DecimalFormat;

public class ConstantsInterfaceAntiPatternFix {

  public static void main(String[] args) {

    // declared as local since class DecimalFormat is not thread-safe.
    DecimalFormat df = new DecimalFormat("#,###,###,##0.00");

    double radius = 3.0;
    double base = 2.0;
    double height = 1.5;

    /**
     * Since Constants interface is inherited, no need to write it as
     * Constants.TRIANGLE_AREA_PREFIX
     */
    double triangleArea = TRIANGLE_AREA_PREFIX * base * height;
    double sphereVolume = SPHERE_VOLUME_PREFIX * PI * pow(radius,
                                               3);

    System.out.println("Area of the triangle = " + df.format(triangleArea));
    System.out.println("Area of the sphere = "  + df.format(sphereVolume));

    // assume that TRIANGLE_AREA_PREFIX &
    // SPHERE_VOLUME_PREFIX
    // get used  many more times throughout this class.
  }
}
```

BP If you overuse the static import feature, it can make your program unreadable and unmaintainable because over a period, you may not understand which static method or static attribute belongs to which class. So use it very rarely under following situations:

1) Use it to declare local copies of java constants. For example, a business application might define a *Constants* class, and import it statically. This would allow *Constant-*

s.NEW_LINE to be referenced as just *NEW_LINE*.

2) When you require frequent access to static members from one or two java classes. For example, a scientific or engineering application might make wide use of *Math.PI*.

BP It is also a bad practice to have one class that contains all constants that are used throughout in your application. It is not a good practice to have unrelated constants in the same class. This creates a coupling between otherwise unrelated components through this class having only constants. This inhibits code reuse as this class may be the only thing they have in common. You may want to later extract a particular component to be used in a different application. This will require you to ship the component classes with constants as well. The best practice is to put the constants where they belong. For example, RebateConstants, ManagedFundConstants, SecurityConstants, etc. Constants should not be used across component boundaries.

Modifiers and where are they applicable?

Q26 Why use modifiers? Why can't you declare a class as both abstract and final? **LF FAQ**

A26 Modifiers allow programmers to control the behavior of classes, object constructors, methods, variables, and even blocks of code. Combinations of modifiers may be used in meaningful ways. Some modifiers will conflict with each other and cannot be used together. Modifiers are applied by prefixing the appropriate keyword for the modifier to the declaration of a class, variable, method or block of code within a method or class.

You cannot create objects of an abstract class. A class marked with an "**abstract**" modifier is meant for extension (i.e. sub classing). A class is declared with a "**final**" modifier to prevent it from being extended (i.e. prevent sub classing). If you mark an abstract class as final, it can neither be extended nor instantiated. So it has no use.

Q27 What are the valid access modifiers? **LF FAQ**

A27 Public, protected, package-private (i.e. no modifier), and private.

Q28 Discuss the significance of the modifiers used in the following class? **LF COQ**

```
package chapter2.com;

final class MyConsts {

  private MyConsts( ){   };

  static final double TRIANGLE_AREA_PREFIX = 1.0/2.0;
  static final double SPHERE_VOLUME_PREFIX = 4.0/3.0;
}
```

A28
- Final classes cannot be extended from outside or within this class (e.g. using a static inner class). An outer class can only either be package-private scoped (i.e. no access modifier) as shown above or public scoped. A package-private scoped class cannot be accessed from outside this (i.e. chapter2.com) package.

```
final class MyConsts { ...}
```

- Private constructors prevent a class from being explicitly instantiated by callers from outside. Classes with a private constructor cannot also be extended from outside, but can be extended within itself using a static inner class.

```
private MyConsts(){ ...}
```

- The variables are package-private scoped so that they can only be visible within the same package i.e. *chapter2.com*.

- The variables are marked static to indicate that they can not be attached to a particular object, but rather to the class as a whole.

- The variables are marked final to indicate that they can be assigned or initialized only once.

Q. How would you go about making the *"MyConsts"* class accessible to the classes in other packages?

A. Firstly, the class should be marked "public" so that it can be accessed from other packages. Secondly, the variables should be marked "public" so that they will be visible to classes in other packages.

Q. What does the following code snippet do? Discuss the modifiers used? **COQ**

```
package chapter2.com;

public final class AnimalFactory {

    static final private AnimalFactory singleton;

    static {
        try {
            //... perform initialization here
            singleton = new AnimalFactory();
        } catch (Throwable e) {
            throw new RuntimeException(e.getMessage());
        }
    }

    private AnimalFactory() {}

    static public AnimalFactory getInstance() {
        return singleton;
    }
}
```

A. **DP** It is an implementation of the singleton design pattern.

- The class is marked final so that it cannot be extended.

- The variable "singleton" is marked private so that it cannot be accessed from outside. It is also marked static and final to indicate that it is a class level variable and can be initialized only once respectively.

- The *getInstance()* method is marked public so that it can be accessed from any class within any package. It is also marked static to indicate that it is not attached to a particular instance (i.e. an object), but to the class itself.

- The *AnimalFactory* is eagerly initialized when the class is loaded, and hence thread-safe. If the construction of *AnimalFactory* was expensive, then it could be lazily initialized using the "**Lazy Initialization Pattern**", but care should be taken to make it thread-safe by making the *getInstance( )* a synchronized method. A method level lock may cause contention issues (e.g. waiting for locks) by locking the whole object, and sometimes can lead to scalability and latency problems. Alternatively, thread-safety can be achieved using block level locks as shown below:

```
package chapter2.com;

public final class AnimalDCLFactory {
    private static volatile AnimalDCLFactory singleton;

    private AnimalDCLFactory() { }

    // Returns instance of the singleton
    static public AnimalDCLFactory getInstance() {
        if (singleton == null) {
            synchronized (AnimalDCLFactory.class) {
                if (singleton == null)
                    singleton = new AnimalDCLFactory();
            }
        }
        return singleton;
    }
}
```

The **Double Checked Lock (DCL)** idiom shown above only works from JDK 1.5 onwards. The **On Demand Holder** (ODH) initialization idiom shown below is thread-safe and also a lot easier to understand.

```
package chapter2.com;

public class AnimalODHFactoryHolder {
    public static AnimalODHFactory instance = new   AnimalODHFactory();

}
```

```
package chapter2.com;
```

189

```
public final class AnimalODHFactory {
   AnimalODHFactory() { }

   // Returns instance of the singleton
   static public AnimalODHFactory getInstance() {
      return AnimalODHFactoryHolder.instance;
   }
}
```

Note: Also do your research on per thread singleton idiom using a *ThreadLocal* class, or the *WeakSingleton* design pattern using weak references.

Q. If you have "*ClassA*" under package "pkga" as shown below, how will you ensure that the method "*processA( )*" is visible to all classes under "pkga" and all classes that extend "*ClassA*" from other packages like "pkgb"? **LF COQ**

```
package pkga;

public class ClassA {

   void processA() {
      //processA ...
   }
}
```

A. Since the method *processA( )* does not have any explicit access modifier, it is "package-private" scoped by default. This means any class in the package "pkga" can access it. In order to enable it to be accessed by any subclasses of "ClassA" from other packages like "pkgb", it needs to be marked with the access modifier "**protected**" as shown below:

```
package pkga;

public class ClassA {

   protected void processA() {
      //processA
   }
}
```

```
}
```

The "*ClassB*" can now access method "*processA( )*" from "*ClassA*" as shown below.

```
package pkgb;

import pkga.ClassA;

public class ClassB extends ClassA {

    public void processB( ) {
        super.processA( );
    }

}
```

Q. Can you access *ClassA*'s "*processA( )*" method from a class "*ClassC*" as shown below that resides in the package "pkgb"? **LF COQ**

```
package pkgb;

import pkga.ClassA;

public class ClassC {

    public void processC( ) {
        new ClassA( ).processA( );
    }
}
```

A. The answer is "No" because the *ClassC* does not extend *ClassA*. The protected scope is only visible to subclasses in other packages. If you want any class from other packages to be able to see it, the access modifier of "*processA( )*" needs to be "public" as shown below:

```
package pkga;

public class ClassA {
```

191

```
public void processA() {
    //processA
  }
}
```

Q. Is there a way to prevent "*ClassB*" from overriding the *processA( )* method from *ClassA*?

A. Yes. Mark the method as final. Final methods cannot be overriden.

```
package pkga;

public class ClassA {

  public final void processA() {
    //processA
  }
}
```

Q29 If you want to extend the *java.lang.String* class, what methods will you override in your extending class? **LF**

A29 You would be tempted to say *equals( )*, *hashCode( )* and *toString( )* methods, but the "*java.lang.String*" class is declared as **final** and therefore it cannot be extended.

Q30 Are 'volatile' and 'const' valid modifiers in Java? **LF FAQ**

A30 Very rarely used modifiers like **strictfp**, **native**, **transient**, and **volatile** are valid modifiers. The modifier "const" is a reserved keyword in Java, but it is not added to the language yet. So currently, const is an invalid modifier.

Q. What is the difference between the modifiers "volatile" and synchronized?

A. Volatile modifier is used on instance variables that may be modified simultaneously by other threads. The modifier volatile only synchronizes the variables marked as volatile whereas synchronized modifier synchronizes all variables. Local variables are not required to be marked as volatile because other threads cannot see them.

Q. If added to Java, how would the modifier "const" differ from a final modifier?

A. A final variable cannot be modified to refer to any other objects other than one it was initialized to refer to. So the final modifier applies only to the value of the variable itself, and not to the object referenced by the variable. The following declarations are real constants as "*String*" is an immutable class and "int" is not an object. So once assigned, it cannot be modified.

```
public static final String SERVICE_NAME = "Financial Service";
public static final int SERVICE_ID = 1;
```

But the following is not a real constant as the referenced object is mutable (i.e. modifiable). The code below shows that the reference "*VAL*" cannot be reassigned_to a different object since it is final, but the object it is referencing to can be modified since it is mutable.

```java
package chapter2.com;

public class MutableConsts {

    //final variables cannot be reassigned once assigned
    private static final MutableBean VAL = new MutableBean();

    //static inner class
    public static final class MutableBean {
        private int val = 5;

        public int getVal() {
            return val;
        }

        public void setVal(int val) {
            this.val = val;
        }
    }

    public static void main(String[] args) {
        System.out.println("before mutating=" + VAL.val);    // prints 5
        VAL.setVal(6);
        System.out.println("after mutating=" + VAL.val);     // prints 6
    }
}
```

This is where the 'const' modifier can come in very useful if added to the Java language. A reference variable or a constant marked as 'const' refers to an immutable object that cannot be modified.

Q. Since the "const" keyword is not yet added to Java, how would you make sure that a static final variable remains a constant? **COQ**

A. By ensuring that the static final variables either refer to primitive data types or immutable objects. The immutable objects will be discussed under section entitled "Objects Essentials".

Q31 How would you go about determining what access levels to use in your code? **BP** **FAQ**

A31 • Declare all your instance variables (aka attributes or fields) as private and provide public getXXX & setXXX access methods. This prevents you from being lazy and grabbing internal things you should not or corrupting a variable. For example, you can implement a fail fast approach to prevent a variable named "age" from incorrectly being assigned with a negative value.

```
package chapter2.com;

public class Person {
  private Short age;                              // best practice

  public Short getAge( ) {
    return age;
  }

  public void setAge(Short age) {
    //fail fast
    if(age == null || age < 0 || age >= 200) {
      throw new IllegalArgumentException("Invalid Age: " + age);
    }
    //the age will never be negative or > 200
    this.age = age;
  }
}
```

If you had declared the variable as follows,

```
public short age;                                // bad practice
```

Then it is easy for any external class to corrupt the age as,

```
personInstance.age = -5;
```

- Don't declare any methods or variables as protected with a view that it may be required in the future. Declare them as protected only if the subclasses absolutely need them to be declared as protected.

- Declare all the methods not in the public interface as private.

- Package private access level is useful if you want to open features to your subclasses within the same package, but want to restrict access outside the package to those who might not understand the full design or consequences of using a feature.

Thinking about the right access modifier to use also forces you to think through how objects and classes are going to interact with each other.

Q32 If you were to give some tips on modifiers, what would they be? **LF**
A32

- *'abstract'* and *'native'* methods have no body. If a method is declared native means, the method implementation is provided external to the JVM in a native language such as C. A class that has at least one abstract method must be declared abstract. A method cannot be declared both 'abstract' and 'native'.

```
abstract void process();
native void process();
```

- *'final'* variables cannot be *'volatile'* and 'volatile' variables cannot be 'final' because final variables cannot be modified, whereas volatile variables can be modified.

- Methods cannot be declared 'native' and 'strictfp' simultaneously.

- Methods that are *'abstract'* cannot be declared *'private'*, *'static'*, *'final'*, *'native'*, *'strictfp'* or *'synchronized'*.

195

- Classes cannot be declared both '*final*' and '*abstract*'.

- A class, method or variable declaration can contain only one of the following access modifiers → *public*, *protected*, or *private*. If it does not have any of the above access modifiers, it is "package-private" scoped by default.

- '*static*' means belong to a class rather than an instance (i.e. an object) of a class. 'static' variables and methods might better have been called per class variables and methods. There is nothing static (unchanging) about them. 'static' refers to a method or variable that is not attached to a particular object, but rather to a class as a whole. When both '*static*' and '*final*' modifiers are applied to a variable, it becomes a constant. All *static* methods are implicitly final, as they cannot be overriden. It is not an error to mark them as *final*, but it is redundant and considered a bad practice. *static methods* can call instance methods only if they use their own object references explicitly, and cannot use the implicit keyword 'this'.

- Surprisingly, the java compiler does not complain if you declare a transient field as static or final. These should be compile-time errors because a "transient" part of an object's state is assumed to be changing within each instance, and it can not be static or final. There is no point in declaring a static member field as transient, since transient means: "do not serialize", and static fields would not be serialized as they belong to a class and not to an individual instance. It is important to keep in mind that the process of serialization is concerned with an object's current state. So declaring a transient variable as static or final does not make any sense.

- Local variables can only be declared as 'final'. Local variables are implicitly private to the block in which they are declared. You cannot use any other access modifiers explicitly. Don't have a synchronized block for local variables as they are always thread-safe. Local variables are stored in a stack and each thread will have its own stack.

Methods and constructors

Q33 What is the difference between constructors and other regular methods? What happens if you do not provide a constructor? Can you call one constructor from another? Are constructors inherited? How do you call a super class's constructor?

LF FAQ

A33 A constructor will be automatically invoked when an object is created using the new keyword whereas a method has to be called explicitly. Constructors are used to initialize the instance variables (aka fields) of an object. Constructors are similar to methods, but with some important differences.

- A constructor must have the same name as the class it is in.
- There is no return type given in a constructor signature. The return value is implicitly **"this"** object itself so there is no need to indicate a return value. There is no return statement in the body of the constructor.
- The **first line of a constructor must** either be a call on another constructor in the same class using **this(..)**, or a call to the super class constructor using **super(..)**. If the first line is neither of these, the compiler automatically inserts a call to the no parameter super class constructor with super( ).

If you don't define a constructor for a class, a default no parameter constructor is automatically created by the compiler at compile time. The default constructor calls the default parent constructor super( ) and initializes all instance variables to default values — zero for numeric types, null for object references, and false for booleans. If you define one or more constructors for your class, no default constructor is automatically created.

```
package chapter2.com;

public class ConstructorParent {
    // a no parameter default constructor will be inserted by the compiler.
}
```

```
package chapter2.com;

public class ConstructorChild extends ConstructorParent {

    private Integer fld1;
    private String fld2;
    private Float fld3;
```

```
//no parameter constructor
public ConstructorChild( ) { }  // implicitly calls parent class' constructor
                                // with the construct → super( );

public ConstructorChild(Integer fld1, String fld2, Float fld3) {
    this(fld1, fld2);          // cannot have both super(...) & this (...) here.
    this.fld3 = fld3;
    // illegal to have super(...) or this(...) anywhere else except in the first line.
}

public ConstructorChild(Integer fld1, String fld2) {
    super( );                  // cannot have both super( ) & this here.
    this.fld1 = fld1;
    this.fld2 = fld2;
}
}
```

Q. Can you call one constructor from another? **LF FAQ**
A. You can call one constructor from another with the **this(...)** construct, but it must be the first line of a constructor.

Q. Are constructors inherited? **LF DC**
A. Constructors are not fully inherited in a sense that you cannot create an instance of a subclass using a constructor of it's superclass. One of the main reasons is because **you probably don't want to override a super class's constructor**, which would be possible if they were inherited. By giving a developer the ability to override a super-class' constructor, you would erode the encapsulation abilities of the language.

Q. How do you call a super class's constructor?
A. You call a super class's constructor with the **super(...)** construct.

Q. Can a constructor throw exceptions?
A. Yes.

Q34 Where and how can you use a private constructor? **LF DP FAQ**

A34 Private constructor is used, if you do not want other classes to instantiate the object, and to prevent subclassing. The instantiation is done by the same class. Not defining any constructors would not work because if you don't define a constructor for a class, a default no parameter constructor is automatically created by the compiler at compile time. Private constructors are

- Used in classes using the singleton design pattern.
- Used in classes using the **static factory methods**. For example, *java.util.Collections* class.
- Used in utility classes. For example, Apache library classes *StringUtils, CollectionUtils*, etc or custom utility classes written by you.

Q35 What are static factory methods? Can you give examples from the Java API? What design patterns does it use? Can you describe the benefits of static factory methods and usefulness of private constructors? **LF DP FAQ**

A35 Static factory methods are an alternative to creating objects through constructors. Unlike constructors, static factory methods are not required to create a new object (i.e. a duplicate object) each time they are invoked. The static factory methods are more testable than complex constructors. They also have a more meaningful names than constructors like:

*Integer.**valueOf**("5"), MyConnection.**newInstance**(..), Arrays.**asList**(..), BigDecimal.-**valueOf**("3.0"),BigInteger.**valueOf**(389)*, String.**valueOf**(5), etc.

Instead of:

```
String[ ] myArray = {"Java", "J2EE", "XML", "JNDI"};
for (int i = 0; i < myArray.length; i++) {
    System.out.println(myArray[i]);
}
```

You can use:

```
String[ ] myArray = {"Java", "J2EE", "XML", "JNDI"};
System.out.println(Arrays.asList(myArray));     // factory method
```

 The following static factory method is an alternative to a constructor. It converts a boolean primitive value to a Boolean wrapper object.

```
public static Boolean  valueOf(boolean b) {
    return (b ? TRUE : FALSE);
}
```

DP The static factory method uses the "**factory method**" design pattern. Common names for factory methods include *getInstance(..)* and *valueOf(..)*. These names are not mandatory - choose whatever makes sense for each case. When you need to create a very large number of objects, each requires an amount of memory to store the objects' state. In some cases, the objects being created may include information that is often duplicated. Immutable instances can be cached and reused. Where this is true, the "**flyweight**" design pattern can be used. The flyweight design pattern often uses a variation on the "factory method" design pattern for the generation of the shared objects. The factory receives a request for a flyweight instance. If a matching object is already in the cache, that particular object is returned. If not, a new flyweight is generated. Usually the full set of available flyweight objects is held within the factory in a collection that can be accessed quickly, such as a *HashMap*. Here is an example of a cache.

```java
package chapter2.com;

import java.util.HashMap;
import java.util.Map;

public class PrefixedWord {

    private String prefix;
    private String word;

    //cache
    private static Map<String, PrefixedWord> wordCache =
                    new HashMap<String, PrefixedWord>(50);

    // cannot be constructed from outside
    private PrefixedWord(String prefix, String word) {
        this.prefix = prefix;
        this.word = word;
    }

    //static factory method that caches values
    public static PrefixedWord valueOf(String prefix, String word) {
        String key = prefix + word;
```

```
    PrefixedWord pWord = null;
    //first check the cache
    if (wordCache.keySet().contains(key)) {
       pWord = wordCache.get(key);
    //construct if not in cache
    } else {
       pWord = new PrefixedWord(prefix, word);
       wordCache.put(key, pWord);
    }
    return pWord;
  }
}
```

Q36 Can you extend a class with a private constructor? For example, a singleton class may have a private constructor. What would you do, if you want to extend a singleton class? DP COQ FAQ

A36 A class with a private constructor cannot be extended from outside.

```
package chapter2.com;

public class MySingletonFactory {

   private static final MySingletonFactory instance = new MySingletonFactory();

   private MySingletonFactory(){}

   public static MySingletonFactory getInstance() {
      return instance;
   }
}
```

Note: It might be a good idea to mark such classes as final as well. The final keyword to the class declaration is purposely omitted to demonstrate that a class with a private constructor cannot be extended **from outside**.

```
package chapter2.com;

public class MyExtSingletonFactory extends MySingletonFactory {
```

```
/**
 * Compile-time error: Implicit super constructor
 * MySingletonFactory( ) is not visible
 */
public MyExtSingletonFactory( ) {
    //implicitly invokes the super class's constructor with super( );
 }
}
```

But, strictly speaking, a non-final class with a private constructor can be extended from inside, using a static inner class as shown below. This is generally not a good practice.

```
package chapter2.com;

public class MySingletonFactory {

    private static final MySingletonFactory instance =
        new MySingletonFactory( );

    private MySingletonFactory( ) {
    }

    public static MySingletonFactory getInstance( ) {
        return instance;
    }

    public static class ExtSingletonFactory extends
        MySingletonFactory {

        public ExtSingletonFactory( ){
            //do something
        }
    }
}
```

So it is a good practice to add the "**final**" keyword to your class declaration. If you want to extend a singleton class from outside, change the access modifier of your constructor from "private" to "protected".

Q37 What are some of the do's and don'ts with respect to constructors in order to write more testable code? What tip would you give your fellow developers to make their code more testable? **BP DP FAQ**

A37 Constructors should predominantly have just field assignments. Constructors should not have any complex object graph construction logic. The complex object graphs should be constructed via a factory or builder design pattern. According to Misko Hevery's "Guide to Writing Testable Code" at http://java.dzone.com/articles/guide-to-writing-testable-code), following are the warning signs to watch out for while writing a constructor:

- The "new" key word in a constructor or at field declarations within a class.
- Anything more than field assignments in constructors.
- Static method calls in a constructor or at field declarations within a class.
- Objects not getting fully initialized on completion of executing the constructors.
- Using an initialization block for object construction.
- Constructors performing complex object graph construction.

Q. What tip would you give your fellow developers to make their code more testable?
A.

- Firstly, use testing frameworks like JUnit, TestNG, DbUnit, and XMLUnit, and mocking frameworks like EasyMock or Mockito. Follow the "**write test cases first**" principle as it not only promotes better coverage of test cases, but also encourages you to write more testable code.

- Most importantly, unit testing is all about testing your code in isolation. To achieve this, care must be taken not to mix **object construction** with **application logic**. You can achieve this isolation through a popular concept known as the **dependency injection,** where a dependency is injected instead of constructing them within an application. So dependency injection makes your application more testable by allowing you to inject a **small subset** of your application in to your unit tests. This small subset can be constructed independently of your whole system due to **looser coupling** between your classes and objects.

Q. What if you have to work with some legacy code, and don't have the luxury to

introduce a dependency injection framework like Spring, Guice, or HiveMind? **DP**
COQ

A. The key aspect of making your code more testable is to "request for services, and not to look for services". Avoid looking for services by instantiating services with the "new" keyword. Request for services with service locators using either JNDI look ups or factories using the factory design pattern. A factory design pattern with "code to interface" design principle can loosely couple a caller from a callee. This will make your code not only more testable, but also more flexible and extendable.

Q38 When is a method said to be overloaded and when is a method said to be overridden? What are their differences? What is a co-variant return type? **LF FAQ**

A38 **Method overloading** is the primary way in which, polymorphism is implemented in Java. Overloading lets you define the same operation in different ways for different data. An overloaded method:

- appear in the same class or a subclass.
- have the same name but,
- have different parameter lists, and,
- can have different return types.

```
class MyClass {
    public void getInvestAmount(int rate) {...}
    public void getInvestAmount(int rate, long principal) { ... }
}
```

The actual method called depends on the number, order, and data types of arguments passed, and determined at **compile-time** (aka **compile-time polymorphism**). It does not depend on the return types or names of the arguments passed.

Method overriding allows a subclass to re-define a non-static method it inherits from its super class. Overriding lets you define the same operation in different ways for different object types. Late-binding also supports overriding. Overriding methods,

- appear in subclasses.
- have the same name as a super class method.
- have the same parameter list as a super class method.

- have the same return type as as a super class method. Until the J2SE 5.0 release, it was true that a class could not override the return type of the methods it inherits from a super class.
- the access modifier for the overriding method must not be more restrictive than the access modifier of the super class method. For example, if the super class method is protected, the overriding method must either be protected or public
- the overriding method can only specify all, none, or a subset of the exception classes (including their subclasses) specified in the throws clause of the overridden method in the super class..

```
class BaseClass{
    public void getInvestAmount(int rate) {…}
}
```

```
class MyClass extends BaseClass {
    @override
    public void getInvestAmount(int rate) { …}
}
```

The actual method called depends on the type on which the method is invoked, and determined at **runt-time** (aka **runtime polymorphism**).

BP It is a best practice to use the override annotation as shown above to ensure that you have not mistyped or used the wrong arguments for your overriding method.

Q39 There is a class X.java and it has a public method. Class Y extends class X. How would you prevent a method in class X from being accessed in class Y using Y's instance? **LF FAQ**

A39 Override the method in class X with the same method name and signature in class Y.

Q. Can you write a new static method in the subclass Y that has the same signature as the one in the super class X?
A. Yes. But this is called "**hiding** or **shadowing**" and not overriding.

Q. Can you also declare a public or protected field in the subclass Y with the same name as the one in the super class X, thus hiding it?
A. Yes. But this approach is not recommended as it breaks encapsulation. Always

declare your fields as private, and provide access via public or protected methods.

Q40 What do you understand by the term "co-variant" in Java? **LF FAQ**

A40 An argument or return type in an overridden method that is made more specialized is called to be co-variant. So you can use co-variant return types to minimize up casting and down casting. For example,

```java
package covariant;

public class Parent {

    Parent process() {
        System.out.println("Parent process() called");
        return this;
    }
}
```

If you were using J2SE5.0 or later version:

```java
package covariant;

public class Child extends Parent {

    /**
     * return type could be either Child or Parent
     */
    Child process() {
        System.out.println("Child process() called");
        return this;
    }
}
```

If you were using a Java version prior to J2SE 5.0:

```java
package covariant;

public class ChildPreJ2SE5 extends Parent {

    /**
```

```
 * Pre J2SE 5.0, a return type of Child will cause a compile-time
 *  error  "The return type is incompatible with Parent.process( )"
 * Hence, same  return type as Parent class is used.
 */
Parent process( ) {
   System.out.println("ChildPreJ2SE5 process( ) called");
   return this;
 }
}
```

```
package covariant;

public class Covarience {

   public static void main(String[ ] args) {

      //Before covariance was introduced
      ChildPreJ2SE5 c1Pre5 = new ChildPreJ2SE5( );
      ChildPreJ2SE5 c2Pre5 = (ChildPreJ2SE5) c1Pre5.process( );
      Parent c3Pre5 = c1Pre5.process( );

      //After covariance was introduced
      Child c1 = new Child( );
      Child c2 =  c1.process( );         // c2 is Child. No casting is required.
      Parent c3 = c1.process( );         // c3 points to Child
   }
}
```

Note: Prior to J2SE 5.0, the return type of the overridden *clone( )* method had to be an *Object* and a cast was necessary. From J2SE 5.0, the return type of the overriding *clone( )* method can be a more specialized subtype.

Q41 How many ways can an argument be passed to a subroutine and explain them? **LF**
A41 2 ways. Pass by value and pass by reference. Java is always pass by value.

Q42 What are varargs? **LF**
A42 This is another handy feature added in J2SE 5.0. The varargs is a variable arguments language feature that makes it possible to call a method with a variable number of arguments. Before making that call, the **rightmost parameter** in the method's

parameter list must conform to the following syntax:

```
type ... variableName
```

The ellipsis (...) identifies a variable number of arguments, and is demonstrated in the following example.

```
package varargs;

public class WithoutVarargs {

    static int sumWithoutVarargs(int[ ] numbers) {
        int sum = 0;
        for (int i = 0; i < numbers.length; i++) {
            sum += numbers[i];
        }
        return sum;
    }

    static int sumWithVarargs(int... numbers) {
        int sum = 0;
        for (int i = 0; i < numbers.length; i++) {
            sum += numbers[i];
        }
        return sum;
    }

    public static void main(String[ ] args) {
        // need to construct the array of numbers first
        int[ ] i1 = { 3, 7, 9, 8 };
        int sum = sumWithoutVarargs(i1);

        // need to construct the array of numbers first
        int[ ] i2 = { 9, 9 };
        sum = sumWithoutVarargs(i2);

        // with varargs, you can pass it directly
        sum = sumWithVarargs(3, 7, 9, 8);
        sum = sumWithVarargs(9,9);
```

```
    }
}
```

Q43 What is the difference between an argument and a parameter? **LF**

A43 The words argument and parameter are often used interchangeably. In Java, **argument** is an expression in the comma-separated list in a method call. For example,

```
sum = sumWithVarargs(3, 7, 9, 8);                    // arguments
```

A **parameter** is an object or reference that is declared in a method declaration or definition (or in a catch clause of an exception handler). For example,

```
static int sumWithoutVarargs(int[ ] numbers) {  // parameter
    int sum = 0;
    for (int i = 0; i < numbers.length; i++) {
        sum += numbers[i];
    }
    return sum;
}
```

Stack versus Heap

Q44 Can you explain what goes on a stack and what goes on a heap for the following code snippet?

```
package heap;

import java.text.SimpleDateFormat;

public class StackVersusHeap {

    private SimpleDateFormat instanceSdf = new SimpleDateFormat();

    public void instanceMethod( ) {
        SimpleDateFormat localSdf = new SimpleDateFormat();
        //...
    }
```

}
}

A44 **Instance variables and Objects are stored on the Heap**. The *SimpleDateFormat* objects go to the heap. The instance variable *instanceSdf* also goes to the heap. Heap is where the state is maintained, and when you get memory leaks, this is where your profiler helps you to find the allocation of memory. Object members or instance variables are stored on the heap along with the object. Therefore, if two threads call a method on the same object instance and this method updates object members, the method is not thread safe.

Local variables and methods are stored on the Stack. So the method *instanceMethod( )* and the local variable *localSdf* go to the stack. Each thread will have its own stack. Local variables and methods are stored in each thread's own stack. That means that local variables are never shared between threads. That also means that all local primitive variables are thread safe. Local references to objects are a bit different. The reference itself is not shared and sits in the stack. But local object referenced is not stored in each thread's local stack. <u>All objects are stored in the shared heap</u>. If an object created locally never escapes the method it was created in, it is thread safe. In fact you can also pass it on to other methods and objects as long as none of these methods or objects make the passed object available to other threads.

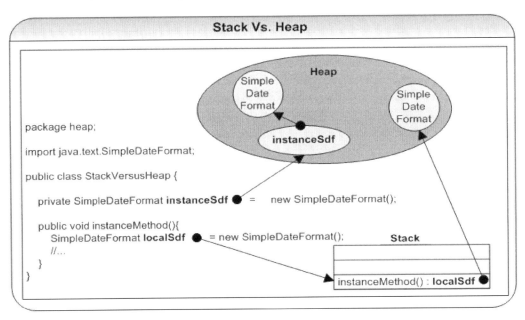

210

Q45 What is the difference between processes and threads?

A45 A process is an execution of a program but a thread is a single execution sequence within the process. A process can contain multiple threads. A thread is sometimes called a lightweight process.

A JVM runs in a single process and threads in a JVM share the heap belonging to that process. That is why several threads may access the same object. Threads share the heap and have their own stack space. This is how one thread's invocation of a method and its local variables are kept thread safe from other threads. But the heap is not thread-safe and must be synchronized for thread safety.

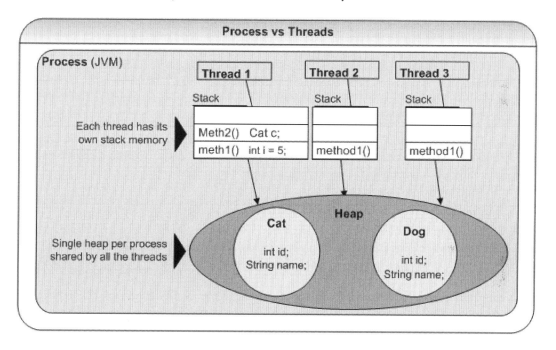

Java is pass-by-value

Q44 Explain the statement Java is always pass by value? **LF FAQ**

A44 Other languages use pass-by-reference or pass-by-pointer. But in Java, no matter what type of argument (i.e. a primitive variable or an object reference) you pass, the corresponding parameter will get **a copy of that data**, which is exactly how pass-by-value (i.e. copy-by-value) works. Even though the definition is quite straight forward, the way the primitives and object references behave when passed by value, will be different. For example, If the passed in argument was a primitive value like int, char, etc, the passed in primitive value is copied to the method parameter. Modifying the copied parameter **will not modify the original primitive value**. On the contrary, if the passed in argument was an object reference, the passed in reference is copied to the method parameter. The copied reference will still be pointing to the same object. So if you modify the object value through the copied reference, **the original object will be modified**. For example,

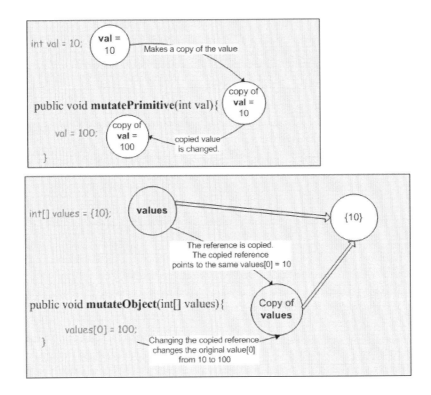

```
package chapter2.com;

public class PassByValue {

    int val = 10;                          // primitive reference
    int[ ] values = {10};                  // object  reference
```

```
public void mutatePrimitive(int val){
   val = 100;
}

public void mutateObject(int[ ] values){
   values[0] = 100;
}

public static void main(String[ ] args) {
   PassByValue instance = new PassByValue( );

   //primitive reference
   System.out.println("val before mutate=" + instance.val);            // prints 10
   instance.mutatePrimitive(instance.val);
   System.out.println("val after mutate=" + instance.val);             // prints 10

   //object reference
   System.out.println("values[0] before mutate=" + instance.values[0]);// prints 10
   instance.mutateObject(instance.values);
   System.out.println("values[0] after mutate=" + instance.values[0]);  // prints 100
  }
}
```

Note: Regardless of what type of array (i.e. primitive array or object array) you're working with, the array identifier is actually a handle to a true object that's created on the heap.

Q45 The value of *Point* p before the following method calls is (10,20). What will be the value of *Point* p after executing the following method calls? **LF COQ**

Scenario 1:

```
static void mutatePoint(Point p) {
    p.x = 50;
    p.y=100;
}
```

Scenario 2:

```
static void mutatePoint(Point p) {
    p = new Point(50,100);
}
```

A45 Scenario 1:

Point p = (**50,100**), as the copied reference will still be pointing and modifying the original *Point (10,2 0)* object through the *mutatePoint( )* method.

Scenario 2:
Point p = (**10,20**), as the copied reference will be creating and pointing to the newly created *Point (50, 100)* object.

Recursive functions

Q46 How would you take advantage of Java being a stack based language? What is a re-entrant method? **LF FAQ**

A46 Recursive method calls are possible with stack based languages and re-entrant methods.

A **re-entrant** method would be one that can safely be entered, even when the same method is being executed, further down the call stack of the same thread. A non-re-entrant method would not be safe to use in that way. For example, writing or logging to a file can potentially corrupt that file, if that method were to be re-entrant.

A function is **recursive** if it calls itself. Given enough stack space, recursive method calls are perfectly valid in Java though it is tough to debug. Recursive functions are useful in removing iterations from many sorts of algorithms. **All recursive functions are re-entrant**, but not all re-entrant functions are recursive.

Stack uses LIFO (**L**ast **I**n **F**irst **O**ut), so it remembers its 'caller' and knows whom to return when the function has to return. Recursion makes use of system stack for storing the return addresses of the function calls.

```
public class RecursiveCall {
```

```java
public int countA(String input) {

    // exit condition – recursive calls must have an exit condition
    if (input == null || input.length( ) == 0) {
        return 0;
    }

    int count = 0;

    //check first character of the input
    if (input.substring(0, 1).equals("A")) {
        count = 1;
    }

    //recursive call to evaluate rest of the input
    //(i.e. 2nd character onwards)
    return count + countA(input.substring(1));
}

public static void main(String[ ] args) {
    System.out.println(new RecursiveCall( ).countA("AAA rating"));    // 3
}
}
```

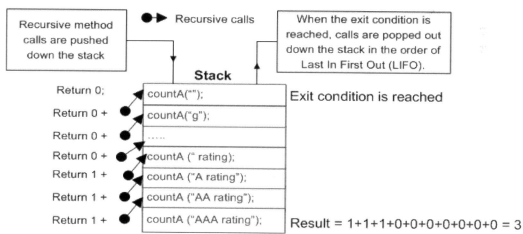

BP PC Recursion might not be the efficient way to code, but recursive functions

215

are shorter, simpler, and easier to read and understand. Recursive functions are very handy in working with tree structures and avoiding unsightly nested for loops. If a particular recursive function is identified to be a real performance bottleneck as it is invoked very frequently or it is easy enough to implement using iteration like the sample code below, then favor iteration over recursion. The iterative approach is shown below:

```java
public class Iteration {

    public int countA(String input) {
        if (input == null || input.length( ) == 0) {
            return 0;
        }

        int count = 0;
        for (int i = 0; i < input.length( ); i++) {
            if(input.substring(i, i+1).equals("A")){
                count++;
            }
        }
        return count;
    }

    public static void main(String[ ] args) {
        System.out.println(new Iteration( ).countA("AAA rating"));    // 3
    }
}
```

Q47 What are idempotent methods? **LF FAQ**

A47 **Idempotent** methods are methods, which are written in such a way that repeated calls to the same method with the same arguments yield the same results. For example, clustered EJBs, which are written with idempotent methods, can automatically recover from a server failure as long as it can reach another server.

```java
package chapter2.com;

import java.util.ArrayList;
import java.util.List;
```

```java
public class IdempotentOperations {

    //member variable
    List<Integer> numbers = new ArrayList<Integer>();

    /**
     * An idempotent operation leaves everything in the same state
     * if you call it once or many times, provided you pass
     * in the same parameters.
     */
    public Integer square(Integer input) {
        return input * input;
    }

    /**
     * An operation that does something like appending to a shared list
     * are not idempotent.
     */
    public List<Integer> add(Integer input) {
        numbers.add(input);
        return numbers;
    }
}
```

Class, instance, and local variables

Q48 What are the different kinds of variables in Java? What are some of the best practices relating to usage of these types of variables? **LF FAQ**

A48 **Local variables** are defined in a method, constructor or block. Local variables (i.e. primitives and object references) are stored in a stack. **Use**: Local variables hold values used in computations in a method. **Lifetime**: Created when a method or constructor is entered and destroyed on exit of a method or a constructor. **Scope/Visibility**: Visible only in the method, constructor, or block in which they are declared. **Declaration/Initial Value**: must be declared, and initialized during declaration or later down the code, but cannot be used if not initialized. **BP** **Best practice/caveat**: Prefer using local variables if you do not really want to maintain any state between method calls. Declare and initialize local variables just before using them. Declaring local variables without using them immediately may unnecessarily increase their scope. This decreases legibility, and increases the likelihood of errors. Local variables are implicitly thread-safe and synchronization is not required. There are exceptional scenarios where the local variables need to be declared before immediately using them. For example,

- When a variable in the *try* block needs to be visible in the *finally* block.
- Some variables that are used within a loop.

```
package chapter2.com;

import java.util.ArrayList;
import java.util.List;
import java.util.Scanner;

public class Declared {

 public static void main(String[ ] args) {
    /**
     * local variable is declared and initialized outside
     * try block to be visible in the finally block
     */
    Scanner sc = new Scanner(System.in);
    try {
       /**
        * local variable 'keepGoing' & 'typedValues" are
        * declared & initialized well before used
        * in the while loop.
        */
       boolean keepGoing = true;
       List<String> typedValues = new ArrayList<String>(20);

       while (keepGoing) {
          System.out.print("Enter Something? [type QUIT to exit] ");
          /**
           * local variable 'answer' is declared &
           * initialized immediately before getting used
           * 'answer' is out of scope outside the while loop.
```

```
        */
      String answer = sc.next();
      if ("QUIT".equalsIgnoreCase(answer)) {
        keepGoing = false;
      }
      typedValues.add(answer);
    }

    /**
     * local variable i is declared and initialized
     * immediately before used. 'typedValues' is declared
     * outside the while loop, hence visible here.
     */
    for (int i = 0; i < typedValues.size(); i++) {
      System.out.println("Input Number " + (i + 1) + " = "
          + typedValues.get(i));
    }
  } finally {
      sc.close();
  }
 }
}
```

Output:

```
Enter Something? [type QUIT to exit] test1
Enter Something? [type QUIT to exit] Test2
Enter Something? [type QUIT to exit] quit
Input Number 1 = test1
Input Number 2 = Test2
Input Number 3 = quit
```

Instance (aka member) variables are declared in a class, but outside a method. They are also called member variables, fields or attributes. These variables are created when an object is created and allocated in the heap. **Use**: Hold values that must be referenced by more than one method. **Lifetime**: Creates when an instance of a class is created with *new*. Destroyed when there are no more references to the containing object, and the garbage collector has removed it from the heap. **Scope/visibility**: Can be seen by all methods in the class. Which other classes can see them depends on the

Language Essentials

access modifiers. **Declaration/initial Value**: Declared anywhere at a class level. Can be initialized at declaration or in constructor. Unlike local variables, these variables are implicitly initialized to its default values (0, 0.0, or false) if not explicitly initialized. **BP** **Best practice/caveat**: Typically declared as private and access is provided to outside classes via public, protected, or package-private scoped methods with proper checks or validation. As the objects can be accessed simultaneously by multiple threads, use these variables in a thread-safe manner. Never use same name for your local, instance, and class variables. If same names were used for an instance variable and a local variable, the local variable **hides** the instance variable, unless the instance variable is prefixed with the "**this**" keyword. Meaning this object's member or instance variable. It is a best practice to use a naming convention to distinguish between the variable types. For example, prefixed with 'this' or a naming convention like m_sameNameVar where 'm' stands for member variable.

```
package chapter2.com;

public class VariableNamingIssue {

    int sameNameVar = 5;                          //instance variable

    public int getSameNameVar() {
        int sameNameVar = 6;                      //local variable
        //do something here....
        /**
         * local variable sameNameVar is returned
         * unless you use the "this" explicitly
         * as --> return this.sameNameVar
         */
        return sameNameVar;            //value of the local variable is returned
    }

    public void setSameNameVar(int sameNameVar) {
        /**
         * prefixing with 'this' improves readability, and uses the instance variable.
         * If "this" is omitted, the local variable gets assigned instead.
         */
        this.sameNameVar = sameNameVar;
    }
}
```

220

```
public static void main(String[ ] args) {
    VariableNamingIssue vni = new VariableNamingIssue( );  //create an object
    vni.setSameNameVar(10);  //instance variable  sameNameVar is set to 10.
    System.out.println("value=" + vni.getSameNameVar( )); //value of the local
                                                //variable 6 is returned.
    }
}
```

Output:

```
value=6
```

Class variables or static variables are declared with the static keyword in a class, but outside a method. There is only one copy per class (strictly speaking, per classloader), regardless of how many objects are created from it. **Use**: Mostly used for constants. It can also be used to aggregate values (e.g. a counter) across objects. **Lifetime**: Created when the program starts (i.e. a class is loaded) and destroyed when the program stops. **Scope/visibility**: Same as instance variables, but are often declared in protected, package or public scope to make constants available to external classes. **Declaration/initial Value**: Declare anywhere at class level. If not explicitly initialized, implicitly initialized to default values (0, 0.0, or false). **BP** **Best practice/caveat**: Global state is harmful to your application design. Sometimes you really do need the globalness of static variables, but don't use it where it would make more sense to just use local variables or create an object with instance variables. Excessive usage of static variables is not a best practice as it can adversely impact maintainability, robustness, scalability, and testability.

BP   Where applicable, prefer making the variables final to prevent changing those values, and consequently making your code less buggy.

Note: Java only allocates primitive data types like int and double, and object references on the stack. All objects are allocated on the heap.

Q49 What will be the output for the following code? **LF COQ**

```
package chapter2.com;

public class AccessingInstanceVariables {
```

```
int a = 6;

public static void main(String[ ] args) {
    System.out.println("a is " + a);
}
}
```

A49   Compile-time error. Since 'a' is an instance variable, you cannot access it without actually creating an instance of an object and qualifying it with the reference.

```
package chapter2.com;

public class AccessingInstanceVariables {

    int a = 6;                                          //instance variable

    /**
     * static method
     */
    public static void main(String[ ] args) {
        AccessingInstanceVariables ref = new AccessingInstanceVariables();
        System.out.println("a is " + ref.a);            // prints 6
        ref.addFive();
    }

    /**
     * non-static (aka instance) method can refer it directly.
     */
    public void addFive() {
        System.out.println("a is " + (a += 5));          // prints 11
        addTwo();
    }

    /**
     * non-static (aka instance) method can refer it directly.
     */
    public void addTwo() {
        System.out.println("a is " + (a += 2));          // prints 13
```

```
        }
}
```

Even though there is no name conflict, improve readability by qualifying it with **"this"** as shown below.

```
package chapter2.com;

public class AccessingInstanceVariables {

    int a = 6; // instance variable

    public static void main(String[ ] args) {
        AccessingInstanceVariables ref = new AccessingInstanceVariables();
        System.out.println("a is " + ref.a);              // prints 6
        ref.addFive();
    }

    public void addFive() {
        System.out.println("a is " + (this.a += 5));       // prints 11
        this.addTwo();
    }

    public void addTwo() {
        System.out.println("a is " + (this.a += 2));       // prints 13
    }
}
```

Section-5:

Classes and Interfaces Essentials

- Working with classes and interfaces
- subclassing, overriding, and hiding
- Designing your classes and interfaces
- Working with abstract classes and interfaces
- Inheritance versus composition
- Applying the design principles
- Class invariant and design by contract
- Working with inner classes
- Packaging your classes to avoid conflicts

This section is for all. If you asked me to pick a section that is most popular with the interviewers, this is it. If you don't perform well in this section, your success rate in interviews will be very low. Good interviewers will be getting you to analyze or code for a particular scenario. They will be observing your decisions with interfaces and classes, and question your decisions to ascertain your technical skills, analytical skills, and communication skills. You can't memorize your answers. This section requires some level of experience to fully understand. It has enough examples for beginners to get some level of familiarization.

Be ready to be asked about some tricky questions around the topics discussed in this section. Java interview questions are meant to analyze your technical bent of mind. You have to tell the way you are going to solve a particular problem with Java or any other programming language of your choice. So the key is to ask the right questions and then apply what you had learned. Keep practicing the examples provided here, and experiment with them until you get a good grasp.

Working with classes and interfaces

Object oriented (i.e. OO) concepts are an important building for creating good services. They provide a common vocabulary to talk about the architecture. Without good understanding of the OO concepts, you could easily implement a procedural programming using classes. All you have to do is create a bunch of classes with nothing but data with getter and setter methods, and some other *Handler* or *Processor* classes to handle the logic with *if/else* and *instanceof* constructs sprayed all over the place. It is important to understand that objects need to not only take care of themselves with data and behavior, but also have to interact with each other.

Q1   Which class declaration is correct if *A* and *B* are classes and *C* and *D* are interfaces? **LF**

a.) class Z extends A implements C, D{}
b.) class Z extends A,B implements D {}
c.) class Z extends C implements A,B {}
d.) class Z extends C,D implements B {}

A1   **a.** class Z **extends** A **implements** C, D{}

A class is a template. A class can extend only a single class (i.e. single inheritance. Java does not support **multiple implementation inheritance**), but can implement multiple interfaces to achieve **multiple interface inheritance**. An interface can also extend more than one other interfaces.

interface E **extends** C,D { //.... }

Q2   What is a class? What are the valid modifiers of a top level class? **LF**

A2   A class is a template for multiple objects with similar features. In another words, A class defines responsibilities (i.e. characteristics and behaviors) that are common to every object.

Modifiers: A top level class can either be public or package-private (i.e. no access modifier) scoped. It can be final concrete, abstract, or non-final concrete (i.e. no final or abstract modifiers).

public class A { ... }   // non-final **concrete** class

```
class A { ... }                      // non-final concrete class
public abstract class A { ... }      // abstract class
public final class A { ... }         // final concrete class
```

Subclassing, overriding, and hiding (aka shadowing)

Q3   What is a subclass? **LF**

A3   A subclass is a class that extends a class. A subclass inherits all of the public and protected members of its parent class, no matter what package the subclass is in. If the subclass is in the same package as its parent, it also inherits the package-private (i.e. no access modifier) scoped members of the parent.

Q4   What can you do in a subclass? **LF FAQ**

A4   You can supplement, override, inherit, and hide/shadow your superclass members.

Supplement:

*   You can declare new fields in the subclass that are not in the superclass.
*   You can declare new methods in the subclass that are not in the superclass.
*   You can write a subclass constructor that invokes the constructor of the superclass, either implicitly or by explicitly using the keyword "super(...)".

Override:

*   You can write a new instance method in the subclass that has the same signature as the one in the superclass, thus overriding it. The ability to override methods allows you to take advantage of **runtime polymorphism**.

Inherit:

*   You can inherit commonly used state and behavior in the super class. One of the benefits of **implementation inheritance** is to minimize the amount of duplicate code in an application by reusing code from the superclass. Since Java does not support multiple implementation inheritance, it becomes a card that can be played only once, and thus it should be used with caution.

Shadow/hide:

*   You can declare a field in the subclass with the same name as the one in the superclass, thus hiding it (not recommended).

- You can write a new static method in the subclass that has the same signature as the one in the superclass, thus hiding it (not recommended).

Q5 What is the output of the following code snippet? Give your reasons and recommendations? COQ

```java
package subclass1;

public abstract class Animal {

    String name = "animal";

    public String getName() {
        return this.name;
    }
}
```

```java
package subclass1;

public class Cat extends Animal {

    String name = "cat";

    public String getName() {
        return this.name;
    }
}
```

```java
package subclass1;

public class Example {

    public static void main(String[] args) {
        Animal animal = new Cat();
        Cat cat = new Cat();

        System.out.println(animal.name);
        System.out.println(cat.name);
        System.out.println(((Cat)animal).name);
```

```
        System.out.println(((Animal)cat).name);

        System.out.println(animal.getName());
        System.out.println(cat.getName());
    }
}
```

A5 The output will be:

```
animal
cat
cat
animal
cat
cat
```

The above code demonstrates implementation of inheritance and polymorphism. But there are a number of bad practices that need to be fixed in the above code.

When both a parent class and its subclass have a field with the same name, this technique is called **variable shadowing**. If the field in the parent class has private access or is in another package and has package-private access, there is no room for confusion because the child class cannot access the field in question of the parent class. In the above example, the variable "name" is defined in both parent and child classes within the same package, and have the package-private scope. Hence, the variable "name" in the parent class *Animal* is accessible to the child class *Cat*. The variable shadowing depends on the **static type** of the variable in which the <u>object's reference</u> is stored and NOT based on the **dynamic type** of the <u>actual object</u> stored. **Note**: The dynamic type will only be resolved at runtime.

Unlike variables, when a parent class and a child class each have a **non-static** method (aka an instance method) with the same signature, the method of the child class overrides the method of the parent class. The **method overriding** depends on the dynamic type of the <u>actual object</u> being stored and NOT the static type of the variable in which the <u>object reference</u> is stored. This can only be evaluated at runtime. As you can see, the rules for variable shadowing and method overriding are directly opposed. This can be demonstrated as shown below:

```
package subclass1;
```

```java
import static java.lang.System.out;

public class Example2 {

    public static void main(String[ ] args) {

        //stored object type = Cat & referencing object type = Animal.
        Animal animal = new Cat( );
        //stored object type = Cat & referencing object type = Cat
        Cat cat = new Cat( );

        out.println("Variable Shadowing: the output depends on");
        out.println("~~  the static type of the variable referencing ~~");
        out.println(animal.name);
        out.println(cat.name);
        out.println(((Cat) animal).name);
        out.println(((Animal) cat).name);

        out.println("\nMethod Overriding: the output depends on ");
        out.println("~~  the dynamic type of the object stored. ~~");
        out.println(animal.getName( ));
        out.println(cat.getName( ));
    }
}
```

Output:

```
Variable Shadowing: the output depends on
~~  the static type of the variable referencing ~~
animal
cat
cat
animal

Method Overriding: the output depends on
~~  the dynamic type of the object stored. ~~
cat
cat
```

Recommendations:

- Firstly, the variable shadowing returns unexpected results. Hence it is a pitfall and should be avoided. Use method overriding instead, which makes possible a powerful object oriented concept known as polymorphism. Both objects of type *Cat* and *Dog* can be stored to the reference of type *Animal*. When you invoke the method *getName( )*, the actual method being invoked depends on the dynamic type of the object stored (i.e. *Cat* or *Dog*) and NOT the static type referencing (i.e. *Animal*) it.

- Secondly, the variable "name" is scoped package-private. This can break encapsulation by allowing incorrect direct assignments like

```
cat.name = null;
```

  from outside classes like *Example2* within this package. Hence, it is recommended to change the variable "name" from package-private scoped to private scoped so that it cannot be directly modified as shown above. The modification is only allowed through a setter method that can validate the input argument(s) before assigning.

- Where it makes sense, to harness the power of polymorphism, code to an abstraction (i.e. interface or an abstract class) and not to an implementation. Hence avoid using

```
Cat cat = new Cat( );
```

  instead use:

```
Animal animal = new Cat( );
Animal animal2 = new Dog( );
```

Where the "*Animal*" could be an interface or an abstract class. The code below incorporates the above recommendations.

```
package subclass1a;
```

```java
public abstract class Animal {

    private String name = "animal"; //since private, cannot be accessed directly
                                    // from outside this class.

    public String getName(){          //accessed via get & set methods.
        return this.name;
    }

    public void setName(String name){   // 'name' is well encapsulated
        //check for valid input
        if(name == null || name.length() == 0){
            throw new IllegalArgumentException("name=" + name);
        }
        this.name = name;
    }
}
```

```java
package subclass1a;

public class Cat extends Animal {

    private String name = "cat";

    public String getName(){
        return this.name;
    }
}
```

```java
package subclass1a;

import subclass1a.Animal;

public class Dog extends Animal {

    private String name = "dog";

    public String getName(){
        return this.name;
```

```
        }
}
```

```
package subclass1a;

import static java.lang.System.out;

public class Example {

    public static void main(String[ ] args) {
        //stored obj type = Cat & referencing obj type = Animal
        Animal animal = new Cat( );
        //stored obj type = Dog & referencing obj type = Animal
        Animal animal2 = new Dog( );

        out.println("Stored obj is a --> " + animal.getName( ));
        out.println("Stored obj is a --> " + animal2.getName( ));
    }
}
```

Output:

```
Stored obj is a --> cat
Stored obj is a --> dog
```

Q6   What happens when a parent class and a child class each have a **static** method with the same signature? ■■

A6   The behavior of static methods will be similar to the variable shadowing, and not recommended. It will be invoking the static method of the referencing static object type, and NOT the dynamic object type being stored.

Designing your classes and interfaces

You need to have a good understanding of the OO concepts, design principles, and certain amount of common sense to design a quality system. Any one can recite the definition of the OO concepts and design principles, but only a few can come up with good class designs for a given problem. It is important to understand when to use an attribute versus a subclass, and when to use a composition or aggregation as opposed to inheritance. For example, if a

233

Dog is a class extending an abstract class *Animal*, how would you design a *Dog* with a mole? As a subclass or as an attribute? If you have a class *Animal*, how would you define its body parts? As a subclass of animal or composition? [Hint: define mole as an attribute like *specialMarks*, and define the body parts as a composition]. A mole won't make a *Dog* to be more specialized. A dog with a mole does not have a **more specialized behavior** compared to dogs without a mole. The body parts of a dog don't have an "is a" relationship with the *Dog*. You can't say that a leg "**is a**" dog. You will have to say a dog has legs. This is a "**has a**" relationship denoting a composition or aggregation. There are more to it, and you will have a better understanding after going through the following Q&As with lots of examples.

Q7   How do you know that your classes are badly designed? `DC OEQ`
A7

- If your application is **fragile** – when making a change, unexpected parts of the application can break.
- If your application is **rigid** – it is hard to change one part of the application without affecting too many other parts.
- If your application is **immobile** – it is hard to reuse the code in another application because it cannot be separated.

Overly complex design is as bad as no design at all. Get the granularity of your classes and objects right without overly complicating them. Don't apply too many patterns and principles to a simple problem. Apply them only when they are adequate. Don't anticipate changes in requirements ahead of time. Preparing for future changes can easily lead to overly complex designs. Focus on writing code that is not only easy to understand, but also flexible enough so that it is easy to change if the requirements change.

Q8   Can you explain if the following classes are badly designed? `OEQ SBQ`

The following snippets design the classes & interfaces for the following scenario. Bob, and Jane work for a restaurant. Bob works as manager and a waiter. Jane works as a waitress. A waiter's behavior is to take customer orders and a manager's behavior is to manage employees.

```
package badrestaurant;

public interface Person {}
```

```java
package badrestaurant;

public interface Manager extends Person {
    public void managePeople();
}
```

```java
package badrestaurant;

public interface Waiter extends Person {
    public void takeOrders();
}
```

```java
package badrestaurant;

public class Bob implements Manager, Waiter {

    @Override
    public void managePeople() {
        //implementation goes here
    }

    @Override
    public void takeOrders() {
        //implementation goes here
    }
}
```

```java
package badrestaurant;

public class Jane implements Waiter {

    @Override
    public List<String> takeOrders() {
        //implementation goes here
    }
}
```

The *Restaurant* class uses the above classes as shown below.

```
package badrestaurant;

public class Restaurant {

    public static void main(String[] args) {

        Bob bob = new Bob();
        bob.managePeople();
        bob.takeOrders();

        Jane jane = new Jane();
        jane.takeOrders();
    }
}
```

A8   The above classes are badly designed for the reasons described below.

- The name should be an attribute, and not a class like *Bob* or *Jane*. A good OO design should hide non-essential details through **abstraction**. If the restaurant employs more persons, you don't want the system to be **inflexible** and create new classes like *Peter*, *Jason*, etc for every new employee.

- The above solution's incorrect usage of the interfaces for the job roles like *Waiter*, *Manager*, etc will make your classes very **rigid** and **tightly** coupled by requiring static structural changes. What if *Bob* becomes a full-time manager? You will have to remove the interface *Waiter* from the class *Bob*. What if Jane becomes a manager? You will have to change the interface *Waiter* with *Manager*.

The above drawbacks in the design can be fixed as shown below by asking the right questions. Basically waiter, manager, etc are roles an employee plays. You can abstract it out as shown below.

```
package goodrestuarant;

public interface Role {

    public String getName();
    public void perform();
}
```

```java
package goodrestuarant;

public class Waiter implements Role {

    private String roleName;

    public Waiter(String roleName) {
        this.roleName = roleName;
    }

    @Override
    public String getName() {
        return this.roleName;
    }

    @Override
    public void perform() {
        //implementation goes here
    }
}
```

```java
package goodrestuarant;

public class Manager implements Role {

    private String roleName;

    public Manager(String roleName) {
        this.roleName = roleName;
    }

    @Override
    public String getName() {
        return this.roleName;
    }

    @Override
    public void perform() {
```

```
    //implementation goes here
  }
}
```

The *Employee* class defines the employee name as an attribute as opposed to a class. This makes the design flexible as new employees can be added at run time by instantiating new *Employee* objects with appropriate names. This is the power of abstraction. You don't have to create new classes for each new employee. The roles are declared as a list using aggregation (i.e. containment), so that new roles can be added or existing roles can be removed at run time as the roles of employees change. This makes the design more flexible.

```
package goodrestuarant;

import java.util.ArrayList;
import java.util.List;

public class Employee {

  private String name;
  private List<Role> roles = new ArrayList<Role>(10);

  public Employee(String name){
    this.name = name;
  }

  public String getName( ) {
    return name;
  }

  public void setName(String name) {
    this.name = name;
  }

  public List<Role> getRoles( ) {
    return roles;
  }

  public void setRoles(List<Role> roles) {
```

```java
      this.roles = roles;
   }

   public void addRole(Role role){
      if(role == null){
         throw new IllegalArgumentException("Role cannot be null");
      }
      roles.add(role);
   }

   public void removeRole(Role role){
      if(role == null){
         throw new IllegalArgumentException("Role cannot be null");
      }
      roles.remove(role);
   }
}
```

The following *Restaurant* class shows how flexible, extensible, and maintainable the above design is.

```java
package goodrestuarant;

import java.util.List;

public class Restaurant {

   public static void main(String[ ] args) {

      Employee emp1 = new Employee ("Bob");
      Role waiter = new Waiter("waiter");
      Role manager = new Manager("manager");

      emp1.addRole(waiter);
      emp1.addRole(manager);

      Employee emp2 = new Employee("Jane");
      emp2.addRole(waiter);
```

```
    List<Role> roles = emp1.getRoles( );
    for (Role role : roles) {
       role.perform( );
    }

    //you can add more employees or change roles based on
    //conditions here at runtime. More flexible.
    }
}
```

Q9 What do you achieve through good class and interface design? **DC OEQ**
A9

- **Loosely coupled** classes, objects, and components enabling your application to easily grow and adapt to changes without being rigid or fragile.
- Less complex and reusable code that increases **maintainability**, **extendability** and **testability**.

Q10 What are the principles of class design used in regards to OOD? **DC**
A10 They are the principles abbreviated as the SOLID principles.

SRP	Single Responsibility Principle	A class should only have a single purpose (i.e. cohesive), and all its methods should work together to achieve this goal.
OCP	Open Close Principle	You should be able to extend a class' behavior, without modifying it.
LSP	Liskov Substitution Principle	Derived classes must be substitutable for their base classes. Derived classes must have the same intent, but different implementation. Another way to look at this principle is to think of design by contract. A sub class should honor the contracts made by its parent classes.
ISP	Interface Segregation Principle	Make fine grained interfaces that are client specific. While SRP addresses high cohesion in the class level, ISP promotes high cohesion in the interface level.
DIP	Dependency Inversion	Depend on abstractions, not on implementations.

	Principle	• Higher level modules should not depend directly on lower level modules. Both should depend on abstractions (interfaces or abstract classes). • Abstractions should not depend on implementations. The implementations should depend on abstractions.

Q11 What are the 3 main concepts of OOP? `DC FAQ`

A11 Encapsulation, polymorphism, and inheritance are the 3 main concepts or pillars of an object oriented programming. Abstraction is another important concept that can be applied to both object oriented and non object oriented programming. [Remember: a pie → **a**bstraction, **p**olymorphism, **i**nheritance, and **e**ncapsulation.]

- **Abstraction** refers to hiding all the non-essential details from the user. Abstraction comes in two forms: abstracting the behavior and abstracting the data. For example, a person driving a car only needs to know about how to use a steering wheel, gear, accelerator, etc, but does not need to know about the internal details like how the engine works? how the transmission works?, how much fuel is released on acceleration?, etc. Thus, abstraction lets you focus on **what** the object does instead of **how** it does.

  Abstraction gives you the ability to conceptualize things by ignoring the irrelevant details. If you refer to an object as a vehicle that can be used in place of an actual vehicle like a car, bus, van, etc, you are making an abstraction. You can make an abstraction at different levels by handling details at different levels. A *Vehicle* class can focus on common behaviors like *forward(..)*, *reverse(..)*, *turn(..)* etc and attributes like make, model, etc of a vehicle. A set of derived classes like *Car*, *Bus*, *Truck*, etc can focus on more specific details of a vehicle. This gives you another level of abstraction by allowing you to refer to an object as a car that can be used in place of different makes like a Toyota, Ford, Volvo, etc and models like Camry, Corolla, etc by capturing the make and model as attributes.

  Abstraction is all about managing complexities at package, class, interface, and method levels. Can you imagine how complex your class hierarchy will become if you represent the make and model as classes instead of attributes within a class? You may end up with thousands of classes from different make and model if not tens of thousands. Good programmers develop this essential skill

241

to logically map a problem to its barest essential through the process of mental exercise. Both the ability to look at the big picture and eye for details of how things work are two essential traits to succeed in software development.

- **Encapsulation** takes abstraction, which allows you to look at an object at a high level of detail a step further by forbidding access to some internal details to minimize complexity. Encapsulation makes your code modular by capturing the data and the function into a single class. Modularity is a goal to treat each class or method like a **black box**. It identifies the parts of an object that should be made public and those that should be made private. The data and methods that an object exposes to every other object is called the object's public interface and the parts that are exposed to its subclasses via its inheritance is called the protected interface. The access modifiers discussed in the previous section are used to restrict access to some of the internal details. Thus, encapsulation is hiding of internal details (e.g. having variables and methods with either private or protected access), and connecting with other objects through well defined narrow boundaries (e.g. well defined methods with package-private or public access) and contracts.

  The question "How would you go about determining what access levels to use in your code?" in "Language Essentials" section demonstrates that a well encapsulated code will maintain the data integrity by preventing any unintentional data corruption.

- **Inheritance** is a way to form new classes using classes that have already been defined. As some believe, the main focus of inheritance is not to achieve code reuse. In a software system, you will often find objects that are much like other objects, except for a few differences. Inheritance is a mechanism used mainly to achieve **categorization**, **modularity**, **clear representation of concepts**, and **separation of concerns**. Categorization is a process in which ideas and objects are recognized, differentiated, and understood. For example, a car, truck, bus, etc are categorized as a vehicle. It implies that objects are grouped into categories for a specific purpose. Using inheritance, you can build a hierarchy of concepts separated in concerns at different levels of abstraction.

  Inheritance also facilitates polymorphism. Another added benefit of inheritance is code reuse. The code reuse is achieved through a type of inheritance known as the **implementation** inheritance to be more specific. But code reuse is NOT the main driver for using inheritance and there is a better approach known as **composition** to achieve code reuse. This will be covered in detail later. There are 2 types of inheritances as shown below:

➤ **Implementation inheritance** (aka class inheritance): You can extend an application's functionality by reusing functionality in the parent class by inheriting all or some of the operations already implemented. In Java, you can only inherit from one superclass using the "**extends**" keyword. **BP** Implementation inheritance promotes code reuse by allowing you to implement the common or shared code in the parent class. But improper use of implementation inheritance can cause programming nightmares by breaking encapsulation, and making future changes a problem. With implementation inheritance, the subclass becomes tightly coupled with the superclass. This will make the design fragile because if you want to change the superclass, you must know all the details of the subclasses to avoid breaking them. So when using implementation inheritance, make sure that the subclasses only change the implementation and not the meaning or intent of the parent class.

➤ **Interface inheritance** (aka type inheritance): This is also known as sub-typing. Interfaces provide a mechanism for specifying a relationship between otherwise unrelated classes, typically by specifying a set of common methods each implementing class must contain. Interface inheritance promotes the design concept of **program to interface not to implementation**. This reduces the coupling or implementation dependencies between systems. In Java, you can implement any number of interfaces with the "**implements**" keyword. **BP** This is more flexible than implementation inheritance because it won't lock you into specific implementations, which can make subclasses difficult to maintain. But care should be taken not to break the implementing classes by modifying the interfaces or forcing the classes to implement a method. The "**Interface Segregation Principle (ISP)**" states that:

"clients should not be forced to implement interfaces they don't use. Instead of one fat interface, many small interfaces are preferred based on groups of methods, each one serving one sub-module."

Unlike implementation inheritance, the interface inheritance does not achieve any code reuse as interfaces can only define behavior, not implement them. It is the responsibility of the class that implements the interfaces to implement the behavior. So how do you achieve code reuse with interface inheritance? It is achieved through a design concept known as the **composition**. Both types of inheritances promote polymorphism.

- **Polymorphism** is the capability to invoke a method without knowing until runtime what kind of object you are dealing with. In a nutshell, polymorphism is a bottom-up method call. The benefit of polymorphism is that it is very easy to add new classes of derived objects without breaking the calling code that uses the polymorphic classes using the implementation inheritance or polymorphic interfaces using the interface inheritance. **COQ** Polymorphism prevents programs to rely on low level details of object implementations. This considerably reduces the dependencies (aka coupling) between modules. Less dependencies means more maintainable and easier to modify programs.

  Polymorphism in Java comes in 2 forms through **method overriding** (aka runtime polymorphism) and **method overloading** (aka compile-time polymorphism). The power of OOP using Java is centered on **runtime polymorphism** using class inheritance or interface inheritance with method overriding. The fact that the decision as to which version of the method to invoke cannot be made at compile time and must be deferred and made at runtime is sometimes referred to as **late binding**. **Note**: Refer Q3, Q20 & Q21 in "Platform Essentials" section and Q38 in "Language Essentials" section.

Q12 What problem(s) does abstraction and encapsulation solve? **DC**

A12 Both abstraction and encapsulation solve same problem of complexity in different dimensions. Encapsulation exposes only the required details of an object to the caller by forbidding access to certain members, whereas an abstraction not only hides the implementation details, but also provides a basis for your application to grow and change over a period of time. For example, if you abstract out the make and model of a vehicle as class attributes as opposed to as individual classes like *Toyota*, *ToyotaCamry*, *ToyotaCorolla*, etc you can easily incorporate new types of cars at runtime by creating a new car object with the relevant make and model as arguments as opposed to having to declare a new set of classes.

Q. How would you go about designing a "farm animals" application where animals like cow, pig, horse, etc move from a barn to pasture, a stable to paddock, etc? The solution should also cater for extension into other types of animals like circus animals, wild animals, etc in the future. **COQ**

A.

```java
package subclass0;

public abstract class Animal {
    private int id;                    // id is encapsulated

    public Animal(int id) {
        this.id = id;
    }

    public int getId() {
        return id;
    }

    public abstract void move(Location location);
}
```

```java
package subclass0;

public class FarmAnimal extends Animal {

    private Location location = null;              // location is encapsulated

    public FarmAnimal(int id, Location defaultLocation) {
        super(id);
        validateLocation(defaultLocation);
        this.location = defaultLocation;
    }

    public Location getLocation() {
        return location;
    }

    public void move(Location location) {
        validateLocation(location);
        System.out.println("Id=" + getId() + " is moving from "
                + this.location + " to " + location);
```

```
        this.location = location;
    }

    private void validateLocation(Location location) {
        if (location == null) {
            throw new IllegalArgumentException("location=" + location);
        }
    }
}
```

```
package subclass0;

public enum Location {
    Barn, Pasture, Stable, Cage, PigSty, Paddock, Pen
}
```

```
package subclass0;

public class Example {

    public static void main(String[] args) {
        Animal pig = new FarmAnimal(1, Location.Barn);
        Animal horse = new FarmAnimal(2, Location.Stable);
        Animal cow = new FarmAnimal(3, Location.Pen);

        pig.move(Location.Paddock);
        horse.move(Location.Pen);
        cow.move(Location.Pasture);
    }
}
```

Output:

```
Id=1 is moving from Barn to Paddock
Id=2 is moving from Stable to Pen
Id=3 is moving from Pen to Pasture
```

In the above example, the class *FarmAnimal* is an abstraction used in place of an actual farm animal like horse, pig, cow, etc. In future, you can have *WildAnimal, Circus-*

Animal, etc extending the *Animal* class to provide an abstraction for wild animals like zebra, giraffe, etc and circus animals like lion, tiger, elephant, etc respectively. An *Animal* is a further abstraction generalizing *FarmAnimal*, *WildAnimal*, and *CircusAnimal*. The *Location* is coded as an enumeration for simplicity. The *Location* itself can be an abstract class or an interface providing an abstraction for *OpenLocation*, *EnclosedLocation*, and *SecuredLocation* further abstracting specific location details like barn, pen, pasture, pigsty, stable, cage, etc. The location details can be represented with attributes like "name", "type", etc.

The *FarmAnimal* class is also well encapsulated by declaring the attribute "location" as private. Hence the "location" variable cannot be directly accessed. Assignment is only allowed through the constructor and *move(Location location)* method, only after a successful precondition check with the *validateLocation(...)* method. The *validateLocation(...)* itself marked private as it is an internal detail that does not have to be exposed to the caller. In practice, the public *move(..)* method can make use of many other private methods that are hidden from the caller. The caller only needs to know **what** can be done with an *Animal*. For example, they can be moved from one location to another. The internal details as to **how** the animals are moved is not exposed to the caller. These implementation details are specific to *FarmAnimal*, *WildAnimal*, and *CircusAnimal* classes.

Working with abstract classes and interfaces

Q13 What do you understand by abstract classes and interfaces? **LF FAQ**

A13 Classes, which contain at least one abstract method, are called **abstract classes**. An abstract class cannot be instantiated as it is meant for extension. Abstract classes may contain a mixture of non-abstract and abstract methods. Non-abstract methods implement the method statements. Any concrete subclass, which extends the class containing abstract methods, must provide the implementation for all the abstract methods.

```
package subclass2;

public abstract class Animal {

    public void about( ) {
        System.out.println("It is a living organism.");
```

```
    }

    public void intro() {
        System.out.println("Animals are eukaryotes.");
    }

    public abstract void sound();
}
```

A concrete class that extends the abstract class is required to provide a concrete implementation to the the abstract method sound( ). If it does not provide a concrete implementation, then the extending class should be marked abstract as well. Also note that the subclasses can achieve code reuse from their parent class by invoking

- a method in the parent directly if that method is not overridden by the subclass and
- using the **super.**_methodName( )_ if a parent class method is overridden by the subclasses.

```
package subclass2;

public class Cat extends Animal {

    @Override
    public void about() {
        super.about();                  //code reuse via implementation inheritance
        intro();                        //code reuse via implementation inheritance
        System.out.println("There are wild and domestic cats.");
    }

    @Override
    public void sound() {
        System.out.println("Meow Meow");
    }
}
```

```
package subclass2;

public class Example {
```

248

```
public static void main(String[ ] args) {
    //stored obj type = Cat & referencing obj type = Animal
    Animal animal = new Cat( );
    animal.about( );
    animal.sound( );
}
}
```

Output:

It is a living organism.
Animals are eukaryotes.
There are wild and domestic cats.
Meow Meow

UML Diagram:

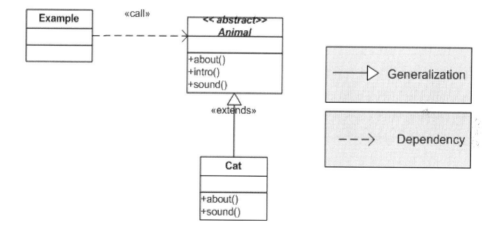

An **interface** is a named collection of method definitions without implementations. An interface defines a set of methods, but does not implement them. A class that implements the interface agrees to implement all of the methods defined in the interface, thereby agreeing to certain behavior. The code reuse for interface inheritance is achieved via **composition**.

```
package subclass2b;

public interface Animal {
   public String getName( );
   public  void about( );
}
```

```
package subclass2b;

public interface Soundable {
   public void sound( );
}
```

The implementing classes must provide the concrete implementation of the interface methods. You can see multiple-interface inheritance in action as the *Cat* inherits methods from both *Animal* and *Soundable*.

```
package subclass2b;

//implements multiple interfaces
public class Cat implements Animal, Soundable {

   private String name = "cat";

   private AnimalHelper helper = new AnimalHelper( );  //composition

   public String getName( ){
      return this.name;
   }

   public void sound( ) {
      System.out.println("Meow Meow");
   }

   public void about( ) {
      helper.about( );          //code reuse via composition
      helper.intro( );          //code reuse via composition
      System.out.println("There are wild and domestic cats.");
   }
```

```
}
```

The *AnimalHelper* class is a composed class, and will be reused for the *Dog* class as shown below.

```
package subclass2b;

//implements multiple interfaces
public class Dog implements Animal, Soundable {

    private String name = "dog";
    private AnimalHelper helper = new AnimalHelper();   //composition

    public String getName(){
        return this.name;
    }

    public void sound() {
        System.out.println("Wow Wow");
    }

    public void about() {
        helper.about();                 //code reuse via composition
        helper.intro();                 //code reuse via composition
        System.out.println("There are wild and domestic dogs.");
    }
}
```

The composed helper class is:

```
package subclass2b;

public class AnimalHelper {

    public void about() {
        System.out.println("It is a living organism.");
    }

    public void intro() {
```

```
        System.out.println("Animals are eukaryotes.");
    }
}
```

Finally, the code snippet that shows interface inheritance and polymorphism in action:

```java
package subclass2b;

import static java.lang.System.out;

public class Example {

    public static void main(String[ ] args) {

        Example example = new Example( );

        Animal cat = new Cat( );                    // Line A
        Animal dog = new Dog( );                    // Line B

        example.aboutAnimal(cat);
        example.makeSound(cat);

        example.aboutAnimal(dog);
        example.makeSound(dog);

        example.printName(cat);
        example.printName(dog);
    }

    //takes an Animal as a parameter
    public void makeSound(Animal animal) {
        if(!(animal instanceof Soundable)){
            throw new IllegalArgumentException(animal + "is not soundable!!");
        }
        ((Soundable) animal).sound( );   // depending on the stored animal, right
                                         // method gets executed polymorphically.

    }

    //takes an Animal as a parameter
```

```
public void aboutAnimal(Animal animal) {
    animal.about();              // depending on the stored animal, right
                                 // method gets executed polymorphically.
}

//takes an Animal as a parameter
public void printName(Animal animal) {
    //depending on the stored animal, right method gets executed polymorphically.
    out.println("Stored obj is a --> " + animal.getName());
}
}
```

Output:

```
It is a living organism.
Animals are eukaryotes.
There are wild and domestic cats.
Meow Meow
It is a living organism.
Animals are eukaryotes.
There are wild and domestic dogs.
Wow Wow
Stored obj is a --> cat
Stored obj is a --> dog
```

The big benefits of programming to interfaces comes when the implementation comes to a object at runtime, for instance via constructor, parameter, factory, dependency injection, etc. In the above example, the methods *makeSound(..)*, *aboutAnimal(..)*, and *printName(..)* takes an instance of an *Animal* object as a parameter at runtime. Depending on the type of animal stored (e.g. *Cat* or *Dog*), the right method gets invoked polymorphically.

UML diagram:

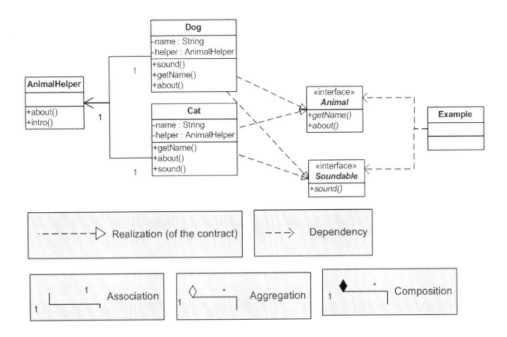

Note: In UML terms, association relationship denotes that two classes are connected with each other. A **navigability** arrow on an association shows which direction the association can be traversed or queried. For example, a *Dog* can be queried about its *AnimalHelper* or traversed to the *AnimalHelper*. The **multiplicity** of an association end is the number of possible instances of the class associated with a single instance of the other end. In the above example, there can be only one *AnimalHelper* for each *Dog*.

Association example,

```
// A Message has an association with a Person
public class Message {
    private Person recipient;
    private Person sender;
    private String text;

    public Message(Person recipient, Person sender, String text) {
        this.recipient = recipient;
        this.sender = sender;
        this.text = text;
    }
}
```

```
}
```

Aggregation and composition are two types of associations. An aggregation is a weaker relationship as shown below where the life cycle of a *Product* is not controlled by the *LineItem*. If a line item is deleted, the associated product does not have to be deleted as well. This product can be used by other line items in other orders.

```
// A LineItem is an aggregate of Product & Quantity
public class LineItem {

    private Product product;
    private Quantity qty;

    public LineItem(Product product, Quantity qty) {
        this.product = product;      // product & qty are created outside this
        this.qty = qty;              //constructor and passed in.
    }

    //...
}
```

Composition is a stronger relationship where the life cycle of the composed class is managed by the composing class as shown below. If an order is deleted, the line item needs to be deleted as well.

```
//An Order is composed of a LineItem and controls life cycle of the LineItem
public class Order {
    private LineItem lineItem;

    public Order() {
        this.lineItem = new LineItem(...);   //lineItem is built in the enclosing
                                             //object's (i.e. Order's) constructor.

    }
    //....
}
```

Conceptually an animal is **composed** of legs, head, heart, etc and **aggregated** (or preferably use associated) with location (i.e. where they live?), toys, breeder, owner, etc.

Q14 What is the significance of abstract classes & interfaces with respect to OO design? `DC FAQ`

A14 In object oriented design, you want the base class to present only an interface for its derived classes. This means, you don't want anyone to actually instantiate an object of the base class. You only want to up cast to it (i.e. implicit up casting, which gives you **polymorphic** behavior), so that its interface can be used. This is accomplished by making a class abstract using the abstract keyword. If anyone tries to make an object of an abstract class, the compiler prevents it. This was demonstrated earlier in this section with the *Animal* class, which is marked abstract.

The interface keyword takes this concept of an abstract class a step further by preventing any method or function implementation at all. You can only declare a method or function, but not provide an implementation. The class, which is implementing the interface, should provide the actual implementation. An interface is a very useful and commonly used aspect in OO design, as it provides the separation of interface and implementation, and enables you to:

- Capture similarities among unrelated classes without artificially forcing a class relationship.

- Declare methods that one or more classes are expected to implement.

- Reveal an object's programming interface without revealing its actual implementation.

- Model **multiple interface inheritance** in Java, which provides some of the benefits of full on **multiple implementation inheritance**, a feature that Java does not support, but some object-oriented languages support by allowing a class to have more than one superclass.

Q15 What can an interface do that an abstract class cannot? What are the differences between abstract classes and interfaces? `LF FAQ`

Abstract class	**Interface**
A class may extend only one abstract class. This gives you implementation inheritance.	A class may implement several interfaces. This gives you multiple interface inheritance.
Has implementation methods and abstract methods.	Has no implementation methods. All methods are abstract.
If you add a new method to an abstract class, you have the option of providing a default implementation of it in the abstract class. Then all implementing classes will continue to work without change. If the new method must be abstract, then you must track down all implementations of this abstract class and provide them with a concrete implementation of this method.	If you add a new method to an interface, you must track down all implementations of that interface in your entire code base and provide them with a concrete implementation of that method.
The visibility of abstract methods can be public, protected or package-private.	The visibility of interface methods can be either public or package-private (i.e. no access modifier).
Represents **is-a/is-an** relationship. For example,	Represents **can-do** or **-able** relationship. For example,

``
class Cat extends Animal {
    public void run( ) {
        ....
    }
}
``
	``
	Class MyDevice implements Runnable {
	    public void run( ) {
	        ....
	    }
	}
	``

This can be read as, a *Cat* **is-an** animal.	This can be read as *MyDevice* is Runn**able** or *MyDevice* **can run** as a separate *Thread*.

Q16 When would you prefer one over the other? **DC DP COQ**

A16 **When to use an abstract class?** In case where you want to use implementation inheritance, then it is usually provided by an abstract base class. Abstract classes are excellent candidates inside of application frameworks. Abstract classes let you define some default behavior in the base class and force subclasses to provide any specific behavior. For example, **template method**(e.g. Struts *RequestProcessor* class) and **composite** (e.g. Swing API component and container classes) design patterns make use of abstract classes. Care should be taken not to overuse implementation inheritance.

When to use an interface? In case where you want to use interface inheritance, where a client wants to only deal with a type and does not care about the actual implementation, use interfaces. If you need to change your design frequently, you should prefer using interfaces instead of abstract classes. Coding to an interface **reduces coupling** and interface inheritance can achieve code reuse with the help of object composition using the helper classes. Another justification for using interfaces is that they solve the 'diamond problem' of traditional multiple inheritance as shown in the diagram. Java does not support multiple inheritance. Java only supports multiple interface inheritance. Interface will solve many of the ambiguities caused by this 'diamond problem'.

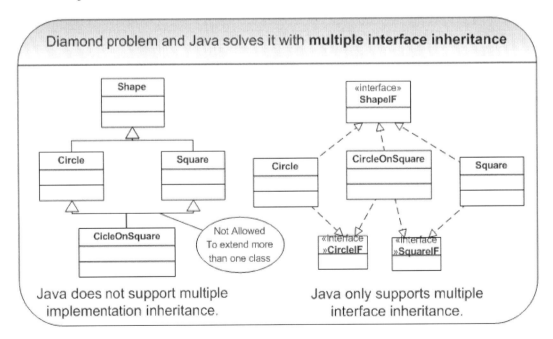

Q17 Can interfaces have constant declarations? **BP DP COQ**

A17 An interface can also include constant (i.e. only public static final) declarations. For example,

```
public interface MyConstants {
    public static final int i = 12;
    int j = 13;
}
```

Every field declaration in the body of an interface is implicitly public, static, and final. However, it is a bad practice (i.e. an anti-pattern) to define your constants via an interface as shown above. Please refer to Q25 – What is a constant interface anti-pattern? How will you avoid it? in section "Language Essentials" for further details.

Q18 What modifiers can be used in an interface? **LF**

A18 An interface can only be public or package-private (i.e. no access modifier) scoped.

Q19 Can you give an example of an interface driven framework in the Java API? **OEQ**

A19 The Java collection framework is an interface based framework. The interfaces used to represent different types of collections are *Collection*, *List*, *Set* and *Map*. The *Comparable* and *Comparator* interfaces address natural and specialized orderings respectively.

Q20 What are marker interfaces in Java? Why to have marker interfaces? **LF FAQ**

A20 The interfaces with no defined methods are called marker interfaces or null interfaces. They just tell the compiler that the objects of the classes implementing the interfaces with no defined methods need to be treated differently. For example, *java.io.Serializable*, *java.lang.Cloneable*, *java.util.EventListener*, *java.rmi.Remote*, etc. Marker interfaces are also known as "tag" interfaces since they tag all the derived classes into a category based on their purpose.

DC PC Now with the introduction of annotations in Java 5, the marker interfaces make less sense from a design standpoint. Annotations are more flexible than marker interfaces. Annotations can have parameters and can not only be applied to classes, but to methods, fields etc. as well. Refer to Q23: Are marker or tag interfaces obsolete with the advent of annotations (i.e. runtime annotations)? in "Platform Essentials" section for more detail.

Inheritance versus composition

Q21 How do you achieve code reuse in your application? **DC**

A21 Through implementation inheritance, composition, and delegation.

Q22 How do you achieve polymorphic behavior? **DC**

A22 Through implementation inheritance or interface inheritance.

Q23 What is the difference between implementation inheritance and composition? **DC**
FAQ

A23 Inheritance is modeled on "**is-a/is-an**" relationship and composition is modeled on "**has-a/has-an**" relationship. There is a weaker composition relationship known as **delegation**. The delegation is modeled on "**uses a/uses an**" relationship. As shown below, the *AnimalHelper* is not composed within the *Cat* class, but the *Cat* class uses an *AnimalHelper* to achieve code reuse.

```java
public class Cat implements Animal, Soundable {

    private String name = "cat";

    public String getName(){
        return this.name;
    }

    public void sound() {
        System.out.println("Meow Meow");
    }

    public void about() {
        AnimalHelper helper = new AnimalHelper();
        helper.about();                          //code reuse through delegation
        helper.intro();                          //code reuse through  delegation
        System.out.println("There are wild and domestic cats.");
    }
}
```

Inheritance happens at compile-time and composition/delegation happens at runtime. Please refer to Q22 - Can you differentiate compile-time inheritance and runtime inheritance with examples and specify which Java supports? in section "Platform Essentials". It is always tempting to create an inheritance hierarchy to get all the functionality provided by a common base class. This is a pitfall and care should be taken in modeling an "is-a" relationship as discussed later. For example,

- A *Dog* or *Cat* "**is an**" *Animal* (Implementation inheritance → in UML: **generalization** and interface inheritance → in UML: **realization**)
- A *Dog* "**has an**" *AnimalHelper* (Composition → in UML: **association**, **composition**, or **aggregation**)
- A *Dog* "**uses an**" *AnimalHelper* (Delegation → in UML: **dependency**)

Q24 What questions do you ask yourself to choose composition (i.e. has-a relationship) for code reuse over implementation inheritance (i.e. is-a relationship)? **DC FAQ SBQ**

A24 **Do my subclasses only change the implementation and not the meaning or internal intent of the base class?** Is every object of type *Dog* really "is-an" object of type *Animal*? Have I checked this for "Liskov Substitution Principle"?

According to **Liskov substitution principle (LSP)**, a *Square* is not a *Rectangle* provided they are mutable. Mathematically a square is a rectangle, but behaviorally a rectangle needs to have both length and width, whereas a square only needs a width.

Another typical example would be, an *Account* class having a method called *calculateInterest(..)*. You can derive two subclasses named *SavingsAccount* and *ChequeAccount* that reuse the super class method. But you cannot have another class called a *MortgageAccount* to subclass the above *Account* class. This will break the Liskov substitution principle because the **intent** is different. The savings and cheque accounts calculate the interest due to the customer, but the mortgage or home loan accounts calculate the interest due to the bank.

Violation of LSP results in all kinds of mess like failing unit tests, unexpected or strange behavior, and violation of open closed principle (OCP) as you end up having if-else or switch statements to resolve the correct subclass. For example,

```
if(shape instanceof Square){
    //....
}
else if (shape instanceof Rectangle){
    //....
```

```
}
```

If you cannot truthfully answer yes to the above questions, then favor using "has-a" relationship (i.e. composition). Don't use "is-a" relationship for just convenience. If you try to force an "is-a" relationship, your code may become inflexible, post-conditions and invariants may become weaker or violated, your code may behave unexpectedly, and the API may become very confusing. LSP is the reason it is hard to create deep class hierarchies.

Always ask yourself, can this be modeled with a "has-a" relationship to make it more flexible? For example, If you want to model a circus dog, will it be better to model it with "is a" relationship as in a *CircusDog* "is a" *Dog* or model it as a **role** that a dog plays? If you implement it with implementation inheritance, you will end up with sub classes like *CircusDog*, *DomesticDog*, *GuideDog*, *SnifferDog*, and *StrayDog*. In future, if the dogs are differentiated by locality like local, national, international, etc, you may have another level of hierarchy like *LocalCircusDog, NationalCicusDog, InternationalCircusDog*, etc extending the class *CircusDog*. So you may end up having 1 animal x 1 dog x 5 roles x 3 localities = 15 dog related classes. If you were to have similar differentiation for cats, you will end up having similar cat hierarchy like *WildCat, DomesticCat, LocalWildCat, NationalWildCat*, etc. This will make your classes strongly coupled.

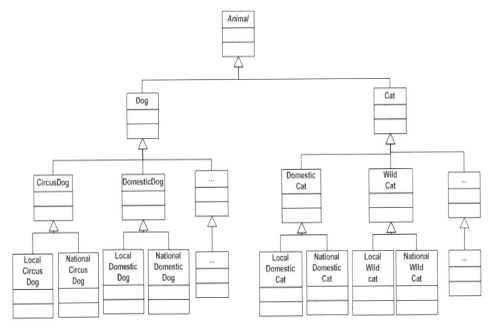

If you implement it with interface inheritance, and composition for code reuse, you can think of circus dog as a **role** that a dog plays. These roles provide an abstraction to be used with any other animals like cat, horse, donkey, etc, and not just dogs. The role becomes a "has a" relationship. There will be an attribute of interface type *Role* defined in the *Dog* class as a composition that can take on different subtypes (using interface inheritance) such as *CircusRole*, *DomesticRole*, *GuideRole*, *SnifferRole*, and *StrayRole* at runtime. The locality can also be modeled similar to the role as a composition. This will enable different combinations of roles and localities to be constructed at runtime with 1 dog + 5 roles + 3 localities = 9 classes and 3 interfaces (i.e. *Animal*, *Role* and *Locality*). As the number of roles, localities, and types of animals increases, the gap widens between the two approaches. You will get a better abstraction with looser coupling with this approach as composition is dynamic and takes place at runtime compared to implementation inheritance, which is static.

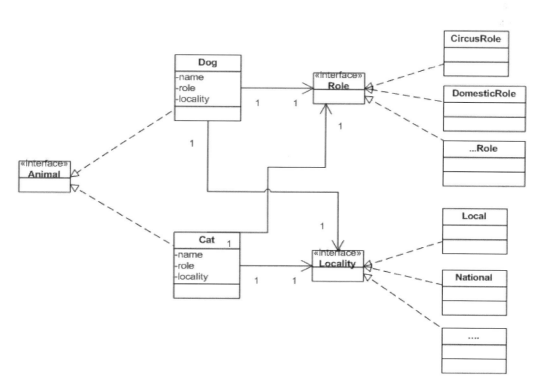

The following code snippet demonstrates the power of interface inheritance with composition. Firstly, define the interfaces,

```
package subclass4;

public interface Animal {
    public String getName();
    public void display();
}
```

```
package subclass4;

public interface Role {
    public void displayRole();
}
```

```
package subclass4;

public interface Locality {
    public void displayLocality();
}
```

Secondly, the concrete classes that implement these interfaces to demonstrate interface inheritance.

```
package subclass4;

public class Dog implements Animal {

    private String name = "dog";

    //composition (strictly speaking in UML terms, this is an aggregation as the
    // life cycle of role and locality are not managed by the Animal.)
    Role role;
    Locality locality;

    public Dog(String name,Role role, Locality locality) {
        super();
        this.name = name;
        this.role = role;
        this.locality = locality;
    }
```

```java
  public String getName( ){
     return this.name;
  }

  public String setName( ){
     return this.name;
  }

  @Override
  public void display( ) {
    System.out.println(getName( ));
    role.displayRole( );
    locality.displayLocality( );
  }
}
```

```java
package subclass4;

public class CircusRole implements Role {

  @Override
  public void displayRole( ) {
     System.out.println("I play on circuses.");
  }
}
```

```java
package subclass4;

public class GuideRole implements Role {

  @Override
  public void displayRole( ) {
    System.out.println("I guide people.");
  }
}
```

```java
package subclass4;
```

```
public class Local implements Locality {

    @Override
    public void displayLocality( ) {
        System.out.println("I am a local dog");
    }
}
```

```
package subclass4;

public class International implements Locality {

    @Override
    public void displayLocality( ) {
        System.out.println("I am an international dog");
    }
}
```

Finally and most importantly, the example class that demonstrates how the combinations can be built on the fly at runtime.

```
package subclass4;

public class Example {

    public static void main(String[ ] args) {
        //code to interface
        Role roleA = new GuideRole( );
        Locality localityA = new Local( );
        Role roleB = new CircusRole( );
        Locality localityB = new International( );

        //you can create different combinations at runtime
        Animal dog1 = new Dog("ABBY", roleA, localityA);
        Animal dog2 = new Dog("ABEL", roleB, localityB);
        Animal dog3 = new Dog("ABERCROMBIE", roleA, localityB);
        Animal dog4 = new Dog("ABRACADABRA", roleB, localityA);

        dog1.display( );
```

```
        dog2.display( );
        dog3.display( );
        dog4.display( );
    }
}
```

Output:

```
ABBY
I guide people.
I am a local dog
ABEL
I play on circuses.
I am an international dog
ABERCROMBIE
I guide people.
I am an international dog
ABRACADABRA
I play on circuses.
I am a local dog
```

Note: The programming language like OT/J from the Object Teams (http://www.objectteams.org/) is a Java extension that implements natively the idea of objects playing roles.

Q25 Can you give an example where composition is favored over implementation inheritance? **DC DP OEQ**

A25 The GoF design patterns favor use of interfaces with composition for code reuse over abstract classes. Design patterns like **strategy** (e.g. Java Collection framework) lets you swap new algorithms and processes into your program without altering the objects that use them. Other popular design patterns that favor interfaces are **decorator** (e.g. the Java I/O classes) and **proxy** (e.g. RMI and EJB).

Q26 Can you give an example of the Java API that favors composition? **DC DP OEQ**

A26 The Java IO classes that use composition to construct different combinations using the decorator design pattern at runtime.

```
//construct a reader
StringReader sr = new StringReader("Some Text....");
```

```
//decorate the reader for performance
BufferedReader br = new BufferedReader(sr);
//decorate again to obtain line numbers
LineNumberReader lnr = new LineNumberReader(br);
```

Applying the design principles

Q27 How will you improve on the following code snippets with appropriate design principles? **DC COQ SBQ**

```java
package principle_srp1;

import java.sql.Connection;
import java.sql.SQLException;
import org.apache.commons.lang.StringUtils;

public class Animal {

    private Integer id;
    private String name;
    private Connection con = null;

    //getters and setters for above attributes go here..

    public boolean validate( ) {
        return id != null && id > 0 && StringUtils.isNotBlank(name);
    }

    public void saveAnimal( ) throws SQLException {
        //save Animal to database using SQL
        //goes here ...
    }

    public Animal readAnimal( ) throws SQLException {
        //read Animal from database using SQL
        //...
        Animal animal = null;
```

```
    //...
    return animal;
  }
}
```

A27 The above class represents 3 different responsibilities.

- Uniquely identifies an animal with id and name.
- Interacts with the database to save and read an animal.
- Validates the animal details.

Hence, the above class violates the **Single Responsibility Principle** (SRP), which states that a class should have only one reason to change. This principle is based on **cohesion**. Cohesion is a measure of how strongly a class focuses on its responsibilities. It is of the following two types:

- **High cohesion:** This means that a class is designed to carry on a specific and precise task. Using high cohesion, methods are easier to understand, as they perform a single task.

- **Low cohesion:** This means that a class is designed to carry on various tasks. Using low cohesion, methods are difficult to understand and maintain.

Hence the above code suffers from low cohesion. The above code can be improved as shown below. The *Animal* class is re-factored to have only a single responsibility of uniquely identifying an animal.

```
package principle_srp1a;

public class Animal {

    private Integer id;
    private String name;

    public Integer getId( ) {
        return id;
    }
    public void setId(Integer id) {
```

```
      this.id = id;
   }
   public String getName( ) {
      return name;
   }
   public void setName(String name) {
      this.name = name;
   }
}
```

The responsibility of interacting with the database is shifted to a data access object (i.e. DAO) class. The data access object class takes an animal object or any of its attributes as input.

```
package principle_srp1a;

public interface AnimalDao {
   public void saveAnimal(Animal animal);
   public Animal readAnimal(Integer id);
}
```

```
package principle_srp1a;

import java.sql.Connection;

public class AnimalDaoImpl implements AnimalDao {

   private Connection con = null;

   // getters and setters for above attributes
   // go here..

   @Override
   public void saveAnimal(Animal animal) {
      // save Animal to database using SQL
      // goes here ...
   }

   @Override
```

```
public Animal readAnimal(Integer id) {
    // read Animal from database using SQL
    // goes here ...
    Animal animal = null;
    // ...
    return animal;
}
}
```

Finally, the responsibility of validating an animal is re-factored to a separate class that takes an animal object as input.

```
package principle_srp1a;

public interface Validator {
    public boolean validate(Animal animal);
}
```

```
package principle_srp1a;

import org.apache.commons.lang.StringUtils;

public class AnimalValidator implements Validator {

    @Override
    public boolean validate(Animal animal) {
        return animal.getId() != null && animal.getId() > 0
            && StringUtils.isNotBlank(animal.getName());
    }
}
```

You now have 3 classes that have clear separation of concerns. The Animal class has been decoupled from database concern and validation concern. The above code is also well encapsulated and highly cohesive.

The challenge with SRP is getting the granularity of a responsibility right. One of the most common complaints about SRP is object explosion. This is a valid complaint, but when things are broken down by concern as shown above, it is far easier to consider the concern in isolation and come up with a better design for that single concern. The art of design is all about striking a good balance by asking the right questions and not blindly following a principle.

Q28 Is there anything wrong with the following code snippet? **DC COQ SBQ**

```java
package principle_ocp1;

public interface Animal {
    //methods are left out for brevity
}
```

```java
package principle_ocp1;

public class Cat implements Animal {
    //methods are left out for brevity
}
```

```java
package principle_ocp1;

public class Spider implements Animal {
    //methods are left out for brevity
}
```

```java
package principle_ocp1;

public class Ostritch implements Animal {
    //methods are left out for brevity
}
```

```java
package principle_ocp1;

import java.util.List;

public class AnimalLegsCounter {

    public int count(List<Animal> animals) {
        int count = 0;
        for (Animal animal : animals) {
            if (animal instanceof Cat) {
```

```
            count += 4;
        } else if (animal instanceof Spider) {
            count += 8;
        } else if (animal instanceof Ostritch) {
            count += 2;
        }
    }
    return count;
}
}
```

```
package principle_ocp1;

import java.util.ArrayList;
import java.util.List;

public class Example {

    public static void main(String[ ] args) {
        List<Animal> list = new ArrayList<Animal>();
        Animal animal = new Cat( );
        list.add(animal);
        animal = new Spider( );
        list.add(animal);
        animal = new Ostritch( );
        list.add(animal);

        int count = new AnimalLegsCounter( ).count(list);
        System.out.println("Total count for " + list.size( )  + " animals = " + count);

    }
}
```

A28 The above code violates the open closed principle (OCP). As time goes on, you may want to add more animals like dog, crab, dragon fly, etc with differing number of legs. This will require you to modify the *AnimalLegCounter* class' *count(...)* method with more else-if statements like:

```
if (animal instanceof Cat || animal instanceof Dog) {
```

```
      count += 4;
} else if (animal instanceof Spider) {
      count += 8;
} else if (animal instanceof Ostrich) {
      count += 2;
} else if (animal instanceof Crab) {
      count += 10;
} else if (animal instanceof DragonFly) {
      count += 6;
}
```

This shows that the class *AnimalLegCounter* is not **closed for modification** as you will have to modify it in order to extend it. In other words, this means it is not **open for extension**. The above example is a trivial one, but in real world applications, the code base might be 10 to 1000 times larger and modifying a class is not a trivial task.

Any time you see big if/else or switch statements, you should think about polymorphism. The code below shows how the real counting logic can be moved to the *count( )* method in individual animal classes, and the *AnimalLegCounter* classes' *count( )* method only makes use of the *count( )* method in the *Animal* classes to make it adhere to the OCP principle using polymorphism as shown below.

```java
package principle_ocp2;

public interface Animal {
    //other methods are left out for brevity
    public abstract int count();
}
```

```java
package principle_ocp2;

public class Cat implements Animal {
    //other methods are left out for brevity

    @Override
    public int count() {
        return 4;
    }
}
```

```java
package principle_ocp2;

public class Ostritch implements Animal {
    //other methods are left out for brevity

    @Override
    public int count() {
        return 2;
    }
}
```

```java
package principle_ocp2;

public class Spider implements Animal {

    //other methods are left out for brevity

    @Override
    public int count() {
        return 8;
    }
}
```

```java
package principle_ocp2;

import java.util.List;

public class AnimalLegsCounter {

    public int count(List<Animal> animals) {
        int count = 0;
        for (Animal animal : animals) {
            count += animal.count();
        }
        return count;
    }
}
```

Classes and Interfaces Essentials

Now, if you want to add more animals like dog, crab, etc, all you have to do is add the relevant classes like *Dog*, *Crab*, etc implementing the same *Animal* interface, and provide the *count(...)* method implementation. The *AnimalLegsCounter* class does not have to be modified at all. In other words, the *AnimalLegsCounter* class is closed for modification by opening it up for extension through adding new classes.

Q29 How can you improve on the following code snippet? **DC COQ SBQ**

```
package principle_dip1;

public class CircusService {

  TigerHandler handler;

  public void setHandler(TigerHandler handler) {
    this.handler = handler;
  }

  public void showStarts() {
    //code omitted for brevity
    handler.handle();
  }
}
```

```
package principle_dip1;

public class TigerHandler {

  TigerHelper helper;

  public void setHelper(TigerHelper helper) {
    this.helper = helper;
  }

  public void handle(){
    //...
    helper.help();
    //...
  }
}
```

276

```
}

package principle_dip1;

public class TigerHelper {

   public void help( ){
      //......
   }
}
```

A29   The above three classes are tightly coupled with each other. The high level class
      CircusService depends on the lower level class *TigerHandler* and the *TigerHandler* in turn
      depends on the lower level class *TigerHelper*. All these classes are directly <u>dependent on
      the implementation</u> as opposed <u>to the abstraction</u>. If some time in the future, the
      circus service needs to deal with an elephant as opposed to a tiger, and you will have to
      change the *CircusService* class to use the newly written *ElephantHandler* instead of the
      TigerHandler. If you want to use an *ImprovedTigerHelper* instead of the *TigerHelper*, you
      will have to change all the handler classes that use the *TigerHelper*. If the *CircusService*
      wants to expand into other animals, then there will be more changes across various
      classes. This shows that the above code is rigid. This situation can be improved by
      applying the dependency inversion principle.

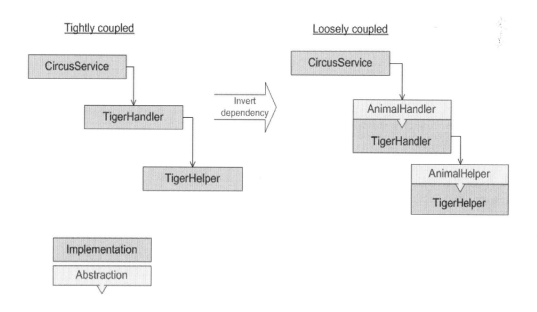

The Dependency Inversion Principle (DIP) states that

- High level modules should not depend upon low level modules. Both should depend upon abstractions.
- Abstractions should not depend upon details. Details should depend upon abstractions.

When this principle is applied, the higher level classes will not be working directly with the lower level classes, but with an abstract layer. This gives us the flexibility at the cost of increased effort. The classes that are less likely to change don't need to apply this principle. Blindly applying this principle can make a system more complex.

The above code can be improved by using the dependency inversion principle (DIP) as shown below:

Firstly define the abstraction layer.

```
package principle_dip2;

public interface AnimalHandler {
    public abstract void handle( );
}
```

```
package principle_dip2;

public interface AnimalHelper {
    public abstract void help( );
}
```

Now the implementation that depends on the abstraction as opposed to the implementation.

```
package principle_dip2;

public class CircusService {

    AnimalHandler handler;
```

```
public void setHandler(AnimalHandler handler) {
    this.handler = handler;
}

public void showStarts() {
    //code omitted for brevity
    handler.handle();
}
}
```

```
package principle_dip2;

public class TigerHandler implements AnimalHandler{

    AnimalHelper helper;

    public void setHelper(AnimalHelper helper) {
        this.helper = helper;
    }

    public void handle(){
        //...
        helper.help();
        //...
    }
}
```

```
package principle_dip2;

public class TigerHelper implements AnimalHelper{

    public void help(){
        //......
    }
}
```

Q30 What is your understanding of some of the following most talked terms like Dependency Inversion Principle (**DIP),** Dependency Injection (**DI)** and Inversion of Control (**IoC**)? **DC COQ FAQ**

A30 **Dependency Inversion Principle** (DIP) is a design principle which is in some ways related to the Dependency Injection (DI) pattern. The idea of DIP is that higher layers of your application should not directly depend on lower layers. Dependency Inversion Principle does not imply Dependency Injection. This principle doesn't say anything about <u>how higher layers know what lower layer to use.</u> This could be done as shown in the above example, or through Dependency Injection by using an IoC container like Spring framework, Pico container, Guice, or Apache HiveMind.

Dependency Injection (DI) is a pattern of injecting a class's dependencies into it at runtime. This is achieved by defining the dependencies as interfaces, and then injecting in a concrete class implementing that interface to the constructor. This allows you to swap in different implementations without having to modify the main class. The Dependency Injection pattern also promotes high cohesion by promoting the Single Responsibility Principle (SRP), since your dependencies are individual objects which perform discrete specialized tasks like data access (via DAOs) and business services (via Service and Delegate classes) .

The **Inversion of Control Container** (IoC) is a container that supports Dependency Injection. In this you use a central container like Spring framework, Guice, or HiveMind, which defines what concrete classes should be used for what dependencies through out your application. This brings in an added flexibility through looser coupling, and it makes it much easier to change what dependencies are used on the fly.

The real power of DI and IoC is realized in its ability to replace the compile time binding of the relationships between classes with binding those relationships at runtime. For example, in Seam framework, you can have a real and mock implementation of an interface, and at runtime decide which one to use based on a property, presence of another file, or some precedence values. This is incredibly useful if you think you may need to modify the way your application behaves in different scenarios. Another real benefit of DI and IoC is that it makes your code easier to unit test. There are other benefits like promoting looser coupling without any proliferation of factory and singleton design patterns, follows a consistent approach for lesser experienced developers to follow, etc. These benefits can come in at the cost of the added complexity to your application and has to be carefully manged by using them only at the right places where the real benefits are realized, and not just using them because many others are using them.

Note: The CDI (Contexts and Dependency Injection) is an attempt at describing a true standard on Dependency Injection. CDI is a part of the Java EE 6 stack, meaning an application running in a Java EE 6 compatible container can leverage CDI out-of-the-box. Weld is the reference implementation of CDI.

Q31 Can you list some of the key principles to remember while designing your classes? **DC** **OEQ**

A31

- Favor composition over inheritance.
- Don't Repeat Yourself (**DRY** principle). Code once and only once.
- Find what varies and encapsulate it.
- Code to an interface, and not to an implementation.
- Strive for loose coupling and high cohesion.

Use design principles and patterns, but use them judiciously. Design for current requirements without anticipating future requirements, and over complicating things. A well designed (i.e. loosely coupled and more cohesive) system can easily lend itself to future changes, whilst keeping the system less complex.

Designing an application or a system

Q32 How would you go about designing a system as described below? **OEQ SBQ**

A barn that contains animals such as cows and horses. A farmer milks the cows in the farm, and the animals eat hay that are stored in the barn. The barn is constructed with wooden planks.

A32 [Hint:]

"is a" relationships

A *Cow* is an animal, and so is a *Horse*.

"has a" relationships

Zero to many (i.e. 0..*) animals live in a *Barn*. The *Barn* is also made of at least 1 and probably many (i.e. 1..*) *WoodenPlanks*. The *Barn* also stores the *Hay* for the animals.

"uses" relationship(s)

A farmer interacts with many (i.e. 0..*) *Cows* by sending messages.

Conceptualize your thoughts with a UML diagram as shown below.

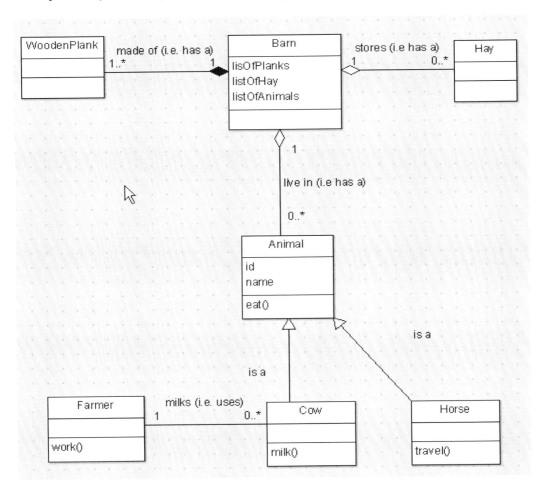

The above class diagram was generated using the open source tool argoUML. In the above design, the animals are tightly coupled to the barn. The above design can be made more flexible to handle other farm animals like hen, etc as shown below. The design below is better because of lower coupling between the animals and the enclosures like *Barn*, *HenHouse*, etc. Similar changes can be applied between the *Enclosure* and the *WoodenPlank* so that the enclosures can be made with other materials like *Mesh*, etc. While designing, you can also think of the design principles discussed above and patterns like factory pattern or dependency injection to promote looser coupling between entities.

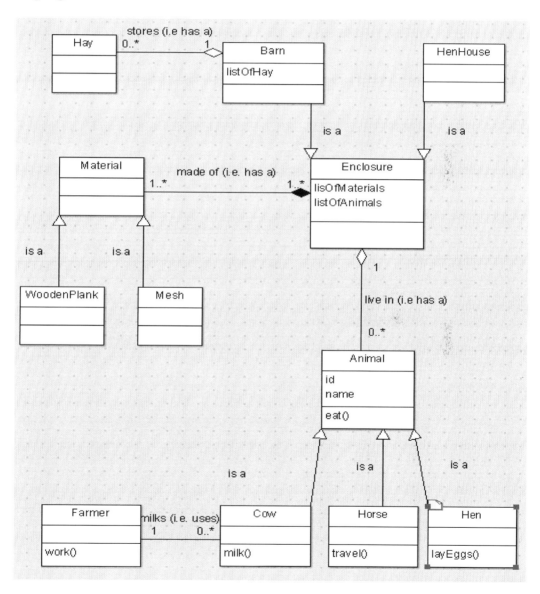

Q33   How would you go about designing a car parking station? **OEQ SBQ**

A33   [Hint: Ask the right questions and map out the requirements.]

Map out the requirements:

- The car park needs to cater for different types of car parks like regular, handicapped, and compact.
- It should keep track of empty and filled spaces.
- It should also cater for valet parking

Map out the classes that would be required. Use a UML class diagram as shown above. Here are some points to get started.

- A *CarPark* class to represent a parking station.
- A *ParkingSpace* can be an abstract class or an interface to represent a parking space, and *RegularParkingSpace*, *HandicappedParkingSpace*, *CompactParkingSpace*, etc are subtypes of a *ParkingSpace*. This means a *RegularParkingSpace* **is a** *ParkingSpace*.
- A *CarPark* **has a** (i.e. composition) finite number of *ParkingSpaces*. A *CarPark* also keeps track of all the parking spaces and a separate list of all the vacant parking spaces.
- A *Vehicle* class **uses a** (i.e. delegation) *ParkingSpace*. The *Vehicle* class will hold attributes using enum classes like *VehicleType* and *ParkingType*. The vehicle types could be *Compact*, *Regular*, and *Handicapped*. The parking types could be *Self* or *Valet*. Depending on the requirements, the self or valet types could be designed as subtypes of the *Vehicle* class.

Note: Care must be taken to have a right balance between over engineering and not engineering at all. All depends on requirements and which parts of the design are most likely to grow in the future phases. The only way to get better at designing is with experience and keeping all the design concepts, principles, and patterns in mind to design a loosely coupled system that is simple, easy to understand, flexible and maintainable.

Class invariant and design by contract

Q34 What is a class invariant? **DC FAQ**

A34 **Class invariant** is -- what must be true about each instance of a class? If an invariant fails then there could be a bug in either calling-method or called-method. It is convenient to put all the expressions required for checking invariants into reusable internal methods that can be called. For example, if you have a class, which deals with only negative integers then you define the *isNegative(..)* convenient internal method as follows:

```
package chapter2.com;

class NegativeInteger {
    Integer value = null;                              //invariant

    // constructor
    public NegativeInteger(Integer val) {

        if (!isNegative(val)) {
            throw new IllegalArgumentException(
                "Invalid negative number = " + val);
        }
        this.value = val;
    }

    public Integer addNumber(Integer val) {
        if (!isNegative(val)) {
            throw new IllegalArgumentException(
                    "Invalid negative number = " + val);
        }

        return this.value + val;
    }

    private boolean isNegative(Integer val) {
        return val.intValue() < 0;
    }
```

```
public static void main(String[ ] args) {
    NegativeInteger val1 = new NegativeInteger(-5);
    System.out.println(val1.addNumber(-3));
    }
}
```

An invariant is more conceptual than a variable. It can be viewed in terms of algorithms and data structures. For example, a binary search tree (i.e. an ordered binary tree) might have the invariant that for every node, the key of the node's left child if not empty is less than the node's own key, and the nodes right child if not empty is more than the node's own key. A correctly written insertion or deletion function for this ordered tree will maintain that invariant.

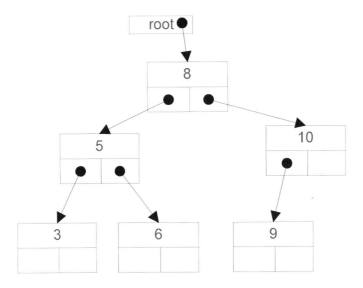

Binary Search Tree (BST)

You could also have a loop invariant that could be verified for being true at the beginning and end of each iteration. For example, you could have a loop that processes a list of orders by moving them from list1 to list2, and you could say that the invariant is *list1.size( ) + list2.size( ) = constant*, at the beginning or end of the loop. If the above invariant check failed, it could indicate that there is a bug in the logic. For example, you may have forgotten to add the processed element from list1 onto list2.

```java
package chapter2.com;

import java.util.ArrayList;
import java.util.List;
import java.util.concurrent.CopyOnWriteArrayList;

import javax.xml.bind.ValidationException;

import org.apache.commons.lang.StringUtils;

public class LoopInvariant {

    public static void main(String[] args) throws ValidationException {
        String[] input = {"age:9", "age=6", "gender:M" , "gender=Male"};
        List<String> outPut = find(input, "=");
        System.out.println(outPut);
    }

    public static List<String> find(String[] input, String toFind) throws
                                                    ValidationException {
        //precondition check
        if(input == null || StringUtils.isEmpty(toFind)){
            throw new IllegalArgumentException("Invlid input !!");
        }

        int initialInputSize = input.length;                        //loop invariant

        List<String> inputList = new CopyOnWriteArrayList<String>(input);  //A
        List<String> outputList = new ArrayList<String>(initialInputSize);

        for (String val : inputList) {
            if(val.contains(toFind)){
                inputList.remove(val);                              //B
                outputList.add(val);
            }

            if(inputList.size () + outputList.size( ) != initialInputSize){    //C
                throw new ValidationException("Loop invariant is violated");
```

287

```
        }
      }
    }

    return outputList;
  }
}
```

Output:

[age=6, gender=Male]

Q. What happens if the line marked with //B is commented?
A. If you comment out the line //B and run the above code, you will get a *ValidationException* as the invariant condition check fails on line //C;

Q. Why *CopyOnWriteArrayList* is used instead of an *ArrayList* or *Arrays.asList(input)*?
A. It is interesting to note that on line marked //A, a concurrent collection class *CopyOnWriteArrayList* is used instead of an *ArrayList* as shown below.

```
List<String> inputList = Arrays.asList(input); //throws UnsupportedOperationException
```

The above line will throw an *java.lang.UnsupportedOperationException* on line \\B. *Arrays.asList( )* returns a list that doesn't allow operations affecting its size. *Array.asList( )* wraps an array in the list interface. The list is still backed by the array. Arrays are fixed size, and they don't support addition or removal of elements, so the wrapper can't either.

If you use the following construct on line //A, you will get a *java.util.ConcurrentModificationException*.

```
List<String> inputList = new ArrayList<String>(Arrays.asList(input));
```

This exception is thrown because the underlying collection is changing while being looped.

BP Programming with invariants is a best practice because you can be confident that your objects are always presented in a consistent state. This will also act as a documentation because programmers often informally write class invariants in documentation or as code comments.

288

Q35 What do you understand by the term "design by contract"? **DC FAQ COQ**

A35 The design by contract ensures code quality by enforcing that the services offered by classes and interfaces adhere to unambiguous contracts. The design by contract is very useful for designing classes and interfaces. These contracts are like checking for an empty or null string, checking for negative numbers, checking for a particular range, etc.

In general the contracts checked are:

- **Pre-conditions:** These are checked when execution enters a method.
- **Post-conditions:** These are checked when execution exits a method.
- **Class invariants:** These must hold at every observable point.

The above contracts have to be followed by the programmer. There is no way to ensure this programmatically.

Contracts are inherited, just like methods. When a method is overridden by a subclass, the subclass may specify its own contracts. This means a subclass may "**weaken the pre-condition and strengthen the post-condition**".

Requirements must be stated in javadoc, and may be enforced by throwing checked or unchecked exceptions when the stated conditions are violated. Using assertions for enforcing requirements is not recommended as assertions can be disabled.

```
package principle_dbc;

import java.math.BigDecimal;

public class Funds {

    private BigDecimal result = null;
    //...

    public BigDecimal calcRate(double rate) {
        //pre-condition check
        if (rate <= BigDecimal.ZERO.doubleValue()
                || rate > BigDecimal.TEN.doubleValue()) {
```

```
        throw new IllegalArgumentException(  "Outside 0.01% - 10.00%");

    }

    // ... logic to calculate the result

    //post-condition check
    if (this.result == null
          || this.result.doubleValue( ) <= BigDecimal.ZERO
              .doubleValue( )) {
        throw new RuntimeException("Invalid result");
    }
    return result;
  }

  //...
}
```

Firstly, in the above code snippet the parameter "rate" is an invariant that must hold true. The *Funds* object's calculation of the result could be incorrect if an invalid "rate" is passed as an argument by its caller. A precondition validation is performed on the "rate" to ensure that the caller fulfills the requirements. Secondly, the implementation of the logic to calculate the result could be defective. So a post-condition validation is performed to verify the correctness of internal logic.

There are a number of frameworks that support "design by contract" like *OVal*, *Jass*, etc. The *OVal* is a validation framework that lets you place the conditions in different ways like annotations, XML, POJO, or scripting languages like Groovy, JavaScript, OGNL (Object Graph Navigation Language – an expression language for getting and setting properties of Java objects), etc and also partly implements programming by contract.

Working with inner classes

Q36 What is an inner class? Can you provide an example from the Java API? When to use inner classes? **LF FAQ**

A36 In Java not all classes have to be defined separate from each other. You can put the definition of one class inside the definition of another class. The inside class is called an inner class and the enclosing class is called an outer class or a top level class. So when you define an inner class, it is a member of the outer class in much the same way as other members like member variables, methods and constructors.

There are two varieties of inner classes, static inner classes and non-static inner classes. The difference is suggested in the name itself, the **static inner classes** are associated with the enclosing class (as any other static member) while the **non-static inner classes** are associated with the "object" of the enclosing class. Inner classes are a phenomenon of the compiler. It converts the inner classes as plain class files with some strange class names like *OuterClass$InnerClass.class*, so that the virtual machine does not distinguish between regular and inner class files.

Access Modifiers: Unlike outer or top most class, which can only use public or package-private (i.e. default) access modifiers, the inner classes can have any access modifiers.

Inner classes can be categorized as below:

1. Static inner class
2. Non-static inner class
   a) member class.
   b) anonymous class.
   c) local class.

Static inner class:

In effect, a **static nested class** is behaviorally a top-level class that has been nested in another top-level class for packaging convenience. Static member classes can be thought of as regular classes that are simply defined inside another class. They have complete access to all the enclosing class's static member variables and methods.

```
package innerstatic;

public class OuterClass {
    private static int d = 7;
    private int e = 6;                          //instance variable
```

```
private static class InnerClass {

    private int i = 2;                          //instance variable

    public static void executeStatic( ) {
        System.out.println("d=" + d);
    }

    public void execute( ) {
        System.out.println("i=" + i);
        System.out.println("e=" + new OuterClass( ).e);
    }
}

public static void main(String[ ] args) {
    OuterClass.InnerClass.executeStatic( );
    OuterClass.InnerClass inner  = new OuterClass.InnerClass( );
    inner.execute( );
}
}
```

Output:

```
d=7
i=2
e=6
```

Q. Can you provide an example from the Java API? **LF OEQ**
A. Static inner classes are a pretty worthless feature because classes are already divided into name spaces by packages. The only real conceivable reason to create a static inner class is that such a class has access to its containing class's private static members. That is both a handy feature and also can be abused since you can, in essence, violate the encapsulation of the outer class by mucking up the outer class's protected and private fields. The most common use of static inner classes is as an auxiliary class that only makes sense when used in conjunction with its enclosing class. For example, the **Map** interface, which includes **Map.Entry** static interface. Although this is an interface, the idea is the same.

Non-static inner class:

292

As with instance methods and variables, an **inner class** is associated with an instance of its enclosing class, and has direct access to that object's methods and member variables. Also, because an inner class is associated with an instance, it cannot define any static members itself. Like with a static inner class, the instance inner class is known as qualified by its containing class name.

Access Modifiers: Since a non-static inner class cannot exist without an enclosing instance, most non-static inner classes are either private or package-private (i.e. no access modifier) scoped.

Q. So what is the real benefit of non-static inner classes? `LF COQ`
A. The inner class instance has access to the instance variables of the containing class instance. These enclosing instance members are referred to inside the inner class via just their simple names, and not via "this" as this in the inner class refers to the inner class instance, and not the associated containing class instance.

```
package inner.nonstatic;

public class OuterClass {
    private static int d = 7;
    private  int e = 6;                       //instance variable


    private void outerMethod(){
        InnerClass ic = new InnerClass();      // create an instance first
        System.out.println("i=" + ic.i);       // accessing inner class variable
        ic.execute();
    }

    private class InnerClass {

        private int i = 2;                     //instance variable

        public void execute() {
            System.out.println("i=" + i);
            System.out.println("e=" + e);      //accessing outer class variables
            System.out.println("d=" + d);      //accessing outer class variables
        }
    }
```

```
    }

public static void main(String[ ] args) {
    OuterClass.InnerClass inner = new OuterClass( ).new InnerClass( );
    inner.execute( );

    OuterClass outer = new OuterClass( );
    outer.outerMethod( );
    }
}
```

Output:

```
i=2
e=6
e=7
i=2
i=2
e=6
d=7
```

Q. Can you provide an example from the Java API? `DP OEQ`
A. The iterator design pattern makes use of a member inner class. For example,

```
public class MyCollection {
    ...
    public Iterator iterator( ) {
        return new MyCollectionIterator( );
    }
    ...
    private class MyCollectionIterator implements Iterator {
        public boolean hasNext( ) { ... }
        public Object next( ) { ... }
        ....
    }
    ...
}
```

This way it can access all the members of the collection, and it is encapsulated so other classes can not access the *MyCollectionIterator* directly. All the classes are not aware of *MyCollectionIterator,* and they just use the *Iterator* interface. The non-static inner classes are also useful as adapters, where the keys or values in a *Map* can be viewed as a *Set* by creating an inner class that implements the *Set* interface.

Q37 Can you have an inner class inside a method and what variables can you access? **LF** **FAQ**

A37 Yes, you can also declare an inner class within the body of a method without naming it. These classes are known as anonymous inner classes.

They can use local variables and parameters of the method, but only ones which are declared "final". This is because the local class instance must maintain a separate copy of the variable, as it may out-live the method. So as not to have the confusion of two modifiable variables with the same name in the same scope, the variable is forced to be non-modifiable.

Q. Can you provide an example from the Java API?
A. Anonymous classes are very powerful, but care must be taken not to over use it as it can clutter up your top level classes and consequently compromise the readability. In certain cases, it can improve readability as shown below.

In Java GUI development where they are attached as listeners:

```
goButton.addActionListener (new ActionListener( )
   {
      public void actionPerformed(ActionEvent e )
      {
         doImportantStuff( );
      }
   }
);
```

Another most common use of anonymous inner class is as comparators inside a method:

```
List<String> listOfValues = new ArrayList<String>( );
Collections.sort(listOfValues, new Comparator<String>() {
      public int compare(String s1, String s2) {
         return s1.compareTo(s2);
```

295

```
        }
    });
```

You can start a simple thread for one-off use inside a method:

```
new Thread(new Runnable( )
    {
        public void run( ){
            // do runnable stuff here
        }
    }
).start( );
```

You can use it for filters:

```
public static FilenameFilter filter(final String regex) {
    //Creation of anonymous inner class:
    return new FilenameFilter( ) {
        private Pattern pattern = Pattern.compile(regex);

        public boolean accept(File dir, String name) {
            return pattern.matcher(new File(name).getName( )).matches( );
        }
    }; // End of anonymous inner class
}
```

Note: In general, defining a class on its own is preferable over anonymous inner classes.

Q38 What is a callback method? **LF**

A38 A callback method is when you register a method with some other object, which that object can call back at a later time.

In Java there is no way to register a method by passing a function pointer like in C/C++. Callback methods are the way of managing life cycle of an instance. Callback methods are those which are called automatically by applications or frameworks when a particular condition has been met. It could be event handling (e.g *actionPerformed( )*) or methods in a Servlet life cycle like *destroy( )* getting called by the container while the container is shutting down.

Most of the languages specify a callback method by passing the address of the subroutine to the system to the request it is calling back from, but Java performs the same thing by using interfaces. Java does not allow passing the address of a subroutine, but allows passing an instance of a class that implements the standard interface. For this purpose, anonymous classes are mainly used as they support a better compact definition of the class that is required as a new class. The following code snippets illustrates a callback method with inner member interface and an anonymous inner class.

```java
package callback;

//Outer class
public class CallBackExample {

    //inner interface
    public interface CallBack {
        int calculate(int a, int b);
    }

    public static void main(String[ ] args) {

        //anonymous inner class
        CallBack adder = new CallBack( ) {
            public int calculate(int a, int b) {
                return a + b;
            }
        };

        CallBack multiplier = new CallBack( ) {
            public int calculate(int a, int b) {
                return a * b;
            }
        };

        System.out.println(adder.calculate(5, 10));        //prints 15
        System.out.println(multiplier.calculate(5, 10));   //prints 50
    }
}
```

DP The callback method is a very powerful technique used by various design patterns. For example, the visitor design pattern uses callback methods. The Java/J2EE job interview companion (400+ Q&A) covers various design patterns with code snippets and examples.

Q. Can you give an example of a callback method from the Java API?
A. To figure out which button was clicked, one could write the code in a monolithic way with ugly if else blocks as shown below:

```java
public class MyGUI extends JFrame implements ActionListener
{
    protected JButton submitButton;
    protected JButton cancelButton;
    //...more buttons

    public void actionPerformed(ActionEvent e)
    {
        //Bad practice
        if(e.getSource() == submitButton)
        {
            // do something
        }
        else if(e.getSource() == cancelButton)
        {
            // do something
        }
        //more else if conditions
    }
    //...
}
```

BP COQ Whenever you see switch statements or large if-else blocks, alarm bells should begin to ring in your mind. In general, such constructs are bad object-oriented design since a change in one section of the code may require a corresponding change in the switch statement. Inner member classes and anonymous classes allow us to get away from the switched *actionPerformed(..)* methods by using an anonymous inner class as shown below:

```
submitButton = new JButton( );
submitButton.addActionListener (new ActionListener( )
  {
     public void actionPerformed( ActionEvent e )
     {
       doImportantStuff( );
     }
  }
);
```

You could also use member inner classes as demonstrated below:

```
public class MyGUI extends JFrame
{
  protected JButton submitButton;
  protected JButton cancelButton;
  //...more buttons

  // inner class definitions
  class SubmitButtonHandler implements ActionListener
  {
    public void actionPerformed(ActionEvent e)
    {
       // do something
    }
  }

  //...define inner member classes for other buttons like cancelButton, etc

  protected void buildGUI( )
  {
    //initialize the buttons
    submitButton = new JButton( );
    cancelButton = new JButton( );
    //...

    // register an inner class action listener instance
    // for each button
    submitButton.addActionListener(new SubmitButtonHandler( ));
```

```
    //.. repeat for each button
    }
}
```

Since inner classes have access to everything in the enclosing class, you can move any logic that would have appeared in a monolithic *actionPerformed(..)* implementation to an inner class.

Packaging your classes to avoid conflicts

Q39 What are the usages of Java packages? How do you go about designing good packages? `LF DC`

A39 The packages

- help you organize files within your project. For example, java.io package does something related to I/O and java.net package does something to do with networking and so on.

- resolve naming conflicts when different packages have classes with the same name. For example, the *StringUtils* class is provided by both the Spring framework and Apache commons library as **org.springframework.util**.*StringUtils* and **org.apache.commons.lang**.*StringUtils* respectively.

If we tend to put all .java files into a single package, as the project gets bigger, it would become a nightmare to manage all your files.

Q40 How do you go about designing good packages? `DC`

A40 The packages exist solely because classes are not sufficient to group code. When designing a package, you will have to ask a number of questions like,

- What if I just want to release the packages (e.g. com.xyz.dao.*) related to just data access?
- What happens if I distribute my jar files (e.g. RMI or Web Service client jars) to the client applications and the totally unexpected thing happens by showing up bugs? I need to be able to determine whether the client had an old version of the package, as the newest version definitely fixed all the remaining bugs. I

want to version my packages in a repository system like CVS or subversion (SVN) to keep track of my changes.

- Can this package be unit tested in isolation?
- Can a change to one package have a knock on effect to a number of other dependent packages? Do I have a cyclic dependency?

Packages create a dependency hierarchy. For example, all the classes related to database operation can be placed in a package called "com.xyz.dao". Another package called com.xyz.client depends on the services offered by the package "com.xyz.dao". Make use of the package UML diagrams to visualize and analyze package dependencies. When designing packages, think of reuse, granularity, release management, unit testing, distribution, and the level of coupling (i.e. dependency) with the other packages. There are a number of principles that can help you design good packages.

- Reuse-Release Equivalence Principle (**REP**) helps you determine the granularity of reuse and release. It states that anything that you reuse must also be released and tracked. If a class depends on another class in a different package, it depends on the entire package. A package can be considered to be the unit of distribution of the software. Releasing a package means an implicit signed contract, that this package will serve as specified. Code should not be reused by copying it from one package and pasting it into another package. Instead, the code should be reused by including a released library in your code. The author of the library retains responsibility for maintaining it, and you should really treat the library like a black box. The author of a library needs to identify releases with different versions. For example, a meta-inf/manifest.mf file, which contains the meta-data about the contents of the jar itself.

```
Manifest-Version: 1.0

Main-Class: com.OnlineMain
Specification-Title: Online Forms Framework
Specification-Version: 2.0
Specification-Vendor: XYZ

Name: com/forms/online/
Implementation-Title: Super Forms Framework
Implementation-Version: 1.0.2
Implementation-Vendor: XYZ
```

```
Name: com/forms/online/ui
Specification-Title: User Interface Framework
Specification-Version: 2.0
Specification-Vendor: Sun
Implementation-Title: User Interface Framework UI classes
Implementation-Version: 1.1.1
Implementation-Vendor: XYZ
```

In general, jar files are hard to distribute, version, and reference. The Java Module System's architecture that will be introduced in Java 7.0 release will provide module definition, the metadata associated with the module, the versioning system and the repositories for storing and retrieving the module definitions. A Java Module is a distribution standard that contains set of classes and resources similar to a JAR (Java ARchive) File. What differs from JAR from a JMS (Java Module System, not Java Messaging System) is that the modules themselves can be versioned. The Java Module System contains a metadata file that contains information about the inclusion of classes, resources and the set of jar files that this module is dependent on. The specification of Java Module System also defines a repository whose Java Module files can be stored, discovered and used by other modules.

- Common-Reuse Principle (**CRP**) helps you decide which classes should be placed into a package. It says that only cohesive classes should be packaged together. It states that the classes that tend to be reused together should be placed in the same package. If a class depends on another class in a different package, it depends on the entire package. Every time the used package is released, the using package must be re-validated and re-released, even though the change was made in a different class. Hence, the classes which are not tightly related to each other should not be in the same package. For example, you can have data access object (i.e. dao) classes and domain (i.e. model) classes for different domains like rebates, commissions, and sales as shown below:

```
com.xyz.dao.rebates
com.xyz.dao.commissions
```

The dao package has the classes like *CommissionsDao*, *CommissionsDaoImpl,* etc for data access logic using pure SQL or Hibernate queries.

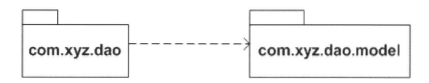

The dao.model package has the domain classes like *CommissionStatement*, *CommissionDetail*, etc. The model classes can not only be used by the dao package classes, but also by the other business service package classes.

com.xyz.dao.model.rebates
com.xyz.dao.model.commissions

- Common-Closure Principle (**CCP**) helps you identify the coupling among the different packages. This principle looks at the maintainability rather than re-usability. The packages should be loosely coupled by not having multiple reasons to change. It's preferable that changes occur in just one package rather than distributed along the whole system. So packages need to be looked at from change and distribution point of view.

- Acyclic-Dependencies Principle (**ADP**) helps you identify the cyclic dependencies among the packages. This is very important from a deployment perspective. For example, the package X depends on package Y, and package Y depends on package X. This causes problems when you have to release a package that was modified. You can break the cycle by introducing a new package Z between X and Y, and move the classes that both X and Y uses to the package Z. One of the ways to break cyclic dependencies is to use dependency inversion principle (DIP).

- Stable-Dependencies Principle (**SDP**) and Stable-Abstractions Principle (**SAP**) help determine the stability of your package. Stability is measured by calculating how easy it is to change a package without impacting other packages within the application. The package stability is measured in terms of the number of classes inside package X that depends on classes outside package X and number of classes outside package X that depend on classes within

303

package X. A package is called stable if it is hard to change, or a lot of classes outside this package depend on it. The diagram below illustrates how to measure instability and how to break cyclic dependency. This principle can go to an atomic level of classes and states that classes should depend only on more stable classes. This where the dependency inversion principle (DIP) comes in handy.

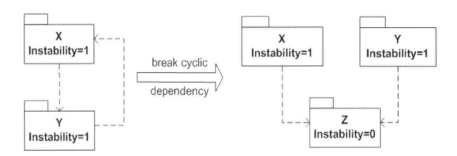

Note: Refactor your packages when it makes more sense to do so by moving classes from one package to another or to a newly created package.

Book recommendation: This has only scratched the surface on design principles. For a more detailed understanding, refer to "Agile Software Development, Principles, Patterns, and Practices" by Robert C. Martin.

Section-6:

Objects Essentials

- Working with objects
- Cloning objects
- Casting objects
- Immutable objects
- Working with enumerations
- Understanding "==" versus equals( )
- Working with the String class
- Type safety with generics
- Serializing your objects
- Garbage collecting your objects

An object (or instance) is an executable copy of a class. In the last section, you looked at the object oriented concepts, design principles, working with classes, and interfaces. It is a must to have a good understanding in working with the objects. You will be performing various operations like creating, cloning, casting, comparing, modifying, serializing, and garbage collecting your objects.

The general preparation for a Java job interview can be summed up in four steps: research, predict questions, prepare answers and practice. The step 2 to predict questions is often not an easy task, but you can always prepare for most common interview questions relating to OO concepts, classes, interfaces, working with objects, and language fundamentals. Still more than 50% of the candidates don't answer these questions right. If you can demonstrate that your fundamentals are solid by answering these questions with examples and illustrations, you will stand a good chance of succeeding. This will be valued a lot more than happening to know or having experience with a sought-after framework the very moment. In other words, if you don't get these fundamental questions right, knowing the sought-after frameworks is not going to do you any good.

Working with Objects

The *java.lang.Object* class is the ultimate super class of all objects. If a class does not explicitly extend a class, then the compiler assumes it extends *java.lang.Object*.

Q01 What are the non-final methods in Java *Object* class, which are meant primarily for extension? Are these methods easy to implement correctly? What are the implications of implementing them incorrectly? **LF**

A01 The non-final methods are *equals( )*, *hashCode( )*, *toString( )*, *clone( )*, and *finalize( )*. These methods are meant to be overridden. The *equals( )* and *hashCode( )* methods prove to be very important, when objects implementing these two methods are added to collections. If implemented incorrectly or not implemented at all, then your objects stored in a collection like a *Set*, *List* or *Map* may behave strangely and also it is hard to debug.

The other methods like *wait( )*, *notify( )*, *notifyAll( )*, *getClass( )*, etc are **final methods** and therefore cannot be overridden. The methods *clone( )* and *finalize( )* have protected access.

Q. Are these methods easy to implement correctly?
A. No. It is not easy to implement these methods correctly because,

- You must pay attention to whether your implementation of these methods will continue to work correctly if sub classed. If your class is not meant for extension, then declare your class as final.
- These methods have to adhere to contracts, and when implementing or overriding a method, the contracts must be satisfied.

Q. What are the implications of implementing them incorrectly?
A. In short, excess debug and rework time. Incorrect implementations of *equals( )* and *hashCode( )* methods can result in data being lost in *HashMaps* and *Sets*. You can also get intermittent data related problems that are harder to consistently reproduce over time.

Q02 If a class overrides the *equals( )* method, what other method it should override? What are some of the key considerations while implementing these methods? **LF COQ**

A02 It should override the *hashCode( )* method. The contract between the *hashCode( )* and *equals( )* methods is clearly defined on the Java API for the *Object* class under respective methods. Here are some key points to keep in mind while implementing these methods,

- The *equals( )* and *hashCode( )* methods should be implemented together. You should not have one without the other.
- If two objects return the same *hashCode( )* integer value does not mean that those two objects are equal.
- If two objects are equal, then they must return the same *hashCode( )* integer value.
- The implementation of the *equals( )* method must be consistent with the *hashCode( )* method to meet the previous bullet points.
- Use @override annotation to ensure that the methods are correctly overridden.
- Favor instanceof instead of *getClass(..)* in the *equals( )* method which takes care of super types and null comparison as recommended by Joshua Bloch, but ensure that the equals implementation is final to preserve the symmetry contract of the method: x.equals(y) == y.equals(x). If final seems restrictive, carefully examine to see if overriding implementations can fully maintain the contract established by the Object class.
- Check for self-comparison and null values where required.

```
package chapter2.com;

public final class Pet {
    int id;
    String name;

    /**
     * use @override annotation to prevent the danger of misspelling
     * method name or incorrect method signature.
     */

    @Override
    public boolean equals(Object that){
        //check for self-comparison
        if ( this == that ) return true;

        /**
         * use instanceof instead of getClass here for two reasons
```

```
 * 1.  it can match any super type, and not just one class;
 * 2.  explicit check for "that == null" is not required as
 *      "null instanceof Pet" always  returns false.
 **/
 if ( ! (that instanceof Pet) )
     return false;

 Pet pet = (Pet)that;
 return  this.id == pet.id  && this != null && this.name.equals(pet.name);


}

/**
 * fields id & name are used in both equals( ) and
 * hashCode( ) methods.
 */

@Override
public int hashCode( ) {
    int hash = 9;
    hash = (31 * hash) + id;
    hash = (31 * hash) + (null == name ? 0 : name.hashCode( ));
    return hash;
}
}
```

Use Apache's *HashCodeBuilder* & *EqualsBuilder* classes to simplify your implementation, especially when you have a large number of member variables. Commonclipse is an eclipse plugin for jakarta commons-lang users. It is very handy for automatic generation of *toString( ), hashCode( ), equals(..), and compareTo( )* methods.

```
package chapter2.com;

import org.apache.commons.lang.builder.EqualsBuilder;
import org.apache.commons.lang.builder.HashCodeBuilder;

public final class Pet2 {
    int id;
    String name;
```

```java
@Override
public boolean equals(Object that) {
    if (this == that)
        return true;

    if (!(that instanceof Pet2))
        return false;

    Pet2 pet = (Pet2) that;
    return new EqualsBuilder().append(this.id, pet.id).append(
        this.name, pet.name).isEquals();
}

/**
 * both fields id & name are used in equals( ),
 * so both fields must be used in hashCode( ) as well.
 */

@Override
public int hashCode() {
    //pick 2 hard-coded, odd & >0 int values as arguments
    return new HashCodeBuilder(1, 31).append(this.id).append(
        this.name).toHashCode();
}
}
}
```

Q03 When should you override a *toString( )* method? `LF COQ`

A03 You can use *System.out.println( )* or *logger.info(...)* to print any object. The *toString( )* method of an object gets invoked automatically, when an object reference is passed in the *System.out.println(refPet)* or *logger.info(refPet)* method. However for good results, your class should have a toString( ) method that overrides Object class's default implementation by formatting the object's data in a sensible way and returning a *String*. Otherwise all that's printed is the class name followed by an "@" sign and then unsigned hexadecimal representation of the hashCode. For example, If the *Pet* class doesn't override the toString( ) method as shown below, by default Pet@162b91 will be printed via *toString( )* default implementation in the *Object* class. The "public class Pet3" can be read as "public class Pet3 extends Object".

```
package chapter2.com;

public class Pet3 {
    int id;
    String name;

    @Override
    public String toString() {
        return new StringBuilder().append("id:" + id).append(
            ",name:" + name).toString();
    }
}
```

Output:

id:<id>, name:<name>

This is by far the easiest method to override. Still you can make mistakes like, say you have the following *toString( )* implementation for the *BasePet class*,

```
@Override
public String toString() {
    return "BasePet - " + "id=" + id + ", name=" + name;
}
```

The above method is fine if not extended by any other class. If the above method is extended by a *Cat* class, the output will still have the hard coded "**BasePet - **". This can be fixed as follows,

```
@Override
public String toString() {
    return this.getClass() + " - " + "id=" + id + ", name=" + name;
}
```

If the above code is called from a *Cat* class, it will print "**Cat - **" followed by the id and name. If it is called from a *Dog* class, it will print "**Dog - **" followed by the id and name.

Q04 Can you override *clone( )* and finalize*( )* methods in the *Object* class? How do you disable a *clone( )* method? `LF COQ`

A04 Yes, but you need to do it very judiciously. Implementing a properly functioning **clone( )** method is complex and it is rarely necessary. You are better off providing some alternative means of object copying through a copy constructor or a static factory method.

```
//copy constructor
public Pet(Pet petToCopy){
   this.setName(petToCopy.getName( ));
   //...
}
```

```
//static factory method
public static Pet newInstance(Pet petToCopy){
   Pet pet = new Pet( );
   pet.setName(petToCopy.getName( ));
   //...
    return pet;
}
```

Q. How do you disable a *clone( )* method?
A. It can be disabled as follows

```
public final Object clone() throws CloneNotSupportedException {
   throw new CloneNotSupportedException( );
}
```

Unlike C++ destructors, the **finalize( )** method in Java is unpredictable, often dangerous and generally unnecessary. Use finally{} blocks to close any resources or free memory. The *finalize( )* method should only be used in rare instances as a safety net or to terminate noncritical native resources. If you do happen to call the finalize( ) method in some rare instances, then remember to follow the following guidelines:

- You should call the finalize method of the super class in case it has to clean up.

```
protected void finalize() throws Throwable {
   try{
      //finalize subclass state
   }
```

311

```
catch(Throwable t){
    //log the exception
}
finally {
    super.finalize( );
}
}
```

- You should not depend on the finalize method being called. There is no guarantee that when (or if) objects will be garbage collected and thus no guarantee that the finalize method will be called before the running program terminates.

- Finally, the code in finalize method might fail and throw exceptions. Catch these exceptions so that the finalize method can continue.

Cloning Objects

The reason for making a local copy of an object is if you're going to modify that object and you don't want to modify the caller's object.

Q05 What is the main difference between shallow cloning and deep cloning of objects? **LF**

A05 **Shallow copy**: If a shallow copy is performed, the contained objects are not cloned. Java supports shallow cloning of objects by default when a class implements the *java.lang.Cloneable* interface. For example, invoking *clone( )* method on a collection like *HashMap*, *List*, etc returns a shallow copy of the *HashMap*, *List*, instances. This means if you clone a *HashMap*, the map instance is cloned but the keys and values themselves are not cloned, but are shared by pointing to the original objects.

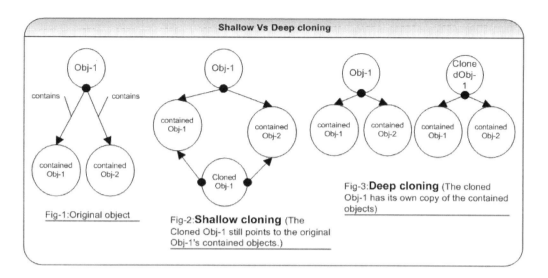

Shallow Vs Deep cloning

Fig-1:Original object

Fig-2:**Shallow cloning** (The Cloned Obj-1 still points to the original Obj-1's contained objects.)

Fig-3:**Deep cloning** (The cloned Obj-1 has its own copy of the contained objects)

Deep copy: If a deep copy is performed, then not only the original object has been copied, but the objects contained within it have been copied as well. Serialization can be used to achieve deep cloning. For example, you can serialize a *HashMap* to a *ByteArrayOutputStream* and then deserialize it. This creates a deep copy, but does require that all keys and values in the *HashMap* to be *Serializable*. The main advantage of this approach is that it will deep copy any arbitrary object graph. Deep cloning through serialization is faster to develop and easier to maintain, but carries a performance overhead. Alternatively, you can provide a static factory method to deep copy as shown below:

```java
public static List deepCopy(List listCars) {
    List copiedList = new ArrayList(10);
    for (Object object : listCars) {
        Car original = (Car)object;
        Car carCopied = new Car();                    //instantiate a new Car object
        carCopied.setColor((original.getColor()));
        copiedList.add(carCopied);
    }
    return copiedList;
}
```

Casting Objects

Understand implicit and explicit casting. Also, be clear about overriding and hiding (aka shadowing). They are two different things.

Q06 What is type casting? Explain up casting vs. down casting? When do you get *ClassCastException*? `LF FAQ`

A06 Type casting means treating a variable of one type as though it is another type.

$$\textbf{byte} \rightarrow \textbf{short} \rightarrow \textbf{char} \rightarrow \textbf{int} \rightarrow \textbf{long} \rightarrow \textbf{float} \rightarrow \textbf{double}$$

(1 byte) (2 bytes) (2 bytes) (4 bytes) (8 bytes) (4 bytes) (8 bytes)

When up casting primitives from left to right, automatic conversion occurs. But if you go from right to left, down casting or explicit casting is required. This was already discussed under "Choosing the right data types" with widening versus narrowing conversions, in "Language Essentials" section.

When it comes to object references, you can always cast from a subclass to a super class because a subclass object is also a super class object. You can cast an object **implicitly** to a super class type (i.e. up casting). If this were not the case, polymorphism wouldn't be possible.

You can cast down the hierarchy as well, but you must **explicitly** write the cast and the object must be a legitimate instance of the class you are casting to. The *ClassCastException* is thrown to indicate that code has attempted to cast an object to a subclass of which it is not an instance. If you are using J2SE 5.0, then "generics" will minimize the need for casting, and otherwise you can deal with the problem of incorrect down casting in two ways:

Using the exception handling mechanism to catch *ClassCastException*:

```
Object o = null;
try {
        o = new Integer(1);
        System.out.println((String) o);
}
catch(ClassCastException cce) {
    logger.log("Invalid casting, String is expected...Not an Integer");
```

```
    System.out.println(((Integer) o).toString( ));
}
```

Using the instanceof statement to guard against incorrect casting:

```
if(o instanceof String) {
    String s2 = (String) o;
}
else if (o instanceof Integer) {
    Integer i2 = (Integer) o;
}
```

The "instanceof" and "typecast" constructs can make your code unmaintainable due to large "if" and "else if" statements, and also can adversely affect performance if used in frequently accessed methods or loops. Look at using generics or visitor design pattern to avoid or minimize these casting constructs where applicable.

Note: You can also get a *ClassCastException* when two different class loaders load the same class because they are treated as two different classes. Refer to "Knowing your way around Java" section under "Gauging your experience with UNIX" where the "Java Linkage Error" is discussed with tips to solve them.

Q07 What do you understand by variable shadowing? `LF FAQ`
A07 When both a parent class and its subclass have a field with the same name, it is called variable shadowing. If the field in the parent class has private access or is in another package and has default (i.e. package private) access, there is no room for confusion. The child class cannot access the field in question of the parent class. So it's clear with which variable any reads and writes in the child class will take place.

However, if the same name variable in the parent class is accessible to instances of the child class, the general rule is that the variable accessed depends on the class to which the variable has been **cast**. For example,

```
package shaddowing;

public class Parent {

    protected String val = "parent";
```

315

```
  public String getVal( ) {
    return val;
  }
}
```

```
package shaddowing;

public class Child extends Parent {

  protected String val = "child";

  public String getVal( ) {
    return val;
  }

  public static void main(String[ ] args) {
    Child c = new Child( );
    System.out.println("val=" + c.val);                //prints "child"

    Parent p = c;                                      //implicitly cast to Parent
    System.out.println("val=" + p.val);                //prints "parent" due to
                                                       //variable hiding
    System.out.println("val=" + p.getVal( ));          //prints "child" due to
                                                       //method overriding
    System.out.println("val=" + ((Child)p).val);       //prints "child" since it is
                                                       //explicitly cast to Child

  }
}
```

Q08 If you have a reference variable of a parent class type, and you assign a child class object to that variable, and then you invoke a **static method** that is present in both parent and child classes, which method will be invoked? `LF FAQ`

A08 Parent's method. Unlike instance methods, you can't override static methods. However, it is possible to write code as shown below, but this is not a method overriding, but a static method shadowing or hiding another static method. You won't get a compile-time error, but the results can be unexpected.

```
package shaddowing;
```

```java
public class Parent {

    public static void sameName() {
        System.out.println("Parent -- sameName()");
    }
}
```

```java
package shaddowing;

public class Child extends Parent {

    public static void sameName() {
        System.out.println("Child -- sameName()");
    }


    public static void main(String[ ] args) {
        Child c = new Child();
        c.sameName();                        // prints: Child – sameName().

        Parent p = c;                        // implicitly cast to Parent.
        p.sameName();                        // prints: Parent – sameName().
    }
}
```

Note: So when you override a method, you get the benefit of polymorphic behavior, but when you hide or shadow, you don't get the polymorphic behavior.

Note: If you happen to have a parameter in a constructor or a method having the same name as an instance variable, you must prefix the instance variable with **"this"** keyword. Otherwise the parameter will be hiding or shadowing your instance variable. For example,

```java
Class Fruit {
    private String name = null;        // instance variable – name

    public Fruit(String name) {        // parameter – name
        this.name = name;              // Correct
        //name = name                  // Wrong. The instance variable is hidden
```

317

```
        // or shadowed by the parameter.
    }
}
```

Immutable Objects

"Classes should be immutable unless there's a very good reason to make them mutable....If a class cannot be made immutable, limit its mutability as much as possible."
    -- by Joshua Bloch

Q09 What is an immutable object? How do you create an immutable type? What are the advantages of immutable objects? `LF BP FAQ`

A09 Immutable objects are objects whose state (the object's data) cannot change after construction. Examples of immutable objects from the JDK include String and wrapper classes like Integer, Double, Character, etc.

Q. How do you create an immutable type?

- Make the class final so that it cannot be extended or use static factories and keep constructors private.

```
public final class MyImmutable { ... }
```

- Make fields private and final.

```
private final int[ ] myArray;
```

- Don't provide any methods that can change the state of the immutable object in any way – not just *setXXX* methods, but any methods which can change the state.

- The "this" reference is not allowed to escape during construction from the immutable class, and the immutable class should have exclusive access to fields that contain references to other mutable objects like arrays, collections and mutable classes like *Date* by:

318

- Declaring the mutable references as private.
- Not returning or exposing the mutable references to the caller. This can be done by defensively copying the objects by deeply cloning them..

Q. What are the advantages of immutable objects?

- Immutable classes can greatly simplify programming by freely allowing you to cache and share the references to the immutable objects without having to defensively copy them or without having to worry about their values becoming stale or corrupted.

- Immutable classes are inherently thread-safe and you do not have to synchronize access to them to be used in a multi-threaded environment. So there are no chances for negative performance consequences as multiple threads can share the same instance.

- Eliminates the possibility of data becoming inaccessible when used as keys in *HashMaps* or as elements in *Sets*. These types of errors are hard to debug and fix.

- Eliminates the need for class invariant check once constructed.

- Allow *hashCode( )* method to use lazy initialization, by caching its return value.

- Cloning is not required.

- Simpler to construct, use, and test due to its deterministic state.

Q10 Why is it a best practice to implement the user defined key class as an immutable object? `LF_COQ`

A10 Immutable objects generally make the best map keys as the keys cannot be modified once they have been added to the *Map*. In general *String*, *Integer*, or *Long* are used as keys, which are immutable objects. If you define your own key class, make sure that they are immutable. Otherwise, if the keys are accidentally modified after adding to a *Map*, you will never be able to retrieve the stored value as the key values have been changed.

This is a common pitfall many Java developers, especially beginners fall for.

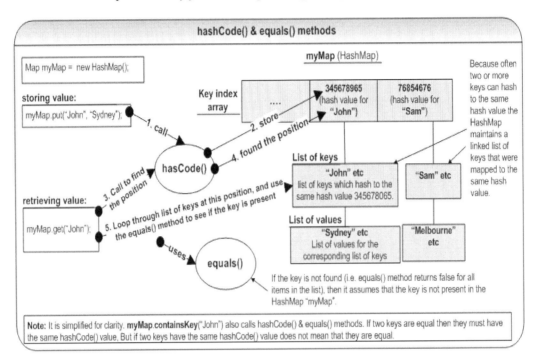

As shown, when *Map*s are used in Java, the *equals( )* and *hashCode( )* methods are implicitly invoked. If these methods are incorrectly implemented or the keys are modified once added to the map, then unpredictable behavior will be experienced, and these behaviors are harder to debug. The *hashCode( )* and *equals( )* methods are implicitly invoked to determine where the key is stored. These methods are called again to retrieve the stored key. If they are implemented inconsistently or the key is mutated, then the stored object cannot be retrieved as the returned values of these methods will vary in between different invocations. To be more specific, the *hashCode( )* method is called to determine the key index (aka the bucket) of the array, and the *equals( )* method is called to retrieve the exact key from the list of keys belonging to that particular key index (or bucket) as the same bucket will be holding multiple keys linked to multiple values. Remember the contract between these two methods? "If 2 objects are equal, they must return the same *hashCode( )* value, but the reverse is not true. Which means, if 2 objects return the same *hashCode( )* value does not mean that those 2 objects are *equal( )*".

Q11 Does the following code produce immutable objects? COQ

```
package chapter2.com;

import java.util.Arrays;

public final class MyImmutable {

    private final Integer[] myArray;

    public MyImmutable(Integer[] anArray) {
        this.myArray = anArray;
    }

    public Integer[] getMyArray() {
        return myArray;
    }

    public String toString() {
        StringBuffer sb = new StringBuffer("Numbers are: ");
        sb.append(Arrays.deepToString(myArray));
        return sb.toString();
    }
}
```

A11 No. The following assignment is incorrect.

```
this.myArray = anArray;
```

If you test the above code with the following code snippet,

```
package chapter2.com;

public class ImmutableTest {
    public static void main(String[] args) {
        Integer[] array = new Integer[] { 1, 2 };
        MyImmutable myImmutableRef = new MyImmutable(array);
        System.out.println("Before constructing " + myImmutableRef);
        myImmutableRef.getMyArray()[1] = 5;                    //mutate value
```

```
        myImmutableRef.getMyArray( )[0] = 7;                          // mutate value
        System.out.println("After constructing " + myImmutableRef);
    }
}
```

Output:

```
Before constructing Numbers are: [1, 2]
After constructing Numbers are: [7, 5]
```

As you can see that the array values have been mutated (i.e. modified) through the references that escaped. You can fix the above code by **defensively copying** the array before returning in the *getMyArray( )* method as well as in the constructor. This is essential because Java's references are passed by value. You can fix the above problem as follows,

```java
package chapter2.com;

import java.util.Arrays;

public final class MyImmutable2 {

    private final Integer[ ] myArray;

    public MyImmutable2(Integer[ ] anArray) {
        this.myArray = anArray.clone( );
    }

    public Integer[ ] getMyArray( ) {
        return myArray.clone( );
    }

    public String toString( ) {
        StringBuffer sb = new StringBuffer("Numbers are: ");
        sb.append(Arrays.deepToString(myArray));
        return sb.toString( );
    }
}
```

Output:

Before constructing Numbers are: [1, 2]
After constructing Numbers are: [1, 2]

Q12 How would you defensively copy a *Date* field in your immutable class? COQ
A12

```java
package chapter2.com;

import java.util.Date;

public final class MyDiary {

    private final Date myDate;

    public MyDiary(Date aDate) {
        this.myDate = new Date(aDate.getTime());    //defensive copying by
                                                    // not exposing the
                                                    // "myDate" reference

    }

    public Date getDate() {
        return new Date(myDate.getTime());          // defensive copying by
                                                    // not exposing the
                                                    // "myDate" reference

    }
}
```

You can try with and without defensive copying by using the following test code,

```java
package chapter2.com;
import java.util.Date;

public class MyDiaryTest {
    public static void main(String[] args) {
        Date myDate = new Date();
        MyDiary ref = new MyDiary(myDate);
        System.out.println("myDate before = " + ref.getDate());
        myDate = ref.getDate();
```

```
    myDate.setDate(25);                          //mutate myDate
    System.out.println("myDate after = " + ref.getDate());
  }
}
```

Q13 How will you prevent the caller from adding or removing elements from pets? How will you make this code fully immutable? COQ

```
package chapter2.com;

import java.util.List;

public class PetCage {
   private final List<Pet> pets;

   public PetCage(List<Pet> pets) {
      this.pets = pets;
   }

   public List<Pet> getPets() {
      return pets;
   }
}
```

A13 An instance of *PetCage* class is not immutable because one can add or remove pets either by obtaining the pets by calling *getPets()* or by retaining a reference to the *List* object passed when an object of this class is constructed. The following change partially solves the immutability problem.

```
package chapter2.com;

import java.util.ArrayList;
import java.util.Collections;
import java.util.List;

public class PetCage {
   private final List<Pet> pets;

   public PetCage(List<Pet> pets) {
```

```
        this.pets = Collections.unmodifiableList(new ArrayList<Pet>(pets));
    }

    public List<Pet> getPets( ) {
        return pets;
    }
}
```

It ensures that you cannot add or remove pets. However, there is no guarantee that the pets are also immutable. To make this instance fully immutable, the *Pet* instance itself must be immutable or use the decorator pattern as a **wrapper** around each of the pets to make them also immutable. For example, The *Integer* wrapper class provides immutability to mutable primitive int value. You could also **defensively deep copy** the list of pets in the constructor and *getPets( )* method.

Q14 What about data that changes sometimes? Is there any way to obtain the benefits of immutability with the added benefit of thread-safety for data that changes less frequently? COQ PC

A14 The Copy-On-Write collections like *CopyOnWriteArrayList* and *CopyOnWriteArraySet* classes from the *util.concurrent* package, introduced in JRE 5.0 are good examples of how to harness the power of immutability while still permitting occasional modifications for **infrequently changing data**. *CopyOnWriteArrayList* behaves much like the *ArrayList* class, except that when the list is modified, instead of mutating the underlying array, a new array is created and the old array is discarded. *CopyOnWriteArrayList* is designed for cases where:

- reads hugely outnumber writes.
- the array is small (or writes are very infrequent).
- the caller genuinely needs the functionality of a list rather than an array.

When you obtain an iterator, which holds a reference to the underlying array, the array referenced by the iterator is effectively immutable and therefore can be traversed without synchronization or risk of concurrent modification. This eliminates the need to either clone the list before traversal or synchronize on the list during traversal. If reads are much more frequent than insertions or removals, which is the case very often, the Copy-on-Write collections and *ConcurrentHashMaps* offer better performance and development convenience. The development convenience is provided not needing to deal with synchronization, deep cloning, or *"ConcurrentModificationException"*. The

ConcurrentModificationException is generally thrown by an *ArrayList*, *HashSet*, or a *HashMap* implementation when you try to try to modify (e.g. remove) an object from a collection while iterating over it.

Working with Enumerations

Q15 Why is it a best practice to use enums over static final int or *String* constants? `LF BP`
A15 The old Java solution for declaring constants is good, but is not a best practice because,

- Allows invalid values. Any integer value can be assigned, although there are only 4 valid choices .

  ```
  season = 25;              // Illogical value, but allowed by the compiler.
  ```

- No easy methods to convert values to and from a string form.
- Less readable and requires more maintaining due to additional look-up code. If there are additions, deletions, or re-orderings to a constant class, the other dependent classes using the constant class will not automatically be readjusted to reflect these changes.
- Fragile for loops as iterating over all values is subject to errors which are not diagnosed at compile time if the values are rearranged, deleted, or added to. There is no way to use the enhanced for loop.
- Only values no behavior.

```
package withoutenum;

import java.util.ArrayList;
import java.util.List;

//not a best practice
public class Weather {
    public static final int WINTER = 0;
    public static final int SPRING = 1;
    public static final int SUMMER = 2;
    public static final int FALL = 3;
```

```java
    public static final int NO_OF_SEASONS = 4; //if new seasons added or
                                               //removed, this value has
                                               //to be adjusted.

    private final int season;                 // not type safe. Allows
                                               // illegal values like 25
    private static final List<Weather> listWeather = new
                                           ArrayList<Weather>();

    private Weather(int season) {
        this.season = season;
    }

    public int getSeason() {
        return season;
    }

    static {
        // Can't use for each loop.
        for (int i = 0; i < NO_OF_SEASONS; i++) {
            listWeather.add(new Weather(i));
        }
    }

    public static List<Weather> getWeatherList() {
        return listWeather;
    }

    public String toString() {
        //no easy methods to convert values to and from string.
        return new Integer(season).toString();
    }
}
}
```

An enum type is a kind of class definition. enums are implicitly final subclasses of *java.lang.Enum*. The possible enum values are listed in the curly braces, separated by commas. By convention the value names are in upper case.

```java
package withenum;
```

```java
import java.util.ArrayList;
import java.util.List;

public class Weather {
    public enum Season {WINTER, SPRING, SUMMER, FALL}

    private final Season season;          //type safe because
                                          //only right seasons can be assigned

    private static final List<Weather> listWeather = new ArrayList<Weather>();


    private Weather(Season season) {
        this.season = season;
    }

    public Season getSeason() {
        return season;
    }

    static {
        //using J2SE 5.0 for each loop
        for (Season season : Season.values()) {
            listWeather.add(new Weather(season));
        }
    }

    public static List<Weather> getWeatherList() {
        return listWeather;
    }

    public String toString() {
        return season.toString();
    }
}
```

Q16 Can enums be used in switch statements? **LF**

A16 Yes. The switch statement was enhanced to allow use of enums. It is important to note that the case values don't have to be qualified with the enum class name, which can be determined from the switch control value.

```
public static void main(String[ ] args) {
    Weather w = new Weather(Season.WINTER);
    switch (w.season) {
    //values are not fully qualified with the enum type Season.
    case WINTER:
      System.out.println("It is Winter");
      break;
    case SPRING:
      System.out.println("It is Spring");
      break;
    case SUMMER:
      System.out.println("It is Summer");
      break;
    case FALL:
      System.out.println("It is Fall");
      break;
    default:
      break;
    }
}
```

Note: The case statements are not fully qualified with the enum name. As shown above it is just *WINTER*, and not *Season.WINTER*.

Q17 How will you get an integer equivalent of an enum value? `LF`
A17 Using the *ordinal( )* method.

```
w.season.ordinal( );
```

Q18 How will you convert a *String* value to an enum value? `LF`
A18 Using the *valueOf( )* method. You can use the methods *name( )* or *toString( )* to convert an enum value back to a string value.

Q19 Would you use *equals( )* or == to compare enum values? `LF`
A19 Both *equals(..)* and == amount to the same thing, and can be used interchangeably as enums are implicitly public static final.

Objects Essentials

Q20 Do you have to override *equals( )* and *hashCode( )* methods for enum? `LF`

A20 No. Since you can only create one instance (i.e. singleton) of each season, you don't have to override these methods. The class *Enum* declares *equals( )*, *hashCode( )*, *clone( )*, and *compareTo( )* methods as final. You can override the *toString( )* method to provide better information for debugging.

Q21 Are enums immutable? `LF DP`

A21 Yes. As with any class, it is easy to provide methods in an enum type which can change the state of an enum constant. Hence, the term "enum constant" is misleading. What is constant is the identity of the enum element, not its state. Perhaps a better term would have been "enum" instead of "enum constant". The enum classes can have behavior, hence the responsibility is on the developers to make it immutable.

Since enum is basically a special class type, and can have methods and fields just like any other class, you can apply the "template method" design pattern to create enumerations that are factories or command objects. Here is a simple example of a "command" enumeration. You can also implement your own method to do a reverse lookup of a weather based on a given weather code as illustrated below.

```java
package withenum;

import java.util.EnumSet;
import java.util.HashMap;
import java.util.Map;

public enum Season {

    WINTER("WT") {
        @Override
        public void execute() {
            System.out.println("Winter...");
        }
    },
    SPRING("SP") {
        @Override
        public void execute() {
            System.out.println("Spring....");
        }
    },
```

```java
SUMMER("SM") {
    @Override
    public void execute( ) {
        System.out.println("Summer...");
    }
},
FALL("FL.") {
    @Override
    public void execute( ) {
        System.out.println("Fall...");
    }
};

private static final Map<String, Season> lookup =
    new HashMap<String, Season>( );

static {
    for (Season s : EnumSet.allOf(Season.class))
        lookup.put(s.getCode( ), s);
}


private String code;

private Season(String code) {
    this.code = code;
}

public String getCode( ) {
    return code;
}

//template method
public abstract void execute( );

//reverse lookup method
public static Season getByCode(int code) {
    return lookup.get(code);
}
}
```

```
}
```

Unsightly switch/case or if/else statements can be minimized or avoided with the help of template method pattern shown above. The client code would use something like *season.execute( )*. The static *getByCode(String)* method provides the reverse lookup by simply getting the value from the Map. The static block that populates the Map, uses a specialized implementation of Set, *java.util.EnumSet*, which has better performance than *java.util.HashSet*. Java 5.0 also provides a more compact and specialized implementation of *Map* for enums with *java.util.EnumMap*.

Understanding "==" versus equals( )

Q22 What is the difference between "==" and equals(..) method? What is the difference between shallow comparison and deep comparison of objects? **LF BP FAQ**

A22 It is important to understand the difference between identity (i.e. ==) comparison, which is a **shallow** comparison that compares only the object references, and the *equals( )* comparison, which is a **deep** comparison that compares the object attributes. The diagram below explains the difference between the two. There are some exceptional conditions when using primitives, *String* objects, and enums. This will be discussed in the ensuing Q&As. Apart from these 3 exceptional conditions, all the other objects in general follow the <u>standard rule</u> depicted by the *Pet* object.

If the *equals(..)* method is not overridden, then the *Object* class's default implementation is invoked, which only compares the object references. Invoking the *equals(..)* method of the *Object* class is equivalent to making a shallow comparison with "==". This is why it is imperative to override the *equals( )* method (, and the *hashCode( )* method) in your custom classes like *Pet*. The Java API objects like *String, Integer, Double,* etc override the *equals(..), hashCode( )* , and the *toString(..)* methods. These methods are meant to be overridden as discussed earlier.

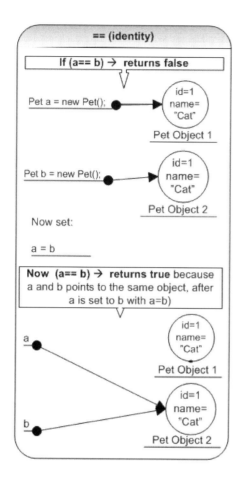

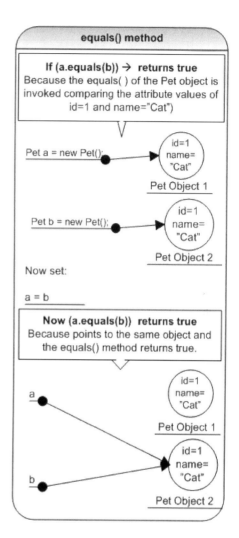

The code snippet below explains how the *String* class follows the standard rule as explained above and a variation to the above rule when the String objects are pooled for performance using the flyweight design pattern.

```
package chapter2.com;

public class String2 {
    public static void main(String[] args) {

        String s1 = new String("A");
        String s2 = new String("A");
```

```
//standard: follows the == and equals() rule applicable to any Java object

if (s1 == s2) {                                    // shallow comparison
    System.out.println("references/identities are equal");  // never reaches here
                                                            // as s1 & s2 point to
                                                            // 2 different objects

}
if (s1.equals(s2)) {                               // deep comparison
    System.out.println("values are equal");        // this line is printed as s1 & s2
                                                    // have the same value of "A"


}

//variation: does not follow the == and equals rule
//Specific to String objects declared as shown below
//This is an example of the fly-weight design pattern.

String s3 = "A";          // goes into a String pool.
String s4 = "A";          // refers to String already in the pool.

if (s3 == s4) {           // shallow comparison
    System.out.println("references/identities are equal");   // this line
                                                             // is printed

}
if (s3.equals(s4)) {                               // deep comparison
    System.out.println("values are equal");        // this line is also printed
    }
}
}
```

Q23 What happens when you run the following code? `LF COQ FAQ`

```
Boolean b1  = new Boolean(false);
Boolean b2  = Boolean.FALSE;

if(b1 == b2) {
    System.out.println("Equal");
}
```

```
else {
    System.out.println("Not Equal");
}
```

A23 Prints "Not Equal".

The == is a shallow comparison that only compares the references. The references are not equal. If you want to print "Equal", perform a deep comparison as shown below, which compares the values.

```
if (b1.equals(b2)) {
    System.out.println("Equal");              //gets printed
}
else {
    System.out.println("Not Equal");
}
```

Q24 Can you discuss the output of the following code? `COQ`

```
public class PrimitiveAndObjectEquals {

    public static void main(String[] args) {
        int a = 5;
        int b = 5;

        Integer c = new Integer(5);
        Integer d = new Integer(5);

        if (a == b) {                                      //Line 1
            System.out.println("primitives a and b are ==");
        }

        if (c == d) {                                      //Line 2
            System.out.println("Objects c and d are ==");
        }

        if (c.equals(d)) {                                 //Line 3
            System.out.println("Objects c and d are equals()");
```

335

```
      }

   if (a == d) {                                                    //Line 4
      System.out
         .println("Primitive a and Object d are == due to auto unboxing");
      }
   }
 }
}
```

A24 Output is:

```
primitives a and b are ==
Objects c and d are equals( )
Primitive a and Object d are == due to auto unboxing
```

- Line 1 is printed as both a and b are primitive data types.
- Line 2 will not get printed as they are comparing the object references (**shallow comparison**). Line 3 will get printed as they are comparing the actual values (**deep comparison**).
- Line 4 is printed because the object reference "d" is auto-unboxed to a primitive int value and then compared with the primitive reference "a". This also illustrates a hidden chance of a *NullPointerException* being thrown if the reference "d" were to be null.

Q25 Can you discuss what gets printed? `LF COQ`

```
public class EnumEquals {

   public enum Action {START, STOP, CONTINUE}

   private static Action action = Action.STOP;

   public static void main(String[ ] args) {

      if(Action.STOP == action){
         System.out.println("Enumurations can be compared to ==.");
      }

      if(Action.STOP.equals(action)){
```

```
      System.out.println("Enumurations can be compared to equals() also.");
    }
  }
}
```

A25 Output is:

```
Enumurations can be compared to ==.
Enumurations can be compared to equals() also.
```

The best practice is to use the referential == for enums as they are safer because you get compile-time errors for incorrect comparisons as described below.

```
public class EnumSaferComparison {

  public enum Action {
    START, STOP, CONTINUE
  }

  public enum Status {
    PENDING, PROCESSED
  }

  private static Action action = Action.STOP;

  public static void main(String[] args) {

    // Does not make sense to compare status with action.
    if (Status.PENDING.equals(action)) {                    //Line 1
      // never gets here.
    }

    // won't compile.
    if (Status.PENDING == action) {                         //Line 2

    }
  }
}
```

Line 1 has been accepted by the compiler even though that condition will never be true.

Line 2 forces the compiler to scream that you can't compare apples with oranges.

Working with the String class

Q26 When do you use a *String* and when do you use a *StringBuffer* or *StringBuilder*?
`LF  PC  FAQ  COQ`

A26 **String** is immutable: you can't modify a string object, but can replace it by creating a new instance. Creating a new instance is rather expensive. For example,

```
//Inefficient version using an immutable String
String output = "Some text"
int count = 100;
for(int i =0; i<count; i++) {
    output += i;
}
return output;
```

The above code would build 99 new *String* objects, of which 98 would be thrown away immediately. Creating new objects unnecessarily is not efficient, and the garbage collector needs to clean up those unreferenced 98 objects.

StringBuffer and **StringBuilder**: are mutable and use them when you want to modify the contents. *StringBuilder* was added in Java 5 and it is identical in all respects to *StringBuffer* except that it is not synchronized, which makes it slightly faster at the cost of not being thread-safe.

```
//More efficient version using a mutable StringBuffer
StringBuffer output = new StringBuffer(110);
output.append("Some text");
for(int i =0; i<count; i++) {
    output.append(i);
}
return  output.toString();
```

338

The above code creates only two new objects, the *StringBuffer* and the final *String* that is returned. BP The *StringBuffer* expands as it reaches its capacity, which can be costly if performed frequently. So it would be better to initialize the *StringBuffer* with the correct size from the start as shown above with the size of 110 if the initial size is known or estimate the size appropriately to minimize the number of times it has to expand.

Note: The creation of extra strings is not limited to the overloaded mathematical operator "+", but there are several other methods like *concat( )*, *trim( )*, *substring( )*, and *replace( )* in the *String* class that generate new string instances. So use *StringBuffer* or *StringBuilder* for computation intensive operations to get better performance.

Q27 Can you write a method that reverses a given *String*? COQ FAQ
A27

```java
public class ReverseString {

    public static void main(String[] args) {
        System.out.println(reverse("big brown fox"));
        System.out.println(reverse(""));
    }

    public static String reverse(String input) {
        if(input == null || input.length() == 0){
            return input;
        }

        return new StringBuilder(input).reverse().toString();
    }
}
```

BP It is always a best practice to reuse the API methods as shown above with the **StringBuilder**(input).**reverse**( ) method as it is fast, efficient (uses bitwise operations) and knows how to handle Unicode surrogate pairs, which most other solutions ignore. The above code handles null and empty strings, and a *StringBuilder* is used as opposed to a thread-safe *StringBuffer*, as the *StringBuilder* is locally defined, and local variables are implicitly thread-safe.

Some interviewers might probe you to write other lesser elegant code using either recursion or iterative swapping. Some developers find it very difficult to handle

339

recursion, especially to work out the termination condition. All recursive methods need to have a condition to terminate the recursion.

```java
public class ReverseString2 {

    public String reverse(String str) {
        // exit or termination condition
        if ((null == str) || (str.length()  <= 1)) {
            return str;
        }

        // put the first character (i.e. charAt(0)) to the end. String indices are 0 based.
        // and recurse with 2nd character (i.e. substring(1)) onwards
        return reverse(str.substring(1)) + str.charAt(0);
    }
}
```

The iterative swapping approach can be demonstrated as shown below.

0	1	2	3	4	5	6
R	e	v	e	r	s	e

lhsIdx   rhsIdx

Swap *lhsIdx* with the *rhsIdx*, and increment the *lhsIdx* and decrement the *rhsIdx*.

0	1	2	3	4	5	6
e	e	v	e	r	s	R

          lhsIdx   rhsIdx

Repeat the above step as long as the lhsIdx is less than the rhsIdx.

e	s	v	e	r	e	R

                 lhsIdx   rhsIdx

e	s	r	e	v	e	R

                       lhsIdx
                       rhsIdx

Now the exit (or loop termination) condition has reached since lhsIdx >= rhsIdx. Let's look at the code:

```java
public class ReverseString3 {

    public String reverse(String str) {
        // validate
        if ((null == str) || (str.length() <= 1)) {
            return str;
        }

        char[] chars = str.toCharArray();
        int rhsIdx = chars.length - 1;

        //iteratively swap until exit condition lhsIdx < rhsIdx is reached
        for (int lhsIdx = 0; lhsIdx < rhsIdx; lhsIdx++) {
            char temp = chars[lhsIdx];
            chars[lhsIdx] = chars[rhsIdx];
            chars[rhsIdx--] = temp;
        }

        return new String(chars);
    }
}
```

Q28 Can you talk through the output of the following code snippet? `COQ FAQ`

```java
package chapter2.com;

public class String1 {

    public static void main(String[] args) {
        StringBuffer sb = new StringBuffer("watering");
        sb.replace(2,6, "WATER");                          // Line 7
        sb.delete(1,4);                                     // Line 8
        String result = sb.substring(2,4);                  // Line 9
        System.out.println("result=" + result);
    }
}
```

A28 Remember two things:

- The start index is 0 based.
- The end index character or value is not included. So replace 2,6 will only include 't', 'e', 'r', and 'i'. The character 'n' on index 6 is not included. The letters "n" and "g" gets pushed out by the letter "R" in the replaced string "WATER"

Indexes	0	1	2	3	4	5	6	7	8	9
sb [2,6 is highlighted for the next step].	w	a	t	e	r	i	n	g		
Line:7 Replace 2, 6 with WATER. [1,4 is highlighted for the next step].	w	a	**W**	**A**	**T**	**E**	**R**	n	g	
Line 8: delete 1, 4. [2, 4 is highlighted for the next step].	w	T	E	R	n	g				
Line 9: substring 2,4	E	R								

Output:

```
result=ER
```

Q29 Can you explain how *Strings* are interned in Java? `LF DP FAQ`

A29 String class is designed with the **Flyweight** design pattern. A pool of *Strings* is maintained by the *String* class. When the intern( ) method is invoked, equals(..) method is invoked to determine if the *String* already exist in the pool. If it does then the *String* from the pool is returned. Otherwise, a new *String* object is added to the pool and a reference to this object is returned. For any two Strings s1 & s2, *s1.intern( ) == s2.intern(s2)* only if *s1.equals(s2)* is true.

Two *String* objects are created by the code shown below. Hence *s1 == s2* returns false.

```
//Two new objects are created. Not recommended.
String s1 = new String("A");
String s2 = new String("A");
```

Instead use:

```
String s1 = "A";
String s2 = "A";
```

s1 and s2 point to the same *String* object in the pool. Hence *s1 == s2* returns true.

Q30 Why *String* has been made immutable in Java? `LF` `SE`

A30
- The main reason for immutability is security. In Java you pass file names, host names, user names, passwords, etc as *String*. For example, had *String* been mutable, 'user1' could log into a Java application using his user-name and password credentials, and then possibly change the name of his password file name, which is a *String* object from 'password1' to 'password2' before JVM actually places the native OS system call to open the file. This is a serious security breach allowing 'user1' to open user2's password file.

- Immutable classes are ideal for representing values of abstract data (i.e. value objects) types like numbers, enumerated types, etc. If you need a different value, create a different object. In Java *Integer*, *Long*, *Float*, *Character*, *BigInteger* and *BigDecimal* are all immutable objects. Immutable classes are inherently thread-safe, hence they are less error prone and can be used safely in a multi-threaded environment for better scalability. Optimization strategies like caching, pooling, etc can be easily applied to improve performance.

Q31 Can you list some escape characters in Java? Where are they generally used? `LF`

A31 Escape characters (also called escape sequences or escape codes) are used to signal an alternative interpretation of a series of characters.

\n	New line (used below)
\t	Tab
\b	Backspace
\r	Carriage return
\f	Formfeed
\\	Backslash
\'	Single quotation mark
\"	Double quotation mark (used below)

All characters can be specified as hexadecimal Unicode characters (\uxxxx) with some as octal characters (\ddd where the first d is limited to 0-3, and the others 0-7 - same as \u0000-\u00ff).

\d	Octal
\ud	Unicode character

Most commonly, escape characters are used to solve the problem of using special characters inside a string declaration.

```
String str = "The question is \"to be or not to be\""

System.out.print("\nCreate a new line before and after.\n");
System.out.print("\nThe Pound symbol is --> \u00A3");
System.out.print("\n The Yen symbol is --> \u00A5");
```

Tip: When using a new line character in your code, it is important to understand that it varies among the different operating systems. For example, Windows uses a "\n\r", Mac uses a "\r", and the UNIX based systems uses a "\n". So, you need to use the "line.separator" property to make your code portable as shown below:

```
private static final String NEWLINE = System.getProperty("line.separator");
```

Q32 How will you split the following string of text into individual vehicle types?

"Car,Jeep, Wagon   Scooter   Truck, Van"

A32
```
package chapter2.com;

public class String3 {
    public static void main(String[] args) {

        String pattern = "[,\\s]+"; //regex pattern – a comma or white space
                                    //repeated 1 or more times
        String vehicles = "Car,Jeep, Wagon   Scooter        Truck, Van";
        String[] result = vehicles.split(pattern);
        for (String vehicle : result) {
            System.out.println("Vehicle = \"" + vehicle + "\"");
        }
    }
}
```

```
}
```

Output:

```
Vehicle = "Car"
Vehicle = "Jeep"
Vehicle = "Wagon"
Vehicle = "Scooter"
Vehicle = "Truck"
Vehicle = "Van"
```

Refer to *java.util.regex.Pattern* class API for regex (i.e. Regular Expression) constructs. The *split( )* method takes a regex pattern to split the given string.

Q33 What are the different ways to concatenate strings? Which approach is most efficient? `LF PC COQ`

A33

- Plus ("+") operator.

  ```
  String s1 = "John" + "Davies";
  ```

- Using a *StringBuilder* or *StringBuffer* class.

  ```
  StringBuilder sb = new StringBuilder("John");
  sb.append("Davies");
  ```

- Using the *concat(...)* method.

  ```
  "John".concat("Davies");
  ```

The efficiency depends on what you are concatenating and how you are concatenating it.

- **Concatenating constants**: Plus operator is more efficient than the other two as the JVM optimizes constants.

  ```
  String s1 = "John" + "Davies";
  ```

345

- **Concatenating *String* variables**: Any one of the three methods should do the job.

```
String s1 = s2 + s3 + s4;
String s1 = "name=";
s1 += name;
```

- **Concatenating in a for/while loop**: *StringBuilder* or *StringBuffer* is the most efficient. Avoid using plus operator as it is the worst offender.

```
StringBuilder sb = new StringBuilder(250);
for( int i=0; i<SIZE; i++ ) {
    sb.append("Item:" + i);
}
```

In summary,

- Use plus ("+") operator for concatenating constants.
- Use *concat( )* method for concatenating 2 string variables.
- Use *StringBuilder* or *StringBuffer* for concatenating a number of *String* variables, and most importantly in loops.
- Prefer *StringBuilder* to *StringBuffer* unless multiple threads can have access to it.

Type safety with Generics

Generics are a big step forward for Java, making it more readable and robust. Having said that, there are a number of limitations and can be tricky to use it correctly in your code. Remembering some of the rules will help you better understand generics.

Q34 Why use generics? **LF**

A34 Generics was introduced in JDK 5.0, and allows you to abstract over types. Without generics, you could put any object into a collection. This can encourage developers to write programs that are harder to read and maintain. For example,

```
List list = new ArrayList( );
list.add(new Integer( ));
list.add("A String");
```

346

```
list.add(new Mango( ));
```

Since you can add any object, you would also not only have to use "instanceof" operator, but also have to explicitly cast any objects returned from this list.

```java
package generics;

import java.util.ArrayList;
import java.util.List;

public class WithoutGenerics {

    public static void main(String[ ] args) {
        //Bad practice to add any object
        List list = new ArrayList( );
        list.add(new Integer(5));           //index 0
        list.add("A String");               //index 1
        list.add(new Float(3.0));           //index 2

        //too many unsightly casts & instanceof constructs
        Integer i = (Integer)list.get(0);
        String s1 = null;
        Object o1 = list.get(1);
        if(o1 instanceof String){
            s1 = (String)o1;
        }

        //if you use the wrong cast, you can get a ClassCastException at runtime
        String s2 = (String)list.get(2);    //index 2 is a Float, not a String .
    }
}
```

Now with generics, your code becomes more robust and readable. **Rule 1:** The type safety is checked during **compile-time**.

```java
package generics;

import java.util.ArrayList;
import java.util.List;
```

```
public class WithGenerics {

    public static void main(String[ ] args) {

        //can only add Integers
        List<Integer> list1 = new ArrayList<Integer>( );
        list1.add(new Integer(5));

        //can only add Strings
        List<String> list2 = new ArrayList<String>( );
        list2.add("A String");

        //can only add Floats
        List<Float> list3 = new ArrayList<Float>( );
        list3.add(new Float(3.0));

        //compile error if you try to add a wrong type
        //list1.add("NOT ALLOWED");     //list1 contains Integers NOT String

        //no casting is needed
        Integer i = list1.get(0);
        String s1 = list2.get(0);
        Float f1 = list3.get(0);
    }
}
```

The for-each loop that was added in JDK 1.5 works well with generics.

```
for(String aString : list2){
    System.out.println(aString);
}
```

Q35 What do you understand by the term "type erasure" with regards to generics? **LF**
FAQ

A35 **Rule 1:** Java generics differ from C++ templates. Java generics (at least until JDK 7), generate only one compiled version of a generic class or method regardless of the number of types used. During **compile-time,** all the parametrized type information within the angle brackets are erased and the compiled class file will look similar to code written prior to JDK 5.0. In other words, Java does not support runtime generics.

Q. Why was it done this way?
A. This was done this way to achieve backward compatibility.

```java
package generics;

import java.util.HashMap;
import java.util.Map;

public class TypeErasure {

    public static void main(String[] args) {
        Map<String, Integer> map = new HashMap<String, Integer>();
        map.put("Key1",new Integer(1));
        Integer val1 = map.get("Key1");          //casting is not required
        System.out.println(val1);
    }
}
```

If you run the compiled class file (i.e. *TypeErasure.class*) with the help of a Java decompiler discussed under platform essentials, you will get the following source code.

```java
package generics;

import java.util.HashMap;
import java.util.Map;

public class TypeErasure
{
    public static void main(String[] args)
    {
        Map map = new HashMap();
        map.put("Key1", new Integer(1));
        Integer val1 = (Integer)map.get("Key1");
        System.out.println(val1);
    }
}
```

As you can see, all the angle brackets have disappeared, and casting has been added.

Q36 What does the following code fragment print? `LF COQ`

```
List<String> list1 = new ArrayList<String>();
List<Integer> list2 = new ArrayList<Integer>();
System.out.println(list1.getClass() == list2.getClass());
```

A36 It prints "true" because of type erasure(i.e. Rule 1), all instances of a generic class have the same runtime class, regardless of their actual type parameter. This also mean, <u>there is no sense in checking generic information at runtime</u>. The following code is illegal.

```
if(list1 instanceof List<String>)                    //illegal
```

The following code will issue a warning.

```
public void unCheckedCastWarning(Object o) {
    List<Integer> l = (List<Integer>)o;              //unchecked cast warning
}
```

The JVM can actually check to see if it's a *List*, but it can't check whether it is a list of *Strings* or *Integers* because the type information in angle brackets have been erased. Never ignore warnings like this from the compiler. You also cannot handle different versions of the same exception as shown below because type erasure does not allow it.

```
//illegal
try {
    //....
}
catch(MyException<Integer> ex1){
    //....
}
catch(MyException<String> ex2){
    //....
}
```

Q37 What are the differences among `LF FAQ`

- raw or plain old collection type e.g. **Collection**
- Collection of unknown e.g. **Collection<?>**
- Collection of type object e.g. **Collection<Object>**

A37 The plain old **Collection**: is a heterogeneous mixture or a mixed bag that contains elements of all types, for example *Integer*, *String*, *Fruit*, *Vegetable*, etc.

The **Collection<Object>**: is also a heterogeneous mixture like the plain old Collection, but not the same and can be more restrictive than a plain old Collection discussed above. It is <u>incorrect</u> to think of this as the super type for a collection of any object types.

Rule 2: Unlike an *Object* class is a super type for all objects like *String*, *Integer*, *Fruit*, etc, *List<Object>* is not a super type for *List<String>*, *List<Integer>*, *List<Fruit>*, etc. So it is illegal to do the following:

```
List<Object> list = new ArrayList<Integer>();          //illegal
```

Though *Integer* is a subtype of *Object*, *List<Integer>* is not a subtype of *List<Object>* because *List* of *Objects* is a bigger set comprising of elements of various types like *Strings*, *Integers*, *Fruits*, etc. A *List* of *Integer* should only contain *Integers*, hence the above line is illegal. If the above line was legal, **then you can end up adding objects of any type to the list, violating the purpose of generics**. So how would you go about adding a method that accepts a collection of any type to iterate through as the following code would not work.

```
package generics;

public interface Fruit {
    public abstract void peel();
}
```

```
package generics;

public class Mango implements Fruit {

    @Override
    public void peel() {
```

```
        System.out.println("peeling " +   this.getClass().getSimpleName());
    }
}
```

```
package generics;

public class Orange implements Fruit {
    @Override
    public void peel() {
        System.out.println("peeling " +   this.getClass().getSimpleName());
    }
}
```

```
package generics;

import java.util.ArrayList;
import java.util.List;

public class Generics3 {

    public static void main(String[] args) {
        List<Fruit> fruitBasket = new ArrayList<Fruit>();
        fruitBasket.add(new Orange());
        fruitBasket.add(new Mango());
        processFruits(fruitBasket);                    //compile-time error
    }

    //Won't work with List<Object> because a List<Object> is not a super
    //type for all fruits (i.e. List<Fruit>).
    public static void processFruits(List<Object> fruitBasket){
        for (Object object : fruitBasket) {
            ((Fruit)object).peel();
        }
    }
}
```

The *processFruits(...)* method can be fixed with the wild card character "?" as discussed next.

The **Collection<?>:** is a homogenous collection that represents a family of generic instantiations of Collection like *Collection<String>*, *Collection<Integer>*, *Collection<Fruit>*, etc.

Rule 3: Collection<?> is the super type for all generic collection as Object[ ] is the super type for all arrays.

```
List<?> list = new ArrayList<Integer>();                  //legal
List<? extends Number> list = new ArrayList<Integer>();   //legal
```

Note: An *Integer* is a sub type of a *Number*.

The *processFruits(...)* method can be fixed as follows to accept any kind of fruit.

```
public static void processFruits(List<? extends Fruit> fruitBasket){
   for (Fruit fruit : fruitBasket) {
      fruit.peel();
   }
}
```

The following code snippet will work with a collection of any type. But very rarely you may have a requirement to do this. It is a bad practice to mix unrelated object types into the same collection.

```
public static void processFruits(List<?> fruitBasket){
   for (Object object : fruitBasket) {
      ((Fruit)object).peel();
   }
}
```

Q. Why not implement the method as follows? LF COQ

```
public static void processFruits(List<Fruit> fruitBasket){
   for (Fruit fruit : fruitBasket) {
      fruit.peel();
   }
}
```

A. If you use *List<Fruit>* instead of *List<? extends Fruit>*, you will not be able to use

353

this method for a *List<Mango>* or *List<Orange>*. As discussed earlier in Rule 2, a *Mango* or *Orange* might be a sub type of *Fruit*, but a *List<Mango>* or *List<Orange>* is not a sub type of *List<Fruit>*. This means the following declaration is illegal.

```
List<Fruit> fruitBasket = new ArrayList<Orange>(); // illegal as per Rule 2.
```

and also, the following *processFruits(List<Fruit> fruitBasket)* as shown below

```
public static void processFruits(List<Fruit> fruitBasket){
  for (Fruit fruit : fruitBasket) {
    fruit.peel();
  }
}
```

will only work if you declare your fruitBasket as follows:

```
List<Fruit> fruitBasket = new ArrayList<Fruit>();          //legal
```

But will throw a compile-time error if you pass a *List<Orange>* as a reference to the processFruits(*List<Fruit>* fruitBasket) method due to Rule 2 as shown below:

```
List<Orange> fruitBasket = new ArrayList<Orange>(); //legal
processFruits(fruitBasket);                         //compile-time error
```

Q. Why was the fruitBasket declared as follows?

```
List<Fruit> fruitBasket = new ArrayList<Fruit>();
```

and not as shown below?

```
List<?> fruitBasket = new ArrayList<?>();                  //illegal
List<?> fruitBasket = new ArrayList<? extends Fruit>();    //illegal
```

A. This is due to the restriction on *Collection<?>* to be used only as a reference.

Rule 4: The *Collection<?>* can only be used as a reference type, and **you cannot instantiate it**. The following statements are illegal.

```
List<?> fruitBasket = new ArrayList<?>();                      //illegal
```

354

```
List<?> fruitBasket = new ArrayList<? extends Fruit>();                //illegal
```

You can use *Collection<?>* to declare it as follows,

```
List<?> fruitBasket = new ArrayList<Fruit>();                          //legal
List<? Extends Fruit> fruitBasket =  new ArrayList<Orange>();  //legal
```

Even if you declare it as above, *Collection<?>* has a restriction (i.e. Rule 5) to add arbitrary objects as shown below.

```
List<? extends Fruit> fruitBasket = new ArrayList<Fruit>();
fruitBasket.add(new Orange());                                      //compile-time error
```

Rule 5: Hence, *Collection<?>* is almost a <u>read-only collection</u> allowing only *remove( )* and *clear( )* operations.

Here is the final implementation that takes notice of the rules.

package generics;

```
import java.util.ArrayList;
import java.util.List;

public class Generics3 {

    public static void main(String[] args) {
        List<Fruit> fruitBasket = new ArrayList<Fruit>();
        fruitBasket.add(new Orange());
        fruitBasket.add(new Mango());
        processFruits(fruitBasket);

        List<Orange> orangeBasket = new ArrayList<Orange>();
        orangeBasket.add(new Orange());
        processFruits(orangeBasket);

        List<Mango> mangoBasket = new ArrayList<Mango>();
        mangoBasket.add(new Mango());
        processFruits(mangoBasket);
```

```
   }

   //I can process any type of Fruit
   public static void processFruits(List<? extends Fruit> fruitBasket){
      for (Fruit fruit : fruitBasket) {
         fruit.peel( );
      }
   }
}
```

Output:

```
peeling Orange
peeling Mango
peeling Orange
peeling Mango
```

Q38 Is it possible to generify your own Java class? LF
A38 Yes.

```
package chapter2.com;

public class MyGenericClass<T> {

   T objType;

   public MyGenericClass(T type) {
      this.objType = type;
   }

   public T getObjType() {
      return objType;
   }

   public void setObjType(T objType) {
      this.objType = objType;
   }

   public static void main(String[ ] args) {
```

```
        MyGenericClass<Integer> val1 = new  MyGenericClass<Integer>(37);
        MyGenericClass<Long> val2 = new MyGenericClass<Long>(250L);
        long result = val1.getObjType( ).longValue( ) +
                                   val2.getObjType( ).longValue( );
        System.out.println(result);
    }
}
```

If you decompile the converted class file, you will get,

```
package chapter2.com;

public class MyGenericClass<T>
{
    T objType;

    public MyGenericClass(T type)
    {
        this.objType = type;
    }

    public T getObjType( ) {
        return this.objType;
    }

    public void setObjType(T objType) {
        this.objType = objType;
    }

    public static void main(String[ ] args) {
        MyGenericClass val1 =
                new  MyGenericClass(Integer.valueOf(37));        //auto-box
        MyGenericClass val2 =
                new MyGenericClass(Long.valueOf(250L));          //auto-box
        long result = ((Integer)val1.getObjType( )).longValue( ) +
                                  ((Long)val2.getObjType( )).longValue( );
        System.out.println(result);
    }
}
```

If you closely examine the above code, you would notice that the compiler has performed auto-boxing as generics does not support primitive types. The angle brackets have been removed for val1 & val2 declarations and appropriate castings have been added to convert from type T to *Integer* and *Long* types.

Tip: If you are not too sure, refer to the compiled class to better understand the code by decompiling it using a Java decompiler.

Q. What do you understand by the term type argument inference? LF
A. Rule 6: The **type inference** happens when the compiler can deduce the type arguments of a generic type or method from a given context information. There are 2 situations in which the type argument inference is attempted during compile-time.

1. When an object of a generic type is created as demonstrated in the *MyGenericClass<T>*.

```
//T is inferred as an Integer
MyGenericClass<Integer> val1 = new  MyGenericClass<Integer>(37);
//T is inferred as  a Long
MyGenericClass<Long> val2 = new MyGenericClass<Long>(250L);
```

2. When a generic method is invoked. For example,

```
package generics;

import java.util.ArrayList;
import java.util.List;

public class MyBasket {

    /**
     * The 'src' is the inferred type T or its sub type and the 'dest' is the
     * inferred type T or its super type.
     */
    public static <T> void copy(List<? extends T> src,
                                        List<? super T> dest) {
        for (T obj : src) {
            dest.add(obj);
```

```
      }
  }

  public static void main(String[] args) {
    List<Orange> orangeBasket = new ArrayList<Orange>(10);
    List<Mango> mangoBasket = new ArrayList<Mango>(10);
    orangeBasket.add(new Orange());
    mangoBasket.add(new Mango());
    List<Fruit> fruitBasket = new ArrayList<Fruit>(10);

    List<Orange> orangeBasket2 = new ArrayList<Orange>(10);
    orangeBasket2.add(new Orange());
    List<Mango> mangoBasket2 = new ArrayList<Mango>(10);
    mangoBasket2.add(new Mango());
    List<Fruit> fruitBasket2 = new ArrayList<Fruit>(10);
    fruitBasket2.add(new Mango());

    MyBasket.copy(orangeBasket2, orangeBasket);   // T is an Orange
    MyBasket.copy(mangoBasket2, mangoBasket);    // T is a Mango

    MyBasket.<Orange> copy(orangeBasket, fruitBasket);   // T is an Orange
    MyBasket.<Mango> copy(mangoBasket, fruitBasket);   // T is a Mango

    MyBasket.copy(fruitBasket2, fruitBasket);                  // T is a Fruit

    MyBasket.copy(fruitBasket, orangeBasket); //compile error - T is a
                                              //Fruit. The 'dest' needs to be
                                              //a Fruit or super type of Fruit
                                              //and Not of type Orange

    MyBasket.<Orange> copy(fruitBasket, orangeBasket); //compile error - T
                                              //is an Orange
                                              //The 'src' needs to
                                              //be an Orange or a
                                              //sub type of an
                                              //Orange and
                                              //NOT of type Fruit

    for (Fruit fruit : fruitBasket) {
```

```
        fruit.peel();
    }
  }
}
```

If you comment the 2 lines that result in compile-time error, you will get the following output,

```
peeling Orange
peeling Orange
peeling Mango
peeling Mango
peeling Mango
```

The **copy(...)** method ensures that fruits from a mixed fruit basket cannot be copied to a basket that only holds oranges or mangoes. But a mixed fruit basket allows fruits to be copied from any basket.

Q39 Is the following code snippet legal? If yes why and if not why not? **LF COQ**

```
public MyGenericClass() {
    this.objType = new T();
}
```

A39 It is not legal as new *T( )* will cause a compile-time error. This is partially because there's no guarantee that the target class for raw type "T" has a constructor that takes zero parameters and partially due to type erasure where the raw type "T" does not have any way of knowing the type of object you want to construct at runtime due to Rule 1 discussed earlier.

Q40 Is the following code snippet legal? If yes why and if not why not? **LF COQ**

```
public class MyGenericClass<T,S> {
    static  T objType;

    public static void process(List<T> list) {
        // ...
    }
}
```

A41 It is illegal as shown bellow.

```
public class MyGenericClass<T,S> {
    static  T objType;                        //compile-time error

    public static void process(List<T> list) {    //compile-time error
       // ...
    }
}
```

Unlike C++, Java uses the same class at runtime for both *MyGenericClass<Integer>* and *MyGenericClass<Long>*. Static members, by definition are bound to the class rather than the instance. If the code above were allowed, then type safety could be compromised if an instance of *MyGenericClass<Integer>* stores an *Integer* value and an instance of *MyGenericClass<Long>* retrieves it as a *Long*.

Rule 7: Static members are not allowed to have reference to their type parameters due to Rule 1. Since the static members are not allowed to have reference to their type parameters, generic enum is also not allowed as enum values are static data members.

```
enum State <T> {                          //illegal
   //....
}
```

Q42 Is it possible to generify methods in Java? **LF**
A42 Yes.

```
package chapter2.com;

import java.util.ArrayList;
import java.util.List;

public class MyGenericMethod {

    //Generified method
    public static <T> void addValue(T value, List<T> list){       //Line A
       list.add(value);
    }
```

```
public static void main(String[ ] args) {
   List<Integer> listIntegers = new ArrayList<Integer>( );
   Integer value1 = new Integer(37);
   addValue(value1, listIntegers);              //T is inferred as an Integer
   System.out.println("listIntegers=" + listIntegers);

   List<String> listString = new ArrayList<String>( );
   String value2 = "Test";
   addValue(value2, listString);                //T is inferred as a String
   System.out.println("listString=" + listString);
  }
}
```

Note: If you had used the wildcard *List<?>* instead of *List<T>* on line A, it would not have been possible to add elements due to Rule 5. You will get a compile-time error. So how does the compiler know the type of "T"? It infers this from your use of the method as discussed in Rule 6. The generated class file looks pretty much the same as the source file without the <Integer> and <String> angle brackets as shown below once decompiled.

```
package chapter2.com;

import java.util.ArrayList;
import java.util.List;

public class MyGenericMethod
{
  public static <T> void addValue(T value, List<T> list)
  {
    list.add(value);
  }

  public static void main(String[ ] args) {
     List listIntegers = new ArrayList( );
     Integer value1 = new Integer(37);
     addValue(value1, listIntegers);
     System.out.println("listIntegers=" + listIntegers);
```

```
        List listString = new ArrayList();
        String value2 = "Test";
        addValue(value2, listString);
        System.out.println("listString=" + listString);
    }
}
```

Q43 Does the following code snippet compile? What does it demonstrate? **LF COQ**

```
public class Generics4<T> {

    public <T> void doSomething(T data) {
        System.out.println(data);
    }

    public static void main(String[] args) {
        Generics4<String> g4 = new Generics4<String>();
        g4.doSomething(123);
    }
}
```

What does "public <T> void doSomething(T data)" really mean?

A43 Yes, the above code snippet does compile. It demonstrates that the type parameter in the class name and the type parameter in the method are actually different parameters. The method signature,

```
public <T> void doSomething(T data)
```

really means:

```
public  void doSomething(Object data)
```

Q44 Can you identify any issues with the following code? **COQ**

```
package generics;

import java.util.ArrayList;
```

363

```
import java.util.Iterator;
import java.util.List;

public class GenericsWithIterators {

    public static void main(String[ ] args) {
        List<Integer> listIntegers = new ArrayList<Integer>( );    //1
        listIntegers.add(5);                                        //2
        listIntegers.add(3);                                        //3

        Iterator it = listIntegers.listIterator( );               //4

        while(it.hasNext( )){                                       //5
            Integer i =  it.next( );                               //6
            System.out.println(i);                                 //7
        }
    }
}
```

A44 Line 4 will cause compile-time error on line 6 as the iterator is not generic. To fix this, replace line 4 with:

```
Iterator<Integer> it = listIntegers.listIterator( );              // fix 1
```

or add an explicit cast to line 6.

```
Integer i =  (Integer) it.next( );                                // fix 2
```

The fix 1 is preferred. When you get an iterator, keyset, or values from a collection, assign it to an appropriate parametrized type as shown in fix 1.

Serializing your objects

Q45 Which Java interface must be implemented by a class whose instances are transported via a Web service?

> a. Accessible

b. BeanInfo

c. Remote

d. Serializable

A45 d. Serializable

Q46 What is serialization? How would you exclude a field of a class from serialization or what is a transient variable? What happens to static fields during serialization? What are the common uses of serialization? What is a serial version id? Are there any disadvantages in using serialization? `LF FAQ`

A46 Object serialization is a process of reading or writing an object. It is a process of saving an object's state to a sequence of bytes, as well as a process of rebuilding those bytes back into a live object at some future time. An object is marked serializable by implementing the *java.io.Serializable* interface. This simply allows the serialization mechanism to verify that a class can be persisted, typically to a file. The common process of serialization is also called **marshaling** or **deflating** when an object is flattened into byte streams. The flattened byte streams can be **unmarshaled** or **inflated** back to an object.

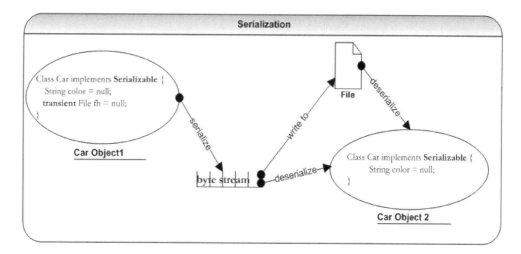

To persist objects, you need to keep 5 rules in mind:

- **Rule #1**: The object to be persisted must implement the *Serializable* interface or inherit that interface from its object hierarchy. Alternatively, you can use an *Externalizable* interface to have full control over your serialization process. For

365

example, to construct an object from a pdf file.

- **Rule #2**: The object to be persisted must mark all non-serializable fields as **transient**. For example, file handles, sockets, threads, etc.

- **Rule #3**: You should make sure that all the included objects are also serializable. If any of the objects is not serializable, then it throws a *NotSerializableException*. In the example shown below, the *Pet* class implements the Serializable interface, and also the containing field types *String* and *Integer* are also serializable.

- **Rule #4**: Base or parent class fields are only handled if the base class itself is serializable.

- **Rule #5**: Serialization ignores static fields, because they are not part of any particular state.

The *Pet* class shown below can be persisted based on the above mentioned rules.

```
package serialization;

import java.io.File;
import java.io.Serializable;

public class Pet implements Serializable {

    private static final long serialVersionUID = 1L;
    //classes Integer and String  implements serializable
    private Integer id;
    private String name;
    //to show that transient fields are not serialized
    private transient File petFile = new File("DummyPet.txt");
    //to show that static fields are ignored
    private static Integer petCount = new Integer(0);

    public Pet(Integer id, String name) {
        this.id = id;
        this.name = name;
```

```
    }

    public Integer getId( ) {
       return id;
    }

    public String getName( ) {
       return name;
    }

    public void incrementCount( ) {
       petCount++;
    }

    @Override
    public String toString( ) {
       return "[id=" + id + ",name=" + name + ",petFile=" + petFile
            + ",petCount=" + petCount + "]";
    }
}
```

You can serialize the *Pet* object as shown below:

```
package serialization;

import java.io.FileOutputStream;
import java.io.IOException;
import java.io.ObjectOutputStream;

public class FlattenPet {

    public static void main(String[ ] args) throws IOException {
        String filename = "C://temp/pet.ser";
        if (args.length > 0) {
            filename = args[0];
        }
        Pet myPet = new Pet(7, "Jimmy");
        myPet.incrementCount( );
        FileOutputStream fos = null;
```

```
   ObjectOutputStream out = null;
   try {
      fos = new FileOutputStream(filename);
      out = new ObjectOutputStream(fos);
      // serialization takes place here
      out.writeObject(myPet);

   } finally {
      if (out != null) {
         out.close();
      }
   }
 }
}
```

You can deserialize the pet.ser byte stream file back to an object as shown below:

```
package serialization;

import java.io.FileInputStream;
import java.io.IOException;
import java.io.ObjectInputStream;

public class InflatePet {

   public static void main(String[ ] args) throws IOException {

      String filename = "C://temp/pet.ser";
      Pet myPet = null;
      FileInputStream fis = null;
      ObjectInputStream in = null;
      try {
         fis = new FileInputStream(filename);
         in = new ObjectInputStream(fis);
         //deserialization occur here
         myPet = (Pet) in.readObject();

      } catch (ClassNotFoundException ex) {
         ex.printStackTrace();
```

```
        }
    finally {
        if (in != null) {
            in.close();
        }
    }
    }
    // print out restored myPet to see what were serialized
    // what were not serialized.
    System.out.println("Inflated pet: " + myPet);
    }
}
```

Output:

Inflated pet: [id=7,name=Jimmy,**petFile=null,petCount=0**]

As you can see in the output, even though the *petCount* was incremented to 1, you got 0 back as static fields will not be serialized. The *petFile* is null, even though is initialized as it is marked transient. Only non-transient and non-static fields "id" and "name" are serialized as shown in the output.

Q47 How would you exclude a field of a class from serialization? `LF FAQ`

A47 By marking it as **transient**. The fields marked as transient in a serializable object will not be transmitted in the byte stream. An example would be a file handle, a database connection, a system thread, etc. Such objects are only meaningful locally. So they should be marked as transient in a serializable class.

Q48 What happens to static fields during serialization? `LF FAQ`

A48 Serialization persists only the state of a single object. Static fields are not part of the state of an object - they're effectively the state of the class shared by many other instances.

Q49 What are the common uses of serialization? Can you give me an instance where you used serialization? `LF FAQ`

A49

- allows you to persist objects with state to a text file on a disk, and re-assemble them by reading this back in. Application servers can do this to conserve memory. For example, stateful EJBs can be activated and passivated using serialization. The objects stored in an HTTP session should be serializable to support in-memory replication of sessions to achieve scalability.

- allows you to send objects from one Java process to another using sockets, RMI, RPC, etc.

- allows you to deeply clone any arbitrary object graph.

Q50 What is a serial version id? **LF FAQ**

A50 Say you create a "*Pet*" class, and instantiate it to "*myPet*", and write it out to an object stream. This flattened "*myPet*" object sits in the file system for some time. Meanwhile, if the "*Pet*" class is modified by adding a new field, and later on, when you try to read (i.e. deserialize or inflate) the flattened "*Pet*" object, you get the *java.io.InvalidClassException* – because all serializable classes are automatically given a unique identifier. This exception is thrown when the identifier of the class is not equal to the identifier of the flattened object. If you really think about it, the exception is thrown because of the addition of the new field. You can avoid this exception being thrown by controlling the versioning yourself by declaring an explicit *serialVersionUID*. There is also a small performance benefit in explicitly declaring your *serialVersionUID* because it does not have to be calculated.

BP So it is a best practice to add your own *serialVersionUID* to your Serializable classes as soon as you define them. If no *serialVersionUID* is declared, JVM will use its own algorithm to generate a default *SerialVersionUID*. The default *serialVersionUID* computation is highly sensitive to class details and may vary from different JVM implementation, and result in an unexpected *InvalidClassExceptions* during deserialization process.

Q51 Are there any disadvantages in using serialization? **LF FAQ**

A51 Yes. Serialization can adversely affect performance since it:

- Depends on reflection.
- Has an incredibly verbose data format.
- Is very easy to send surplus data.

So don't use serialization if you do not have to.

Q52 What is the difference between *Serializable* and *Externalizable* interfaces? How can you customize the serialization process? **LF**

A52 An object must implement either Serializable or Externalizable interface before it can be written to a byte stream. When you use Serializable interface, your class is serialized automatically by default. But you can override *writeObject(..)* and *readObject(...)* methods to control or customize your object serialization process. For example, you can add the following methods to your *Pet* class.

```
private void writeObject(ObjectOutputStream out)
      throws IOException {

   //any write customization goes in this method
   System.out
         .println("Started writing object ...................");
   out.writeObject(this);
}

private void readObject(ObjectInputStream in) throws IOException,
      ClassNotFoundException {

   //any read customization goes in this method
   System.out
         .println("Started reading object ...................");
   in.readObject();
}
```

Note: Both the above methods must be declared private.

No changes are required for *FlattenPet* and *InflatePet* classes. If you re-run *InflatePet* by including the above methods in the *Pet* class, you will get,

Output:

```
Started reading object ...................
Inflated pet: [id=null,name=null,petFile=null,petCount=0]
```

When you use *Externalizable* interface instead of the *Serializable* interface, you have a complete control over your class's serialization process. This interface contains two methods namely *readExternal(...)* and *writeExternal(...)* to achieve this total customization. You can change the *Pet* class to implement the *Externalizable* interface and then provide implementation for following 2 methods.

371

```
public void writeExternal(ObjectOutput out) throws IOException;
public void readExternal(ObjectInput in) throws IOException,
                                          ClassNotFoundException;
```

An example situation for this full control will be to read and write PDF files with a Java application. If you know how to write and read PDF (the sequence of bytes required), you could provide the PDF specific protocol in the *writeExternal(...)* and *readExternal(...)* methods.

Just as before, there is no difference in how a class that implements *Externalizable* is used. Just call *writeObject( )* or *readObject* and, those externalizable methods will be called automatically.

Garbage Collection

A number of recorded questions asked in Java interviews were related to garbage collection.

Q53 What is the difference between final, finally and finalize( ) in Java? **LF FAQ**

A53
- **final** - is a constant declaration.
- **finally** - handles exception. The finally block is optional and provides a mechanism to clean up regardless of an exception is thrown or not.
- **finalize( )** - method helps in garbage collection. This method is invoked before an object is discarded by the garbage collector, allowing it to clean up its state. Should not be used to release non-memory resources like file handles, sockets, database connections, etc because Java has only a finite number of these resources and you do not know when the garbage collection is going to kick in to release these non-memory resources through the *finalize( )* method. The *System.runFinalization( )* is a hint or request to run all the finalizers of eligible objects, but no guarantee is made that finalization will run immediately after the request.

Q54 What do you know about the Java garbage collector? When does the garbage collection occur? **LF FAQ**

A54

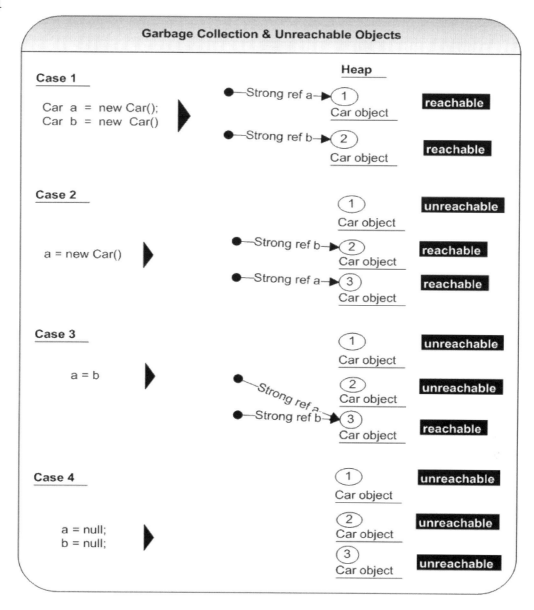

- Java itself does memory management with a concept known as "garbage collection", which implies that objects that are no longer needed by a program are "garbage" and can be thrown away. It is also known as "memory recycling". You do not need to allocate memory at the time of object creation, and also you do not need to free memory explicitly.

- Objects created with new keyword are placed in heap memory. When an object is no longer referenced by the program (i.e. **unreachable**), the heap space it occupies can be recycled so that the space is made available for subsequent new objects. The garbage collector must somehow determine which objects are no longer referenced by the program and make available the heap space occupied by such unreferenced objects.

- Garbage collection helps ensure program integrity and security by preventing Java programmers from accidentally (or purposely) crashing the Java virtual machine by incorrectly freeing memory.

- Garbage collection is an automatic process and cannot be forced. The call *System.gc( )* does NOT force the garbage collection, but only suggests that the JVM may make an effort to do a garbage collection.

- Garbage collection usually adopts an algorithm, which gives a fair balance between how quickly garbage collection thread yields and the speed of memory recovery. It is important for real time systems to use an algorithm that is responsive by quickly yielding the garbage collection thread.

Q55 Explain different types of references in Java? `LF  DP`

A55 The garbage collector treats strong, soft, weak, and phantom objects differently to provide different types of services to your application code. The reference classes include a non-instantiable *Reference* base class and three subclasses that defines 3 different types of weak references like *SoftReference*, *WeakReference*, and *PhantomReference*. A *Reference* is a wrapper around a Java strong reference, using the decorator design pattern. These reference objects are also immutable.

- **Strong reference:** A strong reference is an ordinary Java reference that is used every day.

```
String str = "ABC";
```

The thing that makes them "strong" is how they interact with the garbage collector. Specifically, if an object is reachable via a chain of strong references, it is not eligible for garbage collection because you don't want the garbage collector to destroy the objects you're working on.

- **Weak reference:** A weak reference, simply put, is a reference that isn't strong enough to force an object to remain in memory. Weak references allow you to leverage the garbage collector's ability to determine reachability for you, so you don't have to do it yourself. You create a weak reference like this:

```
Car c1 = new Car();              //referent is c1 is a strong reference
WeakReference<Car> wr = new WeakReference<Car>(c1);
```

A weak reference is a holder for a reference to an object, called the referent. Weak references and weak collections are powerful tools for heap management, allowing the application to <u>use a more sophisticated notion of reachability</u>, rather than the "all or nothing" reachability offered by ordinary (i.e. strong) references. For example,

A *WeakHashMap* stores the keys using *WeakReference* objects, which means that as soon as the key is not referenced from somewhere else in your program, the entry may be removed and is available for garbage collection.

```
package reference;

import java.util.Map;
import java.util.WeakHashMap;
import java.util.concurrent.TimeUnit;

public class WeakerMap {

    private static Map<String, String> map;

    public static void main(String args[]) {
        //substitute with HashMap and compare
        map = new WeakHashMap<String, String>();              //Line A
        map.put(new String("John"), "Smith");
        Runnable runner = new Runnable() {
            public void run() {
                while (map.containsKey("John")) {
                    try {
                        TimeUnit.SECONDS.sleep(1);
                    } catch (InterruptedException ignored) {
```

```
        }
        System.out.println("Checking for John");
        System.gc( ); //nicely ask
    }

    System.out.println("No more John");
    }
};

Thread t = new Thread(runner);      //creates a new thread
t.start( );                         // starts the thread t

try {
    t.join( );          // blocks the main thread until thread t finishes
} catch (InterruptedException ie) {
    ie.printStackTrace( );
    }
  }
}
```

Output:

```
Checking for John
No more John
```

If you replace *WeakHasMap* with *HashMap* on line A, you will have an endless loop printing "Checking for empty" as the entry "*John*" never gets removed from the *HashMap*.

- **Soft reference** is similar to a weak reference, except that it is less eager to throw away the object to which it refers. An object which is only weakly reachable will be discarded at the next garbage collection cycle, but an object which is softly reachable will generally stick around for a while as long as there is enough memory. Hence the soft references are good candidates for a cache.

```
byte[ ] cache = new byte[1024];
//... populate the cache. The referent is  cache
SoftReference<byte[ ]> sr = new    SoftReference<byte[ ]>(cache);
```

The garbage collector may or may not reclaim a softly reachable object depending on how recently the object was created or accessed, but is required to clear all soft references before throwing an *OutOfMemoryError*.

- **Phantom reference:** Unlike soft and weak reference objects, which can optionally be created without associating them with a reference queue, phantom reference objects cannot be instantiated without associating the referent with a reference queue. You can use the arrival of a phantom reference in a reference queue to trigger some action before it becomes unreachable by invoking the *clear( )* method. So phantomly reachable objects are objects that have been *finalized( )* but not reclaimed. The garbage collector will never clear a phantom reference. All phantom references must be explicitly cleared by the program.

```
ReferenceQueue<String> referent = new ReferenceQueue<String>( );
String str = "ABC";
PhantomReference<String> ref = new
               PhantomReference<String>(str, referent);
```

Q56 If you have a circular reference of objects, but you no longer reference it from an execution thread (e.g. main thread), will this object be a potential candidate for garbage collection? **LF**

A56

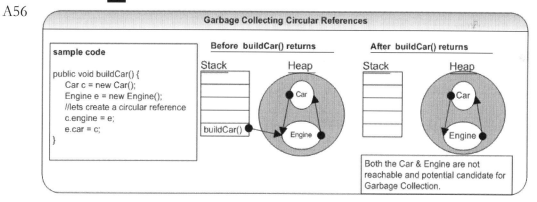

Yes. If you no longer reference it from an executing thread, then this object is unreachable and potential candidate for garbage collection. An object becomes eligible for Garbage Collection when no live thread can access it.

Q57 What are the different ways to make an object eligible for Garbage Collection when it

377

is no longer needed? `LF FAQ`

A57   • Set all available object references to null once the purpose of creating the object is served:

```
String str = "Some value";          // not eligible for GC
str = null;                         //now eligible for GC
```

   • Make the reference variable to refer to another object:

```
String str1 = "Some Value";         // not eligible for GC
String str2 = "Another Value";      // not eligible for GC
str1 = str2;                        // str1 points to str2 "Another Value"
                                    // so "Some Value" is eligible for GC
```

Q58 When does the GC stop? Who controls the GC? Can GC be forced? `LF FAQ`

A58 GC runs on a low priority daemon thread started by the JVM. This thread stops when all non-daemon threads stop.

The JVM controls the GC.

No. The Garbage Collection can not be forced, but there are a few ways by which it can be requested, but there is no guarantee that these requests will be taken care of by the JVM.

```
System.gc() ;
  or
Runtime.getRuntime().gc();
```

Q59 Which part of the memory is involved in Garbage Collection? Stack or Heap? `LF`

A59 Heap.

Q60 How do you know if your garbage collector is under heavy use? What are the best practices to minimize heavy use of garbage collection? `LF MC`

A60 If you see a **jigsaw pattern** in your memory profiler, this is an indication of a memory leak.

   • **Strive for immutable objects** as they not only keep your design simple and thread-safe, but also promotes object reuse through caching.

- The rule of thumb should be to use **object pooling only when their creation consumes significant resources** such as database connection pooling, socket connection pooling (HTTP, RMI, CORBA, Web Service, etc), thread pooling, bitmaps or other graphics objects, etc. If it is about creating a new *String* object, then code readability, maintainability, and simplicity should have higher precedence. Object allocation is relatively fast in JDKs 5 and higher as object creation with the "new" operator is faster (needing 10 instructions) than it used to be, and GC efficiency is also much improved.

- **Premature optimization is the root cause for many other issues**. For example, writing an object pool is not a trivial task. It has its own pitfalls and complexities like,

    - The state of the objects returned to the pool is reset back to a sensible state for the next use of the object.
    - The presence of stale state causes the object to behave differently.
    - The security of your system can be compromised if an object contains confidential data (e.g. credit card numbers) that isn't cleared before the object is passed to a different client.
    - If the objects in the pool are not immutable or thread-safe and accessed concurrently by multiple threads, thread-safety needs to be properly implemented to prevent parallel threads from grabbing and trying to reuse the same object concurrently.

So profile your application first to prove that the GC is over worked. If your GC is over worked, and is using your CPU, then your application will be starved for CPU, causing it to pause. This situation will require your interventions to reduce over working of the garbage collector in one or more of the following means.

    - Allocating the right amount of memory to your JVM at program start-up. There are many approaches to this, but the best thing is to run your program with memory diagnostics, and see how much memory you're really using, then allocate minimum and maximum heap sizes accordingly. In general minimum and maximum values are set to the same value.

- Using the right combination of GC algorithm and other JVM related GC parameters can improve the situation as well. For example, in Java 6 garbage collector, you can use the following combination:

```
-XX:+UseConcMarkSweepGC
-XX:+CMSIncrementalMode
-XX:+PrintGCDetails
-XX:+PrintGCTimeStamps
-XX:+CMSIncrementalPacing
```

- If you had decided that object reuse is the way to go then try it with well proven and tested caching products like, *EHCache*, *Terracotta*, *Tangersol*, *GridGain*, etc.

- Making use of coding best practices discussed already like:

    - Reducing the scope of the variables where possible. For example, local variables are stored in the stack. The stack based allocation is more efficient.

      Based on Brian Goet'z article entitled "Java theory and practice: Urban performance legends, revisited" – **Escape analysis** is an optimization that has been talked about for a long time, and it is finally here -- the current builds of Mustang (Java SE 6) can do escape analysis and **convert heap allocation to stack allocation** (or no allocation) where appropriate. The use of escape analysis to eliminate some allocations results in even faster average allocation times, reduced memory footprint, and fewer cache misses. Further, optimizing away some allocations reduces pressure on the garbage collector and allows collection to run less often.

    - Set your collection data structure with the appropriate initial capacity so that it does not have to resize frequently by discarding the old collection of objects and creating a new collection.

      ```
      Map<Integer,String> mYMap =
              new HashMap<Integer, String> (250);
      ```

Q61 Assume that the following utility method is very frequently accessed by parallel threads, and profiling indicates that this method is causing GC to over work. How would you go about improving the following implementation? **LF COQ**

```java
package simpledate;

import java.text.DateFormat;
import java.text.SimpleDateFormat;
import java.util.Date;

public class ConvertDateUtil {

    private static final String FORMAT = "yyyy-MM-dd";
    public static void format(Date date) {
        DateFormat df = new SimpleDateFormat(FORMAT);
        df.format(date);
    }
}
```

A61 This is only a hypothetical question. For example, the physical memory on the machine could be limited. The above code in general should not cause any performance issue or frequent garbage collection with the modern JVMs. The above code is also easy to read and understand. If the profiler indicates that the GC is being over worked or to understand what options are available for creation of much more complex objects like a bitmap or graphic objects, the above method can be implemented with the following considerations:

- Since *SimpleDateFormat* class is not thread-safe, it was instantiated for each method call as a local variable in the above code. You cannot declare *SimpleDateFormat* as a static variable since it won't be thread-safe. If you want to define it as a static variable to minimize object churn, it has to be appropriately synchronized. Synchronization can introduce thread contention, and is not the best approach. The better approach is to use a *ThreadLocal* class to store dedicated *SimpleDateFormat* object for each thread. This is also known as per-thread caching. This will not only reduce the number of objects created, but also will ensure thread-safety.

381

- As you had seen earlier, soft references get garbage collected only in low memory situations. So it is useful for implementing caches with soft references.

Here is a sample code demonstrating the use of *ThreadLocal* with *SoftReference* for better object and memory reuse.

```java
package simpledate;

import java.lang.ref.SoftReference;
import java.text.DateFormat;
import java.text.SimpleDateFormat;
import java.util.Date;

public class ConvertDateUtil2 {
    private static final String FORMAT = "yyyy-MM-dd";
    private static final ThreadLocal<SoftReference<DateFormat>> repo =
                    new ThreadLocal<SoftReference<DateFormat>>();

    public static void format(Date date) {
        DateFormat df = null;
        SoftReference<DateFormat> softRef = repo.get();
        // if softRef is not garbage collected
        if (softRef != null) {
            df = softRef.get();
        }
        // if garbage collected or not initialized
        else {
            df = new SimpleDateFormat(FORMAT);
            softRef = new SoftReference<DateFormat>(df);
            repo.set(softRef);

        }

        df.format(date);
    }
}
```

Section-7:

Logic and Data structures Essentials

- Java Flow Control
- Java Data structures and algorithms
- Logic Processing
- Exception handling

The data structures and logic processing are prevalently used in programming. It is important to have a basic understanding of the most common data structures like arrays, lists, sets, maps, trees, and graphs, and the basics of the "big-O" algorithmic complexity analysis. You should know why a particular data structure or an algorithm needs to be used for a given usage pattern. You should know the abstract data types such as *List*, *Stack*, or *Set* and the corresponding concrete implementations like *ArrayList*, *HashSet*, *HashMap*, etc.

It is also imperative to understand the performance versus memory tradeoffs between two different concrete implementations of an abstract data structure. The data structures can be traversed iteratively(e.g. arrays, lists, sets) or recursively (e.g. tree). Various sorting, partitioning, and searching algorithms can be applied to various data structures. Most data structures internally use an array or a list to provide a more specialized functionality. Thread-safety and immutability are other two considerations in using different data structures. The following are some common questions answered in this section.

"If Java did not have a *Map* or *Set* implementation, how would you go about implementing your own?"

"What are the common data structures, and where would you use them?"

Java Flow Control

Q1 Why would you prefer a short circuit "&&, ||" operators over logical "& , |" operators? `LF COQ`

A1 Firstly, *NullPointerException* is by far the most common runtime exception. If you use a logical operator, you can get a *NullPointerException*. This can be avoided easily by using a short circuit operator as shown below. There are other ways to check for null, but short circuit && operator can simplify your code by not having to declare separate if clauses.

```
if((obj != null) & obj.equals(newObj)) {   // can cause a NullPointerException
    ....                                    // obj.equals(newObj) is executed
                                            // even if  obj != null returns false.
}
```

Short-circuiting means that an operator only evaluates as far as it has to, not as far as it can. If the variable 'obj' is null, it won't even try to evaluate the '*obj.equals(newObj)*' clause as shown below. This protects the potential *NullPointerException*.

```
if((obj != null) && obj.equals(newObj)) {   // cannot get a NullPointerException
    ...                                      //  because obj.equals(newObj) is
                                             // executed only if obj != null returns true
}
```

`PC` Secondly, short-circuit "&&" and "||" operators can improve performance in certain situations. For example:

```
//the CPU intensive method in bold is  executed  only if number is > 7
if((number <= 7) || (doComputeIntensiveAnalysis (number) <= 13)) {
    ...
}
```

Q2 What can prevent the execution of code in a finally block? `LF COQ`
A2

• An end-less loop.

```
public static void main(String[ ] args) {
    try {
```

```
            System.out.println("This line is printed .....");
            //endless loop
            while(true){
                ...
            }
        }
        finally{
            System.out.println("Finally block is reached.");     // won't reach
        }
    }
```

- *System.exit(1)* statement.

```
public class Temp {

    public static void main(String[ ] args) {
        try {
            System.out.println("This line is printed .....");
            System.exit(1);
        }
        finally{
            System.out.println("Finally block is reached.");     // won't reach
        }
    }
}
```

- Thread death or turning off the power to CPU.
- An exception arising in a finally block itself.
- Process p = Runtime.getRuntime( ).exec("<o/s kill command>");

Q3   What will be the output of the following code snippet? COQ

```
package flow;

public class Finally1 {

    public static void main(String[ ] args) {
        System.out.println("Entering main( )" );
        System.out.println(new Finally1( ).getValue());
```

```
    }

    public String getValue( ) {
        try {
            System.out.println("Entering getValue( )");
            return "Returning the value";
        } finally {
            System.out.println("executing the finally block");

        }
    }
}
```

A3   The finally block is executed before returning the value.

Output:

```
Entering main( )
Entering getValue( )
executing the finally block
Returning the value
```

Q. What value will the following method return?

```
public static int getMonthsInYear(){
  try{
    return 2;
  } finally {
    return 1;
  }
}
```

A. 1 is returned because 'finally' has the right to override any exception/returned value by the try..catch block. It is a bad practice to return from a finally block as it can suppress any exceptions thrown from a try..catch block. For example, the following code will not throw an exception.

```
public static int getMonthsInYear(){
  try{
        throw new RuntimeException( );
```

```
    } finally {
        return 12;
    }
}
```

Q4 What will be the output of the following code snippet? `LF COQ`

```java
package flow;

public class Finally2 {

    public static void main(String[] args) throws Exception {
        try {
            System.out.println("Entered the try block");
            if(1==1){
                throw new Exception("Some exception");
            }
        }
        finally{
            System.out.println("Executing the finally block.");
        }
    }
}
```

A4 The finally block is executed before an exception is thrown.

```
Entered the try block
Executing the finally block.
Exception in thread "main" java.lang.Exception: Some exception
        at flow.Finally2.main(Finally2.java:9)
```

Q5 What is the difference between while and do while loop? `LF`
A5 Do while loop always executes the body of the loop at least once, since the test is performed at the end of the body. The "while" loop always checks the condition first.

```java
while (condition) {
    // reached only if the condition is true.
}
```

```
do {
    // reached at least once even if the condition is false.
} while (condition);
```

Q6   Write a method to print the odd numbers from 1 to 99? COQ

A6

```
public static void printOddNumbers() {
    for ( int i = 1; i < 100; i += 2 ) {
        System.out.println ( i );
    }
}
```

Q7   Can you write a method to print out a multiplication table? COQ

A7

```
static void multiplicationTables ( int max )   {
    for ( int i = 1; i <= max; i++ ) {
        for ( int j = 1; j <= max; j++ ) {
            System.out.print ( String.format ( "%4d", j * i ));
        }
        System.out.println();
    }
}
```

Q8   If you have large if-else or switch-case statements, what would come to your mind? LF
COQ

A8   Replacing the procedural statements with an object oriented approach using polymorphism. Large if-else or switch-case statements are harder to to read, maintain, and extend.

Q. What will be printed with the following code snippet?

```
public static void main(String[ ] args) {
    double value = 3;
    switch (value) {
    case 1:
        System.out.println("A");
        break;
    case 2:
```

```
        System.out.println("B");
        break;
    case 3:
        System.out.println("C");
    default:
        System.out.println("Z");


    }
  }
```

A. The above code will result in a compile-time error. Unlike if-then and if-then-else, the switch statement allows for any number of possible execution paths. But switch works only with enums and primitive data type int or int convertible primitive data types such as byte, short, and char. One of the new features added in Java 7 is the capability to switch on a *String*. The switch statement when used with a String uses the *equals( )* method to compare the given expression to each value in the case statement and is therefore case-sensitive and will throw a *NullPointerException* if the expression is null.

Q. How will you fix the above switch statement?
A. Change the variable "value" from type double to type int. Also, the case 3 statement must have a "break" statement after printing "C", otherwise the default value "Z" will be printed as well.

Q9 What is a conditional operator? **LF**
A9 The conditional operator ?: provides a short-cut to if-else statements. The following if-else statement,

```
if (person != null) {
    return person.getName();
}
else {
    return null;
}
```

can be written more concisely as shown below:

```
return (person != null)) ? person.getName() : null;
```

Note: Future versions of Java may improve null handling with a shortened form of the ternary operator. For example, the code shown below

```
if (person != null) {
    Name name = person.getName();
    if (name != null) {
        return name.getFirstname();
    }
}
```

can be shortened as follows:

```
return person?.getName()?.getFirstname();
```

Q10 What is a fibonacci sequence? Write a method to compute the Nth fibonacci number without using nested loops? COQ

A10 The fibonacci sequence proceeds with the rule that each number is equal to the sum of the preceding two numbers. For example

```
0, 1, 1, 2, 3, 5, 8, 13, 21, 34
```

The code can be written using **recursion** as shown below. A conditional operator is used as the termination or exit condition for the recursive method calls.

```
static long fibonacci(int n) {
    return n <= 1 ? n : fibonacci(n-1) + fibonacci(n-2);
}
```

Java Data structures

Q11 What are the core interfaces of the Java collection framework? LF

A11 *Collection, List, Set, SortedSet, Map, SortedMap, ConcurrentMap, Queue, Dequeue, BlockingQueue, Iterator* (for uni-directional traversal), and *ListIterator* (for bi-directional traversal).

Abstract Data Structure	Concrete Implementation
List	ArrayList, CopyOnWriteArrayList, LinkedList, Stack, etc.
Set	HashSet, EnumSet, CopyOnWriteArraySet, LinkedHashSet, TreeSet, etc
Map	HashMap, ConcurrentHashMap, EnumMap, WeakHashMap, TreeMap, etc
SortedSet	TreeSet
SortedMap	TreeMap
ConcurrentMap	ConcurrentHashMap
Queue	ArrayBlockingQueue, PriorityQueue, PriorityBlockingQueue, SynchronousQueue, etc
BlockingQueue	ArrayBlockingQueue, DelayQueue, PriorityBlockingQueue, SynchronousQueue, etc.
Iterator	Scanner, etc. The implementing class provides the implementation using the iterator design pattern. E.g. myList.*iterator( )*
ListIterator	The implementing class provides the implementation using the iterator design pattern. E.g. myList.*listIterator( )*

Q12 What are the common data structures, and where would you use them? `LF` `COQ` `OEQ`

A12 **Arrays** are the most commonly used data structure. Arrays are of fixed size, indexed, and all containing elements are of the same type (i.e. a homogenous collection). For example, storing employee details just read from the database as *EmployeeDetail[ ]*, converting and storing a string as a byte array for further manipulation or processing, etc. `BP` Wrap an array in a class to protect it from being inadvertently altered. This would be true for other data structures as well.

Lists are known as arrays that can grow. These data structures are generally backed by a fixed sized array and they resize themselves as necessary. A list can have duplicate elements. For example, adding new line items to an order that stores its line items as a list, removing all expired products from a list of products, etc. `BP` Initialize them with an appropriate initial size to minimize the number of resizes.

Sets are like lists but they do not hold duplicate elements. Sets can be used when you have a requirement to store unique elements.

Stacks allow access to only one data item, which is the last item inserted (i.e. Last In First Out - LIFO). If you remove this item, you can access the next-to-last item inserted, and so on. The LIFO is achieved through restricting access only via methods like *peek( )*, *push( )*, and *pop( )*. This is useful in many programing situations like parsing mathematical expressions like (4+2) * 3, storing methods and exceptions in the order they occur, checking your source code to see if the brackets and braces are balanced properly, etc.

Queues are somewhat like a stack, except that in a queue the first item inserted is the first to be removed (i.e. First In First Out – FIFO). The FIFO is achieved through restricting access only via methods like *peek( )*, *offer( )*, and *poll( )*. For example, waiting in a line for a bus, a queue at the bank or super market teller, etc.

LinkedLists are data structures made of nodes, where each node contains data and a reference to the next node, and possibly to the previous node as well for a doubly linked list. For example, a stack or queue can be implemented with a linked list or a doubly linked list because you can insert and delete at both ends. There would also be other situations where data will be frequently inserted and deleted from the middle. The Apache library provides a *TreeList* implementation, which is a good replacement for a *LinkedList* as it performs much better than a *LinkedList* at the expense of using a little more memory. This means a *LinkedList* is rarely a good choice of implementation.

	get	add	insert	iterate	remove
TreeList	3	5	1	2	1
ArrayList	1	1	40	1	40
LinkedList	5800	1	350	2	325

ArrayList is a good general purpose list implementation. An *ArrayList* is faster than a *TreeList* for most operations except inserting and removing in the middle of the list. A *TreeList* implementation utilizes a tree structure internally to ensure that all insertions and removals are O(log n). This provides much faster performance than both an *ArrayList* and a *LinkedList* where elements are inserted and removed repeatedly from anywhere in the list.

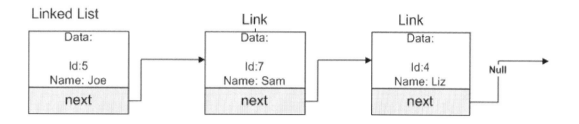

```
package bigo;

class Link {
    public int id;           // data
    public Sring name;       // data
    public Link next;        // reference to next link
}
```

HashMaps are amortized constant-time access data structures that map keys to values. This data structure is backed by an array. It uses a hashing functionality to identify a location, and some type of collision detection algorithm is used to handle values that hash to the same location. For example, storing employee records with employee number as the key, storing name/value pairs read from a properties file, etc. **BP** Initialize them with an appropriate initial size to minimize the number of resizes.

Trees are the data structures that contain nodes with optional data elements and one or more child elements, and possibly each child element references the parent element to represent a hierarchical or ordered set of data elements. For example, a hierarchy of employees in an organization, storing the XML data as a hierarchy, etc. If every node in a tree can have utmost 2 children, the tree is called a **binary tree**. The binary trees are very common because the shape of a binary tree makes it easy to search and insert data. The edges in a tree represent quick ways to navigate from node to node.

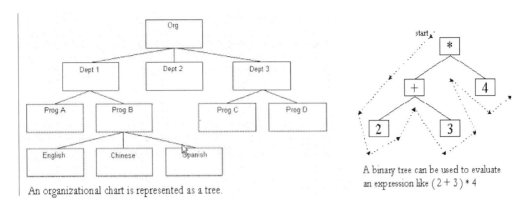

An organizational chart is represented as a tree.

A binary tree can be used to evaluate an expression like $(2 + 3) * 4$

Java does not provide an implementation for this but it can be easily implemented as shown below. Just make a class *Node* with an *ArrayList* holding links to other *Nodes*.

```java
package bigo;

import java.util.ArrayList;
import java.util.List;

public class Node {
    private String name;
    private List<Node> children = new ArrayList<Node>();
    private Node parent;

    public Node getParent( ) {
        return parent;
    }

    public void setParent(Node parent) {
        this.parent = parent;
    }

    public Node(String name) {
        this.name = name;
    }


    public void addChild(Node child) {
```

```
      children.add(child);
   }

   public void removeChild(Node child) {
      children.remove(child);
   }

   public String toString( ) {
      return name;
   }
}
```

Graphs are data structures that represent arbitrary relationships between members of any data sets that can be represented as networks of nodes and edges. A tree structure is essentially a more organized graph where each node can only have one parent node. Unlike a tree, a graph's shape is dictated by a physical or abstract problem. For example, nodes (or vertices) in a graph may represent cities, while edges may represent airline flight routes between the cities.

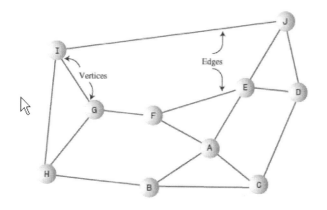

The vertices (or nodes) A - J could represent the destinations and the edges could represent a flight path of an air lines.

To make a Java graph class, you will have to work out the way in which the information can be stored and accessed. A graph will be using some of the data structures mentioned above. The Java API does not provide an implementation for this. But there are a number of third party libraries like JUNG, JGraphT, and JDSL (does not seem to support generics). The following example shows one of many ways to represent a graph data structure.

395

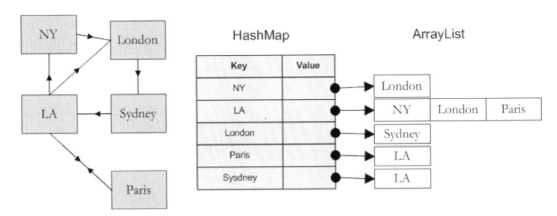

A graph must represent its vertices and edges in the code. Two vertices in a graph are adjacent if they form an edge. The vertex objects can be placed in a *Map* as shown above. A map is used for a fast retrieval by vertex name. Edges can be represented with an adjacency value list as shown above. A path is a sequence of vertices in which each successive pair is an edge as in LA → NY → London → Sydney → LA. To be more specific, this is a cyclic path because the first and last vertices are the same. The following code shows a very basic graph class.

```
package bigo;

import java.util.ArrayList;
import java.util.HashMap;
import java.util.List;
import java.util.Map;
import java.util.Set;

public class Graph {

    protected Map<String, List<String>> adjacencyMap;

    public Graph(int size) {
        this.adjacencyMap = new HashMap<String, List<String>>(size);
    }

    public boolean addVertex(String vertex) {
        if (adjacencyMap.containsKey(vertex))
            return false;
```

```java
        adjacencyMap.put(vertex, new ArrayList<String>( ));
        return true;
    }

    public boolean addEdge(String vertexStart, String vertexEnd) {
        addVertex(vertexStart);
        addVertex(vertexEnd);
        List<String> l = (ArrayList<String>) adjacencyMap.get(vertexStart);
        l.add(vertexEnd);
        return true;
    }


    public int getVerticesCount( ) {
        return adjacencyMap.size( );
    }

    public int getEdgeCount( ) {
        int count = 0;
        Set<String> keys = adjacencyMap.keySet( );

        for (String key : keys) {
            if (key != null) {
                List<String> edges = (ArrayList<String>) adjacencyMap
                        .get(key);
                count += edges.size( );
            }
        }
        return count;
    }

    public static void main(String[ ] args) {
        Graph g = new Graph(10);
        g.addEdge("NY", "London");
        g.addEdge("LA", "NY");
        g.addEdge("LA", "London");
        g.addEdge("LA", "Paris");
        g.addEdge("London", "Sydney");
        g.addEdge("Paris", "LA");
```

```
    g.addEdge("Sydney", "LA");

    System.out.println("no of vertices = " + g.getVerticesCount());
    System.out.println("no of edges = " + g.getEdgeCount());
  }
}
```

The map of string objects shown above can be replaced with a map of *Vertex* objects and a graph class with an adjacency matrix. The *hasVisited* boolean flag can be used in an algorithm to systematically start at a specific vertex and then move along the edges to other vertices, and when it is done you know that you have traversed through every vertex. An adjacency matrix is shown below.

	LA	NY	London	Sydney	Paris
LA	0	1	1	0	1
NY	0	0	1	0	0
London	0	0	0	1	0
Sydney	1	0	0	0	0
Paris	1	0	0	0	0

Note: 1 means an edge between two vertices (i.e. adjacent), and 0 means not adjacent.

```
package bigo;

class Vertex {
    public String name;                //(e.g. "LA", "London", etc)
    public boolean hasVisited;

    public Vertex(String  name)
    {
        this.name = name;
        hasVisited = false;
    }
}
```

```
package bigo;

class Graph2 {
```

```java
    private final int MAX_VERTICES = 5;
    private Vertex vertexList[ ];          // array of vertices
    private int adjMat[ ][ ];              // adjacency matrix
    private int noVertices;                // current no. of vertices

    public Graph2( ) { // constructor
        vertexList = new Vertex[MAX_VERTICES];
        // adjacency matrix
        adjMat = new int[MAX_VERTICES][MAX_VERTICES];

        noVertices = 0;
        //O (n²) complexity
        for (int i = 0; i < MAX_VERTICES; i++)
            //set adjacency
            for (int j = 0; j < MAX_VERTICES; j++)
                // matrix to 0
                adjMat[i][j] = 0;
    }

    public void addVertex(String name) {
        vertexList[noVertices++] = new Vertex(name);
    }

    public void addEdge(int start, int end) {
        adjMat[start][end] = 1;        // '1' means an edge between two vertices
        adjMat[end][start] = 1;        // '1' means an edge between two vertices
    }
}
```

Note: Many interview candidates fail to mention Tree and Graph data structures.

Q12 What do you know about the big-O notation and can you give some examples with respect to different data structures? `LF OEQ`

A12 The Big-O notation simply describes how well an algorithm scales or performs in the worst case scenario as the number of elements in a data structure increases. The Big-O notation can also be used to describe other behavior such as memory consumption. At times you may need to choose a slower algorithm because it also consumes less memory. Big-o notation can give a good indication about performance for large amounts of data, but the only real way to know for sure is to have a performance benchmark with large data sets to take into account things that are not considered in Big-O notation like paging as virtual memory usage grows, etc. Although benchmarks are better, they aren't feasible during the design process, so Big-O complexity analysis is the choice.

The algorithms used by various data structures for different operations like search, insert and delete fall into the following performance groups like constant-time $O(1)$, linear $O(n)$, logarithmic $O(\log n)$, exponential $O(c^n)$, polynomial $O(n^c)$, quadratic $O(n^2)$ and factorial $O(n!)$ where n is the number of elements in the data structure. It is generally a tradeoff between performance and memory usage. Here are some examples.

Example 1: Finding an element in a *HashMap* is usually a constant-time, which is $O(1)$. This is a constant time because a hashing function is used to find an element, and computing a hash value does not depend on the number of elements in the *HashMap*.

Example 2: Linear search of an array, list, and *LinkedList* is linear, which is $O(n)$. This is linear because you will have to search the entire list. This means that if a list is twice as big, searching it will take twice as long.

Example 3: An algorithm that needs to compare every element in an array to sort the array has polynomial complexity, which is $O(n^2)$. A nested for loop is $O(n^2)$. An example is shown under sorting algorithms.

Example 4: Binary search of a sorted array or *ArrayList* is logarithmic, which is $O(\log n)$. Searching an element in a *LinkedList* normally requires $O(n)$. This is one of the disadvantages of *LinkedList* over the other data structures like an *ArrayList* or array offering a $O(\log n)$ performance, which offers better performance than $O(n)$ as the number of elements increases. A logarithmic running times mean, if 10 items take at most x amount of time, 100 items will take say at most 2x amount of time, and 10,000 items will take at most 4x. If you plot this on a graph, the time decreases as n (i.e. number of items) increases.

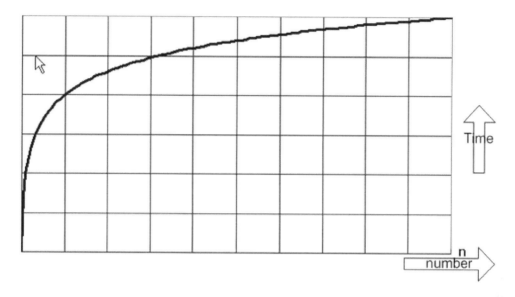

Q. What can you tell about the performance of a *HashMap* compared to a *TreeMap*? Which one would you prefer?

A. A balanced tree does have O (log n) performance. The *TreeMap* class in Java maintains key/value objects in a sorted order by using a red-black tree. A red-black tree is a balanced binary tree. Keeping the binary tree balanced ensures the fast insertion, removal, and lookup time of O (log n). This is not as fast as a *HashMap*, which is O(1) , but the *TreeMap* has the advantage of that the keys are in sorted order which opens up a lot of other capabilities.

Which one to choose? PC

The decision as to using an unordered collection like a *HashSet* or *HasMap* versus using a sorted data structure like a *TreeSet* or *TreeMap* depends mainly on the usage pattern, and to some extent on the data size and the environment you run it on. The practical reason for keeping the elements in sorted order is for frequent and faster retrieval of sorted data if the inserts and updates are frequent. If the need for a sorted result is infrequent like prior to producing a report or running a batch process, then maintaining an unordered collection and sorting them only when it is really required with *Collections.sort(...)* could sometimes be more efficient than maintaining the ordered elements. This is only an opinion, and no one can offer you a correct answer. Even the complexity theories like Big-O notation like O(n) assume possibly large values of n. In practice, a O(n) algorithm can be much faster than a O(log n) algorithm, provided the data set that is handled is sufficiently small. One algorithm might perform better on an AMD processor than on an Intel. If your system is set up to swap, disk performance need to be considered. The only way to confirm the efficient usage is to test and measure both performance and memory usage with the **right data size**. Measure both the approaches on your chosen hardware to determine, which is more appropriate.

Q13 What is the tradeoff between using an unordered array versus an ordered array? `OEQ`

A13 The major advantage of an ordered array is that the search times are much faster with O (log n) than an unordered array, which is O (n) for larger values of n. The disadvantage of an ordered array is that the insertion takes longer (i.e. O (n)) because all the data with higher values need to be moved to make room. The insertion for an unordered array takes constant time of O(1). This means, it does not depend on the number of elements. The following code snippet demonstrates adding an element to both ordered and unordered array.

Inserting an element into an unsorted array

```java
package bigo;
import java.util.Arrays;

public class InsertingElementsToArray {

    public static void insertUnsortedArray(String toInsert) {

        String[] unsortedArray = { "A", "D", "C" };

        String[] newUnsortedArray = new String[unsortedArray.length + 1];
        System.arraycopy(unsortedArray, 0, newUnsortedArray, 0, 3);
        newUnsortedArray[newUnsortedArray.length - 1] = toInsert;
        System.out.println(Arrays.toString(newUnsortedArray));
    }

    public static void main(String[] args) {
        insertUnsortedArray("B");
    }
}
```

Inserting an element into a sorted array

```java
package bigo;

import java.util.Arrays;

public class InsertingElementsToArray {

    public static void insertSortedArray(String toInsert) {

        String[] sortedArray = { "A", "C", "D" };

        /*
         * Binary search returns the index of the search item
         * if found, otherwise returns the minus insertion point. This example
         * returns index = -2, which means the elemnt is not found and needs to
         * be inserted as a second element.
         */
        int index = Arrays.binarySearch(sortedArray, toInsert);

        if (index < 0) {                                    // not found.

            // array indices are zero based. -2 index means insertion point of
            // -(-2)-1 = 1,  so insertIndex = 1
            int insertIndex = -index - 1;

            String[] newSortedArray = new String[sortedArray.length + 1];
            System.arraycopy(sortedArray, 0, newSortedArray, 0,  insertIndex);
            System.arraycopy(sortedArray, insertIndex,
                    newSortedArray, insertIndex + 1,  sortedArray.length - insertIndex);
            newSortedArray[insertIndex] = toInsert;
            System.out.println(Arrays.toString(newSortedArray));
        }
    }

    public static void main(String[] args) {
        insertSortedArray("B");
    }
}
```

So the decision depends on the usage pattern. Ask yourself the following questions.

Do I have more inserts/deletes or search? What is the maximum number of elements likely to be stored in this array? How often do I need the sorted data? And finally what does my performance benchmark show?

Q. How would you choose between a *LinkedList* and an *ArrayList*? PC
A. It depends on the use case, and the following table summarizes it.

Algorithm	Access at			Insert at		
	front	**back**	**middle**	**front**	**back**	**middle**
ArrayList	O (1)	O (1)	O (1)	O (N)	O (1)	O (N)
LinkedList	O (1)	O (1)	O (n)	O (1)	O (1)	O (1)

Unless you have lots of inserts in the front and middle and the performance bench marks clearly shows that *LinkedList* is the way to go, it is better to use an *ArrayList*.

Q14 Describe typical use cases or examples of common uses for various data structures provided by the *Collection* framework in Java? LF OEQ
A14 You choose data structures based on your projected usage patterns, memory and performance considerations.

Usage patterns :

- Use arrays when the amount of data is reasonably small and the amount of data is predictable in advance. If insertion speed is important, use an unordered array. An array cannot be used for everything because searching an unordered array is slow with O(n), and deletion of both ordered and unordered array takes O(n) to fill the hole.

- If the initial collection size cannot be determined upfront, the primary implementations like *ArrayList*, *HashMap*, or *HashSet* should do the job unless you require a special usage pattern. Those special usage patterns are like access sequences like FIFO, LIFO, etc, duplicates are allowed or not, and ordering needs to be maintained or not, etc.

- Use a *List* if duplicates are allowed, and a *Set* if duplicates are not allowed.

- Use a stack for Last In First Out (LIFO) access. For example, you may want to track online forms as a user opens them and then be able to back out of the open forms in the reverse order. That is, you may want to store form references in the stack and then, as the user clicks the OK button on each form, bring the correct form to the top by popping out the most recent form from the stack. You could also build your own application profiler by storing the current time in the stack for each method as you push it on to the stack and then subtracting that from the current time as you pop it out from the stack to find out how long it took to execute that method. The *Stack* implementation class in Java extends the *Vector* class, which has all methods synchronized. Hence it is not recommended to use the *Stack* implementation. A more complete and consistent set of LIFO stack operations is provided by the **Dequeue** interface, which stands for **double-ended queue** and its implementations.

- If you conceptually have a producer-consumer pattern, for example a producer thread produces a list of jobs for a number of consumer threads to pick up, then a *Queue* implementation is more appropriate. This of course could be done with a synchronized *LinkedList*, but a queue will provide a better concurrency optimization by eliminating random access. The *BlockingQueue* is an efficient implementation of a typical *Queue* interface. There are other specific implementations like *DelayQueue, PriorityQueue, SynchronousQueue*, etc. to cater for the variations in the usage.

- If you need to frequently insert and remove elements at arbitrary positions in a sequence, you could choose a *LinkedList*. For example, If you have a very large collection where many elements need to be added to both the beginning and end of a collection, a *LinkedList* should be faster than an *ArrayList*. However, an *ArrayBlockingQueue* is even faster. Generally use an array, *List*, or a *BlockingQueue* (this is from the *java.util.concurrent* package) depending on the other needs, and use a *LinkedList* only if your performance tests show that a *LinkedList* can offer a better performance. Practically, this is very rare, if not never.

- Use a *TreeSet* or *TreeMap* if you like your objects to be in sorted order by using a balanced red-black tree. A red-black tree is a balanced binary tree, meaning a parent node has maximum 2 children and as an entry is inserted, the tree is monitored as to keep it well-balanced. Balanced binary tree ensures fast lookup time of O(log n). A *HashSet* or a *HashMap* has a much faster access time of O(1), but won't maintain the entries in a sorted order.

- A *WeakHashMap* is good to implement canonical maps. If you want to associate some extra information to a particular object that you have a strong reference to, you put an entry in a *WeakHashMap* with that object as the key, and the extra information as the map value. Then, as long as you keep a strong reference to the object, you will be able to check the map to retrieve the extra information. Once you release the strong reference to the key object, the map entry will be cleared and the memory used by the extra information will be released.

- A cache is a memory location where you can store data that is otherwise expensive to obtain frequently from a database, ldap, flat file, or other external systems. A *WeakHashMap* is not good for caching because a *WeakHashMap* stores the keys using *WeakReference* objects that means as soon as the key is not strongly referenced from somewhere else in your program, the entry may be removed and be available for garbage collection. This is not good, and what you really want to have is your cached objects removed from your map only when the JVM is running low on memory. This is where a *SoftReference* comes in handy. A *SoftReference* will only be garbage-collected when the JVM is running low on memory and the object that the key is pointing to is not being accessed from any other strong reference. The standard Java library does not provide a *Map* implementation using a *SoftReference*, but you can implement your own by extending the *AbstractMap* class.

- Implementing your own cache mechanism is often not a trivial task. Cache needs to be regularly updated, and possibly distributed. A better option would be to use one of the third-party frameworks like OSCache, Ehcache, JCS and Cache4J.

- Use an immutable collection (aka unmodifiable collection) if you don't want to allow accidental addition or removal of elements once created. The objects stored in a collection needs to implement its own immutability if required to be prevented from any accidental modifications.

Threading considerations: CC

If accessed by a single thread, synchronization is not required, and arrays, lists, sets, stacks, etc can be used as a local variable. If your collections are used as a local variables, the synchronization is a complete overkill, and degrades performance considerably. On the contrary, it is a bad practice to assume that the application is always going to be single threaded and use data structures in a thread unsafe manner, for example declaring it as an instance or static variable. What if the application needs to scale to handle concurrent access from multiple threads?

If accessed by multiple threads, prefer a concurrent collection like a copy-on-write lists and sets, concurrent maps, etc over a synchronized collection for a more optimized concurrent access. Stay away from the legacy classes like *Vectors* and *HashTables*. In a multi-threaded environment, some operations may need to be atomic to produce correct results. This may require appropriate synchronizations (i.e. locks). Improper implementation in a multi-threaded environment can cause unexpected behaviors and results.

Performance and memory considerations: `PC MC`

The choices you make for a program's data structures and algorithms affect that program's memory usage (for data structures) and CPU time (for algorithms that interact with those data structures). Sometimes you discover an inverse relationship between memory usage and CPU time. For example, a one-dimensional array occupies less memory than a doubly linked list that needs to associate links with data items to find each data item's predecessor and successor. This requires extra memory. In contrast, a one-dimensional array's insertion/deletion algorithms are slower than a doubly linked list's equivalent algorithms because inserting a data item into or deleting a data item from a one-dimensional array requires data item movement to expose an empty element for insertion or close an element made empty by deletion. Here are some points to keep in mind.

- The most important thing to keep in mind is scalability. Assuming that a collection will always be small is a dangerous thing to do, and it is better to assume that it will be big. Don't just rely on the general theories (e.g. Big-O theory) and rules. Profile your application to identify any potential memory or performance issues for a given platform and configuration in a production or production-like (aka QA) environment.

- Initialize your collection with an appropriate initial capacity to minimize the number of times it has to grow for lists and sets, and number of times it has to grow and rehash for maps.

```
List list = new ArrayList(40);
Map map = new HashMap((int) (40/ 0.75 + 1));
```

Q15 What method(s) should you override for objects you plan to add to sets or maps? LF FAQ

A15 *equals(…)* and *hashCode( )* methods.

Q16 How do you get an immutable collection? LF DP

A16 This functionality is provided by the Collections class, which is a wrapper implement-ation using the decorator design pattern.

```
public class ReadOnlyExample {
    public static void main(String args[]) {
        Set<String> set = new HashSet<String>( );
        set.add("Java");
        set.add("JEE");
        set.add("Spring");
        set.add("Hibernate");
        set = Collections.unmodifiableSet(set);
        set.add("Ajax");                          // not allowed.
    }
}
```

Q17   What is the difference between *Collection* and *Collections*? LF

A17 The *Collection* is a super interface for the other interfaces like *Set, List, Queue, SortedSet*, etc, and implemented by many classes like *HashSet, ArrayList, LinkedList, BlockingQueue, Stack*, etc.

The *Collections* class is a utility class like the *Arrays* class. Whilst the *Arrays* class provides a series of static factory methods for working with fixed size indexed data structures, the *Collections* class provides static factory methods for different collections that can grow. The *Collections* class provides wrapper implementations using the decorator design pattern for flexibility, performance, and robustness. It supports,

- **Polymorphic algorithms** – sorting, shuffling, reversing, binary search, etc.

408

- **Set algebra** - such as finding subsets, intersections, and unions between objects.
- **Immutability** - when immutability is required, wrapper implementations are provided for making a collection immutable.

For example, to prevent addition and removal of elements:

```
Collections.unmodifiableSet(set);
```

To return an empty set:

```
shoppingBasket.assignNewBasket(Collections.emptySet( ));
```

To remove all occurrences of "SHOE" from a list.

```
shoppingBasket.removeAll(Collections.singleton("SHOE"));
```

To add 12 copies of cereal boxes:

```
shoppingBasket.addAll(Collections.nCopies(12, "CerealBox"));
```

To sort a given list **naturally**:

```
Collections.sort(shoppingBasket);
```

To **custom** sort a given list:

```
Collections.sort(shoppingBasket, new Comparator<List<String>>() {
   public int compare(List<String> o1, List<String> o2) {
      return o2.size( ) - o1.size( );
   }
});
```

To search for a specific item:

```
int pos = Collections.binarySearch(shoppingBasket, itemToSearch);
```

Note: Refer to the *Collections* API for more useful utility methods like reverse, copy, fill, addAll, swap, min, max, etc.

Q18 What does the following code do? Can the *LinkedHashSet* be replaced with a *HashSet?* COQ

```java
import java.util.ArrayList;
import java.util.LinkedHashSet;
import java.util.List;

public class CollectionFunction {
    public <E> List<E> function (List <E> list) {
        return new ArrayList<E>(new LinkedHashSet<E>(list));
    }
}
```

A18 The above code removes duplicates from a supplied list by passing it through an implementation of a *Set* interface. In this case, a *LinkedHashSet* is used to honor the ordering by implementing a *SortedSet* interface. If ordering is not required, the *LinkedHashSet* can be replaced with a *HashSet*.

Q19 What are some of the best practices relating to the Java Collection framework? BP
A19

- **Choose the right type of data structure** based on usage patterns like fixed size or required to grow, duplicates allowed or not, ordering is required to be maintained or not, traversal is forward only or bi-directional, inserts at the end only or any arbitrary position, more inserts or more reads, concurrently accessed or not, modification is allowed or not, homogeneous or heterogeneous collection, etc. Also, keep multi-threading, atomicity, memory usage and performance considerations discussed earlier in mind.

- **Don't assume that your collection is always going to be small** as it can potentially grow bigger with time. So your collection should scale well.

- **Program in terms of interface not implementation:** For example, you might decide a *LinkedList* is the best choice for some application, but then later decide *ArrayList* might be a better choice for performance reason.

   Bad:

```
ArrayList<String> list = new ArrayList<String>(100);
```

Good:
```
// program to interface so that the implementation can change
List<String> list = new ArrayList<String>(100);
List<String> list2 = new LinkedList<String>(100);
```

- **Return zero length collections** or arrays as opposed to returning a null in the context of the fetched list is actually empty. Returning a null instead of a zero length collection is more error prone, since the programmer writing the calling method might forget to handle a return value of null.

```
List<String> emptyList = Collections.emptyList( );
Set<Integer> emptySet = Collections.emptySet( );
```

- **Use generics** for type safety, readability, and robustness.

- **Encapsulate collections**: In general, collections are not immutable objects. So care should be taken not to unintentionally expose the collection fields to the caller. The caller may not perform any necessary validation.

Bad Approach:

```
package encapsulation;

import java.util.HashSet;
import java.util.Set;

public class BadCarYard {
    //no duplicates allowed, hence use a Set
    private Set<Car> carsCol = new HashSet<Car>(10);

    //exposes the carsCol to the caller
    public Set<Car> getCars( ) {
        return carsCol;
    }
    ...
}
```

Good Approach:

```java
package encapsulation;

import java.util.Collections;
import java.util.HashSet;
import java.util.Set;

public class GoodCarYard {

    private Set<Car> carsCol = new HashSet<Car>();

    public void addCar(Car car) {
        // throw exception early
        if (car == null) {
            new IllegalArgumentException("Cannot add null");
        }
        //more checks here to add a valid Car
        carsCol.add(car);
    }

    public void removeCar(Car car) {
        if (car == null) {
            new IllegalArgumentException("Cannot add null");
        }
        //... more checks here before removing a car
        carsCol.remove(car);
    }

    public Set<Car> getCars() {
        // prevent addition or removal from outside this class
        return Collections.unmodifiableSet(carsCol);
    }
}
```

- **Immutable objects should be used as keys** for the *HashMaps*. Generally you use *java.lang.Integer* or *java.lang.String* class as the key, which are immutable Java objects. If you define your own key class, then it is a best practice to make the key class an immutable object. If you want to insert a new key, then you will always have to instantiate a new object as you cannot modify an immutable object. If the keys were made mutable, you could accidentally modify the key after adding to a *HashMap*, which can result in you not being able to access the object later on. The object will still be in the *HashMap*, but you will not be able to retrieve it as you have the wrong key (i.e. a mutated key).

- **Use copy-on-write classes and concurrent maps** for better scalability. It also prevents *ConcurrentModificationException* being thrown while preserving thread safety.

- **Memory usage and performance can be improved by setting the appropriate initial capacity** when creating a collection. For example,

If you are likely to have an *ArrayList* with say 11 elements, but if you initialize the *ArrayList* as follows,

```
List<String> myList = New ArrayList<String>( );
```

By default, the capacity is 10. When you add the 11th element to the array list, it will have to resize or grow using the following formula (oldCapacity * 3)/2 + 1. This will be equal to 10*3/2+1=16. So it creates a new array with size of 16 and and copies all the old 10 elements to the new array and adds the 11th element to the new array. The old array with 10 elements become eligible for garbage collection. So resizing too many times can adversely impact performance and memory. So it is a best practice to set the initial capacity to an appropriate value so that the lists don't have to resize too often. The above declaration for 11 elements can be improved by setting the initial capacity to either 11 or greater.

```
List<String> myList = new ArrayList<String>(11);
```

Same is true for *HashMaps* as well. As a general rule, the default load factor of 0.75 offers a good tradeoff between time and space costs. Higher load factor values decrease the space overhead, but increases the lookup cost through methods like *get( )*, *put( )*, etc. The expected number of entries in the map and its load factor should be taken into account when setting its initial capacity, so as to minimize the number of rehash operations. If the initial capacity is greater than the maximum number of entries divided by the load factor, no rehash operations will ever occur. This means the load factor should not be changed from 0.75, unless you have some specific optimization you are going to do. Initial capacity is the only thing you want to change, and set it according to number of items you want to store. You should set the initial capacity to (no. of likely items / 0.75) + 1 to ensure that the table will always be large enough, and no rehashing will occur. For 11 items it will be (11/0.75) + 1 = 16.

```
Map<String> myMap = new HashMap<String>(16);
```

Q20 If Java did not have a *HashMap* implementation, how would you go about writing your own one? SBQ COQ

A20 Writing a *HashMap* is not a trivial task. It is also not a good practice to reinvent the wheel. The interviewer is trying to evaluate your level of technical knowledge and thought process. What really important here are, how you approach the problem?, how good your understanding of the data structures are?, and how well you can logically think and code?.

- Firstly, decide on the backing data structure. Arrays are fast and memory efficient. Hence an array can be used to back up the map. This will be an indexed bucket.
- Decide on a hashing algorithm to index the array and store the entries in a particular slot of the array.
- Decide on a strategy to store two or more keys that result in the same hash code value. More objects can be linked with each other occupying the same index. This means each bucket can contain 0..N entries. This linking strategy is shown in the diagram.
- Decide on an approach to evaluate the hash code, which determines the array bucket index to use.

```
int index = Math.abs(key.hashCode( ) % buckets.length);
```

- Come up with a strategy for resizing the backing array when the capacity is reached. This process is known as rehashing whereby existing items are mapped to new bucket locations.
- Consider implementing the *Map* interface and fill in the empty methods that need to be implemented.

414

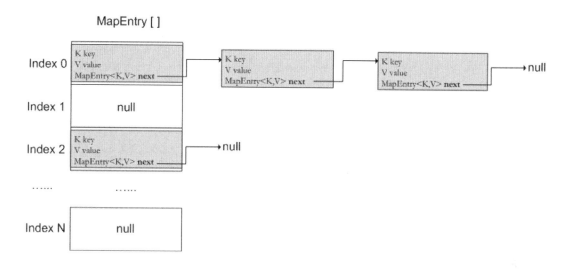

MapEntry [ ]

The following code snippets demonstrate how you could go about implementing your own *HashMap* class.

```java
package bigo;

public class MapEntry <K, V> {        // K --> Key, V--> Value

    private final K key;                    //mutating the key is bad
    private V value;
    private MapEntry<K, V> next;       //next entry in the same bucket

    public MapEntry(K key, V value){
        this.key = key;
        this.value = value;
    }

    // getters and setters are ignored for brevity
}
```

Next, the *HashMap* class that is composed of the *MapEntry*.

```java
package bigo;
```

```java
import java.util.Collection;
import java.util.Map;
import java.util.Set;

public class MyHashMap<K, V> implements Map<K, V> {

    private MapEntry<K, V>[] buckets = null;

    public MyHashMap() {
        this(10);
    }

    @SuppressWarnings("unchecked")
    public MyHashMap(int capacity) {
        buckets = new MapEntry[capacity];
    }

    @Override
    @SuppressWarnings("unchecked")
    public V get(Object key) {
        // check for pre-condition.
        if (key == null)
            throw new IllegalArgumentException( "The key cannot be null");

        MapEntry<K, V> entry = getMatchingEntry((K) key);
        return entry != null ? entry.getValue() : null;
    }

    @Override
    public V put(K key, V value) {
        // check for pre-condition.
        if (key == null)
            throw new IllegalArgumentException("The key cannot be null");

        MapEntry<K, V> entry = getMatchingEntry((K) key);

        if (entry != null) {                    //if the key is found
            entry.setValue(value);
        }
```

```
    else {                                    //if the key is not found
       int index = evalBucketIndex(key);
       if (buckets[index] != null) {          //if the bucket is already allocated
          entry = linkEntry(buckets[index] , key, value); //link it to an entry already
                                                          //attached to that bucket

       } else {                                          //if the bucket is not allocated
          entry = new MapEntry<K, V>(key, value); //allocate a new bucket
          buckets[index] = entry;
       }
    }
    return entry.getValue( );
}

/**
 * Hashing function. The more spaced out the indices are, the better the
 * performance is. Only positive values can be used as an array index.
 */
private int evalBucketIndex(K key) {
   int index = Math.abs(key.hashCode( ) % buckets.length);
   return index;
}

/**
 * Return the matching entry if found, otherwise return null
 */
private MapEntry<K, V> getMatchingEntry(K key) {
   MapEntry<K, V> entry = buckets[evalBucketIndex((K) key)];

   // same index can have more entries linked by "next" attribute
   // in the MapEntry class. So find the one where key matches
   while (entry != null && !key.equals(entry.getKey( ))) {
      entry = entry.getNext( );
   }

   // conditional operator
   return entry != null ? entry : null;
}
```

```
/**
 * Create a new entry and link it to the given bucket entry
 */
private MapEntry<K, V> linkEntry(MapEntry<K, V> entry, K key, V value){
    boolean linked = false;

    while(!linked){
        if(entry.getNext() == null){                            //if not linked
            entry.setNext(new MapEntry<K, V>(key, value));     //Create a new entry &
                                                                // link it

            linked = true;
        }
        else{
            entry = entry.getNext();
        }
    }

    return entry;
}

//other methods that need to be implemented for the
//Map interface not shown for brevity.
}
```

Q20 If Java did not have a Stack implementation, how would you go about implementing your own? SBQ COQ

A20
- Determine the backing data structure (e.g. array, linked list, etc).
- Determine the methods that need to be implemented like *pop( )*, *push( )*, *peek( )*, *clear( )*, *empty( )*, etc.
- Determine how you are going to keep track of the last item added. For example, keeping track with an index variable "*topIndex*".
- Determine what to do if the capacity is reached? Double the capacity of the backing array.
- Drawing a diagram as shown below could make things clearer.

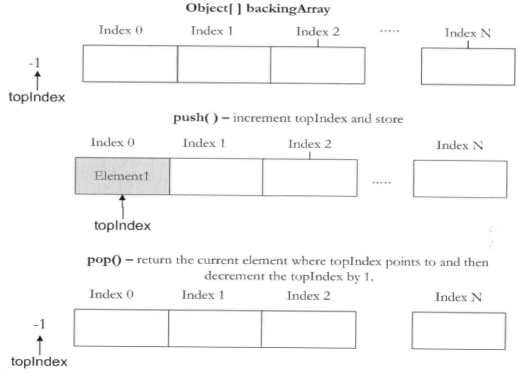

Object[ ] backingArray

push( ) – increment topIndex and store

pop() – return the current element where topIndex points to and then decrement the topIndex by 1.

Here are some code snippets to get started. Define the interface first.

```java
package bigo;

public interface Stack<E> {
    E push(E item);
    E pop();
    boolean empty();
    //other methods like peek( ), etc omitted for brevity
}
```

Now provide the implementation class.

```java
package bigo;

public class MyStack<E> implements Stack<E> {
```

```java
private Object[] backingArray;
private int topIndex;
private static final int DEFAULT_CAPACITY = 10;

public MyStack() {
    this.backingArray = new Object[DEFAULT_CAPACITY];
    topIndex = -1;
}

@Override
@SuppressWarnings("unchecked")
public E pop() {
    if (empty()) {
        throw new RuntimeException("No data is found");
    }
    // return the index element and reset the index by -1
    return (E) backingArray[topIndex--];
}

@Override
public E push(E item) {
    doubleTheArrayIfLimitIsReached();
    //increment the index and store the item
    this.backingArray[++topIndex] = item;
    return item;
}

@Override
public boolean empty() {
    return topIndex == -1;
}

/**
 * If the array capacity is reached, double it
 */
private void doubleTheArrayIfLimitIsReached() {
    if (topIndex + 1 == this.backingArray.length) {
        Object[] newArray = new Object[backingArray.length * 2];
```

```
        // copy the existing elements to the new expanded array
        System.arraycopy(backingArray, 0, newArray, 0,
            backingArray.length);
        // set the backingArray to the expanded array
        backingArray = newArray;
        System.out.println(
                "The backing array has been expanded to " + backingArray.length);
    }
  }
}
```

Note: A queue can be implemented in a similar fashion by declaring a *backingArray*, a *frontIndex*, a *backIndex, and a currentSize*. Initialize the *frontIndex* to 0 and the *backIndex* to -1. You will have to provide the relevant methods like *enque( )*, *deque( )*, etc.

enqueue( ):

- If the *currentSize* == *backingArray.length* extend the backing array capacity by doubling it.
- Increment the *backIndex* by 1. If the incremented index is equal to the array length (*backingArray.lenth*), set the *backIndex* to 0 (i.e. imagine it as an endless circular array).
- Set the element to the backIndex (i.e. *bacckingArray[backIndex]* = *element*).
- Increment the *currentSize* by 1 (i.e. *currentSize++*).

dequeue( ):

- Decrement the *currentSize* by 1 (i.e *currentSize--*).
- Return the value that *frontIndex* points to (i.e. *backingArray[frontIdex]*).
- Increment the *frontIndex* by 1. If the *frontIndex* == *backingArray.length*, set the *frontIndex* to 0 (i.e. imagine it as an endless circular array).

Note: Use the LIFO operations provided by the *Deque* interface and its implementations as opposed to the *Stack* implantation, which extends the legacy *Vector* class.

Sorting Elements

Q21 If I mention the interface names *Comparable* or *Comparator*, what does come to your mind? Why do we need these interfaces? **LF**

A21 Sorting. *SortedSet* and *SortedMap* interfaces maintain sorted order. The elements are sorted as you add or remove them. The other interfaces like *List* or *Set* don't sort elements as you add or remove. So you need to sort them on a as needed basis.

If you store objects of type *String* or *Integer* in a *List* or *Set*, and would like to occasionally sort them, say for reporting purpose, you can do so as shown below as *String* or *Integer* by default implements the *Comparable* interface and provides a *compareTo(..)* method to be called while sorting.

```java
package sorting;

import java.util.ArrayList;
import java.util.Collections;
import java.util.List;

public class Sorting1 {

    public static void main(String[] args) {
        List<String> myShoppingList = new ArrayList<String>();
        myShoppingList.add("Cereal");
        myShoppingList.add("Apples");
        myShoppingList.add("Soap");
        myShoppingList.add("Brush");
        System.out.println("Before sorting: " + myShoppingList);
        // invokes compareTo method implemented in the String class.
        Collections.sort(myShoppingList);
        System.out.println("After sorting: " + myShoppingList);
    }
}
```

Output:

Before sorting: [Cereal, Apples, Soap, Brush]
After sorting: [Apples, Brush, Cereal, Soap]

As you can see that the items are sorted lexicographically. This is the default imple-ment provided by the *compareTo(...)* method in the *java.lang.String* class. What if you have a special reporting requirement to sort by length of the item name. This is where the **Comparator** interface comes in handy by giving you more control over ordering. You can define your own ordering logic through the *compare(...)* method as shown below using the *Comparator* interface.

```java
package sorting;

import java.util.ArrayList;
import java.util.Collections;
import java.util.Comparator;
import java.util.List;

public class Sorting2 {

    public static void main(String[] args) {
        List<String> myShoppingList = new ArrayList<String>();
        myShoppingList.add("Cereal");
        myShoppingList.add("Apples");
        myShoppingList.add("Soap");
        myShoppingList.add("Brush");
        myShoppingList.add(null);
        System.out.println("Before sorting: " + myShoppingList);

        //Anonymous inner class.
        Collections.sort(myShoppingList, new Comparator<String>() {
            @Override
            public int compare(String o1, String o2) {
                if(o1 == null) {
                    o1 = "";
                }
                if(o2 == null) {
                    o2 = "";
                }
                return new Integer(o1.length( )).compareTo(o2.length( ));
            }
        });
```

```
        System.out.println("After sorting: " + myShoppingList);
    }
}
```

Output:

```
Before sorting: [Cereal, Apples, Soap, Brush]
After sorting: [Soap, Brush, Cereal, Apples]
```

Note: The above class is using an anonymous class to sort, but if you require to reuse the sorting in a number of places, you must move the *compare(...)* method to its own class as shown below.

```
import java.util.Comparator;

public class NameLengthComparator implements Comparator<String> {

    public int compare(String o1, String o2) {
        //implementation goes here. same as above
    }
}
```

You can use it as follows

```
Collections.sort(myShoppingList, new NameLengthComparator( ));
```

Q. What if your collection contains custom objects like a *Pet* class?
A. You can provide the default sorting behavior by having the *Pet* class implement the *Comparable* interface and implementing the *compareTo(...)* method as shown below:

```
public class Pet implements Comparable<Pet> {

    int id;
    String name;

    public Pet(int id, String name) {
        this.id = id;
        this.name = name;
    }
}
```

```java
    // getters and setters go here

    //invoked during sorting
    public int compareTo(Pet o) {
        Pet petAnother = o;
        // natural alphabetical ordering by name
        return this.name.compareTo(petAnother.name);
    }


    //invoked when the list is printed
    public String toString() {
        return "[id=" + id + ", name=" + name + "]";
    }
}
```

Take note of generics being used above. The above *Pet* class can be used as shown below.

```java
package sorting;

import java.util.ArrayList;
import java.util.Collections;
import java.util.List;

public class Sorting3 {

    public static void main(String[] args) {
        List<Pet> myPetList = new ArrayList<Pet>();
        myPetList.add(new Pet(1, "Dog"));
        myPetList.add(new Pet(2,"Rabit"));
        myPetList.add(new Pet(3,"Cat"));
        myPetList.add(new Pet(2, "Hamster"));
        System.out.println("Before sorting: " + myPetList);
        //compareTo method gets invoked on Pet.class
        Collections.sort(myPetList);
        System.out.println("After sorting: " + myPetList);
    }
}
```

Output:

Before sorting: [[1,Dog], [2,Rabit], [3,Cat], [2,Hamster]]
After sorting: [[3,Cat], [1,Dog], [2,Hamster], [2,Rabit]]

So far so good. What if you have an additional special sorting requirement to sort first by id and then by name. You can use the *Comparator* interface to sort based on multiple attributes as shown below.

```java
package sorting;

import java.util.ArrayList;
import java.util.Collections;
import java.util.Comparator;
import java.util.List;

public class Sorting4 {

    public static void main(String[ ] args) {
        List<Pet> myPetList = new ArrayList<Pet>( );
        myPetList.add(new Pet(1, "Dog"));
        myPetList.add(new Pet(2, "Rabit"));
        myPetList.add(new Pet(3, "Cat"));
        myPetList.add(new Pet(2, "Hamster"));
        System.out.println("Before sorting: " + myPetList);
        Collections.sort(myPetList, new Comparator<Pet>( ) {
            @Override
            public int compare(Pet o1, Pet o2) {
                int byIds = o1.getId( ).compareTo(o2.getId( ));
                // if ids are same, compare by name
                if (byIds == 0) {
                    return o1.getName( ).compareToIgnoreCase( o2.getName( ));
                }
                return byIds;
            }
        });
        System.out.println("After sorting: " + myPetList);
    }
}
```

```
}
```

Output:

Before sorting: [[1,Dog], [2,Rabit], [3,Cat], [2,Hamster]]
After sorting: [[1,Dog], [2,Hamster], [2,Rabit], [3,Cat]]

Note: The above class is using an anonymous class to sort, but if you require to reuse the sorting in a number of places, you must move the *compare(...)* method to its own class.

Q. What contract do you need to watch out for when writing your own comparator?
A. As per the Java API for *java.util.Comparator,* caution should be exercised when using a comparator capable of imposing an ordering inconsistent with the *equals(...)* method.

```
if compare(o1,o2) == 0   then   o1.equals(o2)   should be true.
if compare(o1,o2) != 0   then   o1.equals(o2)   should be false.
```

Algorithms

Q22 Can you write an algorithm to.....? COQ
A22 **Swap two variables?**

```
package algorithms;

public class Swap {

    public static void main(String[ ] args) {
        int x = 5;
        int y = 6;

        //store 'x' in a temp variable
        int temp = x;
        x = y;
        y = temp;
```

```
      System.out.println("x=" + x + ",y=" + y);
   }
}
```

Bubble sort → { 30, 12, 18, 0, -5, 72, 424 }?

```
package algorithms;
import java.util.Arrays;

public class BubbleSort {

   public static void main(String[ ] args) {
      Integer[ ] values = { 30, 12, 18, 0, -5, 72, 424 };
      int size = values.length;
      System.out.println("Before:" + Arrays.deepToString(values));

      for (int pass = 0; pass < size - 1; pass++) {
         for (int i = 0; i < size - pass - 1; i++) {
            // swap if i > i+1
            if (values[i] > values[i + 1])
               swap(values, i, i + 1);
         }
      }

      System.out.println("After:" + Arrays.deepToString(values));
   }

   private static void swap(Integer[ ] array, int i, int j) {
      int temp = array[i];
      array[i] = array[j];
      array[j] = temp;
   }
}
```

Q. Is there a more efficient sorting algorithm? COQ
A. Although bubble-sort is one of the simplest sorting algorithms, it's also one of the slowest. It has the $O(n^2)$ time complexity. Faster algorithms include quick-sort and heap-sort. The *Arrays.sort( )* method uses the quick-sort algorithm, which on average

has $O(n * \log n)$ but can go up to $O(n^2)$ in a worst case scenario, and this happens especially with already sorted sequences.

```
package algorithms;
import java.util.Arrays;

public class QuickSort {

    public static void main(String[] args) {
        Integer[] values = { 30, 12, 18, 0, -5, 72, 424 };
        System.out.println("Before:" + Arrays.deepToString(values));
        Arrays.sort(values);
        System.out.println("After:" + Arrays.deepToString(values));
    }
}
```

Q. How will you partition the following numbers 7 3 6 8 2 9 5 4 around the pivotal number of 5 so that the lower values are in front of it and higher values are behind it? COQ

7	3	6	8	2	9	5 (pivot)	4
^							^

Start two pointers, one at array index 0 and the other at array index 7, which is the last element in the array. Advance the left pointer forward until a value greater than the pivot (i.e. 5) is encountered. Advance the right pointer backwards until a value less than the pivot (i.e 5) is encountered. In this case, the current left pointer value 7 is greater than pivot (i.e. 5) and the right pointer value 4 is less than the pivot (i.e. 5), so swap them as shown below before advancing as shown below with the shading. The pointers have also advanced to the next position. Also note that the left pointer has skipped the value "3" as it is less than pivot value"5". The right pointer has skipped the values "5" and "9" as they are equal and greater than the pivot value of "5" respectively.

4	3	6	8	2	9	5 (pivot)	7
		^		^			

The left pointer value 6 is greater than pivot (i.e. 5) and the right pointer value 2 is less than the pivot (i.e. 5), so swap them as shown below before advancing.

4	3	2	8	6	9	5 (pivot)	7

^ ^

When the pointers are pointing to the same value as shown above, swap it with the pivot value as shown below.

4	3	2	5 (pivot)	6	9	8	7

^ ^

As you can see now, the smaller values (or numbers) are in front of the pivot value "5" and higher values are behind it. This array is now called **partitioned**. The partitioning is used recursively by the quick sorting algorithm to sort elements. The above partitioning algorithm can be applied as shown below.

```java
package algorithms;

public class Partition {

    public static int partition(int[] values, int leftIndex,
        int rightIndex, int pivotIndex) {

        int i = leftIndex;
        int j = rightIndex;

        while (i < j) {
            //moving from left to right
            while (i <= j && values[i] <= values[pivotIndex])
                i++;
            //moving from right to left
            while (j >= i && values[j] >= values[pivotIndex])
                j--;

            if (i < j)
                swap(values, i, j);
        }

        //swap the current index value with the pivot index value
        swap(values, i, pivotIndex);
        return i;                               // return the pivot index
    }
```

```
public static void swap(int[ ] values, int i, int j) {
    int temp = values[i];
    values[i] = values[j];
    values[j] = temp;
}

public static void main(String[ ] args) {
    int[ ] values = { 7, 3, 6, 8, 2, 9, 5, 4};
    //pivot value is 5, left index value is 7 and right index value is 4
    partition(values, 0, values.length -1, values.length - 2 );

    //prints 4,3,2,5,6,9,8,7
    for ( int i = 0; i < values.length; i++ ) {
        System.out.print(values[i]);
        if(i < values.length-1)
            System.out.print(",");
    }
}
}
```

Alternatively, a single pointer can be used by moving from left to right by ensuring that the pivot index is always the last index (i.e. at the end) as demonstrated below:

| 7 | 3 | 6 | 8 | 2 | 9 | 5 (pivot) | 4 |

Send the pivot item to the back.

| 7 | 3 | 6 | 8 | 2 | 9 | 4 | 5 (pivot) |

Move from left to right, and swap with the pointer if the current value is less than the pivot value "5". 3 is less than the pivot value of 5, so swap it with the pointer value. After swapping, move the pointer forward one index.

| 3 | 7 | 6 | 8 | 2 | 9 | 4 | 5 (pivot) |

Skipping values "6" and "8" as they are greater than the pivot value of "5". 2 is less than the pivot value, so swap it with the current pointer value. After swapping, move the pointer forward one index.

3	2	6	8	7	9	4	5 (pivot)

4 is less than the pivot value, so swap it with the current pointer value and move the pointer forward one index.

3	2	4	8	7	9	6	5 (pivot)

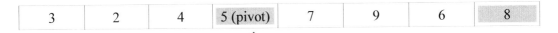

No more smaller values than the pivot value of "5" can be found, so swap the pivot value with the current pointer value.

3	2	4	5 (pivot)	7	9	6	8

The code for the above explanation can be written as shown below:

```java
package algorithms;

public class Partition2 {

    public static int partition(int[] values, int leftIndex,
                        int rightIndex, int pivotIndex) {

        int pivotValue = values[pivotIndex];
        // send pivot item to the back
        swap(values, pivotIndex, rightIndex);

        // keep track of where the front is
        int index = leftIndex;
        // check from the front to the back
        for (int i = leftIndex; i < rightIndex; i++)
        {
            // swap if the current value is less than the pivot
            if (values[i] < pivotValue) {
                swap(values, i, index);
                index++;
            }
        }
    }
}
```

```
        // put pivot item in the middle
        swap(values, rightIndex, index);
        return index;                               // return the current index
    }

    public static void swap(int[ ] values, int i, int j) {
        int temp = values[i];
        values[i] = values[j];
        values[j] = temp;
    }

    public static void main(String[ ] args) {
        int[ ] values ={ 7, 3, 6, 8, 2, 9, 5, 4};
        partition(values, 0, values.length - 1, values.length - 2);

        //prints 3,2,4,5,7,9,6,8
        for (int i = 0; i < values.length; i++) {
            System.out.print(values[i]);
            if(i < values.length-1)
                System.out.print(",");
        }
    }
}
```

Q. How would yo go about applying the QuickSort algorithm to sort the values 7 3 6 8 2 9 5 4 without using the *Arrays.sort(...)*.

A. The key steps involved are:

- **Partition** the array with respect to a random element.
- **Partition** the left part of the array.
- **Partition** the right part of the array.
- Recursively perform the above steps until the exit condition is reached.

Since this is a recursive algorithm, you need a terminating or exit condition that does not make a recursive call. The terminating condition is when the *rightIndex* is less than or equal to the *leftIndex*.

```
package algorithms;
```

```java
public class QuickSort2 {

    //... partition and swap methods as shown before omitted for brevity.

    public static int[] quicksort(int[] values, int leftIndex,  int rightIndex) {

        // This is a recursive algorithm and the terminating condition is
        if (rightIndex > leftIndex) {
            // partition the array with respect to a random element
            int pivotIndex = (leftIndex + rightIndex) / 2;
            int newPivotIndex = partition(values, leftIndex, rightIndex, pivotIndex);

            // partition the left part of the array, using quicksort( ).
            quicksort(values, leftIndex, newPivotIndex - 1);

            // patition the right part of the array, using quicksort( ).
            quicksort(values, newPivotIndex + 1, rightIndex);
        }
        return (int[ ]) values;
    }

    public static void main(String[ ] args) {
        int[ ] values = { 7, 3, 6, 8, 2, 9, 5, 4 };
        quicksort(values, 0, values.length - 1);

        // prints 2,3,4,5,6,7,8,9
        for (int i = 0; i < values.length; i++) {
            System.out.print(values[i]);
            if (i < values.length - 1)
                System.out.print(",");
        }
    }
}
```

Q. Did you make any assumptions in the above code? `COQ`
A. Yes, the supplied array is not already sorted, it is a large array, and the sorting is always in ascending order.

Q. Can you write a function that checks if a given array is already sorted either in ascending or descending order? COQ

A.

```java
package algorithms;

public class AlgorithmUtils {

    public static boolean sorted(int[] input) {

        if (input == null || input.length == 0) {
            throw new IllegalArgumentException("Invalid Input.");
        }

        boolean ascending = false;
        int first = input[0];
        int second = input[1];
        // ascending
        if (first < second)
            ascending = true;

        for (int i = 0; i < input.length-1; i++) {
            if ((ascending && input[i] > input[i + 1])
                    || (!ascending && input[i] < input[i + 1]))
                return false;
        }

        return true;
    }

    //...
}
```

Q. How will you ensure that the above code is functioning it correctly? COQ BP

A. By writing unit tests that cover positive scenarios like an array sorted in ascending order and an array sorted in descending order and also a negative scenario like an unsorted array. Also, test for exceptional conditions like a null or empty array.

Q. Can you write a code to search for number 5 in 7 3 6 8 2 9 5 4? COQ

435

Logic and Data structures Essentials

A. The code below uses the linear search algorithm. The linear search algorithm's two advantages are simplicity and the ability to search either sorted or unsorted one-dimensional arrays. Its sole disadvantage is the time spent in examining the elements. The average number of elements to examine is half the array size, and the maximum is to examine the entire array. For example, a one-dimensional array with 1 million elements requires a linear search to examine an average of 0.5 million elements and a maximum of 1 million elements. The linear search has the complexity of O(n).

```
package algorithms;

public class LinearSearch {

    public static boolean found(int[] input, int number) {
        if(input == null || input.length == 0) {
            throw new IllegalArgumentException("Invalid Input");
        }

        for (int i = 0; i < input.length; i++) {
            if(number == i) {
                return true;
            }
        }
        return false;
    }
    //...
}
```

For very large values of n, the binary search gives a better complexity of O(log n). It uses the divide and conquer strategy to achieve better performance for very large arrays. For example, a one-dimensional array with 1,048,576 elements requires binary search to examine a maximum of 20 elements. Binary search algorithm's two disadvantages are increased complexity and the need to presort the one dimensional array prior to searching. To search for the value of 5:

Unsorted values.

7	3	6	8	2	9	5	4

Firstly sort it, using the quick sort algorithm discussed earlier.

0	1	2	3	4	5	6	7
2	3	4	5	6	7	8	9

left idx   mid idx   right idx

Divide the array into two halves around the center (left idx + right idx)/2 = (0 + 7)/2 = 3. In this case, the idx 3 (which has the value of 5) is the middle index. Compare the search value of 5 with the mid idx. If the search value (i.e. 5) is greater than mid idx value, then the search value may or may not be on the RHS of the mid idx. The LHS can be safely ignored. If the search value is less than the mid idx, then the search value may or may not be on the LHS of the idx. The RHS can be safely ignored. If the search value is neither less than or greater, then the search value is the mid idx. In this example, the value of 5 is in the mid idx, and hence will be found immediately. To illustrate this, search for a value of 8 as shown below.

0	1	2	3	4	5	6	7
2	3	4	5	6	7	8	9

left idx   mid idx   right idx

The search value (i.e. 8) is greater than the mid idx value of 5, so set the left idx to mid idx + 1 = 4, and then recompute the new mid idx to (left idx + right idx)/2 = (4 + 7)/2 = 5

0	1	2	3	4	5	6	7
2	3	4	5	6	7	8	9

                                  left idx   mid idx   right idx

The search value of 8 is still greater than the mid idx, hence the left idx becomes mid idx + 1 = 5 + 1 = 6, and the new mid idx becomes (left idx + right idx) / 2 = (6 + 7) / 2 = 6.

0	1	2	3	4	5	6	7
2	3	4	5	6	7	8	9

                                                      left idx   right idx

                                                        mid idx

The search value of 8 is equal to the value of the mid idx, hence the value is found. Also, note that the if the value were not be found, the terminating condition is the left idx > right idx. The code snippet below demonstrates the binary search.

```
package algorithms;

public class BinarySearch {

    public static boolean found(int[ ] input, int number) {
        if (input == null || input.length == 0) {
            throw new IllegalArgumentException("Invalid Input");
        }

        int leftIdx = 0;
        int rightIdx = input.length - 1;
        int midIdx;

        while (leftIdx <= rightIdx) {
            midIdx = (leftIdx + rightIdx) / 2;
            if (number > input[midIdx])
                leftIdx = midIdx + 1;
            else if (number < input[midIdx])
                rightIdx = midIdx - 1;
            else
                return true;
        }
        return false;
    }

    //...

}
```

Q. Is there a way to improve the above code snippet? COQ
A. The above code snippet only handles int values, and the code can be made more reusable by making it handle binary search of any *Comparable* object as shown below:

```
package algorithms;

public class BinarySearch2<T>{
```

```java
@SuppressWarnings("unchecked")
public static boolean found(Comparable[] input, Comparable compare) {
    if (input == null || input.length == 0) {
        throw new IllegalArgumentException("Invalid Input");
    }

    int leftIdx = 0;
    int rightIdx = input.length - 1;
    int midIdx;
    while (leftIdx <= rightIdx) {
        midIdx = (leftIdx + rightIdx) / 2;
        if (compare.compareTo(input[midIdx]) > 0)
            leftIdx = midIdx + 1;
        else if (compare.compareTo(input[midIdx]) < 0)
            rightIdx = midIdx - 1;
        else
            return true;
    }

    return false;

}

// ....
}
```

The above code can be used with an *Integer, BigDecimal, String*, and any custom class that implements the interface *Comparable*.

Note: There are other algorithms for sorting like merge sort, heap sort, insert sort, etc. Also do your research on the interpolation search, which is a slight variation from the binary search algorithm. This algorithm is a bit more complex and efficient than the binary search algorithm.

Q23 What are the different binary tree traversal mechanisms? COQ

A23 Traversing a tree means visiting all the nodes of a tree in order. Many different binary tree algorithms involve traversals. For example, if you wish to count the number of employees in an organizational chart you must visit each node. If you wish to find the highest salary or add all the salaries of your employees by department, you must examine the value contained in each node. Report generation is an important task of Web based applications. A tree structure can be used to model the layout of nested reports and traverse the tree to produce nested results and offer aggregation functions.

There are two fundamentally different kinds of binary trees traversals - those that are **depth-first** and those that are **breadth-first**. There are three different types of depth-first traversals, which are preorder, inorder, and postorder. There is only one kind of breadth-first traversal, which is the level order traversal. Trees can be traversed recursively or iteratively. Recursive traversal is the best known and most frequently used. Recursive algorithm uses method call stack in order to keep the state of the traversal for every level of a tree.

Preorder traversal

Preorder traversal gets its name from the fact that it visits the root first. In the case of a binary tree, the algorithm is → visit the root first, and then traverse the left subtree, and then traverse the right subtree.

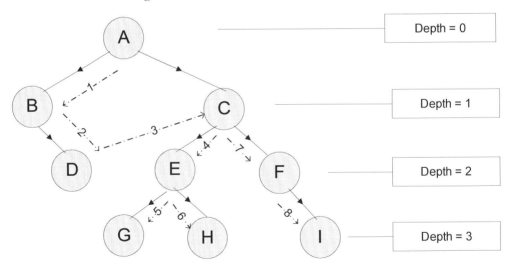

Prints: ABDCEGHFI

In preorder traversal, each node is visited before any of its children. The code snippet for recursion is shown below.

440

```
//preorder traversal for a binary tree
public void traverse(Node node) {
    //Exit condition for recursion
    if (node == null) {
        return;                            //otherwise this will be an endless loop
    }

    System.out.println(node.getName( ));
    traverse(node.getLeft( ));             //recurse left node
    traverse(node.getRight( ));            //recurse right node

}
```

The above algorithm can be achieved iteratively without recursion as shown below by using a *Dequeue* (i.e. LIFO using a double-ended queue).

```
public static void preorderIterative(Node node) {
    Deque<Node> s = new ArrayDeque<Node>(10);
    s.push(node); // push the root node

    while (!s.isEmpty( )) {
        node = s.pop( );
        System.out.print(node.getValue( ));

        if (node.getRight( ) != null) {   // push the right node first,
            s.push(node.getRight( ));     // as a stack is LIFO
        }

        if (node.getLeft( ) != null) {    // push the left node last,
            s.push(node.getLeft( ));      // as a stack is LIFO
        }
    }
}
```

The diagram below shows how a double ended queue is used for traversal. Each pass within the while loop will have a value popped up (e.g. A), and its children pushed in (e.g. B and C).

Logic and Data structures Essentials

The values that are popped out of the stack and printed .

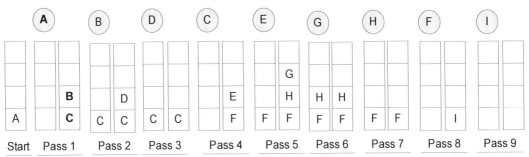

In-order traversal

In a binary tree in-order traversal, left child tree is visited first, then visit the parent node, and then visit the right child tree.

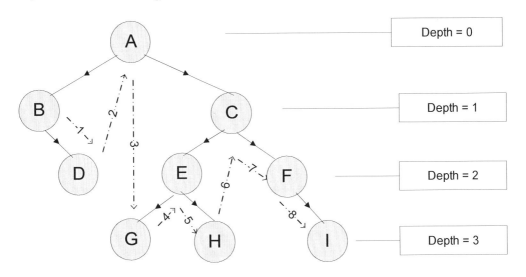

Prints: BDAGEHCFI

The recursive approach is shown below.

```
//inorder traversal for a binary tree
public void traverse(Node node) {
    //Exit condition for recursion
    if (node == null) {
```

```
        return;                              //otherwise this will be an endless loop
    }

    traverse(node.getLeft( ));               //recurse left node
    System.out.println(node.getName( ));
    traverse(node.getRight( ));              //recurse right node
}
```

The iterative approach is shown below using a LIFO approach:

```
public static void inorderIterative(Node node) {
    Deque<Node> s = new ArrayDeque<Node>(10);
    while (!s.isEmpty() || null != node) {
        if (null != node) {
            s.push(node);
            node = node.left;
        } else {
            node = s.pop();
            System.out.print(node.getValue());
            node = node.right;
        }
    }
}
```

The diagram below shows how a double ended queue is used for traversal. All depends on how the elements are popped in and popped out.

The values that are popped out of the stack and printed .

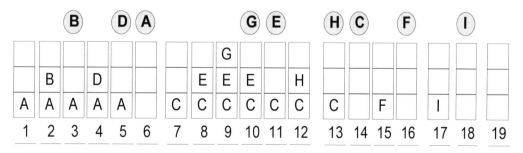

Postorder traversal

In a binary tree postorder traversal, the left and right subtrees are visited before the parent node.

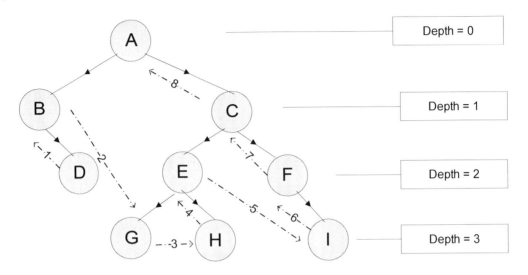

Prints: DBGHEIFCA

```
//postorder traversal for a binary tree
public void traverse(Node node) {
   //Exit condition for recursion
   if (node == null) {
      return;                            //otherwise this will be an endless loop
   }

   traverse(node.getLeft());            //recurse left node
   traverse(node.getRight());           //recurse right node
   System.out.println(node.getName());
}
}
```

Q. What is an expression tree?
A. An expression tree is a binary tree that represents a mathematical expression. It is shown below to demonstrate tree traversals discussed above.

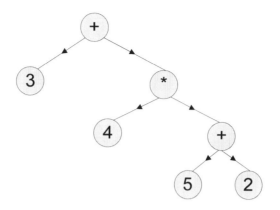

Preorder traversal: + 3 * 4 + 52
Inorder traversal: 3 + 4 * 5 + 2
Postorder traversal: 3452+*+

Note: Check the sample classes *treetraversal.Node* and *treetraversal.NodeTest* to try the non-recursive approach for inorder and postorder traversals.

Q. Can you give some real life examples of these tree traversals?
A.

Preorder traversal can be used to create or clone an existing tree. The parent needs to exist before the children can be added. Evaluation of expressions in prefix notation and processing of the abstract syntax trees by compilers (e.g. JavaCC, ANTLR, etc) are based on preorder traversal. The *DefaultMutableTreeNode* is a general purpose tree data structure in the package j*avax.swing.tree*. The *getNextNode( )* method in this class returns the node that follows a preorder traversal. A *JavaScript* method like *getElementsBy-TagName(...)* could use a preorder traversal to return the elements from a HTML DOM (Document Object Model) tree. It can also be used in your web pages for the site map, menus, and the bread crumb navigation due to its simplicity of retrieving parents and children.

Postorder traversal is used for evaluating of expressions in post-fix, and by the Reverse Polish Notation (RPN), which is used by the compilers. For example, a machine language will require a notation like 2 3 +. A postorder is required for destroying a tree. All the children needs to be destroyed before the parent can be destroyed.

```
public void destroy(Node node) {
    if (node == null)
        return;                    // exit condition

    destroy(node.left)
    destroy(node.right)

    freeCurrentNode(node)
}
```

Any situations where sub tasks need to be performed before the parent tasks. For example, nested pop up menus where child menus need to be closed before the parent menus can be closed. In a build process or a Gantt chart, sub tasks or processes need to be completed before the parent tasks or processes can be completed.

Inorder traversal can be used to search for an item in a balanced binary tree using the binary search algorithm. You can also print all of their data in alphanumeric order.

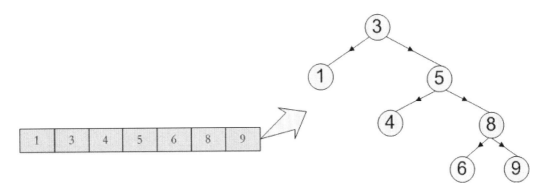

The WHERE clause SQL expressions can be parsed using inorder tree traversal. For example the SQL expression

SELECT * from employees WHERE emp.name = 'john' and emp.age > 10

can be parsed for WHERE clause using an in-order traversal as shown below:

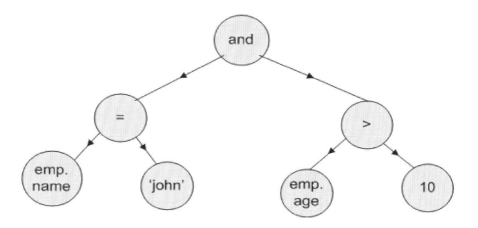

emp.name = 'john' and emp.age > 10

Note: The **level-order** is another traversal option that will be discussed next.

Q24   What are the different searching methodologies for trees that may not have any particular ordering? Which approach will you use if you are likely to find the element near the top of the tree? Which approach will you be using if you are likely to find the element near the bottom of the tree? COQ SBQ

A24   There are 2 types of searches known as BFS and DFS.

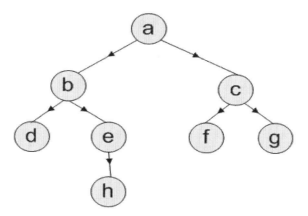

Breadth First Search (BFS) aka level-order traversal.

The BFS searches through a tree from the root and moves from nodes left to right at each level (i.e depth 0, depth 1, etc) until either the search element has been found or all the nodes have been looked at. As per the diagram, it will be searched in the order of a, b, c, d, e, f, g, and h. The preorder traversal uses a stack, and the BFS uses a queue. The queue (FIFO) and stack (LIFO) are pretty much opposite. The *LinkedList* class can be used as a queue for storing children on the same level. The code snippet below demonstrates the BFS for a binary tree.

```java
public boolean bfsSearch(Node root, String search) {
    if (root == null) {
        return false;
    }

    Queue<Node> q = new LinkedList<Node>();              // FIFO
    q.add(root);

    Node tmp;

    while (q.size() > 0) {
        tmp = q.remove();                       //removes from head of the queue

        if (tmp.getName().equals(search)) {
            return true;
        }

        if (tmp.getLeft() != null) {
            q.add(tmp.getLeft());               //add to the end of the queue
        }

        if (tmp.getRight() != null) {
            q.add(tmp.getRight());              //add to the end of the queue
        }
    }

    return false;
}
```

Depth First Searching (DFS)

A DFS searches through a tree starting at the root, and goes straight down a single branch until a leaf is reached. Then, it repeats the same process with its nearest ancestor that has not been searched through yet. As per the diagram, it will be searched in the order of a, b, d, h, e, c, f, and g.

The code snippet below demonstrates the DFS for a binary tree.

```
public boolean dfsSearch(Node node, String search) {
    //exit condition for recursion
    if (node == null) {
        return false;
    }

    //exit condition for recursion
    if (node.getName( ).equals(search)) {
        return true;
    }

    //recursive calls
    return dfsSearch(node.getLeft( ), search) || dfsSearch(node.getRight( ), search) ;
}
```

Logic Processing

The interviewers are not only looking for your logic processing and coding capability, but also your reasoning ability and engineering skills. Think aloud where possible with the logical steps and key considerations like readability, maintainability, performance, memory utilization, possible test scenarios – both positive and negative unit tests, alternative approaches, pros, and cons for each alternative, etc. Don't compromise on readability, extendability, and maintainability for a small performance gain.

Your approach is as important if not more important than getting it right. The interviewers will also be looking to see if you are willing to change your code without the "I know it all" attitude and your willingness to learn. Time limitation and nervousness can play a part in arriving at the most efficient solution, but your approach and engineering skills can give interviewers the confidence that you are on the right track and can get the job done if they know how you are thinking.

Q25 Write a program that allows you to create an integer array of 5 elements with the following values: int numbers[ ]={5,2,4,3,1}. The program computes the sum of first 5 elements and stores them at element 6, computes the average and stores it at element 7 and identifies the smallest value from the array and stores it at element 8. COQ

A25 Remember that the arrays are zero based.

```java
package chapter2.com;

public class Numbers {

    public static void main(String args[ ]) {
        // last three zeros are for the result
        int numbers[ ] = { 5, 2, 4, 3, 1, 0, 0, 0 };

        //set the minimum to a max value
        numbers[7] = Integer.MAX_VALUE;

        for (int i = 0; i < 5; i++) {
            // sum the numbers
            numbers[5] += numbers[i];
            // track the lowest
            if (numbers[i] < numbers[7]) {
                numbers[7] = numbers[i];
            }
        }
        // average the numbers
        numbers[6] = numbers[5] / 5;
        System.out.println("Total is " + numbers[5]);
        System.out.println("Average is " + numbers[6]);
        System.out.println("Minimum is " + numbers[7]);
    }
}
```

Output:

```
Total is 15
Average is 3
Minimum is 1
```

Q26 Write a program that will return whichever value is nearest to the value of 100 from two given int numbers. COQ

A26 You can firstly write the pseudo code as follows:

- Compute the difference to 100.
- Find out the absolute difference as negative numbers are valid.
- Compare the differences to find out the nearest number to 100.
- Write test cases for +ve, -ve, equal to, > than and < than values.

```java
package chapter2.com;

public class CloseTo100 {

    public static int calculate(int input1, int input2) {
        //compute the difference. Negative values are allowed as well
        int iput1Diff = Math.abs(100 - input1);
        int iput2Diff = Math.abs(100 - input2);

        //compare the difference
        if (iput1Diff < iput2Diff) return input1;
        else if (iput2Diff < iput1Diff) return input2;
        else return input1;                        //if tie, just return one
    }

    public static void main(String[] args) {
        //+ve numbers
        System.out.println("+ve numbers=" + calculate(50,90));

        //-ve numbers
        System.out.println("-ve numbers=" + calculate(-50,-90));

        //equal numbers
        System.out.println("equal numbers=" + calculate(50,50));

        //greater than 100
        System.out.println(">100 numbers=" + calculate(85,105));
        System.out.println("<100 numbers=" + calculate(95,110));
    }
}
```

Output:

```
+ve numbers=90
-ve numbers=-50
equal numbers=50
>100 numbers=105
<100 numbers=95
```

Q27 Write a program that will return factorial of n (usually written as *n!*), which is the product of all integers up to and including n (1 * 2 * 3 * ... * n). Can you explain both recursive and iterative approaches? Which approach would you prefer? COQ

[Hint: if n=5, n!= 5 * 4 * 3 * 2 * 1 and *0! == 1! == 1*]

A27 **Considerations:**

- n! can be written as n * (n-1) * (n-2) ….... * 1.
- factorials for negative numbers are undefined.
- 0! is equal to 1.
- Should be able to handle factorials for large numbers like 20.
- Write test scenarios for 0, a larger value like 20, and a negative value.

Recursive approach:

```
package chapter2.com;

public class Factorial1 {
    public static int evaluate(int input) {
        if (input < 0) {
            throw new RuntimeException("Undefined for -ve: " + input);
        }

        //0! == 1! == 1
        if (input <= 1) {
            return 1;                                //recursion exit condition.
        }
        return input * evaluate(input - 1);
```

```
    }

    public static void main(String[ ] args) {
        // zero
        System.out.println("0! = " + evaluate(0));
        // non-zero +ve number
        System.out.println("5! = " + evaluate(5));
        // Large +ve number
        System.out.println("20! = " + evaluate(20));        // wrong - data over flows
    }
}
```

Output:

```
0! = 1
5! = 120
20! = -2102132736                                          //wrong – data over flows
```

Improved recursive approach:

The above solution will not work for large numbers as the maximum limit will reach quickly, and will over-flow after 12! (i.e. 12! = 479001600). The above issue can be fixed by using a *BigInteger* where the values are limited only by the amount of memory. The revised code is as shown below.

```
package chapter2.com;

import java.math.BigInteger;

public class Factorial2 {
    public static BigInteger evaluate(int input) {
        if(input < 0) {
            throw new RuntimeException("Undefined for -ve: " + input);
        }

        BigInteger result = BigInteger.valueOf(input);

        //0! == 1! == 1
        if (result.intValue( ) <= 1) {
```

```
        return BigInteger.ONE;                               //recursion exit condition.
    }
    return result.multiply(evaluate(result.intValue( ) -1));
}

public static void main(String[ ] args) {
    //zero
    System.out.println("0! = " + evaluate(0));
    //non-zero +ve number
    System.out.println("5! = " + evaluate(5));
    //Large +ve number
    System.out.println("20! = " + evaluate(20));            //right
    }
}
```

Output:

```
0! = 1
5! = 120
20! = 2432902008176640000
```

Iterative approach:

MC Writing a recursive factorial method may not be the recommended approach as recursive solution's memory usage is $O(N)$ instead of $O(1)$. Recursive functions are more suited in situations where the iterative approach will either be more complex or harder to understand. For example, nested loops that are more than 2 levels deep. Recursive functions are more suited for composite objects having a tree or hierarchical structure. Since recursion takes stack memory space, it should be used carefully. If your tree is very large, the traversal function should be implemented iteratively. The iterative approach is illustrated below.

```
package chapter2.com;

import java.math.BigInteger;

public class Factorial3 {
    public static BigInteger evaluate(int input) {
        if(input < 0) {
```

```
        throw new RuntimeException("Undefined for -ve: " + input);
    }
    if(input == 0) {
        return BigInteger.ZERO;
    }

    BigInteger result = BigInteger.ONE;

    while(input != 0) {
        result = result.multiply(BigInteger.valueOf(input));
        input = input - 1;
    }

    return result;
}

public static void main(String[ ] args) {
    //zero
    System.out.println("0! = " + evaluate(0));
    //non-zero +ve number
    System.out.println("5! = " + evaluate(5));
    //Large +ve number
    System.out.println("20! = " + evaluate(20));
    }
}
```

Output:

```
0! = 1
5! = 120
20! = 2432902008176640000
```

Q28 Write a method which takes the parameters (int[ ] inputNumbers, int sum) and checks input to find the pair of integer values which totals to the sum. If found returns true, else returns false? COQ

A28 **Considerations:**

- Should it work for negative integers?
- How big is the *inputNumbers* array? How often does this method gets called?

455

- What scenarios need to be tested? +ve numbers, negative numbers, positive sum, negative sum, etc.?
- What are the possible approaches to achieve this?

Approach 1: using nested loops:

- Pick one number from the array of *inputNumbers* and compare against other numbers in the array of *inputNumbers* to see if 2 numbers add up to the given *sum*.
- If the picked number adds up to the given *sum* with at least one other number from the array, return true. Otherwise repeat this process by picking the next number from the array of *inputNumbers* to see if it adds up to the given *sum*.
- If none of the 2 numbers in the array add up to the given *sum*, return false.

```
package chapter2.com;

public class FindPairWithSum1 {

    public static boolean hasSum(int[ ] inputNumbers, int sum) {
        //nested for loops.
        //int n = inputNumbers.length. max loops --> O(n²)
        for (int i = 0; i < inputNumbers.length; i++) {
            for (int j = i + 1; j < inputNumbers.length; j++) {
                if (inputNumbers[i] + inputNumbers[j] == sum) {
                    return true;
                }
            }
        }
        return false;
    }

    public static void main(String[ ] args) {
        System.out.println(hasSum(new int[ ]{3,5,8,9},8));
        System.out.println(hasSum(new int[ ]{3,5,8,9},7));
        System.out.println(hasSum(new int[ ]{3,5,8,9,8,9,7,8,9},3));
        System.out.println(hasSum(new int[ ]{9,8,5,3},8));
        System.out.println(hasSum(new int[ ]{9,8,-5,3},4));
        System.out.println(hasSum(new int[ ]{9,8,-5,-3},-8));
```

```
                System.out.println(hasSum(new int[ ]{9,8,-5,-3},5));
        }
}
```

Output:

```
true
false
false
true
true
true
true
```

Pros: Works for negative numbers as well. Easy to read and understand.

Cons: Not suited for larger arrays and frequent invocations of the method as its maximum loop count is $O(n^2)$. Say for an array with 500 numbers, max loop count is 500*500 = 250000 times. Hence not at all efficient for larger arrays.

Note: If negative numbers are not required to be supported, you can add a check to speed things up a bit further as shown below:

```
for (int i = 0; i < inputNumbers.length; i++) {
    /negative numbers are not supported.
    //fail fast and throw exception early.
    //class invariant must be satisfied
    if(inputNumbers[i] < 0){
        throw new RunTimeException("No -ve numbers");
    }

    if(inputNumbers[i] > sum){
        continue;
    }

    for (int j = i + 1; j < inputNumbers.length; j++) {
        if (inputNumbers[i] + inputNumbers[j] == sum) {
            return true;
        }
    }
```

457

```
        }
    }
}
```

Approach 2: using another collection:

- Pick one number from the array of *inputNumbers*.
- Evaluate the *requiredNumber* (*sum* – picked number) to add up to the given *sum*. Store this *requiredNumber* in a set (e.g. a *HashSet*) for later use.
- Pick the next number, and see if it is one of the *requiredNumbers* by checking it in the previously stored set (i.e. *setNumbers*). If found return true.
- Continue this process for all the numbers in the *inputNumbers* array.
- If all the numbers are processed, and no match was found, return false.

```java
package chapter2.com;

import java.util.HashSet;
import java.util.Set;

public class FindPairWithSum2 {

    public static boolean hasSum(int[ ] inputNumbers, int sum) {
        //using a set.
        //int n = inputNumbers.length. max loops --> n
        Set<Integer> setNumbers = new HashSet<Integer>( );
        for (int i = 0; i < inputNumbers.length; i++) {
            int requiredNumber = sum - inputNumbers[i];
            if(setNumbers.contains(inputNumbers[i])) {
                return true;
            }
            else{
                setNumbers.add(requiredNumber);
            }

        }
        return false;
    }

    public static void main(String[ ] args) {
        System.out.println(hasSum(new int[ ]{3,5,8,9},8));
```

```
System.out.println(hasSum(new int[ ]{3,5,8,9},7));
System.out.println(hasSum(new int[ ]{3,5,8,9,8,9,7,8,9},3));
System.out.println(hasSum(new int[ ]{9,8,5,3},8));
System.out.println(hasSum(new int[ ]{9,8,-5,3},4));
System.out.println(hasSum(new int[ ]{9,8,-5,-3},-8));
System.out.println(hasSum(new int[ ]{9,8,-5,-3},5));
    }
}
```

Output:

```
true
false
false
true
true
true
true
```

Pros: Easy to read and understand. More efficient than nested loops for larger arrays. Its maximum loop count is n. Say for an array with 500 numbers, max loop count is 500 times.

Cons: Require additional memory consumption to store *requiredNumbers* in a separate collection.

Note: If negative numbers are not required to be supported, an additional optimization can be made by adding the following line just after the for loop line.

```
//class invariant check
if(inputNumbers[i] < 0){
    throw new RunTimeException("No -ve numbers");
}
if(inputNumbers[i] > sum){
    continue;
}
```

Approach 3: using two pointers:

459

- Sort the array of *inputNumbers* in ascending order.
- Define two pointers – one starts from the beginning and the other starts from the end.
- Loop through the array of *inputNumbers* until either numbers pointed by start and end pointers add up to the given *sum* or both the pointers point to the same element in the array.
- If the elements pointed by the start and end pointers add up to the given *sum*, return true. If the given *sum* is greater, move the start pointer forward to the next element. If the given *sum* is lesser, move the end pointer backwards to the previous element.
- If sum is found, return true, and otherwise return false.
- A simple diagram as demonstrated in the algorithms section would make things clearer.

```java
package chapter2.com;

import java.util.Arrays;

public class FindPairWithSum3 {

    public static boolean hasSum(int[] inputNumbers, int sum) {
        //using two pointers.
        //int n = inputNumbers.length. max loops --> n-1
        int start = 0;                              //left pointer
        int end = inputNumbers.length -1;           //right pointer
        Arrays.sort(inputNumbers);                  //sort the array
        while (start != end) {
            if(sum == inputNumbers[start] + inputNumbers[end]) {
                return true;
            }
            else if(sum > inputNumbers[start] + inputNumbers[end] ) {
                ++start;                            // move forward the lhs pointer
            }
            else {
                --end;                              // move backward the rhs pointer
            }
        }
        return false;
```

```
        }
    }

    public static void main(String[ ] args) {
        System.out.println(hasSum(new int[ ]{3,5,8,9},8));
        System.out.println(hasSum(new int[ ]{3,5,8,9},7));
        System.out.println(hasSum(new int[ ]{3,5,8,9,8,9,7,8,9},3));
        System.out.println(hasSum(new int[ ]{9,8,5,3},8));
        System.out.println(hasSum(new int[ ]{9,8,-5,3},4));
        System.out.println(hasSum(new int[ ]{9,8,-5,-3},-8));
        System.out.println(hasSum(new int[ ]{9,8,-5,-3},5));
    }
}
```

Output:

```
true
false
false
true
true
true
true
```

Pros: Easy to read and understand. More efficient than nested loops for larger arrays. Its maximum loop count is n-1. Say for an array with 500 numbers, max loop count is 499. Can be used for negative numbers.

Cons: Array of numbers must be sorted prior to use. Using a quick sort algorithm will incur an additional $O(N * \log N)$ performance.

Which approach to choose? Using another collection or two pointers. Incorporate performance and memory usage benchmarks.

Q29 Can you write a code to *evaluate( )* a simple mathematical calculation as shown below using a binary tree? COQ

$$3 + 4 * (5 + 2) = 31$$

A29 A binary tree is made of nodes, where each node contains a "left" pointer, a "right" pointer, and a data element (e.g. operand, operator, etc). The "root" pointer points to the topmost node in the tree. The left and right pointers recursively point to smaller "subtrees" on either side. A null pointer represents a binary tree with no elements (i.e. an empty tree).

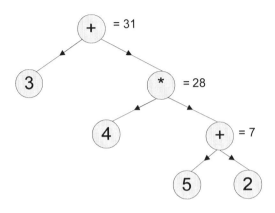

```
package binarytree1;

public class Node {

    enum OPERATOR {  ADD, SUBTRACT, MULTIPLY, DIVIDE  };

    //store the values
    private Integer lhsValue, rhsValue;

    // operator node that links value nodes
    private OPERATOR operator = null;
    private Node lhsNode, rhsNode;

    public Node() {}

    public void link(Node lhsNode, Node rhsNode) {
        this.lhsNode = lhsNode;
        this.rhsNode = rhsNode;
    }

    // ... relevant getters & setters
```

```java
public int evaluate( ) {
    int result = 0;
    int lhs = 0, rhs = 0;

    if (lhsNode != null) {
        lhs = lhsNode.evaluate( );
    }

    if (rhsNode != null) {
        rhs = rhsNode.evaluate( );
    }

    if(lhsNode == null && lhsValue != null){
        return lhsValue;
    }

    if(rhsNode == null && rhsValue != null){
        return rhsValue;
    }

    if (operator == null) {
        throw new IllegalArgumentException("Invalid Operator: " + operator);
    }

    switch (operator) {
    case ADD:
        result = lhs + rhs;
        break;

    case SUBTRACT:
        result = lhs - rhs;
        break;

    case MULTIPLY:
        result = lhs * rhs;
        break;

    case DIVIDE:
```

```
        result = lhs / rhs;
        break;
    }

    return result;
  }
}
```

The above code can be used as shown below:

```
package binarytree1;

public class TreeCalculator {

  public static void main(String[ ] args) {
    // 3 + 4 * (5+2)
    Node five = new Node( );
    five.setLhsValue(5);

    Node two = new Node( );
    two.setRhsValue(2);

    Node operation1 = new Node( );
    operation1.setOperator(Node.OPERATOR.ADD);
    operation1.link(five, two);
    System.out.println("operation1=" + operation1.evaluate( ));   // 7

    Node four = new Node( );
    four.setLhsValue(4);
    Node operation2= new Node( );
    operation2.setOperator(Node.OPERATOR.MULTIPLY);
    operation2.link(four, operation1);
    System.out.println("operation2=" + operation2.evaluate( ));   // 28

    Node three = new Node( );
    three.setLhsValue(3);
    Node operation3= new Node( );
    operation3.setOperator(Node.OPERATOR.ADD);
    operation3.link(three, operation2);
```

```
        System.out.println("operation3=" + operation3.evaluate()); // 31
    }
}
```

The above solution is not ideal. The biggest problem with the *Node* class is that all the code and logic are enclosed in a single method. What if you need to add another operation like a modulus operation? A cleaner solution is to use polymorphism instead of if/else or switch conditionals as shown below. The above code is not open for extension. When ever you see large switch or if/else statements, polymorphism and open-closed principle should come to mind. The following solution is also more testable.

```
package binarytree2;

public interface Node {
    int evaluate();
}
```

```
package binarytree2;

public abstract class AbstractOperationNode implements Node {

    protected Node left, right;

    public AbstractOperationNode(Node left, Node right){
        this.left= left;
        this.right = right;
    }
}
```

```
package binarytree2;

public class OperandNode implements Node {

    Integer value;

    public OperandNode(Integer value){
        this.value = value;
    }
}
```

465

```
  @Override
  public int evaluate( ) {
    return value;
  }
}
```

```java
package binarytree2;

public class AddOperationNode extends AbstractOperationNode {

  public AddOperationNode(Node left, Node right){
    super(left, right);
  }

  @Override
  public int evaluate( ) {
    return left.evaluate( ) + right.evaluate( );
  }

}
```

```java
package binarytree2;

public class MultiplyOperationNode extends AbstractOperationNode {

  public MultiplyOperationNode(Node left, Node right){
    super(left, right);
  }

  @Override
  public int evaluate( ) {
    return left.evaluate( ) * right.evaluate( );
  }
}
```

```
//... similar code for the other operational nodes
```

The above code can be used as shown below with polymorphism in action. If a new operation was added, all you have to do is to add a new operation node and provide an appropriate implementation via the the *evaluate( )* method. This shows that the above code is open for extension and closed for modification. It also harnesses the power of OO concept known as "**polymorphism**".

```
package binarytree2;

public class TreeCalculator {

    public static void main(String[ ] args) {
        // 3 + 4 * (5+2)

        Node five = new OperandNode(5);
        Node two = new OperandNode(2);
        Node result1 = new AddOperationNode(five, two);
        System.out.println("node result1=" + result1.evaluate( ));  // 7

        Node four = new OperandNode(4);
        Node result2 = new MultiplyOperationNode(four, result1);
        System.out.println("node result2=" + result2.evaluate( ));  // 28

        Node three = new OperandNode(3);
        Node result3 = new AddOperationNode(three,result2);

        System.out.println("node result3=" + result3.evaluate( ));  // 31
    }
}
```

Q30 Can you suggest the most appropriate data structure for each of the following scenarios given below?

A30 **Q.** A Java program to read a text file and print each of the unique words in alphabetical order together with the number of times the word occurs in the text?

A. A *TreeMap* automatically sorts new keys on insertion, no sorting after wards is needed. So it can store the words in alphabetical order. Alternatively, you can use a *TreeBag*, which is an implementation of a *Bag* interface provided by the Apache Commons' collection framework. A bag can hold a number of copies of each object. For example,

```
public static void main(String[ ] args) {
    Bag bag = new TreeBag( );
    String text = "A small cat jumped over a small fence";
    String[ ] wordArray = text.split("\\s");              // split on white space
    for (String string : wordArray) {
        bag.add(string.toLowerCase());
    }

    // iterate over the unique set
    for (Object word : bag.uniqueSet()) {
        System.out.println("word '" + (String) word + "' has " + bag.getCount(word) + "
                                                        occurrence(s).");
    }
}
}
```

Output:

```
word 'a' has 2 occurrence(s).
word 'cat' has 1 occurrence(s).
word 'fence' has 1 occurrence(s).
word 'jumped' has 1 occurrence(s).
word 'over' has 1 occurrence(s).
word 'small' has 2 occurrence(s).
```

Q. A Java program to <u>undo</u> a last n number of tasks performed on a user interface?
A. Use a *Stack* implementation like a *Dequeue* that gives a LIFO capability.

Q. A Java program to represent a bus network for a travel company?
A. Cities can be model as nodes in a graph and the roads connecting the cities as edges. It will be a **directed** graph as you need to show the direction of the edges as either unidirectional or bidirectional. In this example, it is important to associate some cost with the connection from one node to another. The travel cost will vary between the cities .If you wanted to determine the shortest distance and route from one city to another, you first need to assign a cost from traveling from one city to another. The logical solution would be to give each edge a weight, such as how many kilo meters it is from one city to another. So, it will be a directed weighted graph to be more specific.

The directionality and weightedness of a graph can have one of the following four arrangements of edges,

- Directed, weighted edges
- Directed, unweighted edges
- Undirected, weighted edges
- Undirected, unweighted edges

Note: There are many other real life examples for a graph data structure like a city regional telephone network, a flight network, a courier service network, a link structure of a web page where the nodes are the web pages available at the website and links from one page to another as directed edges, etc.

Q. How would you represent an image in the form of a bitmap?
A. You need to use a one-dimensional array of pixel data. Each entry in the array represents a single pixel in the image.

```
int[ ] pixels = new int [width*height];
```

The two-dimensional pixel data are flattened into a one-dimensional array by placing the pixel at position (x, y) into the array at position (y * width+x).

Q. What data structure would you use to store any arbitrary two dimensional data from a database table?
A. Create a Java bean class named *"ColumnData"* that has a *Map* to represent column names as *Map* keys, and column values as *Map* values. The row data will be represented as a list of *"ColumnData"*.

```
List<ColumnData> list = new ArrayList<ColumnData>(100);
```

Q. Customers waiting for a teller in a bank?
A. In real life a line of customers waiting for service of some kind is represented by a Queue. The rule that determines who goes next is called a queuing discipline. The simplest queuing discipline is called **FIFO**, for "first-in-first-out". The other most common queuing discipline is **priority queueing**, in which each customer is assigned a priority, and the customer with the highest priority goes first, regardless of the order of arrival. The priority can be based on anything: what time a flight leaves, how many groceries the customer has, how important the customer is, or if you are traveling with young children, etc.

Note: A printer spooler is another example to use a queue so that the print jobs can be printed in the order of their arrival.

Exception handling

Exception handling is used to prevent application from being stuck due to unusual occur-rences. If the exceptions are handled properly, the application will never get terminated abruptly. Bad exception handling can make your application harder to read, maintain and debug.

Q31 Why does Java have exceptions? What is the difference between checked and unchecked exceptions? LF FAQ

A31 Java does have exceptions to handle exceptional situations.

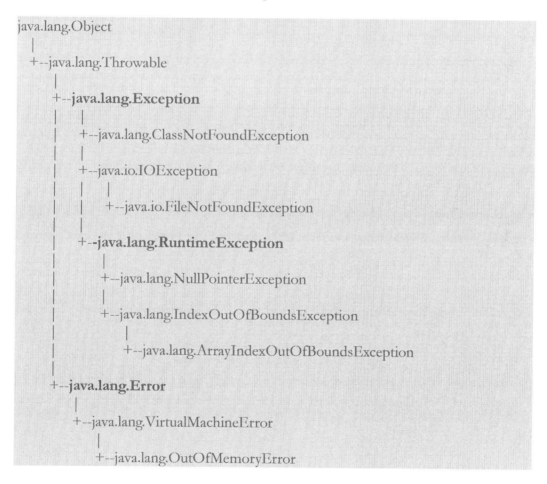

```
java.lang.Object
   |
   +--java.lang.Throwable
       |
       +--java.lang.Exception
       |   |
       |   +--java.lang.ClassNotFoundException
       |   |
       |   +--java.io.IOException
       |   |   |
       |   |   +--java.io.FileNotFoundException
       |   |
       |   +--java.lang.RuntimeException
       |       |
       |       +--java.lang.NullPointerException
       |       |
       |       +--java.lang.IndexOutOfBoundsException
       |           |
       |           +--java.lang.ArrayIndexOutOfBoundsException
       |
       +--java.lang.Error
           |
           +--java.lang.VirtualMachineError
               |
               +--java.lang.OutOfMemoryError
```

In Java, there are basically two types of exceptions: **Checked** exceptions and **unchecked** exceptions.

- A checked exception is any subclass of *java.lang.Exception* (or *java.lang.Exception* itself). An unchecked exception is any subclass of *java.lang.Runtime*Exception (or *java.lang.Runtime*Exception itself).

- A checked exception can throw compile-time errors to force the calling code to either catch the exception or declare it in a throws clause. For example, *ClassNotFoundException*, *FileNotFoundException*, *IOException*, *SQLException*, *PersistenceException*, etc are checked exceptions. These exceptions occur mainly due to conditions that are not in programmer's control. These include conditions such as connection errors to database, LDAP servers, external services, and other network failures.

  In case of an unchecked exception, the compiler doesn't force client programs (aka calling programs) to either catch the exception or declare it in a throws clause. In fact, client programs may not even have to know that the exception could be thrown. For example, *StringIndexOutOfBoundsException*, *ClassCastException, ArrayIndexOutOfBoundsException*, *NullPointerException*, etc are unchecked exceptions. If you wish, you can handle them. Unchecked exceptions occur mainly due to programming errors like invoking a method on a null object (*NullPointerException*), an invalid argument is passed to a method (*IllegalArgumentException*), trying to access an array index beyond the allocated memory (*ArrayIndexOutOfBoundsException*), etc.

Checked exception example:

```
package exceptions;

import java.io.File;
import java.io.FileWriter;
import java.io.IOException;

public class CheckedDemo {
```

```java
//must throw or catch checked IOException.
//Otherwise you will get a compile-time error
public void writeFile() throws IOException  {
    File file = new File("C://temp/demo.txt");
    FileWriter fw = new FileWriter(file);          //Can throw IOException
    fw.write("test");
    fw.close();                                    //Can throw IOException
}

//must throw or catch checked IOException.
//Otherwise you will get a compile-time error
public static void main(String[ ] args) {
    try {
        new CheckedDemo().writeFile();             //Can throw IOException
    }
    catch(IOException ioe) {
        ioe.printStackTrace();
    }
}
}
```

Unchecked exception example:

```java
package exceptions;

public class UnCheckedDemo {

    // If you wish, you  can handle unchecked exceptions
    // but, it will not be necessary as shown here.
    public int getValue() {
        int[ ] i = { 0, 2 };
        return i[3];                   //throws ArrayIndexOutOfBoundsException
    }

    // If you wish, you  can handle unchecked exceptions
    // but, it will not be necessary as shown here.
    public static void main(String[ ] args) {
        new UnCheckedDemo().getValue();        //throws runtime exception
                                          //ArrayIndexOutOfBoundsException
```

473

```
    }
}
```

There are no **throws** or **catch** clauses for the unchecked exceptions as shown above.

Q32   Will the following code compile? `COQ`

```
public static void writeFile(String filePath, String text) {
    try {

        //some File handling implementation

    } catch (Exception t) {
        System.out.println("catch 3");
        t.printStackTrace();
    } catch (IOException ioe) {
        System.out.println("catch 2");
        ioe.printStackTrace();
    } catch (FileNotFoundException fnf) {
        System.out.println("catch 1");
        fnf.printStackTrace();
    }
}
```

A32   No. The *FileNotFoundException* is extended (i.e. inherited) from the *IOException*, and *IOException* is extended from the *Exception* class as shown below. So subclasses have to be caught first.

```
+--java.lang.Exception
    |   |
    |   +--java.lang.ClassNotFoundException
    |   |
    |   +--java.io.IOException
    |   |   |
    |   |   +--java.io.FileNotFoundException
```

Exception handling in Java is **polymorphic** in nature. For example, if you catch or throw type *Exception* in your code, then it can catch or throw its descendent types like

IOException and *FileNotFoundException* as well. So if you catch the type *Exception* before the type *IOException*, then the type *Exception* block will catch all its sub class types as well, and *IOException* block will never be reached. In order to catch the type *IOException* and <u>handle it differently</u> to type *Exception*, *IOException* should be caught before catching the type *Exception*. The *FileNotFoundException* should be caught before *IOException*, if you want to handle it differently to type *IOException*. For example,

```
package exceptions;

import java.io.File;
import java.io.FileNotFoundException;
import java.io.FileWriter;
import java.io.IOException;

public class ExceptionsArePolymorphic {

    public static void writeFile(String filePath, String text)
        throws IOException {

        File file = new File(filePath);
        FileWriter fw = null;
        try {
            if (text == null || text.length() == 0) {
                throw new IllegalArgumentException(
                    "Nothing to write: text= " + text);
            }
            fw = new FileWriter(file);      // can throw FileNotFoundException.
            fw.write(text);                 // can throw IOException.

        } catch (FileNotFoundException fnfe) {
            throw fnfe;
        } catch (IOException ioe) {
            throw new RuntimeException("Error writing: " + ioe);
        } catch (Exception ex) {
            throw new RuntimeException("Unexpected error: " + ex);
        } finally {
            if (fw != null) {
                fw.close();                 //always cleanup in a finally block.
            }
```

```
        }
      }
   }

   public static void main(String[ ] args) {
      try {
         // there is no folder called onpurpose
         writeFile("c:\\onpurpose\\demo.txt", "Testing...");
      } catch (IOException ioe) {
         if(ioe instanceof FileNotFoundException){
            System.out.println("Check FilePublisher Cron Job: ...");
         }
         throw new RuntimeException(ioe);        //exception wrapping
      }
   }
}
```

Note: When you catch exceptions, subclasses must be caught first. When you throw an exception, throwing the base class will handle all the subclasses as well. Throwing an *IOException* will handle *FileNotFoundException* as well. But the reverse is not true. Throwing a *FileNotFoundException* will not handle an *IOException* being thrown. Throwing a base exception type will minimize the need for the client code to change when a new exception is added or removed as long as   the added or removed exception extends or implements the base exception type.

Q33 When do you want to use checked exceptions and when do you want to use unchecked exceptions? `LF FAQ BP`

A33 There is no obvious answer for this. The industry and the experts are divided in their opinions. As a general recommendation, checked exceptions should be used when the calling code can take an alternate action to recover from that exception. For example, a caller can recover from a *TimeOutException* in a network call by retrying a number of times.

Unchecked exceptions are used when there's a critical exception (e.g. *NullPointerException, ClassCastException, SQLException*, etc) that the calling code is unlikely to be able to recover from it. For example, the client code will never come to know why a particular *SQLException* occurred as it has no knowledge of underlying implementation details and internal database design. So it is not worth forcing a client to handle an exception it does not know about.

When writing exception handling, always ask yourself – What action can the client code take when a particular exception occurs?

Why favor unchecked exceptions? Unchecked exceptions make your code more readable by not cluttering your code with try-catch blocks and aggregated throws clauses. The less you handle exceptions, the less chance of writing bad error handling code like sloppy catch blocks that suppress the exception, using exceptions for flow control, not properly abstracting throws clauses, etc. Some of the important points to keep in mind if you take this approach are:

- Unlike checked exceptions, unchecked exceptions are not self-documenting. The client will not have sufficient information as to what exceptions can be thrown from a given method. Hence document all unchecked exceptions with the Java-doc.

```
package exceptions;

public class UncheckedExcDocument {

    /**
     * @param name
     * @param range
     * @throws IllegalArgumentException if input is empty
     * @throws NegativeAgeException if age is negative
     */
    public void someMethod(String name, int age){
        if(name == null || name.length( ) == 0){
            throw new IllegalArgumentException("input=" + name);
        }

        if(age <= 0){
            throw new NegativeAgeException(age);
        }
    }
}
```

- Write negative unit tests that can also act as documentation. It will serve as a documentation that can also be executed as shown below:

477

```
package exceptions;

import org.junit.Before;
import org.junit.Test;

public class UncheckedExcDocumentTest {

    UncheckedExcDocument ref = null;

    @Before
    public void setUp(){
        ref = new UncheckedExcDocument();
    }

    @Test(expected=IllegalArgumentException.class)
    public void negativeTestBadName(){
        ref.someMethod(null, 5);
    }

    @Test(expected=NegativeAgeException.class)
    public void negativeTestBadAge(){
        ref.someMethod("John", -1);
    }
}
```

- Remember to provide clean up code in a finally block.

```
public void createUser() {
    //...
    try {
        jdbcUtil.createUser(...);  //can throw unchecked exceptions
    }
    finally{
        //clean-up code
        if(jdbcUtil != null){
            jdbcUtil.closeConnection()
        }
    }
}
```

Note: No catch blocks as it only throws unchecked exceptions.

Why favor checked exceptions?   Checked exceptions are self-documenting with appropriate throws clauses, but be aware of the following pitfalls and bad practices.

- When forced to catch or throw exceptions, developers can write sloppy catch blocks as shown below:

```
//Bad practice to suppress exceptions. It hides bugs.
try {
    methodCallThatCanTrowException( );
}
//catch and suppress the exception. Very bad.
catch(Exception ex){
}
```

- The above code not only sweeps checked exceptions under the carpet, but also the unchecked exceptions. It's okay to ignore exceptions that are thrown from a finally block. This is because the code in the finally block is intended to be "cleanup" code, and you could decide to treat exceptions occurring there as secondary, and to put an explicit catch and just log the exception. This is one of the few cases where it's fairly legitimate to just ignore the exception. A finally block should also not have a return statement as it can discard exceptions.

- Don't expose implementation details to the client. For example, an *SQLException* revealing internal database schema details. This could provide a potential loop hole for security breach through potential SQL injection attack. It is better to wrap these exceptions with more appropriate exceptions like *UserNotFoundException*, *RedrawLimitExceededException*, etc. Try not to over do it as you may end up having long stack traces.

- When using checked exceptions, adding or removing an exception from a method can break the client code. This will make your method signature very fragile and can cause its own scheduling and versioning nightmares if the code is already deployed to production. So abstract out the throws clause.

For example, your *UserDao* interface should throw *UserNotFoundException* as opposed to throwing an implementation specific exception like *SQLException* if the data is stored in database, *IOException* if the data is stored in a file system, or a *RemoteException* if the data is stored via a RMI call to an EJB. You can catch the implementation specific exceptions like *SQLException* in your *UserDaoImpl* class by catching them and re-throwing them as a *UserNotFoundException*. This enables your implementation details to change without impacting the contract with the client. The client will always get a *UserNotFoundException* regardless of your implementation using a database server or a file system.

- Don't make your interfaces vague by throwing type *Exception*. It will be unclear as to which exceptions can be thrown from the methods. Use classes derived from the type *Exception*. For example *IOException*.

- Don't use exceptions for flow control as shown below:

```
public void processMaxCount() {
  try {
    while(true) {
      increment();
      //do something
    }
  }
  catch(CountLimitReachedException e) {}

  //continue with rest of the code
}


public void increment() throws CountLimitReachedException {
  if(count > Constants.MAX_COUNT) {
    throw new CountLimitReachedException();
  }

  ++count;
}
```

The above code uses an infinite loop to increase the count until the user defined checked exception *CountLimitReachedException* is thrown. This difficult to read code can be replaced with a while loop that compares count against the MAX_COUNT.

```
while(count <= Constants.MAX_COUNT) {
    increment( );
    //do something
}
```

- Avoid catch blocks that just re-throw a caught exception. This just increases your code size without adding any real value.

```
public void method1( ) {
  try {
    //Do something
  }
  catch(SomeException ex){
    throw ex;
  }
}
```

If you prefer a balanced approach by mixing both approaches based on its merits, strive for consistency as mixing exception types often results in confusions and inconsistent use. For example, on a per package basis as suggested by Rod Johnson.

Q34 What is the difference between exception and error? LF
A34 When a dynamic linking failure or some other "hard" failure in the JVM occurs, the JVM throws an *Error. Errors* are unchecked. Typical Java programs should not catch *Errors*. In addition, it's unlikely that typical Java programs will ever throw *Errors* either. A typical example for this would be an *OutOfMemoryError* thrown when the JVM cannot allocate an object because it is out of memory, and no more memory could be made available by the garbage collector.

Q35 What is a user defined exception? When would you define your own exception? LF FAQ
A35 User defined exceptions are custom exceptions defined by either extending the *Exception* or *RuntimeException* classes. It can also extend any other subclass of *Exception*.

481

User defined unchecked exception:

```
package exceptions;

public class NegativeAgeException extends RuntimeException {

    // Exception class implements Throwable interface
    // and Throwable interface implements Serializable interface
    private static final long serialVersionUID = 1L;

    private int age;

    public NegativeAgeException(int age) {
        this.age = age;
    }

    public int getAge() {
        return age;
    }

    public String toString() {
        return "Age cannot be negative" + " " + age;
    }
}
```

User defined checked exception:

```
package exceptions;

import java.util.Arrays;

public class MyAppException extends Exception {

    private static final long serialVersionUID = 1L;

    private String errorCode;
    private String errorDescription;
    private String[] variables;
```

```java
    public MyAppException(String errorCode, String errorDescription,
        String[ ] variables) {
      this.errorCode = errorCode;
      this.errorDescription = errorDescription;
      this.variables = variables;
    }

    public String getErrorCode( ) {
      return errorCode;
    }

    public String getErrorDescription( ) {
      return errorDescription;
    }

    public String[ ] getVariables( ) {
      return variables;
    }

    @Override
    public String toString( ) {
      return "errorCode=" + errorCode + ",erorDesc="
          + errorDescription + ",variables= " + Arrays.deepToString(variables);

    }
  }
```

Q. When would you define your own exception? OEQ

A. Provide custom exceptions only if you have useful information to the calling code. For example, the client code can query for *errorCode* and other additional variables as shown above. Alternatively, the calling code can catch a specific exception type like *TimeOutException* to recover from it. But if you are not going to add any extra inform-ation or handle it in a special way, then just throw a standard exception like:

```java
throw new RuntimeException ("Error processing charge details: " + ...);
```

Q36 What are the best practices in regards to exception handling? BP

A36 In addition to the pitfalls and best practices covered under checked versus unchecked exceptions,

- **Throw an exception early** because the exception stack trace helps you pinpoint where an exception occurred by showing you the exact sequence of method calls that leads to the exception. By throwing your exception early, the exception becomes more accurate and more specific. Avoid suppressing or ignoring exceptions. Also avoid using exceptions just to get a flow control.

  Instead of:

  ```
  // assume this line throws an exception because filename == null.
  InputStream in = new FileInputStream(fileName);
  ...
  ```

  Use the following code because you will get a more accurate stack trace:

  ```
  ...
  if(filename == null) {
      throw new IllegalArgumentException("file name is null");
  }

  InputStream in = new FileInputStream(fileName);
  ...
  ```

- **Catch an exception late**. You should not try to catch an exception before your program can handle it in an appropriate manner. The natural tendency when a compiler complains about a checked exception is to catch it so that the compiler stops reporting errors. It is a bad practice to sweep the exceptions under the carpet by catching it and not doing anything with it. The best practice is to catch the exception at the appropriate layer (e.g. an exception thrown at an integration layer can be caught at a presentation layer in a catch {} block), where your program can either meaningfully recover from the exception and continue to execute or log the exception only once in detail, so that user can identify the cause of the exception.

- **Don't lose your stack trace**. Throwing a new exception from a catch block without passing the original exception into the new exception can cause some part of the stack trace to be lost, and can make debugging less effective.

```java
public void method1( ) {
  try {
    //Do something
  }
  catch(SomeException ex){
    throw new RuntimeException(ex.getMessage( ));   //Bad: stack trace
                                                    //will be lost
  }
}

public void method1( ) {
  try {
    //Do something
  }
  catch(SomeException ex){
    throw new RuntimeException("Error " + ex);          //Good
  }
}
```

Note: The Java 7 may have an improved catch clause by allowing you to catch multiple exceptions and handle them the same way.

```java
try {
    return klass.newInstance( );
} catch (InstantiationException | IllegalAccessException e) {
    throw new RuntimeException(e);
}
```

Section-8:

Matching patterns with regular expressions

    –   The reason regular expressions are so useful is that they can be used to target what you need in any string with the flexibility of being able to use your matches to process the given string. Regular Expressions are integrated into many programmer tools and programming languages.

    –   Regular expressions are used to search, replace, filter, and validate data. Each time you use Regular Expressions, you are invoking a powerful search engine. This search engine is one that searches through text looking for specific patterns.

    –   Many find regular expressions to be a bit tricky, but if you can learn how to handle regular expressions you will have one of the most simplest, cleanest and efficient tools in your arsenal to take on a variety of problems.

    –   Regular Expressions can be used to match just about anything. Regular expressions are a language study all to themselves.

Matching patterns with Regular Expressions

The regular expressions are very powerful and it can be used in your Java code, shell scripts, UNIX commands, build scripts like ANT, XSD restrictions, IDEs, TEXT editors, and other tools. Here are a few reasons to motivate yourself to learn regular expressions (aka **regex**)

- Regex are everywhere. Even many experienced programmers are intimidated by it, and knowing how to use regexp effectively will help you stand out from the crowd.
- Regex help you write short code.
- Regex saves time.
- Regex are fast if written with performance in mind.

Note: Please refer to the java.util.regex.**Pattern** class API for the summary of regular expression constructs.

Q01 How will you go about implementing the following validation rules for a user name?

- user name must be between 2 and 17 characters long.
- valid characters are A to Z, a to z, 0 to 9, . (full-stop), _ (underscore) and - (hyphen)
- user name must begin with an alphabetic character.
- user name must not end with a . (full stop) or _ (underscore) or - (hyphen).

A01 The above rules can be implemented with a regular expression as shown below:

```
package regex;

import java.util.regex.Matcher;
import java.util.regex.Pattern;

public class UserNameRegex {

    public static final String PATTERN =
                "^[a-zA-Z][a-zA-Z0-9._-]{0,15}[a-zA-Z0-9]$";
    public static final Pattern p = Pattern.compile(PATTERN);
```

```
public static boolean apply(String userName) {
    Matcher matcher = p.matcher(userName);
    return matcher.find();
  }
}
```

PC Not compiling the regular expression can be costly if *Pattern.matches( )* is used over and over again with the same expression in a loop or frequent method calls because the *matches( )* method will re-compile the expression every time it is used. You can also re-use the *Matcher* object for different input strings by calling the method *reset( )*.

What does this pattern mean?

^	[a-zA-Z]	[a-zA-Z0-9._-]{0,15}	[a-zA-Z0-9]	$
Beginning of a line	Valid start characters. Should start with an alphabet. Must occur once.	Valid characters in the middle. Minimum occurrences 0 and max occurrences 15.	Valid end characters. Should not end with "." "-" or "_". Must occur once.	End of a line.

How will you test this? Test with JUnit. The junit.jar file must be in the classpath.

```
package regex;

import org.junit.Assert;
import org.junit.Test;

public class UserNameRegexTest {

  @Test
  public void testMinLength() {
    Assert.assertFalse("can't be <2", UserNameRegex.apply("P"));
  }

  @Test
  public void testMaxLength() {
    Assert.assertFalse("Can't be >17", UserNameRegex
```

```
            .apply("Jonathon-Christopher"));
}

@Test
public void testCantEndWith() {
    Assert.assertFalse("can't end with . - _", UserNameRegex
        .apply("s.g.r."));
}

@Test
public void testMustStartWith() {
    Assert.assertFalse("Must start with an alphabet",
        UserNameRegex.apply("23Lucky"));
}

@Test
public void validNames() {
    Assert.assertTrue("Min Length 2", UserNameRegex.apply("Jo"));
    Assert.assertTrue("Max Length 17", UserNameRegex
        .apply("Peter-Christopher"));
    Assert.assertTrue(". - _ allowed in the middle",
        UserNameRegex.apply("s.g-h_k.r"));
    Assert.assertTrue("end with numeric", UserNameRegex
        .apply("Lucky23"));

}
}
```

Q02 How would you go about validating a supplied password in your code that must adhere to the following conditions?

- Must contain a digit from 0-9.
- Must contain one uppercase character.
- Must contain one lowercase character.
- The length must be between 6 to 15 characters long.

A02 It can be achieved with a regular expression. But unlike the previous question, this is a bit more complicated than it looks. You might be tempted to write something like,

```
[0-9A-Za-z]{6,15}
```

But the above regex is not going to meet the requirement. The above regex will only ensure that the valid characters are used and the password is of correct length (i.e. between 6 and 15 characters). But it won't ensure that there is at least one digit from 0-9, one lower case and one uppercase. So, the above regex will return true for passwords like

- Johnpwd   //no digit in the password
- john123   //no uppercase character in the password

This is where the regex with **look ahead** comes to the rescue. The pattern below uses "look ahead" with the syntax **?=**. The regex pattern with look ahead is shown below:

((?=[A-Za-z]*[0-9])(?=[0-9A-Z]*[a-z])(?=[0-9a-z]*[A-Z])){6,15}

```
public static void correct() {
    String PATTERN =
        "((?=[A-Za-z]*[0-9])(?=[0-9A-Z]*[a-z])(?=[0-9a-z]*[A-Z])){6,15}";
    Pattern p = Pattern.compile(PATTERN);
    Matcher matcher = p.matcher("John123");
    System.out.println(matcher.find());                //prints true;
    matcher = p.matcher("john123");
    System.out.println(matcher.find());                //prints false;
    matcher = p.matcher("johnpwd");
    System.out.println(matcher.find());                //prints false;
}
```

Don't be overwhelmed by long regex patterns as shown above. Once you divide them into smaller chunks as shown below, things become much clearer.

(?=[A-Za-z]*[0-9])	?= → means look ahead for * → means 0 to many [A-Za-z]* → means zero to many valid characters like A-Z and a-z. [0-9] → means followed by a digit. The [0-9] can also be substituted with "\d" meaning a digit. When used within Java, you need to use "\\d", the first back slash is to escape the "\" in "\d" since "\" is an escape

	character in Java.
(?=[0-9A-Z]*[a-z])	Similar.. Positively look ahead for presence of a-z followed by 0 or many valid characters like 0-9 and A-Z.
(?=[0-9a-z]*[A-Z])	Similar.. Positively look ahead for presence of A-Z followed by 0 or many valid characters like 0-9 and a-z.
((?=[A-Za-z]*[0-9])(?=[0-9A-Z]*[a-z])(?=[0-9a-z]*[A-Z])){6,15}	The overall length must be at least 6 characters and maximum allowed length is 15.

Note: The look ahead and look behind constructs are collectively known as "**look around**" constructs. Unlike the **greedy quantifiers** discussed in previous Q&A, the "look arounds" actually match characters, but then give up the match and only return the result with "match" or "no match". That is why they are called "assertions". They do not consume characters in the string like [0-9A-Za-z]{6,15}, but only assert whether a match is possible or not.

The **look ahead** constructs are **non-capturing**. If you want to capture the values matched, for example to debug or use the captured values, the above regex can be modified with additional parentheses to capture the matched values. The capturing parentheses are in bold.

((?=([A-Za-z]*)([0-9]))(?=([0-9A-Z]*)([a-z]))(?=([0-9a-z]*)([A-Z]))){6,15}

You can display the captured values as shown below:

```
public static void correctWithGroup() {
    String PATTERN =
     "((?=([A-Za-z]*)([0-9]))(?=([0-9A-Z]*)([a-z]))(?=([0-9a-z]*)([A-Z]))){6,15}";
    Pattern p = Pattern.compile(PATTERN);
    Matcher matcher = p.matcher("John123");
    System.out.println(matcher.find());

    int count = matcher.groupCount();
    //0, and 1 are outside parentheses, which will be empty
    for (int i = 2; i <= count; i++) {
        System.out.println(matcher.group(i));
    }
```

```
}
```

Outputs:

```
true
John
1
J
o

J
```

As you can see,

- (?=([A-Za-z]*)([0-9])) matches **John** followed by **1**, i.e. presence of a digit.
- (?=([0-9A-Z]*)([a-z])) matches **J** followed by **o**, i.e. presence of a lower-case alphabet.
- (?=([0-9a-z]*)([A-Z])) matches nothing followed by **J**, i.e. presence of an uppercase letter.

Q03 What does .*, +, and ? mean with respect to regular expressions? Where do you look for the summary of Java regular expression constructs?

A03 *, +, and ? are known as (greedy) quantifiers as they quantify the preceding character(s). For example,

> . → matches any character.
> .* → matches any character repeated 0 or more times.
> .+ → matches any character repeated 1 or more times.
> .? → matches any character repeated 0 or 1 time. This means optional.
>
> [a-zA-Z]* → Any alphabet repeated 0 or more times.
> [a-zA-Z]+ → Any alphabet repeated 1 or more times.
> [a-zA-Z]? → Any alphabet repeated 0 or 1.

Note: These are not wild characters. *, +, and ? are **regex repetitions**. The {x,y} is also used for repetition. For example, [a]{3,5} means the letter "a" repeated at least 3 times or a maximum of 5 times. In fact, internally the *Pattaren.java* class implements,

- **a*** as a{0, 0x7FFFFFFF}
- **a+** as a{1, 0x7FFFFFFF}

The values in square brackets (i.e. [ ]) are known as character sets. The ., *, ?, etc are escaped and used as literal values within the square brackets. Here are some examples of the character sets.

- [aeiou] → matches exactly one lowercase vowel.
- [^aeiou] → matches a character that ISN'T a lowercase vowel (^ inside [ ] means NOT) .
- ^[a-z**&&**[^aeiou]]*$ → matches any character other than a vowel anchored between start (^) and end ($). This is a character class **subtraction regex**. The "&&" means intersection.
- [a-d[m-p]] → Matches characters a to d and m to p. This is a **union regex**.
- [a-z&&[d-f]] → Matches only d, e, and f. This is an **intersection regex**.
- [x-z[**p{Digit}**]] → matches x-z and 0-9. Similar to [x-z0-9] or [x-z[\\d]]. The "\p" stands for POSIX character classes.
- ^[aeiou] - matches a lowercase vowel anchored at the beginning of a line
- [^^] → matches a character that isn't a caret '^' .
- ^[^^] → matches a character that isn't a caret at the beginning of a line.
- ^[^.]. → matches anything but a literal period, followed by "any" character, at the beginning of a line
- [.*]* → matches a contiguous sequence of optional dots (.) and asterisks (*)
- [aeiou]{3} - matches 3 consecutive lowercase vowels (all not necessarily the same vowel)
- \[aeiou\] → matches the string "[aeiou]". "\" means escape.

Q04 What does grouping mean with regards to regular expressions? Would you prefer capturing or non-capturing group?

A04 A group is a pair of parentheses used to group sub patterns. For example, c(a|u)t matches cat or cut. A group also captures the matching text within the parentheses. The groups are numbered from left to right, outside to inside. For example, (x(y*))+ (z*) has 3 explicit and 1 implicit groups. The implicit group 0 is the entire match.

- implicit group 0: (x(y*))+(z*)
- explicit group 1: (x(y*))

- explicit group 2: (y*)
- explicit group 3: (z*)

Capturing groups are numbered by counting their opening parentheses from left to right. The captured sub sequence may be used later in the expression, via a back reference, and may also be retrieved from the matcher once the match operation is complete. Groups beginning with ?: are pure, non-capturing groups that do not capture text and do not count towards the group total. For example, (?:x(?:y*))+(?:z*) will only have group 0 being the entire match.

```java
package regex;

import java.util.regex.Matcher;
import java.util.regex.Pattern;

public class RegexGroup {

    public static void main(String[] args) {
        CharSequence inputStr = "xyyxyyzz";
        String patternCapturing = "(x(y*))+(z*)";
        String patternNonCapturing= "(?:x(?:y*))+(?:z*)";
        System.out.println("====Capturing=====");
        apply(inputStr,patternCapturing);
        System.out.println("====Non Capturing=====");
        apply(inputStr,patternNonCapturing);
    }

    public static void apply(CharSequence inputStr, String patternStr) {
        // Compile and use regular expression
        Pattern pattern = Pattern.compile(patternStr);
        Matcher matcher = pattern.matcher(inputStr);
        boolean matchFound = matcher.find();

        if (matchFound) {
            // Get all groups for this match
            for (int i = 0; i <= matcher.groupCount(); i++) {
                System.out.println("group " + i + " --> "
                        + matcher.group(i));
            }
        }
```

```
        }
    }
  }
}
```

Output:

```
====Capturing=====
group 0 --> xyyxyyzz
group 1 --> xyy
group 2 --> yy
group 3 --> zz
====Non Capturing=====
group 0 --> xyyxyyzz
```

The following sample code illustrates substitution, where the captured group numbers can be used for the subsequent matches. For example, the term "marketing" and "sales" can be captured and reused as these terms appear more than once. Once within the URL and once outside the URL as per the code snippet shown below.

```java
package regex;

import java.util.regex.Matcher;
import java.util.regex.Pattern;

public class CapturingParenthesis {

    /**
     * To match a URI that starts with one of the following:
     * http://www.site.com/marketing/ or http://www.site.com/sales/
     */
    public static void main(String[] args) {
        final String input = "You can try either "
                + "http://www.site.com/marketing/ for marketing related "
                + "queries or http://www.site.com/sales/ for sales "
                + "related queries and further information.";

        System.out.println("========Capturing==========");
        String capPat1 = "http://www.site.com/(marketing|sales)/";
        execute(input, capPat1);
```

```java
        System.out.println("=====Capturing with substitution=====");
        String capPat2 = "http://www.site.com/(marketing|sales)/.*\\1";
        execute(input, capPat2);

        System.out.println("========Non capturing=========");
        // can be more efficient
        String nonCapPat1 = "http://www.site.com/(?:marketing|sales)/";
        execute(input, nonCapPat1);

        System.out.println("===Non capturing no substitution==");
        // can't use it for substituting the previous match
        String nonCapPat2 = "http://www.site.com/(?:marketing|sales)/.*\\1";
        execute(input, nonCapPat2);
    }

    public static void execute(String input, String pattern) {
        Pattern p = Pattern.compile(pattern);
        Matcher matcher = p.matcher(input);

        while (matcher.find()) {
            System.out.print("Start index: " + matcher.start());
            System.out.print(" End index: " + matcher.end() + " ");
            System.out.println("group= " + matcher.group());
        }
    }
}
```

Output:

```
========Capturing==========
Start index: 19 End index: 49 group= http://www.site.com/marketing/
Start index: 83 End index: 109 group= http://www.site.com/sales/
=====Capturing with substitution====
Start index: 19 End index: 63 group= http://www.site.com/marketing/ for
marketing
Start index: 83 End index: 119 group= http://www.site.com/sales/ for sales
========Non capturing==========
Start index: 19 End index: 49 group= http://www.site.com/marketing/
```

Start index: 83 End index: 109 group= http://www.site.com/sales/
===Non capturing no substitution==

Note: The "\1" (group 1) captures either "marketing" or "sales" when the capturing pattern is used. Since "\" has to be escaped in Java, it is represented as "\\1". The .* matches the word "for" as it means match any character 0 or more times.

PC Group capturing incur a small-time penalty each time you use them. If you don't really need to capture the text inside a group, prefer using non-capturing groups.

Q05 What do you understand by greedy, reluctant, and possessive quantifiers? What do you understand by the term "backtracking"?

A05

Greedy	Reluctant	Possessive
[a-z][A-Z]* [a-z][A-Z]+ [a-z][A-Z]? [a-z][A-Z]{1,2} [a-z][A-Z]{2,} [a-z][A-Z]{,6}	[a-z][A-Z]*? [a-z][A-Z]+? [a-z][A-Z]?? [a-z][A-Z]{1,2}? [a-z][A-Z]{2,}? [a-z][A-Z]{,6}?	[a-z][A-Z]*+ [a-z][A-Z]++ [a-z][A-Z]?+ [a-z][A-Z]{1,2}+ [a-z][A-Z]{2,}+ [a-z][A-Z]{,6}+
As the name implies a greedy quantifier will first try to **match as many characters as possible** from an input string, even if this means that the input string will not have sufficient characters left in it to match the rest of the regular expression. If this happens, the greedy quantifier will **backtrack**, returning characters until an overall match is found or until there are no more characters.	As the name implies a reluctant (or lazy) quantifier, on the other hand, will first try to **match as few characters in the input string as possible**.	As the name implies a possessive quantifier always match the entire input string, trying once (and only once) for a match. **Unlike the greedy quantifier, the possessive quantifiers never backtrack**, even if doing so would allow the overall match to succeed.

```java
package regex;

import java.util.regex.Matcher;
import java.util.regex.Pattern;

public class GreedyReluctantPossessive {

    public static void main(String[] args) {
        String input = "xfooxxfooxxxxfooxxxxxxxxfoofo";

        // this is the default for *, +, and ?.
        // fetches the whole String eagerly and then start to backtrack
        String eagerPattern = ".*foo";
        System.out.println("=======Greedy========");
        execute(input, eagerPattern);

        // Backtrack to the beginning and start fetching one at a time
        String reluctantPattern = ".*?foo";
        System.out.println("=======Reluctant========");
        execute(input, reluctantPattern);

        // fetches the whole String eagerly, but won't let go of what was fetched
        String possessivePattern = ".*+foo";
        System.out.println("=======Possessive========");
        execute(input, possessivePattern);

        // possessive pattern is more suited for matching text in quotes.
        String input2 = "a=\"xfoo\" some text b=\"xfooo\""
                        + "some more text c=\"xfo\"";
        possessivePattern = "\"xfoo\"*+";
        System.out.println("=====Possessive match for text in quotes=====");
        execute(input2, possessivePattern);
    }

    private static void execute(String input, String pattern) {
        Pattern p = Pattern.compile(pattern);
        Matcher matcher = p.matcher(input);
```

499

```
    while (matcher.find( )) {
      System.out.print("Start index: " + matcher.start( ));
      System.out.print(" End index: " + matcher.end( ) + " ");
      System.out.println("group= " + matcher.group( ));
    }
  }
 }
}
```

Output:

```
=======Greedy=========
Start index: 0 End index: 27 group= xfooxxfooxxxxfooxxxxxxxxfoo
=======Reluctant=========
Start index: 0 End index: 4 group= xfoo
Start index: 4 End index: 9 group= xxfoo
Start index: 9 End index: 16 group= xxxxfoo
Start index: 16 End index: 27 group= xxxxxxxxfoo
=======Possessive===============Possessive match for text in
quotes=====
Start index: 2 End index: 8 group= "xfoo"
Start index: 21 End index: 26 group= "xfoo
```

Q. Why did the string "xfooxxfooxxxxfooxxxxxxxxfoofo" return no match when used with a possessive quantifier?

A. Even if you try to match "xfooxxfooxxxxfooxxxxxxxxfoo" without the last "fo", the possessive quantifier would match nothing because the possessive quantifiers will not give up the matches on a **backtrack**, and the .*+ matches your entire string including the last "foo" and then there's nothing for "foo" to match in the pattern ".*+foo". So use possessive quantifiers only when you know that what you've matched should never be backtracked. For example, "[^f]*+.*foo" or more importantly matching text in quotes as demonstrated above with "\"xfoo\"*+".

PC BP Always test your regular expressions with negative and positive test cases. Generally the possessive quantifiers are more efficient than the reluctant quantifiers, and the reluctant quantifiers are more efficient than the greedy quantifiers. When a regex is used in a performance critical area of your application, it would be wise to test it first. Write a benchmark application that tests it against different inputs. Remember to test different lengths of inputs, and also inputs that almost match your pattern.

Like most regex engines, Java uses NFA (Non deterministic Finite Automaton) approach. This means the engine scans the regex components one by one, and progresses on the input string accordingly. However, it will go back in order to explore matching alternatives when a "dead end" is found. Alternatives result from regex structures such as quantifiers (*, +, ?) and alternation (e.g. a|b|c|d). This exploration technique is called **backtracking**. In a more simpler term, backtracking means return to attempt an untried option.

`PC` The .* and alternation (e.g. a|b|c) regexes must be used sparingly. For example, if you want to retrieve everything between two "@" characters in an input string, instead of using "@(.*)@", it's much better to use "@([^@]*)@". This regex can be further optimized by minimizing the backtracking with the help of a possessive quantifier "*+" instead of a greedy quantifier "*". Say you are using the pattern "@([^@]*)@" with a long input string that does not have any "@". Because "*" is a greedy quantifier, it will grab all the characters until the end of the string, and then it will backtrack, giving back one character at a time. The expression will fail only when it can't backtrack anymore. If you change the pattern to use "@([^@]*+)@" with a possessive quantifier "*+", the new pattern fails faster because once it has tried to match all the characters that are not a "@", it does not backtrack; Instead it fails right there. Take care not to compromise correctness for a small optimization.

`PC` Regular expressions like "(COLON|COMMA|COLUMN)" have a reputation for being slow, so watch out for them. Firstly, the order of alternation counts. So, place the more common options in the front to be matched faster. Secondly, extract out the more common ones. For example, CO(MMA|L(ON|UMN)). Since COMMA is more common, it is used first. The "CO" and "L" are extracted out as they are more common.

Q06 Can your write a function that will replace all tokens delimited by @ with a given String?

Sample Input = "Hello @name@, where are you @name@?"

A06

```
package regex;

import org.apache.commons.lang.StringUtils;
```

```
public class RegexDelimiter {

    public static void main(String[] args) {
        String input = "Hello @name@, Where are you @name@?";
        System.out.println(function(input));

    }

    public static String function(String input) {
        if (StringUtils.isEmpty(input)) {
            return input;
        }
        String pattern = "@[^@]*+@";
        String output = input.replaceAll(pattern, "John");
        return output;
    }
}
```

Output:

Hello **John**, Where are you **John**?

Note: The pattern "@[^@]*+@" could be written as "@.*?@" as well, but where possible avoid ".*" as they can backtrack a lot. You could also see possessive quantifier *+ in action as it is more efficient than the reluctant quantifier *?. The greedy quantifier cannot be used here as it would provide a wrong result "Hello John?" by matching the text between the very first and very last "@" characters.

Q07 Can you discuss what the following regular expression does?

`<[\s]*a[\s]*[^>]*?href[\s]*=[\"\'\s]*(.*?)[\"\'\s]*[^>]*?> (.*?)<[\s]*/[\s]*a[\s]*>`

A07 The above code matches input Strings like:

```
<a href='#'>My Link</a>
< a href='#'>My Link</a>
< a class=\"myclass\" href = '#' >My Link< / A >
```

The code sample below implements the above regular expression. It converts the input to lowercase before matching.

```java
package regex;

import java.io.PrintStream;
import java.util.regex.Matcher;
import java.util.regex.Pattern;

import org.apache.commons.lang.StringUtils;

public class AnchorRegularExpr {

    public static void main(String[] args) {
        PrintStream out = System.out;
        out.println(function("< a HREF = '#' >My Link< / A >"));
    }

    public static boolean function(String input) {
        if (StringUtils.isEmpty(input)) {
            return false;
        }
        String pattern = "<[\\s]*a[\\s]*[^>]*?href[\\s]*=[\"'\\s]*"
                + "(.*?)[\"'\\s]*[^>]*?>"
                + "(.*?)<[\\s]*/[\\s]*a[\\s]*>";
        Pattern p = Pattern.compile(pattern);
        Matcher m = p.matcher(input.toLowerCase());
        return m.find();
    }
}
```

It may look complicated, but if you dissect it, it seems very straight forward.

\\s → White space character including newline, carriage return, etc.
    [\t\n\x0B\f\r].

[\\s]* → Matches one or more white spaces.

[^>]*? → This one matches anything that's not '>'. The '^' character inside
    '[ ]' directs a negative match. Add a '?' after the '*' to make it a

reluctant quantifier, otherwise it wouldn't stop at 'href' because the html tags could have attributes like rel, id, class, target, etc before or after the "href" attribute. It can be in any order.

(.*?) → is used to reluctantly match any characters including spaces and newlines, which might be present in the anchor text or value. It also captures the anchor text and value with the group numbers 1 & 2.

Q08 How will you go about matching comments in an XML or HTML file?

A08 It can be achieved using either regex or XPath. Initial instinct for this requirement would be to write something as shown below:

```
public static void wrong( ) {
    String PATTERN = "^<!--(.*)-->$";
    final String COMMENT =
                "<!-- <tag-1>abc</tag-1><tag-2>abc</tag-2> -->";
    Pattern p = Pattern.compile(PATTERN, Pattern.MULTILINE);
    Matcher matcher = p.matcher(COMMENT);
    boolean matchFound = matcher.find( );
    System.out.println(matchFound);
    if (matchFound) {
        System.out.println(matcher.group(1));
    }
}
```

Even though the above code snippet returns true, the above pattern will not work if you have multi-line comments as shown below, which would be the case in real life XML or HTML comments.

```
final String COMMENT =
  "<!--<tag-1>abc</tag-1>\n<tag-2>abc</tag-2> -->";
```

This can be corrected with the help of **negative look ahead** construct as shown below to assert that a "-" is <u>not followed by</u> a "->", which means not the end of comment tag.

```
public static void correct( ) {
    String PATTERN = "^<!--(([^-]+|-(?!->))*)-->$";
    final String COMMENT =
```

```
            "<!--<tag-1>abc</tag-1>\n<tag-2>abc</tag-2> -->";
    Pattern p = Pattern.compile(PATTERN, Pattern.MULTILINE);
    Matcher matcher = p.matcher(COMMENT);
    boolean matchFound = matcher.find();
    System.out.println(matchFound);
    if (matchFound) {
        System.out.println(matcher.group(1));
    }
  }
}
```

Output:

```
true
<tag-1>abc</tag-1>
<tag-2>abc</tag-2>
```

^<!--	Starts with "<!--"
(([^-]+|-(?!->))*)	The outside parenthesis in bold is to capture the match as group 1.
[^-]	Means **Not** hyphen (-). A ^ inside a [...] means NOT.
([^-]+|-(?!->))	?! → means **negative look ahead**. "|" means or. The regex in bold means a "-" not followed by a "->".
([^-]+|-(?!->))*	Means 0 to many characters that are either not a hyphen or if it is a hyphen, then it must not be followed by a "->".
-->$	Ends with "-->"

Note: The positive and negative look aheads are very powerful if you want to match something "followed by" or "not followed by" respectively.

Important: It is not a best practice to parse an XML document with regexes. An XML is not a regular language. You cannot parse it using a regular expression. An expression that you think will work will break when you get nested tags, then when you fix that it will break on XML comments, then CDATA sections, then processor directives, then name spaces, etc. So favor using an XMLParser and XPath to parse XML documents.

Q. Write a regex to determine a http URL using a positive **look behind**?
A. (?<=http://)\\S+

(?<=http://)	?<= → positively look behind for "http://"
\\S+	Zero or more non-white character i.e. [^\s].

Q09 How would you configure the Java regex engine to be case insensitive?

A09 The *Pattern* class has a number of constants to configure the engine for case insensitive search, multi-line search, comments included in regex, etc.

```
public static void main(String[] args) {
    String PATTERN = "john";
    final String COMMENT = "John";
    Pattern p = Pattern.compile(PATTERN, Pattern.CASE_INSENSITIVE);
    Matcher matcher = p.matcher(COMMENT);
    boolean matchFound = matcher.find();
    System.out.println(matchFound);
}
```

The above **CASE_INSENSITIVE** pattern constant can be re-written with the configuration flags to be included within the regex pattern as shown below:

```
public static void main(String[] args) {
    String PATTERN = "(?i)john";              //?i means ignore case
    final String COMMENT = "John";
    Pattern p = Pattern.compile(PATTERN);
    Matcher matcher = p.matcher(COMMENT);
    boolean matchFound = matcher.find();
    System.out.println(matchFound);
}
```

If you want to include comments for the above pattern, you can configure the matching engine as shown below:

```
// i --> ignore case, x --> allow comments
String PATTERN = "(?ix)john #look for john ignoring case";
```

Note: Here are the other configurations that can be used:

(?m) → **Multi-line mode**. Toggle treats newlines as white space. The ^ and $ expressions will no longer match to the beginning and end of a line, respectively, but will match the beginning and end of the entire input sequence or string.

(?s) → Toggle dot (i.e. '.') to match any character including the new line characters. By default a "." matches everything except a new line character.

(?u) → Toggle Unicode standard case matching. By default, case-insensitive matching assumes that only characters in the US-ASCII char-set are being matched.

(?d) → Enables UNIX line mode in which only the '\n' line terminator is recognized in the behavior of ., ^, and $.

The pattern below will ignore case, will set the "." character to include newlines, and allows comments in patterns.

```
String PATTERN = "(?isx)john.* #look for john ignoring case";
```

Note: (?idmsux-idmsux) → Turns match flags on - off for entire expression.

Q10 Can you give me some real life scenarios where you used regular expressions? OEQ
A10 The generic regular expression concept has been implemented on many different languages and many different tools. Here are some practical examples. The open ended questions are a great opportunity to sell your experience.

1. Finding relevant exceptions and counting occurrences of any values in log files using the UNIX grep command, which stands for "Global Regular Expression Print".

The command shown below prints all exceptions except the "NullPointer".

```
$ cat error.log | grep -e Exception | grep -v NullPointer
```

The command below counts the occurrences of *SecurityException*.

```
$ cat error.log | grep -c "SecurityException"
```

Note: Refer to "Gauging Your Experience with UNIX" in section entitled "Knowing your way around Java" for more practical examples using regular expressions in UNIX.

2. Validating user input fields like name, password, phone numbers, email addresses, social security numbers, tax file numbers, etc. The example below validates the product codes for presence of invalid characters and length.

```java
public static void main(String[] args) {
    List<String> products = new ArrayList<String>(10);
    products.add("CFX.GHS");            //valid
    products.add("CFX GHS");            //Not valid. Whitespace is not allowed.
    products.add("CFXGHSXXXXX");  //Not valid. Longer than 10 characters.
    products.add("CFX.GHS.XX");       //valid

    for (String product : products) {
        if(product.matches("^[a-zA-Z.]{2,10}")) {
            System.out.println(product + " code is valid");
        }
        else {
            System.out.println(product + " code is NOT valid");
        }
    }
}
```

The regex validations can be performed on client side and server side.

3. Regex can be used in URL rewrite filters to convert a RESTful URL to an application specific URL and vice versa. For example, you could use third-party frameworks like tucky filter, which allows you to configure URL rewrite rules via inbound and outbound configurations in XML files. For example,

Inbound rules:

```xml
<rule>
  <from>^/accounts/$</from>
  <to>/account/list.do</to>
</rule>
<rule>
```

```
   <from>^/accounts/([a-z0-9]+)/$</from>
   <to>/accounts/display.do?accountId=$1</to>
</rule>
<rule>
   <from>^/accounts/([a-z0-9]+)/edit$</from>
   <to>/accounts/edit.do?accountId=$1</to>
</rule>
```

As per the above example, a RESTful URL like "/accounts/005678924/" will be forwarded "/accounts/display.do?accountId=005678924"

Outbound rules:

```
<outbound-rule>
   <from>^/accounts/list.do$</from>
   <to>/accounts/</to>
</outbound-rule>
<outbound-rule>
   <from>^/accounts/display.do\?accountId=([a-z0-9]+)$</from>
   <to>/accounts/$1/</to>
</outbound-rule>
<outbound-rule>
   <from>^/accounts/edit.do\?accountId=([a-z0-9]+)$</from>
      <to>/accounts/$1/edit</to>
</outbound-rule>
```

The outbound URL rule will revert "/accounts/display.do?accountId=005678924" back to the RESTful URL "/accounts/005678924/" to be displayed on the client side browser. As you can see the rules are based on regex.

4. Regex can be used to split files containing delimited data. For example, extracting values from a CSV file (i.e. a file containing comma separated values).

```
package regex;

public class SplitCSV {

  public static void main(String[] args) {
    String line = "John A, Peter O`Sullivan,\"James, Junior \",\"\"\"";
```

509

```
//the limit is set to -1, if the limit n is greater than zero
//then the pattern will be applied at most n - 1 times
String[ ] tokens = line.split("\\s*,\\s*(?=([^\"]*\"[^\"]*\")*[^\"]*$)");

for (int i = 0; i < tokens.length; i++) {
    System.out.println(tokens[i]);
}
}
```

Output is:

```
John A
Peter O`Sullivan
"James, Junior "
""
```

\\s*,\\s*	Look for comma preceded or followed by white spaces. The \\s will trim any leading or trailing white spaces. If white spaces are not required to be trimmed then just use a ',' without the \\s* on either side of the comma.
(?=([^\"]*\"[^\"]*\")*[^\"]*$)	You can read the regex as a **positive look ahead** for zero or more occurrences of "Some text in double quotes" preceded or followed by some text without double quotes.

The positive look ahead with construct ?= is required to eliminate any text within double quotes with a comma. For example, the comma within "James, Junior" <u>will fail</u> the positive look ahead assertion and will not incorrectly split it into 2 separate values as

  • "James
  • Junior".

The "," before the "James, Junior " will pass the followed by (i.e. positive look ahead) assertion to |

	correctly split it as a single word → "James, Junior"
[^\"]*	Means 0 or more occurrences of any character other than double quotes.
\"	Means a double quote. The \ is used to escape double quotes.

Q. How would you go about implementing the above without using the *String.split( )* function?

A. As sown below,

```
package regex;

import java.util.regex.Matcher;
import java.util.regex.Pattern;

public class SplitCSV2 {

    public static void main(String[] args) {
        String line = "John A, Peter O`Sullivan,\"Peter, James \",\"\"";
        Pattern p = Pattern
            .compile("\\s*,\\s*(?=([^\"]*\"[^\"]*\")*[^\"]*$)");
        Matcher m = p.matcher(line);

        int i = 0;
        while (m.find( )) {
            System.out.println(line.substring(i, m.start( )));
            i = m.end( );
        }
        if(i< line.length( ))
            System.out.println(line.substring(i));
    }
}
```

5. Regex can be used in Maven pom.xml or Ant build.xml files. For example, maven ant-run plug-in can use the ant task "replaceregexp" to find and replace values in files using regular expressions as shown below:

511

```
<replaceregexp file="target/myapp/WEB-INF/web.xml"
    flags="m" byline="false"
    match="^(\s*)(&lt;!--START--)((?:[^-]+|-(?!-&gt;))*)(--END--&gt;)(\s*)$"
    replace="" />
```

Note: The above regex is similar to the one that was discussed earlier to match XML or HTML comments with difference being that the above regex is defined in an XML file. Since the regex is defined within an XML file, the XML characters "<" and ">" are replaced with the corresponding entity references "<" and ">" respectively.

6. Regex can be used in text editors like UltraEdit, TextPad, Notepad++, etc to find and replace values. For example, in notepad++, if you want to swap the "link location" and display values from

Some text <a href="**display value**">**http://mytitle.com.au**</a> blah blah

to,

Some text <a href="**http://mytitle.com.au**">**display value**</a> blah blah

The following quick and dirty regex can be used to achieve the expected results. The \ 1 and \2 are captured group numbers used to swap the link location with the display value.

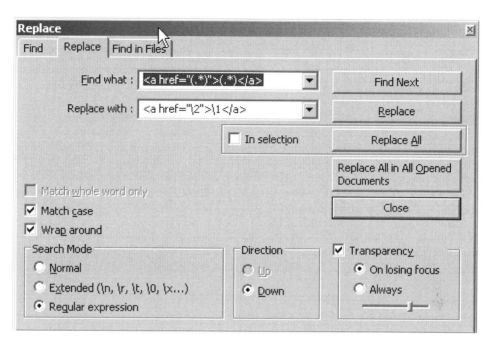

7. Regex can be used to assert data in regression and load testing tools like selenium and JMeter to assert values. Also note that these tools support assertion using an XPath, which would be more appropriate than using a regex in many situations. A selenium based JUnit test in Java would look something like:

```
boolean result = selenium.isTextPresent("regexp:" + "\\$4,925\\.87");
assertTrue(result);
```

where $ has a special meaning (i.e. end of line) in regex, hence it is escaped with "\$", and "." has a special meaning in regex (i.e. match any character), and it is escaped with "\.". Since "\" has a special meaning (i.e. escape character) in Java, it has to be escaped with an additional "\" as shown above with "\\$" and "\\.". The above regex verifies presence of amount "$4,925.87" in a web page.

In JMeter regex tester, to extract "name" and "value" from a web page containing something like,

```
<input type="text" name="firstname" value="Peter" />
```

you could use a regex like,

```
name="([^"]+)".*value="([^"]+)"
```

Where [**^"**] means NOT quotes. In JMeter, it can be used to extract values from a response page and pass it on as a query string in the subsequent requests.

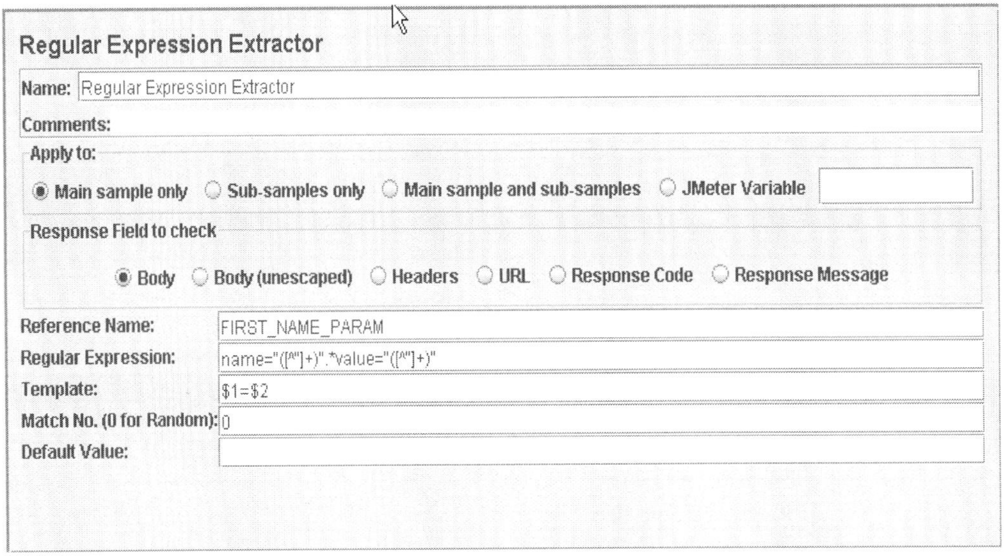

The extracted value can be used as a query string for the subsequent request. The $1 is group 1 that captures the name "firstname" and $2 is group 2 that captures the value "Peter". The extracted pattern ($1=$2) is stored with the reference name "FIRST_NAME_PARAN" to be used later.

As shown below, the value stored in the FIRST_NAME_PARAM is added to the path as a query string.

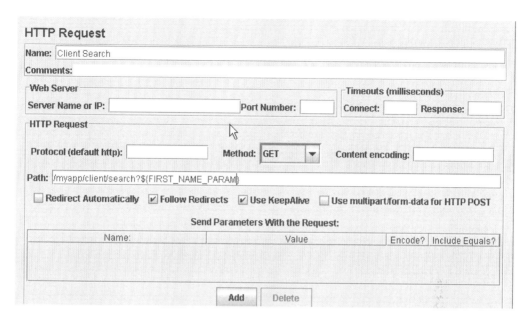

The substituted path will be:

/myapp/client/search?firstname=Peter

8. Modern databases often offer built-in regular expression features that can be used in SQL statements to filter columns using a regular expression. For example, MySQL's REGEXP operator works just like the LIKE operator, except that it uses a POSIX Extended Regular Expression. Oracle Database 10g adds 4 regular expression functions that can be used in SQL and PL/SQL statements to filter rows and to extract and replace regex matches.

9. The W3C standard for XQuery 1.0 and XPath 2.0 Functions and Operators defines three functions **fn:matches**, **fn:replace** and **fn:tokenize** that take a regular expression as one of their parameters.

Note: There are also tools like *RegexBuddy* and *RegexMagic* that would assist with learning, creating, understanding, and testing regular expressions.

Q11 Write a regular expression for the following scenarios?

A11

Q. Replace multiple spaces in a string with a single space?

A.

```
String str = "String   to replace   multiple   spaces with a single space.";
System.out.println(str.replaceAll("\\s{2,}", " ")); \\ "\s" means white space
```

Q. Write a regex to match a hexadecimal color code?

A. The six-digit hexadecimal representation of a color is of the form #RRGGBB, where RR, GG, and BB are the hexadecimal values for the red, green, and blue values of the color. Using a hexadecimal code is the most reliable of the several ways you can define colors in HTML or style sheets.

```
^#([A-Fa-f0-9]{6}|[A-Fa-f0-9]{3})$
```

Q. Can you describe what the following *replace( )* function does?

```
public static void main(String[] args) {
    String input = "23/06/1954";
    String output = replace(input);
    System.out.println(output);
};


public static String replace(String input) {
    String output = input.replaceAll("(0?[1-9]|[12][0-9]|3[01])/(0?[1-9]|1[012])/
                        ((19|20)\\d\\d)","$2/$1/$3");

    return output;
}
}
```

A. It replaces a date input in dd/mm/yyyy format to mm/dd/yyyy format.

(0?[1-9]|[12][0-9]|3[01])/	Matches dates in the form of 01-09 or 1-9 or 10-19 or 20-29 or 30, 31. Whatever in the parenthesis will be group 1 denoted in the replace string by $1. The "/" divides the day and month fields.
(0?[1-9]|1[012])/	Matches months 01-09 or 1-9, or 10, 11, 12. This will be

	group number 2, and denoted in the replace string as $2. The "/" divides the month and year fields.
((19|20)\\d\\d)	Matches 19[0-9][0-9] or 20[0-9][0-9]. Matches years starting with 19 or 20. This group will be captured as group 3, and denoted in the replace string by $3.

Q. How will you represent time in both 12 hour and 24 hour format using regex?
A.

12 hour format:

(1[012]\|[1-9]):([0-5][0-9])\\s?(?i)(am\|pm)

(1[012]|[1-9])	The group 1 is the hour. Matches 10, 11, 12 or 1-9.
:	Hour minute separator
([0-5][0-9])	Matches 00 to 59.
\\s?	Optional white spaces.
(?i)	Next checking is case insensitive
(?i)(am|pm)	Matches am, AM, aM, Am, pm, PM, pM, or Pm.

24 hour format:

([01]?[0-9]\|2[0-3]):[0-5][0-9]

([01]?[0-9]|2[0-3])	Matches $0-9$, $1-9$, $00-09$, $10-19$, or $20-23$.
:	Matches ':' .
[0-5][0-9]	Matches 00 to 59.

Q. Write a regex to match image files?
A.

([^\s]+(\.(?i)(jpg\|png\|gif\|bmp))$

([^\s]+	Group #1 starts with the parenthesis. 1 or more non white space characters.

(\.(?i)	Group #2 starts, and followed by a dot ".". Ignore case checking (?i).
(jpg|png|gif|bmp)	Group #3 containing possible image file extensions "jpg", "png", "gif", or "bmp".
)$)	End of group #2, end of the string and end of group #1.

Q12 Which of the following will be matched by the regex ".*[^ a-zA-Z0-9].*" ?

    a) ON_LINE
    b) ONLINE
    c) online9
    d) on-line
    e) on line

A12 a) and d) will match true due to presence of "_" and "-" respectively. The regex reads NOT blank space, a-z, A-Z or 0-9 preceded or followed by zero or more characters. The above regex is looking for presence of any character other than a-z, A-Z, 0-9, and a blank space.

Q13 Which of the following will be matched by the regex ".*[^0-9].*" ?

    a) 12345678
    b) 123-456
    c) 123 456

A13 b) and c) will be matched due to presence of "-" and blank space respectively. The above regex is looking for presence of anything other than a digit.

Q14 If you had a special requirement to strip out currencies from a specific report, how would you go about stripping it out?

A14 There are many ways to achieve this like using a *Formatter* like a *DecimalFormatter*, etc. It can also be achieved using a regular expression like:

```
String output = input.replaceAll("\\p{Sc}", "");
```

Where,

\ → Java escape character
\p{Sc} → A currency symbol

Section-9

Job Interview Tips

- Interviews are not technical contests...
- Don't wait to be asked ….
- Think out loud and brainstorm with the interviewers ….
- Sometimes knowing something is better than knowing nothing …
- Interviewers place a lot of value in "I don't know" over inventing answers
- An interview is a two way street …
- Open-ended questions are your opportunity to …..
- Books can impart knowledge, but cannot give you the much needed experience …

Interviews are not technical contests...

to see who gets the most technical questions right. It is all about hiring the right person who can get the job done. To get the job done, relevant technical skills must be complemented with good soft-skills, right attitude, and passion. Open ended questions are your ideal opportunity for you to make a statement about your technical and non-technical abilities to get the job done.

Q. Why do you like software development?
A. [Hint:]

- Have special interest in pro-actively and re-actively resolving thread-safety issues, performance issues, design gaps, and general development issues, where I get to apply and expand technical, analytical, researching, problem-solving, communication, and people skills.

- Enjoy analyzing the pros, cons, and trade-offs of each design and development alternatives to arrive at an effective and workable solution that can adapt to growing and changing business needs.

- Software development can be complex as there are so many moving parts, and it is quite satisfying to get your work through the SDLC (Software Development Life Cycle) phases like design, development, deployment, testing, documentation, support, and hand-over. There is always a variety of tasks and responsibilities to be performed. Opportunity to applying agile practices where appropriate, makes your journey even more enjoyable by interacting more closely with the multidisciplinary teams.

- Motivated by having something new to be learned in every project in terms of domain knowledge, technologies, frameworks, tools, best practices, anti-patterns, business processes, development processes, and people. For example, Java 5.0 features like annotations, generics, enhanced for loop, auto-boxing, enums, and java.util.concurrent packages take ease of development to a new level.

- It involves both the technical side as well as the people side to have your project completed successfully.

Job Interview Tips

Q. What do you enjoy the most about your job?
A. [Hint:]

- Identifying and fixing issues relating to design, thread-safety, performance, security and memory management.

- Access to plethora of frameworks and libraries that can improve productivity and quality of a software. There is always something new to learn.

- Developing custom frameworks or libraries where appropriate with tools like annotation processing tool, Java reflection API, ANTLR, Javaassist, etc to improve productivity.

- Working on the first iteration of a typical use case to come up with the full vertical slice (i.e. end to end), where key decisions need to be made and vital tasks need to be executed. For example,

    ✔ Choice of technologies, frameworks, and tools.

    ✔ Validating the baseline architecture.

    ✔ Analyzing the pros and cons of design alternatives, and identifying gaps in requirements and design.

    ✔ Custom frameworks or utility classes are to be written for ease of development.

    ✔ Processes need to be put in place for build management, dependency management, deployment management, change management, release management, automated testing, etc.

- Writing code for multiple platforms. Separating protocol dependent code from business logic dependent code to promote code reuse.

- Introducing agile practices where appropriate in multidisciplinary team environments.

- Improving development and build processes through better requirements management, change management, dependency management, and release management.

- Capturing the existing domain knowledge and managing it systematically. Understanding the primary business objectives, core assets, organizational units responsible for these assets, and how they are interrelated.

- Getting the work through inception, elaboration, construction, and transition phases, and to finally see it meeting customers' needs.

Don't wait to be asked ....

Many interviewers don't know what questions they will be asking -- it will depend on your resume, and where you take them to. You can bring up certain topics yourself that are relevant to the position you are being interviewed for. Open-ended questions give you a great opportunity to sell your-self.

Q. Tell me about your self? Can you describe your current and past contributions?
A. [Hint]

These questions are always asked, and be prepared with a unique selling proposition that meets the job specification. Your unique selling proposition should match your accomplishments and strengths to prospective employers' needs. Some employers give more weight to technical skills. Some other employers take a more balanced approach by giving equal importance to technical skills, soft skills, and personality. You need to sell your self in all areas. Pick 4 – 5 of your top most accomplishments and strengths that are relevant to the position.

Strengths and accomplishments relevant to the position:

- If you know that the position you're applying for might possibly involve managing others, and you have been working towards management previously, pointing that out in your answer aligns your plans with the company's goals.

- If you have been using the technologies and frameworks required by the employer, then highlight your experience with those technologies and frameworks.

- If you have the domain and business knowledge required by your prospective employer, mention it.

Strengths and accomplishments common to most positions:

- Experience and accomplishments in process improvements. This could be development process, build process, deployment process, requirements and change management process, and release management process.

- Accomplishments in key areas like fixing thread-safety issues, designing and developing custom frameworks to improve productivity, identifying performance bottlenecks and tuning performance, fixing memory leaks, fixing bugs relating to language fundamentals, etc.

- Being proactive in identifying potential gaps in business requirements, functional requirements, non-functional requirements, architecture, and design. Taking initiatives to get things moving. Mentoring junior developers.

- Your resume should already have a personal statement that discusses your qualities - in the most positive terms possible. Make sure you are familiar with your resume. If you need to learn more about this, refer to my book entitled "Java/J2EE Resume Companion" at http://www.lulu.com/java-success, which is full of examples.

Think out loud and brainstorm with the interviewers ....

Technologies/frameworks/tools are very vast. Nobody will know everything. The interviewer certainly won't know everything either. Interviewers are interested in evaluating how good your basics are?, what experience and skills you have?, and how well you can think through a problem?

Q. How would you go about writing your own HashMap?
A. [Hint]

- It is not a good practice to reinvent the wheel. The interviewer is trying to evaluate your level of technical knowledge and thought process. He/she is only expecting you to know the approach. Consider it as a brain storming session.

- Firstly, code to interface. Create a class that implements the *java.util.Map* interface with empty methods.

- Decide on the backing data structure. Arrays are fast and memory efficient. Hence an array can be used to back up the map. This will be an indexed bucket.

- Decide on a hashing algorithm to index into the array and store an object in that slot of the array.

```
long bucketIndex = function(key, arrayLength);
```

- Come up with a strategy to detect and resolve collisions. Collisions can be detected by having each slot of the array point to a LinkedList. That contains key-value pairs. You can create a class called *Entry* that has attributes key and value as type *Object*.

- Come up with a strategy for resizing when the capacity is reached. This process is known as rehashing whereby existing items are mapped to new bucket locations.

- Fill in the empty methods that need to be implemented.

- Think about performance and thread safety.

Note: An example is provided in the section "Logic and Data structures".

Q. If the time is 3.15pm, what is the angle between the hour and minute hands?
A.
- The minute hand will be on 3.
- The hour hand will be ¼ of the way between 3 and 4.
- Between 3 and 4, there are 5 minutes (or divisions). The ¼ of 5 is 1.25.
- One full circle is 360 degrees.
- This means each minute (or division) is 360/60 = 6 degrees.
- Hence 1.25 minutes (or divisions) = 1.25 * 6 degrees = 7.5 degrees.

Systematically thinking aloud and drawing or making a pictorial representation can contribute to answers quickly. Even if you don't solve it completely, it shows that you are prepared to take on the challenge without being put off by it. It reveals your determination and positive attitude. If you can at least get some of the premises and steps correct, the interviewer will be convinced that you will eventually get it right if more time is given. Be prepared to bounce ideas off the interviewer. This shows that you are prepared to solve things collaboratively.

Sometimes knowing something is better than knowing nothing ...

If you are only familiar with something, then be honest about it. You could say that your familiarity is limited to just working on tutorials and learning the basic concepts. If you are confident, you could say that you believe that you have a good grasp on it, and happy for the interviewer to ask any technical questions relating to it.

Q. Do you have any experience with JSF?
A. [Hint:]

My experience with JSF is limited to working with a few tutorials and learning the basics, but I am happy for you to ask any technical questions on it.

But, I do have 2 year commercial hands on experience with similar component based Web development using the Tapestry framework. I am a quick learner, and will be motivated to learn JSF, if given the opportunity.

Interviewers place a lot of value in "I don't know" over inventing answers ...

Many interviewers strongly believe that a smart and experienced developer can pickup new frameworks, APIs, tools, etc. So, be honest.

Q. Do you have any experience with JBoss Seam?
A. [Hint:]

Sorry, I have not used it before. It will be a good skill to have and I am motivated to learn it.

An interview is a two way street ...

You will have to ask intelligent questions as well. Questions that will determine if a particular job is inline with your career goals and aspirations. Questions that will bring out your strengths and achievements relevant to the job requirements. Questions that will show that you are passionate about what you do. Questions that can hand back the control to you in a nicer way. Don't over do it. Don't come across as inflexible, arrogant, or someone with a wrong attitude.

Q. Do you have any questions for us?
A. Yes.

[Hint:]

You: If I am successful, what technologies/frameworks/architectures will I be exposed to?

Interviewer: You will be using Java 6, EJB3, JAX-WS, and ANT.

You: I am currently using all those technologies/frameworks in a Service Oriented Architecture. I was instrumental in developing a service delivery framework that improves developer productivity. If you like, I am happy to elaborate on this service delivery framework.

[Hint:]

You: The job specification states that experience with Service Oriented Architecture (SOA) would be an advantage, and I do have hands-on experience with the SOA technologies like XML, XSD, WSDL, JAX-WS, Services Bus, XQuery, and XPath. Would this experience considered favorably?

Other questions that can be asked are:

* How will you assess that I'm doing a good job? Would there be opportunities to grow if I can prove myself?
* What are the key challenges in the first few months of the role?
* What are the reasons that the job came about? What is the size of the current team?

- Do you follow any agile practices or have plans to introduce them?
- What are the prospects for growth and advancement?
- Is there any areas of my skills and experience you would like me to further clarify?
- What kind of work can I expect to be doing in the first year?
- If I am extended a job offer, how soon would you like me to start?
- What is the next step in the selection process from here and when should I expect to hear from you next?

Open-ended questions are your opportunity .....

- to make a statement about your ability to get the job done.
- to prove based on your past experience, achievements, and extra-curricular activities that:

  - ✔ You are technically capable.
  - ✔ You can analyze, research, and solve problems.
  - ✔ You can work as a team.
  - ✔ You can communicate at all levels. Both oral and written communication.
  - ✔ You can learn quickly, mentor, and take initiatives.
  - ✔ You can look at things from both business & technology perspective.
  - ✔ You can look at both the bigger picture and also have the attention to details.
  - ✔ You are flexible, and have the right attitude and enthusiasm to get things done.

Books can impart knowledge, but cannot give you the much needed experience ...

This book has highlighted potential problems, best practices, do's and don'ts. You can read them and understand them. Most accomplished professionals are self-taught. If you want to really master them, you need to pro-actively apply them to experience it. Once you experience it, you will remember it, and be good at what you do. I have included so many examples for you to try and experience it. In many cases the decisions have to be made from a number of choices. Firstly, you need to have the knowledge to come up with the valid choices. You will have to work out the pros and cons for each choice. Nothing is black and white in real world. There are trade-offs to be made. Only experience can give you the expertise to make the the right decision under a given circumstance. So, I urge you to not just read it, but apply it. Once you experience it, you may not even agree with some of my reasoning. When you start to do so, you start to think and act like an experienced professional. If you are already an experienced professional, use it as a quick refresher as it is not easy to remember everything. Whether you are already an accomplished professional or not, always remember that good technical skills must be complemented with good soft skills and right attitude. Be passionate about what you do, but don't be inflexible. Understand the importance of good communication skills, and remember that the software development is a team sport.

Glossary & Index

Abbreviation	Description
aka	Also Known As
ANTLR	ANother Tool for Language Recognition
AOP	Aspect Oriented Programming
API	Application Programming Interfaces
APT	Annotation Processing Tool
BCEL	Byte Code Engineering Library
EE	Enterprise Edition
ETL	Extract Transform Load
FIFO	First In First Out
i.e.	That is
IDE	Integrated Development Environment
JAR	Java ARchive
JAX-WS	Java API for XML Web Services
JAXB	Java Architecture for XML Binding
JAXP	Java API foe XML Processing
JDK	Java Development Kit
JIT	Just In Time
JMX	Java Management eXtension
JPA	Java Persistence API
JRE	Java Runtime Environment
JSR	Java Specification Request
JVM	Java Virtual Machine
LIFO	Last In First Out
MBean	Managed Bean
ME	Micro Edition

NPE	NullPointerException
OO	Object Oriented
OOA	Object Oriented Analysis
OOD	Object Oriented Design
OS	Operating System
POJO	Plain Old Java Object
Regex	Regular Expressions
SAAJ	SOAP with Attachments API for Java
SE	Standard Edition
SNMP	Simple Network Management Protocol
SQL	Structured Query Language

Index

Glossary & Index

Glossary & Index

Glossary & Index

539

Glossary & Index

Please email any suggestions or errors to java-interview@hotmail.com. For other career making resources, please visit http://www.lulu.com/java-success. The career companions and essentials will compliment each other to lift your career a few notches.

"Any intelligent fool can make things bigger, more complex, and more violent. It takes a touch of genius -- and a lot of courage -- to **move in the opposite direction**."
- Albert Einstein

"If you can't explain it to a six year old, you don't understand it yourself."
- Albert Einstein

Glossary & Index

1032437R00288

Made in the USA
San Bernardino, CA
29 October 2012